AUTHORING
YOUR LIFE

AUTHORING YOUR LIFE

Developing an INTERNAL VOICE to Navigate Life's Challenges

MARCIA B. BAXTER MAGOLDA
FOREWORD BY SHARON DALOZ PARKS

STERLING, VIRGINIA

Sty/us

Published by Stylus Publishing, LLC
22883 Quicksilver Drive
Sterling, Virginia 20166-2102

Library of Congress Cataloging-in-Publication-Data
Baxter Magolda, Marcia B., 1951-
   Authoring your life : developing an internal voice to
navigate life's challenges / Marcia B. Baxter Magolda.
— 1st ed.
       p. cm.
   Includes bibliographical references and index.
   ISBN 978-1-57922-271-0 (hardcover : alk. paper)
1. Maturation (Psychology)—Case studies. 2. Autonomy
(Psychology)—Case studies. 3. Self-reliance—Case studies.
4. Adulthood—Psychological aspects—Case studies. I. Title.
   BF710.B396 2009
   155.2'5—dc22

                                                    2008055005

13-digit ISBN: 978-1-57922-271-0 (cloth)

Printed in the United States of America

Illustrations Copyright © 2009 Matthew Henry Hall

All first editions printed on acid free paper
that meets the American National Standards Institute
Z39-48 Standard.

Bulk Purchases

Quantity discounts are available for use in workshops
and for staff development.
Call 1-800-232-0223

First Edition, 2009

10 9 8 7 6 5 4 3 2 1

Dedication

To my mother, Marjorie Baxter, and my husband, Peter Magolda, for their resilience in navigating life's challenges.

CONTENTS

List of Tables and Maps   ix

Acknowledgments   xi

Foreword   xv

Note to Readers   xix

Introduction   1

1   Challenges of Adult Life   21

2   Dawn's Story—Bringing out the Truth
    in a Character   45

3   Mark's Story—Developing a Spiritual
    Philosophy of Life   75

4   Kurt's Story—Being True to the Man
    in the Glass   103

5   Sandra's Story—Living Her Faith   133

6   Lydia's Story—External Chaos;
    Internal Stability   161

7   Evan's Story—Being the Best
    You Can Be   189

8   How to Be Good Company for Your
    Own Journey   215

9   Partnerships: How to Provide Good
    Company for Others' Journeys
    toward Self-Authorship   249

10 Diverse Self-Authorship Stories   281

11 Mapping Your Journey   311

12   A Theory of Self-Authorship
        Development   321

        Longitudinal Study Methodology and Methods   347

        Notes   355

        Index   365

TABLES AND MAPS

Key Locations in the Journey
Toward Self-Authorship   4

Map: Journey toward
Self-Authorship   5

Learning Partnerships:
A Tandem Bicycle Experience   14

Map: Journey toward Self-Authorship   20

Dawn's Journey toward
Self-Authorship   44

Mark's Journey toward
Self-Authorship   74

Kurt's Journey toward
Self-Authorship   102

Sandra's Journey toward
Self-Authorship   132

Lydia's Journey toward
Self-Authorship   160

Evan's Journey toward
Self-Authorship   188

ACKNOWLEDGMENTS

This book is about authoring your life—or developing an internal voice to navigate life's challenges. It is the result of the journeys of 30 adults who have been generous in sharing their lives with me for over 20 years since they began college. I have been privileged that these adults have given freely of their innermost reflections and details of their lives to educate me and others about the journey toward and through self-authorship. I am grateful for the opportunity to share in their lives and the trust they have placed in me to use their insights to help others navigate this journey.

As my participants were navigating the challenges of adult life, I was navigating the challenges of interpreting what their experiences meant for adult development. I have been privileged to have many good partners on that journey. I am deeply indebted to all who have partnered with me over that 20-year period and helped in the writing of two prior books. Here I express my appreciation for those who have been regular partners in the creation of the present book.

Opportunities to explore ideas at length with Kelli Zaytoun, Lisa Boes, and Blythe Clinchy enriched my understanding of the nuances of developing an internal voice. Their writing continues to inspire me to pursue the complexities of how the internal voice evolves. The opportunity to participate in analyzing longitudinal interviews with Vasti Torres and Ebelia Hernandez, and sustained conversations with Elisa Abes and Jane Pizzolato about their self-authorship studies deepened my insight into the multiple dynamics of self-authorship, particularly those related to identity. Collaborating with Patricia King and the Wabash National Study of Liberal Arts Education research team offered rich dialogues that challenged my thinking about the intricacies of adult development in multiple contexts. Partnering with Elizabeth Creamer and Peggy Meszaros on the relationship of self-authorship to career decision making enriched my sense of how educators might help adolescents develop internal voices. Working with Terry Wildman and Barbara Bekken on the Earth Sustainability project affirmed that self-authorship is possible during college if educational environments are shaped to enable it. Collaborating with Carolyn Haynes and Kari Taylor to shape our own campus environment to promote self-authorship reinforced that belief. All of these collaborative partnerships reminded me of the value of sharing the stories from my longitudinal study.

In the summer of 2007, Patricia King, Vasti Torres, and Elizabeth Creamer read this book manuscript and we met for two days of conversation. Pat came to the meeting wearing a T-shirt displaying a "map of life." It occurred to us that a map might be a useful metaphor for the journey toward and through self-authorship. The conversation turned to what the book was intended to accomplish. When I said that I hoped the participants' stories would inspire others in their twenties and thirties to work on cultivating their internal voices, we agreed that rewriting the book for that audience was necessary. Doing so posed a challenge for me, given my history of writing for educators. Fortunately I had two excellent mentors with whom I worked on the *About Campus* magazine: Jean Henscheid and Kari Taylor. Watching these exceptional writers edit manuscripts to arrive at a clear, engaging story helped me learn how to alter the book manuscript to achieve that aim. Kari Taylor subsequently edited this book; I am grateful for her expertise and substantive contribution to the manuscript. Kari has also been an invaluable intellectual partner in talking through developmental concepts and how multiple dynamics of development intertwine. I am also indebted to John von Knorring, President of Stylus Press, whose intellectual vision and editing acumen helped me achieve a balance of scholarly research and readability in this book. The eloquence with which participants told their stories made this possible.

Because writing is only a small portion of my teaching position at the university, time to write is made possible by colleagues who contribute to other aspects of my work. Brianne MacEachran, Leah Reynolds, and Taran Cardone have been exceptional partners in completing important work that enabled me to focus on writing. Jan Clegg's expertise in transcribing audiotapes and sharing her perspectives was invaluable.

Although many of the colleagues noted here are also friends, I am equally appreciative of friends and family who have been good partners on this journey. My walking partners, Kristy Drobney and Kari Taylor, have been mainstays in processing life in general and sustaining exercise when time is in short supply. My art fair partner, Michele Welkener, provides a creative perspective on life. My father-in-law, Charles Magolda, who spent his last years in our household, gently reminded me of the importance of taking time to rest amidst the chaos of life. My sister and brother-in-law, Ardath and David Sunderland, each a 35-year veteran of teaching, modeled a lifelong commitment to education.

Two people have been central to my ability to navigate life's challenges. My mother, Marjorie Baxter, enabled me to develop my internal voice early in life and has steadfastly supported it throughout my life. Her courage, resilience, and "can do" attitude is an on-going inspiration to me. My spouse, Peter Magolda, has modeled for me what Mark (chapter three) calls "grace in the dance with reality." Peter's ability to remain centered regardless of life circumstances enables us to move productively around the obstacles of life. I am grateful to both these partners for their unconditional love and support.

FOREWORD

We live at a hinge time in history, a threshold time when societies and cultures are being recomposed. We are learning that the way life used to work—or the way we thought it should—doesn't work any longer. The twenty-something years are among the primary hinge moments in the human lifespan, a time when a person may be recomposed. When you are between the ages of (roughly) 18 and 32, no longer a child or adolescent and moving into your adult years, it may become more and more apparent that life—specifically *your* life—is not unfolding as you had assumed.

"It's up to you—you make the decision," your work supervisor says, underscoring the expectations. "Stop worrying about what other people think," your well-meaning friend admonishes. "What do you *really* want?" asks your counselor. "Why don't you just . . . ?" your parent suggests (again). "Why didn't you pay attention to your *own* feelings?" another friend asks incredulously. You try to ignore a gnawing voice at the back of your mind that secretly wonders: "Do I really fit in this job?" A journalist with a microphone stops you on the street, mentions a hot public issue, and asks: "What is *your* position?" Living with these kinds of questions, expectations, and demands is far easier said than done, and as we move into adulthood, doing so may become increasingly wearing, frustrating, bewildering, and urgent—even overwhelming or depressing.

Indeed, moving into adulthood asks something more of us—more than choosing a job, profession, or career, and becoming financially independent; more than finding a partner and caring for children; more than gaining more marketable knowledge, skills, and credentials. Especially in today's world, becoming an adult requires us to navigate a vast sea of choices and constraints. In our complex and diverse society, the moral terrain can be obscure and sometimes treacherous. Further, big questions that call for complex and vital decision making don't always wait to appear until you are "ready." Though still young, you may encounter a health crisis. Or the job doesn't work out as you hoped.

Or a vital relationship gets rocky. You discover you have to make decisions that will affect other people—some you love and others you have never met. Parents, friends, religious figures, or other voices may still have authority in your life, but simply following their lead no longer yields success, contentment, satisfaction, confidence—or joy. The difficult and glorious reality is that becoming an adult requires finding and including your own voice in the arena of authority—developing an inner sense of your own truth and authority that you (and others) can trust.

Many people live all of their "adult" lives without really becoming grown-ups—remaining forever dependent upon others to determine the course of their lives. Sometimes this happens in obvious ways, and sometimes it is very subtle. They may feel they are happy and even effective, but if life throws them a curve ball, they can easily become disoriented and lost—even angry or despairing. Others become restless and dissatisfied with simply going along with the external voices. They begin to notice their "own voice," but then get stuck because they are not quite able to dare to take their own voice too seriously. Still others are sure that they don't want to be dependent on all the outside voices that claim to have the answers; yet although they know how to be "against" those external voices, they don't know quite what to be "for." Thus they also get stuck.

Getting beyond the stuck place requires good company and the realization that recomposing ourselves as adults takes time—longer than we may wish. Learning how to listen to "our own insides" and how to consciously and responsibly make meaningful sense of self and world is a kind of journey.

In this book Marcia Baxter Magolda offers a map for that journey. If you are in your twenties or thirties, this map will provide some confidence, comfort, and cues. Better yet, it is more than a map. It generously and respectfully provides true stories of real and diverse people who have traveled through the same territory. The stories take you inside the stress of the kinds of real dilemmas and dramas that are similar to your own. These stories can serve as a flashlight—illumining your own path as they shine light on familiar feelings and boost your courage.

Following this path, we discover that our journey—our life—is a part of a bigger story. That bigger story is the story of human becoming, a story that moves through uncertainty, pain, and shadowlands, but one that doesn't have to stop in those places. The tension, bewilderment, and hurt of those places may be resolved within ourselves in ways we couldn't have expected.

There is also a story within the story. That deeper story is about how we become authors of our own stories, our own lives—how we become self-authoring. Like authoring a book, writing a play, or composing a song, authoring our own lives requires learning and practice, practice, practice. It helps if we don't try to do it entirely alone. Marcia Baxter Magolda provides good company on the path of learning and practice, whether you are just setting out or have already been on this path for a while. In either case, this book will make the journey less lonely. It will assist you in finding learning partners, mentors, guides, and also help you become the same for others.

But this is not simply a self-help book. We live in a time when we need more grown-ups. We need citizens who do not just "go with the flow" and who can think for themselves about the questions not only of our individual lives but also of the changing life of our society, our world, our planet. Each one of us is a special blend of heredity, experience, talent, pain, and hope. Each of us holds a distinct angle of vision and a unique voice that we can bring to the conversation of the twenty-first century. If any one of us fails to speak in our authentic voice—our self-authored voice—something vital for our collective life that can only come through us will be lost, missing from the conversation that is now needed. Whatever our age, it is critical that we each become fully adult and provide good company for others on the way. As we live in this hinge time of great cultural change, Marcia Baxter Magolda reminds us how much is at stake in the journey toward full adulthood—toward a more meaningful and purposeful life for each of us as individuals and for all of us together, as each of us is invited—called—to participate in the composing of a more sustainable, just, and prosperous world. This book matters for all of us.

Sharon Daloz Parks,
Author of: *Big Questions, Worthy Dreams: Mentoring Young Adults in Their Search for Meaning, Purpose and Faith;* and *Leadership Can Be Taught: A Bold Approach for a Complex World.*

NOTE TO READERS

The purpose of this book is to help adults in their twenties and thirties shift from dependence on authority to the development of their internal voices to meet life's challenges. I envision you, the reader, as someone in your twenties or thirties and concerned with managing the direction of your life. Perhaps you are not entirely fulfilled in your work, or want more from your personal or professional relationships, or sometimes not feeling in control of your life. This book provides you with a way to reflect on your life and use what you learn about yourself to develop an internal foundation that will provide a sense of direction. That foundation is what I call "self-authorship."

I also address this book to the family members, friends, college teachers and student affairs personnel, mentors, coaches, and employers of adults starting out on their journey toward self-reliance, as well as those beyond that point who are confronting problems for which they don't feel adequately prepared. If you are one of these other readers, this book provides insights to help others shift from dependence on authority to developing their internal voices to meet life's challenges—in other words, to achieve "self-authorship."

The book contains stories from over 1,000 interviews that I conducted with a group of adults over the last 22 years—from the time they were 18 to their current age of 40. They report that succeeding in adult life required them to develop their *internal voices*—to decide within themselves what to believe, who to be, and how to relate to others. As a college educator for 25 years, I typically address my writing about these interviews to college educators so that we can do a better job of helping students develop their internal voices to be successful in adult life. However, listening to these interviews over the years and talking with the interviewees about their life stories convinced me that we each have a role to play in meeting our own life challenges, just as we all have a role in helping others do so. In fact, it takes personal initiative and the support of family, friends, coworkers, employers, teachers, coaches, and a multitude of others to develop one's internal voice and use it to guide one's life. As a result, I write this book to those of you in your twenties and thirties who are probably working on developing your internal voices and to readers in all roles that support you in that process. You likely also play some of these support roles for others.

As a result of my interest in reaching a broad audience with these stories, I have avoided language that may be unfamiliar to those of you who do not read regularly about adult development. I introduce terms that I see as necessary for understanding the stories and how to use them. For those of you who have read my earlier books, I hope to model a way to make the ideas educators routinely share with each other interesting and useful to a wider range of readers. Chapter 12 includes a theory of adult development and educational practice intended to help college educators promote students' internal voices during college.

INTRODUCTION

THE PURPOSE OF THIS BOOK IS TO PROVIDE YOU WITH A COMPASS for the journey through your twenties and thirties as a foundation for your life. In your teens, parents, teachers, and other adults help you find your way. The journey through adolescence is often like riding a tandem bicycle; the adolescent rides on the back while a guide (e.g., parent, teacher, coach) directs the journey from the captain's seat up front. Generally at the end of secondary schooling, whether you go to work or college, the unstated expectation is that you will move up to the captain's seat (or take to your own bicycle) to find your own way through life's challenges.

This book offers insights and strategies to find meaning in your life, develop your adult identity, and handle significant transitions and often challenging circumstances in your life. The strategies and insights I describe in this book come from a study I started in 1986 with 101 students as they entered college. Now, over 20 years later, 35 of them still participate in our annual interview as they are turning forty. Their stories offer a variety of ways to think about key questions, including the following: *Who am I? What do I want in relationships? How do I know what to believe?* Figuring out how you feel about these issues is an important part of standing back from the external influences that shaped you as an adolescent and deciding who you want to be and what your purpose in life will be. As you encounter new experiences and responsibilities, you may find that the way you are living your life is incompatible with your developing sense of self. The career path that looked so promising turns out to be disappointing, a relationship falls apart, or your way of making

1

sense of the world becomes insufficient to navigate life's transitions. Developing your internal voice will help you work through these challenges, help you face unexpected circumstances that are beyond your control—career setbacks, personal illness, or loss of loved ones—and enable you to go forward with confidence. Finally, developing your internal voice will help you build an internal, psychological "home" that will serve as the foundation for your future.

This book offers a road map of the various paths available to you to *author* your life. The stories reveal numerous paths that you can take, from depending on adult guides for what to think and do to finding your own internal voice to guide what to think and do. By following participants on their paths and seeing the resemblances among their paths and your own, I am confident that their stories will help you uncover core personal values to inform your own complex life decisions. Using your internal voice and core personal values to guide your life is what I have come to call *self-authorship*.

This book will also be useful to those of you who have personal or professional relationships—as partners, parents, supervisors, mentors, teachers, or counselors—with others who are working to author their lives. You can provide good company to others by helping them explore their experiences, listen to their own thoughts and feelings, and work through challenges to develop suitable solutions. The key to being good company is to take the back seat of the bike— to offer guidance and support but encourage the rider up front to sort out the key questions and make decisions. Understanding the twists and turns of the journey to self-authorship will help you be a better partner.

A MAP AND TRAVEL GUIDE TO SELF-AUTHORSHIP

My participants' stories from when they were in their twenties and thirties, though they offer a variety of diverse pathways to self-authorship, share an overall shift from relying on *external formulas* to *self-authorship*. Before we explore this shift in more detail, it is important to consider how developmental change happens.

How Developmental Change Happens

As we travel along our developmental journey, we interpret things we see along the way through the perspectives we have acquired—rules of how we have come to think about the world and ourselves. Generally speaking, we do not consciously think about these rules unless something unexpected happens that surprises us. When we have an experience that contradicts our rule, we usually see it as an exception rather than seriously questioning the rule we have come to trust. Only when we have encountered a number of exceptions do we stop to consider whether our rule needs to be changed. We tend not to throw out rules too quickly, but instead alter them just enough to account for the exceptions. Family expectations are an example of rules. Growing up, we see our family's expectations as the rule; we do not question these because they are our only experience. When we meet the families of schoolmates, friends, or eventually coworkers, we notice that not all families have the same expectations. Initially, other families' expectations are an exception. When we realize that many different families have different sets of expectations, we decide that different expectations are unique to different families. We now have a new rule about family expectations. Developmental psychologists describe this process as giving up one way of making meaning to adopt a more complex one.

We are generally not conscious of this process of operating on the basis of one rule, noting its exceptions, and revising it to better account for our experience. As we travel we are absorbed in the daily activities of the trip. We get caught up in the immediacy of the trip itself. Riding our bike along the path, we do not consciously think about how we are riding—our balance, the movement of our feet, the way we shift the gears, the way we interact with our tandem partner. It isn't until we have a chance to stop, get off the bike, look at the map, and think about where we have been that we are able to stand back from the journey to reflect on it. It is this ability to extract ourselves from how we operate in the world to analyze it that reflects movement along the developmental journey. For example, we are not able to extract ourselves from family expectations until we stop and reflect on the multiple expectations we experienced, as well as on the situation to decide what to think about it. The developmental journey is the continual process of finding those parts of ourselves that we cannot see (e.g., family expectations), pulling them out to reflect on them, and deciding what to make of them.

This process occurs over and over as we encounter new experiences. These sets of rules mark our place on the various locations along the journey toward self-authorship. Table I.1 offers descriptions of these key locations and the general order in which they appear on the journey.

TABLE I.1 KEY LOCATIONS IN THE JOURNEY TOWARD SELF-AUTHORSHIP

External Formulas	Trust authorities to decide what to believe, follow others' visions for how to succeed. External voices (those of others) in the foreground drown out internal voice.
Crossroads	Torn between following others' versus own visions and expectations.
Listening to Internal Voice	Recognize the importance of hearing one's internal voice and begin work to identify it. Attempt to get internal voice into conversation with external voices.
Cultivating Internal Voice	Use internal voice to sort out beliefs, establish priorities, and put the puzzle of who you are together. Work to reduce reliance on external authorities.
Self-Authorship	Trust yourself to decide what to believe, follow your vision for how to succeed. Internal voice in the foreground coordinates information from external voices.
Trusting the Internal Voice	Realize that reality is beyond your control, but you can control your reaction to reality; use internal voice to shape reaction.
Building an Internal Foundation	Use internal voice to make internal commitments and build them into a foundation or philosophy of life to guide action.
Securing Internal Commitments	Live out internal commitments in everyday life.
Key: **Bold** = phases *Italics* = elements within phases	

The corresponding map illustrates the various paths my participants experienced in the journey.

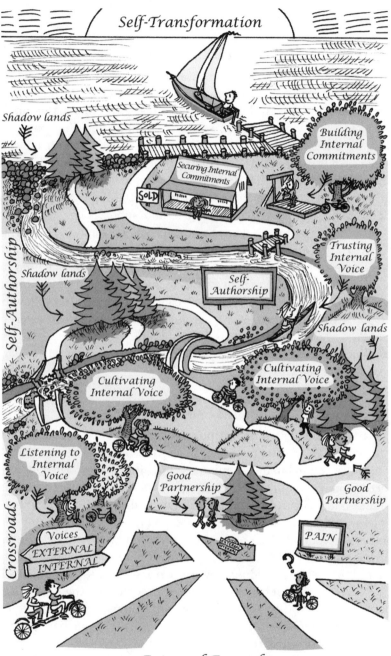

THE JOURNEY TO SELF-AUTHORSHIP

External Formulas

The participants in my study entered college heavily reliant on external authorities for what to believe, how to learn, how to define themselves, and how to build relationships with others (this phase is located at the bottom of the map). They made decisions based on what they thought others expected of them rather than on self-determined criteria. They did realize that their parents and professors did not always have the answers, but they trusted these authorities for guidance more than they trusted themselves—which is not surprising, given the guidance and supervision afforded by those authorities during adolescence. As college seniors, 80 percent of the group still relied heavily on external authorities to decide what to believe.[1] Some were aware that they were responsible for deciding what to believe. However, they had not acquired the capacity to do so. Thus, most of them left college believing that following the plans they had acquired from authorities (what I call *external formulas*) would yield success in adult life. On the map you will notice participants traveling north from external formulas toward the area marked *Crossroads*.

The Crossroads

My participants agreed to continue our annual interviews after their graduation. They took positions in a wide array of occupations—from education to business and everything in between. They became teachers, chefs, real estate managers, salespeople, and accountants, to name a few. Some enrolled in graduate and professional education to become doctors, lawyers, therapists, and ministers. Some married, some divorced, and some had children in their twenties. Despite the variation in their life circumstances, they shared one commonality. Their plans, despite yielding various degrees of professional and personal success, invariably brought them to a challenging crossroads: one path continued to point them toward others' visions and expectations (*external formulas*) while another path branched off and pointed them toward their own vision and expectations (*internal voice*). The sign that says "pain" on the map conveys that some kind of pain "stopped" people on their journey to figure out how to face life's challenges. Following external formulas guided by others' visions left participants feeling unfulfilled; they recognized that an important piece was missing—their own voices.

Listening to the Internal Voice. In an attempt to resolve this pain, participants focused on learning to *listen to their internal voices*. They tried a variety of strategies to stop, get off their bikes, and listen to how they felt rather than to what everyone else wanted from them. Some wrote journals to identify their feelings; others sought experiences (e.g., travel, relationships, work roles) that would help identify their own thinking. No matter what strategy they used, participants focused on identifying what made them happy, examining their own beliefs, finding parts of themselves that were important to them, and establishing a distinction between their feelings and external expectations. It was not easy. Some had good partners to help them sort out their ideas and move forward (more about this later). Others had to find their own way and sometimes got stuck or sidetracked in what one participant called the shadow lands.

Cultivating the Internal Voice. As participants began to hear their internal voices more clearly, they worked hard at *cultivating those voices*. This involved developing parts of themselves they valued, establishing priorities, sifting out beliefs and values that no longer worked, and putting pieces of the puzzle of who they were together. The challenges they encountered at work and in relationships offered opportunities to identify their professional and personal goals and work toward a clearer vision of who they wanted to be. Again, the road ahead often ran through the shadow lands.

Most participants spent their twenties *listening to and cultivating their internal voices* in order to devise their own plans for the future.[2] They worked at varying paces and levels of intensity to address the driving questions of their twenties: how do I know, who am I, and how do I relate to others? As participants gained clarity in their internal voices, they were able to exit the winding pathways in the crossroads and travel toward the next major phase of the journey—*self-authorship*.

Self-Authorship

In the center of the map you see a bridge crossing the river that separates the *Crossroads* from *Self-Authorship*. Mark described *self-authorship* like this:

> Making yourself into something, not what other people say or not just kind of floating along in life, but you're in some sense

a piece of clay. You've been formed into different things, but
that doesn't mean you can't go back on the potter's wheel and
instead of somebody else's hands building and molding you, you
use your own, and in a fundamental sense change your values
and beliefs.[3]

Moving into self-authorship means using your own hands to build
and mold who you are and to firmly establish your internal voice.
Although participants did not always change the fundamental basis
of their values and beliefs, they used their own hands to make their
values and beliefs their own. Participants crossed the bridge when
they began to *trust their internal voices*.

Trusting the Internal Voice. Trusting your internal voice is
the key task of this first phase of self-authorship. At this point in the
journey, participants reported a significant insight that helped them
move forward. They realized that reality, or what happened around
and to them, was often beyond their control. At the same time, they
realized that their reactions to reality were within their control.
This realization helped them choose effective responses to obstacles
they encountered, enabling them to "go with the flow" rather than
try to remove or change experiences that blocked their paths. It took
numerous experiences in various parts of their lives to gain enough
confidence to trust the internal voice. It was a relatively smooth
process for some and a rocky one for others, depending in large part
on the quality of company available for the journey. Visits to the
shadow lands were normal in this part of the journey.

Building an Internal Foundation. When participants
trusted their internal voices enough to guide their lives, they moved
on to the next phase of self-authorship—*building an internal foundation*. Participants used their internal voices to make internal
commitments and shape them into a philosophy or a framework—
an internal foundation—to guide them in responding to reality. This
involved examining how they had organized their lives and rethinking attitudes or behaviors that conflicted with their internal voices.
Sometimes this meant changing careers; other times it meant
rebuilding or leaving relationships. Participants accepted their talents and used them to shape their lives. They used their internal
authority to refine their beliefs, identities, and relationships, and to
make internal commitments to them. The process of building the
internal foundation, and at the same time using it to guide their
actions, often identified issues that had to be resolved. Similar to

any construction project, it is typical for the builder to return for additional materials or to revise a blueprint to address some unanticipated issue. Participants sometimes had to go back to build up more trust as they constructed their internal psychological home. Construction problems also meant visits to the shadow lands to reflect on how to proceed.

Securing Internal Commitments. Participants reported that establishing their internal commitments, which they did as they built their internal foundations, differed considerably from living their internal commitments. *Securing internal commitments* meant living them in every aspect of their lives. Some described this as the difference between having the commitments in their heads versus in their hearts. The commitments and foundations shifted from something being constructed to a solid home in which to live. As participants adopted the commitments in every aspect of their lives, the commitments became second nature. They intuitively "knew" what to do in various situations and were confident they could handle whatever came their way. Being secure in these internal commitments left participants feeling less afraid of change, more open to deep relationships with others, and more open to continued personal growth. The village near the top of the map reflects participants' feeling of being at home with themselves and those around them. The landing above the village reflects the experience of a few participants nearing age 40, who were considering additional personal growth (see Dawn's story in chapter 2).

The journey toward self-authorship is complicated by the fact that multiple layers of development take place at the same time.

Three Dimensions of Development

As we travel along our developmental journeys, we recognize that we need to figure out what to believe and value, who we are, and what kinds of relationships we want with others. These three tasks reflect three dimensions of our overall development as people.

Deciding what to believe and value represents our *cognitive development* or the assumptions we hold about knowledge and how it is acquired. For example, early on we tend to adopt the beliefs and values of our families, teachers, or faith leaders who ride on the front of our tandem bicycles. Along the journey we meet others who have beliefs and values that differ from ours. As we explore these new ideas, we realize that we need to explore why we believe what we do and settle on whether it really works for us or whether we might alter it in some way.

Figuring out who we are represents our *intrapersonal development* or how we view ourselves. As is the case with beliefs and values, where we grow up, our families, and our school experiences shape our identities. When we are younger our identities are strongly influenced by the expectations of those around us, particularly those who are in the front seat of the tandem bicycle. In adult life we are faced with determining how to reshape our identities so that they reflect our internal voices.

Building relationships with others, *our interpersonal development*, requires knowing how we want to interact with them. Parent-child relationships, in which the parent is on the front seat of the bicycle, involve certain expectations of both parties. Adult-adult relationships involve different sets of expectations of each party. As adults we are challenged to figure out what kinds of expectations we have for others in our lives and how we want to react to their expectations of us. As our internal voices grow, we sometimes need to renegotiate expectations with loved ones.

Sorting out how we feel about our beliefs and values, our identities, and our relationships is an on-going part of the journey as we continually work on these tasks as our internal voice develops.

As participants entered their thirties, some had made major career and personal life changes that pushed them to bring their lives into balance with their new internal voices. Many of these challenges of their thirties would test their internal voices and require further work to establish foundations to withstand the uncertainties and complexities of life in twenty-first century society. They faced major health problems, family tragedies, career upheaval, and the "normal" adjustments of work, personal relationships, and parenting. The overarching challenge of their thirties was to integrate their beliefs, values, identities, and relationships into a core sense of self or psychological home from which to function in the disruptions reality introduced into their daily lives. Talking with participants over the course of their thirties, I learned how some were fortunate to find supervisors, colleagues, friends, and family who could serve as good company for the process of using their own hands and voices to shape who they are. Thus, despite the pain that was often involved in developing an internal foundation for their lives, they were able to accept what they could not control and manage what they could. This sense of internal authority helped them maintain hope for the future. Those who were less fortunate in finding good company had to work harder to develop internal foundations. In some cases, even when nearing their forties, participants wondered if they really had the power to influence their futures.

LEARNING PARTNERSHIPS: HOW TO FIND—AND PROVIDE—GOOD COMPANY

Having been down this path myself some 15 years ahead of my participants, I knew some of the dangers of professional and personal commitments made on the basis of external formulas. As the participants and I talked annually throughout their twenties, I often wished their college experiences would have brought them to the crossroads earlier to save them some of the anguish they experienced encountering it later. As we explored both their successes and frustrations, they often reported feeling somewhat alone in facing the challenges of adult life. They found that significant people in their lives often tried to solve their problems rather than listen to how they felt about them. They found our conversations helpful to reflect on these issues, and some labeled our talks therapeutic. I became, in a way, a companion on their journeys. Together we began to develop the story of possible pathways in the journey to self-authorship, and I learned how to be good company for their journeys.

These stories inspired me to organize my study's participants' insights into a model of learning partnerships[4] to help family members, friends, educators, and employers to become better company for the journey toward self-authorship. The model shows the qualities of good company so that you can develop it for yourself or provide it to those you care about.

My study's participants described good partners as those who offered guidance from the back seat, encouraging them to steer the bicycle and shift the gears while the partner contributed to the forward motion by pedaling. Participants felt supported when partners:

- Respected their thoughts and feelings,
- Helped them sort through their experiences, and
- Collaborated with them to help them solve their own problems.

Gwen's supervisor is a good example of a partner who had these supportive characteristics:

> She helps me think through some situations as issues arise and I'm trying to decide what to do. Her management style I just admire immensely. I present the problem, then I say, "So here's where I am." Her first question always is, "So what do you read on this? What do you think?" In the beginning it was frustrating because I wanted her to say, "Okay. Well, here's how you handle that," because I didn't know. I'd never run across any of that before. She's very good at, "Okay, well, have you thought about this? Have you thought about this? Okay." And then suddenly everything is like, "Oh, so that's what I'm supposed to do." Very good at helping you reach your own conclusions.[5]

Gwen's supervisor respected Gwen's thoughts and feelings and helped Gwen identify them through the questions she asked. Asking whether she had thought about one angle or another helped Gwen sort out her experience and thinking. Thus the supervisor collaborated with Gwen to help Gwen reach her own conclusions. The supervisor stayed on the back seat and encouraged Gwen to drive the bicycle.

This support was crucial for participants to meet the demands of their everyday lives. They found themselves challenged to:

- Deal with complex issues at work and in personal life,
- Develop their own personal authority, and
- Work collaboratively with others to solve mutual issues.

Sandra encountered these challenges in her work as a therapist. She described how her team functioned:

> We have peer review meetings for two hours every week. We discuss cases. The team perspective, ideas about what to try, is really terrific. I rely more on them than on my supervisor. If I have a lot of experience, I make my own decisions; that is

LEARNING PARTNERSHIPS: A TANDEM BICYCLE EXPERIENCE

part of gaining confidence as a therapist. I don't ask about chemical-dependency issues because I have a good base of knowledge and can make good decisions. If it is new ground I'll ask a colleague who has more experience for their opinion. Usually I say, "Here is what I was thinking about doing, what do you think?" to see if it sounds like a good clinical decision.[6]

Working with clients presented complex issues that Sandra felt pressured to handle effectively. Her employer expected her to develop her own personal sense of authority to handle her therapy sessions well. However, employees were also expected to contribute to the team's efforts to make the best decisions for all clients, thus she had to work collaboratively with her teammates. This meant that she sometimes rode in the front seat with support from her teammates, and other times she took the back seat as she supported others on the team. In later years (see Sandra's detailed story in chapter 5), Sandra continued to face these challenges as she worked with many players to address her clients' needs. The support Sandra received from her peers helped her cope with these challenges. Partners can push us to challenge ourselves to help us grow if the challenges are not automatically present in our work or personal lives.

The figure on the next page captures the essence of a learning partnership.

My study participants did not have to go out of their way to look for the challenges—they arose automatically in relationships, in the course of parenting, at school, and at work. Relationships and parenting required balancing multiple people's needs, including their own. Professors and employers expected participants to bring their personal authority to bear on complex problems, decisions, and plans. Working with colleagues required negotiating multiple ideas to form mutually agreeable courses of action. Thus the demand for self-authorship was ever present in all aspects of their lives. Participants did, however, have to look for partners who could be good company to help them develop self-authorship. So how do you go about finding this kind of support for the challenges you face?

First, knowing the kind of support you need helps you recognize it when it is available in others around you. Reading the detailed stories in this book will help you envision what this support looks like so you can take advantage of it when you come across it. Second, knowing what you need helps you communicate clearly with potential partners about what would be beneficial to you. Letting partners know that you would appreciate the opportunity to share your thinking, to get guidance in thinking through situations yourself, and to learn the processes you might use to solve problems gives them a better sense of how to support you. Sharing the challenges you are facing and explaining your need to develop the personal authority to face them helps potential partners understand your needs in the relationship. When you ask for support, clarify that you are not asking for answers and do not intend to give up the front seat.

Knowing the qualities of a good partner also helps you be a good partner to others. Draw out their thinking and listen carefully rather than offering advice. Ask questions to help them sort out experiences they find challenging. Help them reflect on and organize their ideas to come up with workable solutions. Remind yourself to stay in the back seat. The stories in this book reveal numerous ways to offer good company.

THE IMPORTANCE OF DEVELOPING SELF-AUTHORSHIP AND GOOD COMPANY

I contend it is a pressing and significant problem when adults in their twenties still view themselves and the world through external formulas. I do not say this to be critical of my participants or of those of you who use external formulas; I make this observation based on the educational and societal demands that the world today places on adults in their twenties. There is nothing wrong with operating from external formulas in and of itself. Problems arise, however, when the demands of your environment require the exercise of personal authority that you have had no opportunity or preparation to develop. As Robert Kegan, a developmental psychologist, argued, the demands of contemporary society for self-authorship are well over the heads of much of the adult population.[7] That is to say that these demands ask something of us that we have not yet developed the capacity to do. Kegan explains this dilemma with the analogy of driving an automatic versus a standard transmission automobile. Knowing how to drive an automatic is sufficient as long as plenty of automatics are available to do the gear shifting for us.

However, if only standard transmissions are available, we would be at a disadvantage without this ability to shift gears ourselves. Societal demands for work and personal life often require that we learn to shift the gears ourselves.

A synthesis of reports about desired college-level learning outcomes (e.g., the ability to think critically, a strong sense of identity, and functioning in mature interdependent relationships) supports the notion that the goals of higher education demand self-authorship rather than authority-dependence.[8] My participants clearly encountered contexts after college (and sometimes during college) that required them to become independent of external authority and develop their own voices. They were faced with this challenge while simultaneously holding major responsibilities at work and home. As teachers, accountants, attorneys, doctors, social workers, et cetera, they had responsibilities that had significant effects on others' lives; and at the same time, in their roles as spouses, partners, and parents, they had responsibilities towards those with whom they had mutual relationships. The major issues participants faced (see Chapter 1 for detailed examples) reveal the dilemmas involved in adult roles and choices made in the midst of trying to find and cultivate one's internal voice.

The reliance on external formulas that was so prevalent among my participants into their twenties was more a result of schooling and societal dynamics than about their lack of capacity. Their work and advanced educational settings required them to analyze information and make complex decisions; identify and act on their values; and collaborate effectively with a wide range of other people. Their ability to quickly rise to this challenge suggests that they were capable of self-authorship when it was demanded of them and when they had appropriate support. Their stories of college experiences and family contexts indicated that they were neither sufficiently challenged nor supported to develop their internal voices earlier. Thus my report of their college experiences described the *growth that occurred* in contexts in which there was not sufficient challenge and support for self-authorship rather than the *growth that is possible* when there is sufficient challenge and support for self-authorship. Because we know that adult life demands self-authorship, we all must work toward achieving it and helping others do so. I hope this book helps you promote your own and others' self-authorship so that you can face the challenges of your life successfully.

How to Use this Book

The stories contained in this book are rich descriptions of my study participants' lives in their twenties and thirties. They offer windows into how my participants established and maintained successful careers, developed meaningful relationships, made life decisions, handled the joys and challenges of parenting, and faced unexpected tragedies. In talking about these experiences, participants share how they worked their way out of external formulas, through the crossroads, and developed self-authorship. Although their individual paths have been unique, you will notice common patterns among them. Their paths have not been linear, but instead full of detours and steps back along the way. As you read their stories, consider how their experiences correspond with yours and how their interpretations might help guide you.

The first part of this book addresses the challenges of adult life and the role of self-authorship in meeting them. Chapter 1 introduces the challenges participants encountered in their thirties and the various ways they experienced them. Their placement on the map shows how their stories illustrate in detail each location on the journey. The degree to which they trusted their internal voices affected making career choices, blending parenting with careers, finding and maintaining significant relationships, deciding whether to have children, parenting, and coping with major health crises. Chapters 2 through 7 present in-depth stories of six participants' experiences as they developed and learned to trust their own voices, built internal foundations for their lives, and secured their internal commitments. The details of these stories are intended to enable you to enter into the participants' experiences and share the complexity of their journeys over time.

The next two chapters focus on how you and your partners can support developing self-authorship. The in-depth stories in Chapter 8 illustrate the various circumstances that stimulated and supported the development of self-authorship for the participants. These stories illustrate how you can use similar circumstances to promote your own development. The in-depth stories in Chapter 9 demonstrate how partners can support others in developing their own internal voices.

These stories illustrate using the Learning Partnerships Model to support partners who are still dependent on external formulas, or are at the crossroads struggling to develop self-authorship. They also demonstrate various approaches to developing learning partnerships appropriate to particular personal characteristics or social contexts. The result is a compass to help you navigate the multiple pathways on the map of your life, and to guide you through the myriad and complex forms that your journey toward developing internal voice may take.

Despite the richness of my study participants' stories, all lives are unique and no one group can possibly capture everyone's experience. Thus it is important to place participants' stories in the larger context of other studies of self-authorship to draw in other perspectives that might relate to your experience. Chapter 10 includes stories from these other studies to further explore the nature of self-authorship among students who are currently in postsecondary education, among older adults, and among persons who experience marginalization (for example, due to race, gender, or sexual orientation). These stories convey the multiple factors that interact to help people internally author their own lives. If you did not find your particular identity in earlier parts of the book, you might find themes here that address aspects of your experience. In Chapter 11 I attempt to draw out the key insights and strategies from these stories and offer you an opportunity to reflect on how they relate to your experience. Despite the messiness of the journey toward self-authorship, thinking through these questions will help you consider the factors in your life that affect the development of your internal voice.

The last chapter of the book is a postscript written for readers who follow studies of college student and adult development and others who are professionally interested in how we might interpret these collective stories. I bring together the storylines from all the participants to form a theory of the development of internal voice. I outline an overarching storyline that involves three components of self-authorship as well as the diverse patterns of how people move within these components. The circular nature of this storyline; the intersections among how participants approached the key questions about knowing, identity, and relationships; and the role of personal characteristics in development combine to create multiple possibilities for the journey toward and through self-authorship.

I hope you will find your story, or at least parts of it, within these pages. And I hope you will come away with a sense of how to improve your life and the lives of those around you.

INDIVIDUALS' PHASES ON THE JOURNEY

CHAPTER 1

CHALLENGES OF ADULT LIFE

ATTAINING CAREER SUCCESS, ATTAINING FINANCIAL STABILITY, MAINTAINING EXISTING RELATIONSHIPS, and building new ones, as well as managing constant change and ambiguity, rank among the obvious challenges of adult life. There is a less noticeable challenge, however, that is at the root of all of these. One of my interviewees, Cara, described it at age 28:

> I have had a good intuitive sense but have ignored it; like in bad relationships, my stomach would clench. Then I'll have a logical or rational voice saying you are overreacting. In the last six months I've tried to listen more; spend twenty minutes a day and do breathing exercises. I'm used to reading to help myself, read what someone else is saying rather than listening to myself. The more I'm listening to myself, I'm allaying fears. I'm paying more attention to me than to other people. I made some bad decisions as a result of listening to others. I changed my major to psychology to stay at home with a boyfriend. I'm sick of listening to others! Then I think, "I'm not honest with my parents." When am I going to stand up for myself and be who I am instead of trying to make people happy? Or share my reaction when people aggravate me? Expression of my opinion is seen as creating a scene. If a man said it, they'd say "good point." I am at the start of this—not there—an invisible force, I'm pushing against it, what is it? I don't know, but it is there though.[1]

This invisible force of external influence complicated Cara's experience in her doctoral program and her decisions about whether to marry and have children (a more detailed account of Cara's story appears in chapter 8). At age 28, Cara stood at the crossroads of external influence and her own internal voice. Cara had begun to develop her internal thoughts and feelings—her internal voice—yet she found it difficult to use it consistently. If you have experienced this invisible force, you know how difficult it is to overcome it. In this chapter, I recount interviewees' stories to preview the challenges of adult life and how one's location on the journey helps or hinders facing these challenges. I chose the parts of their stories that highlight specific locations on the journey to give you a better idea of what it is like to experience each location. Although everyone experiences these differently, reading these stories is intended to help you reflect on your life to see if you identify with any of these locations. Reading about participants' experiences and how they developed their internal voices will help you consider how to develop your internal voice to manage similar challenges in your life. The map from the introduction is repeated on page 20 with the participants in this chapter stationed throughout the journey.

DREAMS MEET REALITY

Many interviewees spent their twenties figuring out who they wanted to become and what they wanted to do with their lives. Living out these dreams was more challenging than most anticipated. Even for those who in a sense got what they wanted in their careers or personal lives, life's uncertainties complicated living out their dreams. Career choices were central to most interviewees in their thirties. Some found their work fulfilling and continued on paths they had set out on shortly after college. Others changed paths in search of more fulfilling work; some found it, and others did not. The impact of external realities on interviewees' workplaces often changed the nature of their work environments in ways that were beyond their control. Companies were sold to new management, supervisors came and went, and school principals needed educators to teach different grades or at different schools. When interviewees were promoted, they sometimes found themselves in new types of work that did not suit their personal styles or priorities.

Personal life choices were equally salient. Some interviewees yearned for life partners they could not find. Those who found partners early had to work through the stresses that personal growth creates in relationships. Some were able to reframe relationships to grow with their development; others made decisions to move on. The question of whether to have children was a big issue, as was the ability to do so. Some couples' infertility led to exploring *in vitro* fertilization, surrogates, and adoption. For those who did have children, particularly women, tension between career and parenthood demands ensued. Most were torn about making the choice and concerned about the effect of childcare on their children's development. Even those who had no economic choice but to continue working still struggled with the decision, often felt guilty about it, and had to handle the pressures day care brings. Parenting in and of itself was another challenge. It came easier for some than others, yet most wondered if they were handling things effectively. Many worried about the competitiveness of schooling and safety issues. The aging and health of their own parents and grandparents was often another challenge.

In addition to these "typical" challenges that one would expect in one's thirties, interviewees faced other issues they did not anticipate. The incidence of major health problems struck me as unusually high for this group. Dawn was diagnosed with multiple sclerosis (MS); Reginald with bipolar disorder. Lauren had an emergency hysterectomy resulting from complications of childbirth, Alice contracted Guillain-Barré and was completely paralyzed during her second pregnancy, and Cara had two miscarriages. Will was diagnosed with leukemia at the age of 37 and died when he was 38. Other interviewees struggled with major health crises of their spouses—Adrian's husband contracted an incurable disease, Gennesse's spouse had a heart attack at 35, Anne's husband developed a neurological disease that required him to walk with a cane, and Justin's wife experienced a mental health crisis. Others endured the major health problems of their children. Pamela's daughter had rheumatoid arthritis by the age of two, Lydia's son had an extreme food allergy that resulted in regular emergency runs to have his esophagus unblocked, and both Kelly and Mark had children who had surgery in the first year of life. Rosa lost her 35-year-old sister to cancer. These health problems and their implications led interviewees to reconsider their perspectives on life, their identities, and their relationships. Facing the real possibility of death or long-term disability prompted rethinking priorities and defining them internally.

Some interviewees reported feeling depressed because of the stresses of life. Many reported that the attacks of September 11, 2001, affected their perspectives on life. That situation affected some interviewees directly—Evan was in his Manhattan office a block away from the World Trade Center when it fell, Kelly's husband subsequently served an 18-month tour of duty in Iraq, and Lydia's husband's military career was affected by the war. Interviewees' ability to cope with these life events and the uncertain futures that accompanied them varied in relation to the support systems available to them and to the degree to which they had developed their internal authorship at the time they encountered these challenges. The stories that follow offer insights into how interviewees experienced and processed both the expected and unexpected challenges of their professional and personal lives.

As you read these stories, observe how some of these adults struggled to value and act on their own aspirations as they set out on their life paths. Many felt bound to the opinions of others and found it difficult to put their own aspirations in the foreground of their decision making. You will notice that many made sense of their circumstances by distinguishing between what they could and could not control. The ability to accept what they could not control and to focus on what they could control helped them create a foundation for authoring their lives. Pay particular attention to how some of these adults turned challenges like a lack of fulfillment at work or an encounter with a major setback to their benefit. Some were able to use these challenges to develop internal authority that then sustained their confidence through stressful situations and helped them feel grounded despite these challenges. Finally, pay close attention to who these adults were able to draw on for support along the way.

Genesse's Story: Struggling to Listen to the Internal Voice

Genesse took a job as a marketing representative upon graduation. It would be the first of many jobs in which she encountered conflicts stemming from her personal values and with unethical supervisors. After a year of unsatisfying work in that role, she decided to try her hand at retail sales. She found herself in a glorified cashier job at her first company, so she began to explore other possibilities. When her boss learned that she was considering leaving, he coerced her into resigning. She obtained an assistant manager position with another retail company but found herself at odds again with her supervisor. The supervisor was upset that Genesse's store did not always meet its sales goals, and Genesse was uncomfortable with the aggressive sales approach her supervisor wanted her and her staff to employ. Despite being promoted to store manager during the next year, the stress of the job made Genesse physically sick, so she left for a position in a temporary agency in personnel. She noted that the only benefit of her retail days was meeting her future husband. Marriage was a bright spot in Genesse's mid-twenties.

Initially her job at the temporary agency made for a more normal life, but soon her interactions with the head of the agency turned into a nightmare. The situation was so bad that she sought therapy to process it and soon after left the position for the benefit of her mental health. She obtained a human relations position in the company where her father-in-law worked and thought she had finally found an enjoyable career. She felt that this work environment was helping her "adjust the way I'm thinking . . . I'm working toward being more autonomous."[2] Just as Genesse was settling into a good work environment, downsizing left her unemployed. After three months of searching, she found a position in customer service. It was not an ideal job, but it was workable. As Genesse turned 30, she reported that work had been the negative theme of her twenties, that she had learned that she could not trust everyone, and that she had to stand up for herself. She recognized that she needed to listen to her internal voice instead of listening to others. Circumstances in her life would continue to complicate her ability to hear her internal voice.

Turning 30 also brought the question of children to the forefront. Genesse and her husband, Greg, felt ready to have children, but she was having trouble getting pregnant. She took several rounds of fertility drugs, after which her doctor suggested *in vitro* fertilization. Worried about the expense, Genesse began reading about adoption. In the midst of their explorations, she became pregnant. The pregnancy turned out to be a challenge. She was routinely sick, ended up on extended bed rest, had to have a Caesarian section, and contracted a staph infection in the hospital. Genesse was thrilled to have a child, but as seemed to be the pattern in her life, it did not go easily.

Her daughter, Jennie, cried all night unless Genesse slept with her. Genesse consulted her doctor about what to do and he told her to let Jennie cry. Genesse tried but reported being "a basket case," sitting in the hallway crying herself. She then felt guilty taking Jennie into her bed because others said it was not wise. Not trusting herself to determine what to do, Genesse consulted her mother and mother-in-law, both of whom wavered between following the doctor's advice and telling Genesse that she should do what she felt was best. Genesse wavered as well and would sometimes make it through a night letting Jennie cry. Most nights, she ended up giving in.

The struggles with sleeping, which did not completely resolve until Jennie was four, were only the beginning of the challenges Genesse would face. Financial problems led Genesse and Greg to accept his parents' offer to keep Jennie while they worked. Jennie loved her grandparents and often did not want to come home with Genesse at the end of the day. Genesse worried that too much individual attention was not good for Jennie's development. Genesse's and Greg's concerns that Jennie needed to learn to get along with other children led them to put her in day care. She cried incessantly, and the day care staff became noticeably frustrated with her after a month. One day, two other children bit her because of their frustrations with her crying, and Genesse moved Jennie to another day care. After a month, the director recommended that she be removed because of her continual crying. Genesse's in-laws volunteered to take on the day care role again and even came to Genesse's house to pick Jennie up every morning.

The years of work-related and parenting stress left Genesse depressed and inhibited her ability to trust her feelings. Her internal voice was not yet strong enough to manage the stress, and thus she felt unable to control her reactions. She knew that she needed to take action about her bouts of crying and anger, so she began to take antidepressants. She observed that September 11 had affected her perspective, helping her frame her work problems as minimal in comparison to larger world issues. She was able to let go of some of her work-related stress and was relieved to have a good child care arrangement. She had an opportunity to acquire what appeared to be a better job. The management-oriented training for the job was extensive and enjoyable, and she made good friends in the process. At the end of training, however, she and her new co-workers were stationed in cubicles to call clients to sell their company's services. Supervisors timed their calls, and they were chastised if there was too much down time. She found herself back in a negative work environment similar to those she had experienced in her twenties. She struggled in this job for a few months, and then took a position as an administrative assistant for an investment broker. To complicate matters, her husband had quadruple bypass surgery at age 35. She described it as horrifying, particularly in light of her father's death from a massive heart attack when she was 16. She and her husband went on a diet and began exercising. After a time they "fell off the wagon," leaving Genesse feeling guilty. She said "I don't feel like I'm an adequate wife or mother, I don't give 100 percent to my job, I can't please anybody [laughs]."

Genesse's strongest supporter was her husband. Now she feared for his life:

> I don't feel joy really in anything much. I guess it is kind of a numb existence. If I had any hopes of ever quitting work, they're gone because he's not insurable. So I feel trapped. So that's what I'm going through right now. Fear of the unknown. Fear that everything is fine with Greg right now, but there may be something working that we don't know anything about. I had a scare earlier this year. I found a lump, freaked out about that, went for mammogram, they found something on the other side in a group of cysts that were together, so went back in and had that drained, so I don't know what I've got frankly.

Greg had an independent business, so they relied on Genesse's job for health insurance. Having never had a fulfilling work life, she was disillusioned about having to work. Genesse saw her husband's fragile health as something to fear because it was beyond her control; she was unable to find a sense of groundedness amid uncertainty, in part because she had not been able to listen to her internal voice to strengthen it.

Still struggling to listen to her own voice given the magnitude of challenges, Genesse found herself at odds with her mother over parenting practices but was indebted to her mother because she paid for half of the tuition to send Jennie to private school. Genesse also found herself overwhelmed with keeping up with checking Jennie's homework, checking the class Internet site nightly as the teacher expected for Jennie's first grade class, getting gifts for birthday parties, and getting her child ready for school. In our twentieth interview, I asked Genesse how she coped with all this stress. She replied:

> It's like you're on autopilot—just function day to day. I was telling you about my friend at my previous job and we were both so depressed over the whole thing. A couple of times we sat in her car at lunch and talked about how we never thought our lives would be like this. You turn off to protect yourself mentally— shield yourself; you do it because you have to.

In response to my question about whether she felt she had the power to change things, Genesse said:

> Um, no. Honestly [laughs], I wish I did. That's what my friend and I talked about too, the ability to even dream, to have any dreams to think that things could be different. No, I don't even let myself. I can't. I think I used to, but I can't remember back that far now. Now, I avoid that for fear that I'll get my hopes set on something that won't come true. Better to not even—it's a self-protection thing. Not thinking about things. But then on the other hand I think I'm very introspective, too.

The progress Genesse had made trying to listen to her voice in her late twenties had been eroded by the events of her thirties. The continual stresses of unfulfilling work, parenting concerns, financial constraints, and now her husband's health had driven her to give up her dreams. Her voice had been drowned out by the challenges in her life for which there was insufficient support. Because of her introspective nature, Genesse was aware that her voice had been drowned out. As she approached age 40, she was engaged in therapy to try to recover it.

Barb's Story: Straddling Motherhood and Law Partnership Tracks

After college, Barb worked in marketing research full time and attended law school part time. She found it challenging to focus her energy in two different areas, so after a year, she took a part-time law clerk position and attended law school full time. During her post-graduation year clerkship, she was offered a position in a law firm in another city. She struggled with the decision to move because her mother had MS and was deteriorating. Her father encouraged her to accept the job and her husband supported the move. Barb's mother died two months after Barb started with the law firm. This put life in perspective and made Barb wonder if work warranted the priority she had always given it. She also worried whether her personal style, which was nonconfrontational, was going to be a fit with law. Although she reported gaining confidence in her first year with the firm, she reported that she needed to change caring "too much about what other people think." When I asked Barb if her concern about what others thought determined what she thought, she replied, "This could be the number one misery in my life. At least once a day, someone says, 'Stop worrying about what other people think.' I probably won't be happy until I can forget that. I've been working on this."

For the rest of her twenties, Barb worked on increasing her confidence, becoming more assertive in her work role, and positioning herself to work on the kind of projects that would help her become a partner in the firm. She reported being single-mindedly career-focused until her first child was born when she was 29. Her original plan was to return to work full time, but after her daughter was born, she felt an emotional need to spend as much time as possible with her. After a four-month maternity leave, she returned to work part time. She framed the part-time work solution as a compromise that gave rise to a number of problems, not the least of which was giving up the partnership track:

> The thing I find hardest—I don't feel like I'm the best mom because I work, yet not the best lawyer because I'm part time. I can't do either perfectly—I can't do it all. Jimmy understands me wanting to be both mom and career. He likes the fact that I work, likes the money, but doesn't like that I'm exhausted. He says do whatever, but I would like him to say [one way or the other]. I can't be best at either, but have best of both—have some of both. There's no real answer.

Barb's mixed feelings come through clearly here. She didn't resent changing her focus at work and putting the partner option aside but was bothered by being less respected and felt she was making a sacrifice by working part time. She wanted to be a good mother but felt that could not be her sole role. She felt she wasn't fulfilling either role to the extent that she would have liked but appreciated having both. Her last comment is telling: She began to say she had the best of both worlds and then revised her comment to some of both worlds. Her struggle to listen to her own feelings is evident here, as is her concern about others' perceptions of her. She stood at the crossroads. She simultaneously appreciated her husband's understanding yet wished he would just "say one way or the other" because she had not cultivated her internal voice sufficiently to make the choice herself.

Barb continued part-time work and had a son two years later. As a result of changing her focus at work, she made an effort to carve out a niche for herself in the firm. She succeeded, as she reported in our fifteenth interview:

> I've found my niche, and that's what makes my job enjoyable. I have a narrow focus that gives me the confidence that I need at work to do well because I feel like I know more than most people about my small area. And so with what I'm doing, it's more talking people through issues and coming to a common understanding of things, which is easier to me than more of a confrontational type of an atmosphere. I don't get the same type of stress that I would get when I was doing things that weren't really a good fit for my personality.

This niche worked well because it gave Barb confidence and fit her personality. She also reported gaining confidence through motherhood. A year later, she reported considering returning to work full time in order to strive toward becoming a partner. Because she often worked late at night after her children were in bed, she figured that going from 32 to 40 hours was not going to be much of a change, and it would help her "make the compensation that I should be making as a full-time person and get back on partnership track. And then when my kids are in school, I'll be back where I should be." Barb still had mixed feelings about motherhood and partnership, in part because she was not sure how her employers and colleagues would respond to the balance she struck between the two roles. Worrying about the stigma associated with part-time work, Barb showed that she still cared what other people thought:

> I think I'm doing a pretty good job at this point of balancing [parenting and work]. I think I'm still looked at pretty favorably at work. I'm just afraid the longer that . . . if it's temporary, I think people are more accepting of it. The whole stigma of part-time bugs me, so I'll be anxious to get rid of that. And to be honest, my friend just had a baby and I know she's planning on coming back full-time. And I think it's going to be hard for

me because I know that she's going to probably work as much as I do and she'll be considered (for partner) just because she's coming back full-time. I don't know. I kind of liked having that one day [off] for a while. It'll be hard to give that up.

She was also feeling some stress about increased expectations at work. She remained hesitant to "take the ball and run with it" on her own. Barb's perspective on work and how to balance it with parenting revealed that she was still working at cultivating her internal voice. As she had predicted, caring too much about what others thought remained the main misery in her life. Continuing to focus on what others thought of her hindered her ability to organize her life to align with her top priorities, as well as to give advice to clients based on her gut instincts and previous experiences. A sense of tension and a tendency to second-guess herself permeated her day-to-day activities.

Reginald's Story: Finding his Calling

Reginald attended seminary immediately after college and was confident that becoming a pastor was his calling. Reginald spent considerable energy during seminary working through what he believed, listening to and cultivating his internal voice. Thus, he entered his first position as an associate pastor with confidence. He soon learned that the senior pastor was more authoritarian than Reginald had expected. Reginald found himself losing confidence initially but worked to express his beliefs. Although he found support from others in the church team, he became increasingly at odds with the senior pastor. After two years in this situation, Reginald crossed the bridge into self-authorship when he decided to stand up for his beliefs, resulting in routine confrontations between the senior pastor and him. As they were working with their bishop to resolve their differences, Reginald's father took him aside and suggested that he be tested for bipolar disorder. Because this condition was prevalent in his family and he respected his father, he went to see a doctor, though he was convinced it was unnecessary. Unfortunately, he was diagnosed as having bipolar disorder and began treatment. Prior to his diagnosis, Reginald thought he could work out the differences with his senior pastor. After the diagnosis, he decided it best for his health that he resign. After a brief break, he was placed in an interim pastor position in another church. Dealing with his diagnosis, trying to separate it from his feelings about his first pastoral experience, and being in a transitional role all shook his confidence and sent him into uncertainty of the shadow lands. At age 30, he considered giving up the ministry and becoming a teacher. He started education classes while in his interim role but was called to a church and took that assignment. While at his interim assignment, he met the woman who would later become his wife.

Reginald decided to stay in the ministry but continued to struggle in team ministries. The church hesitated to put him in an individual ministry because of his bipolar disorder diagnosis, despite the fact that he controlled it with medication. After much negotiation, the church agreed to put him back in the call process. He was called to interview in another part of the country and learned that the bishop's office had sent a letter outlining his bipolar diagnosis and suggesting that he be placed only in a team ministry.

Reginald had to work through this undermining of his respect for church authority. He was disappointed that representatives of the church he loved treated him the way they did, and given the strength of his internal voice at the time, had the courage and confidence to directly confront the bishop to express his view of the situation. He reconciled the tension between obeying church authority and standing up for his own rights by concluding that acting on his principles was the best he could do. He accepted that church authority was fallible and pursued what he viewed as the right process even when the outcome was not what he had hoped for. Indeed, Reginald's life in the church was not at all what he had expected it to be.

Reginald's personal life was not what he expected either. He married a woman who was divorced with two children. Although Reginald readily accepted the children, their father did not want them to move across the country where Reginald accepted a new call. Over the next few years, Reginald and his wife had two children together, at which point her children did move in with them, and they worked with the issues blended families encounter. Fortunately, Reginald was already building an internal foundation from which to handle these transitions and complex relationships. He also enjoyed a good partnership with his senior pastor during these years, and he and his family blossomed in their new community.

In our twentieth interview, Reginald shared that he was in transition again. His church had concluded a year earlier that they could not support two pastors. The senior pastor left so that Reginald could stay; however, the community had mixed feelings about whether Reginald should become the lead pastor. Although some members of the congregation encouraged him to ask for the call, he was hesitant to do so because he believed it would splinter the congregation. Despite the divisions in his congregation about the future direction of their church, Reginald's confidence and commitment to his ministry were not shaken this time. He explained that the problems in his congregation were "not about me" but rather about the political nature of the church. Reginald trusted his internal voice and had built a sufficient internal foundation to withstand the problems his congregation was experiencing. He did not take it personally, and it did not interfere with his role as he saw it; however, he was still in search of a pastoral assignment that held greater possibilities than those he had experienced thus far. Now that he had built a sufficient internal foundation, Reginald's next challenge was to find a professional home that fit with his psychological home.

Anne's Story: Getting Off the Career Treadmill

Anne took a job as an accountant for a paper manufacturing company after college. She was transferred twice in the first few years and ended up on the East Coast. In her mid-twenties she married, became a certified public accountant, and was promoted in her company. A combination of experience and good supervisors enabled her to become adept at thinking through problems, and she gained confidence in her internal voice; however, she became bored in her job, and despite a counter-offer from her company, she accepted a new job in the Midwest closer to her and her husband's families. She found out quickly that she had made a mistake, saying, "They wanted people to be mediocre. They thought I wanted to know too much."[3] Anne quit the job, started taking courses for her master's degree in business, and took a job in the international division of another company. Reflecting on her experience with the negative work environment, she realized that—much like Barb and Genesse—she had cared too much about what others thought of her. She recognized that she lost some of her confidence in that environment.

Anne regained her confidence in an environment that supported it. Anne found her new job to have a positive environment and enjoyed opportunities to travel to Argentina and London. At age thirty, she was reconsidering the role work played in her life and making internal commitments:

> With my new job, I was telling a friend that I am really fortunate: happy marriage, nice house, a job I love, and close to family. I'm more content. Maybe it is the way I think about things. I was always concerned about others and comparing myself and how fast they are rising; now, I don't do that as much. I'm more concerned with improving myself and enjoying myself. I am happy with where I am right now; I have met some of my expectations. I've calmed down with the rush to promotions. I'm seeing and doing new things, meeting people from all different countries. I feel like I could do this forever and be more satisfied with what I have and not so greedy. I'm busy because we are opening operations all over the world, so I don't have as much time at home as I want to. It's important to me that what I am doing at work matters. I also define myself too much by my work; I'm working on it. I measure myself a lot by my work. Unhappiness at my previous job pulled on my confidence and spread to my home life. I do need to work on this; I realize that I am more than just my job.

Anne had met some of her own expectations and thus was more relaxed about her work and less concerned about promotions. She recognized the central role her work played in her identity and the value of broadening her sense of herself beyond work. At the same time, she needed to engage in work that had value and was invested in setting the foundation for her career. In her early thirties, she received an offer to return to her original company. She scrutinized the offer carefully and judged it too good to pass up because she knew the company culture fit her values. Thus, she was acting on the internal foundation as she was building it. The arrival of her first child during this time further altered her thinking on career issues and helped her continue to build the internal foundation:

> It puts a new perspective on things. Things that were once really important to me aren't as much now because I consider her all the time now, too, what would be best for her. I used to want to run the company or be in charge, in a high position and

a high title, and honestly now I really don't care. I don't care if I'm the CFO. It's more important to me to go someplace where they're flexible. As long as the money's decent and I can come and go and the work is challenging and the people are nice, that's fine. I never thought I'd be saying that, but she's more important to me now. I have no interest in traveling like I did before to Argentina or Europe for a week or two. It is more important to me to have the time to be with her, and if I have a little less money, that's fine. We've changed our standard of living, gone from two incomes to one income and don't have some of the stuff that maybe I would like, but to me it's more important that she's sleeping in her own crib and with someone that loves her, so that's a change. I used to be—still am a little bit—more materialistic, and right now it's more important that she's home. I feel like I'm not around her enough, and sometimes I feel pretty torn about going to work, but I think it's made it easier just knowing Dad's home with her and when I leave she's in her crib sleeping.

Anne's husband had returned to school, so he stayed home with the baby. His presence at home made it palatable for Anne to go to work, even though she wanted to spend more time with her daughter. Anne still valued her career but now placed it in the context of her role as a mother. She valued her daughter being at home more than material possessions. Financially, the choice she and her spouse made was clearly the most logical. Despite Anne's confidence in her internal foundation and the decisions she had made based on it, she sometimes wished things were different. Her husband continued to stay home after their second child, and living on one income meant some sacrifices. She worried that they could not give their children some of the material things their friends had. Anne was clear that they could not afford these luxuries, yet she wanted her children to be happy.

In her late thirties, Anne and her husband encountered another challenge that altered their lives. Her husband learned that he had a hereditary neurological disease that affected his balance. This, in turn, affected his activities with the children. Anne reported how they were handling it:

We are trying to make the best of it. It's not fatal, but it definitely changed our lives. The doctors said sometimes it can get worse and people wind up in wheelchairs or this may be it. No one can really say. Right now, he doesn't feel comfortable walking without a cane. Not very bright for the future, but I just keep telling myself people are getting cancer and a girl I went to school with died of an aneurism two weeks after her child was born and this is not so much frightening. But sometimes I get to feeling sorry for myself, like what did I do to deserve all this crap going on? Last night, when I was feeling a little bit sorry for myself, Alan said, "You've got a great job and wonderful kids and it's okay." Yet he seems kind of depressed about it . . . he's kind of shut himself off a lot from the world. I'm trying to get him to do stuff, go somewhere, but he's afraid of falling.

Understandably, Anne sometimes got discouraged; however, despite her worries, Anne had constructed a sufficient internal foundation to forge ahead and try to keep a positive attitude. She and her husband did what they felt was best for their family and their children even though it differed from traditional societal norms and sometimes from their own desires.

Al's Story: Finding Peace and Calm

Al succeeded in his first postcollege career as a computer consultant where he spent time automating systems to help people do their work more efficiently. Finding this unfulfilling, he returned to school to take science courses to prepare for medical school. In his twenties, he completed his medical training, married, and joined a medical practice as a family doctor. Perhaps more importantly, he sorted out his values; learned to engage in mutual decision making with his wife, colleagues, and patients; and learned to trust his internal voice. Over the course of his twenties, Al had come to the conclusion that worrying didn't solve anything, saying, "Keeping things that matter in focus yields a sense of peace and calm; you don't need to get worked up."[4] He combined this attitude, along with his belief that Christ is there to help, to become comfortable with medical decision making. At thirty-three, he described his comfort with uncertainty in his work saying, "As long as I know I'm doing as much as I can, and I'm getting help when it is over my head, I'm comfortable with the unpredictability of a situation."[5] Al's confidence in his skills helped him build his internal foundation, which in turn enabled him to ask for help without hesitation. His confidence in himself also enabled him to share authority with his patients. He explained that he did not discourage patients from getting another opinion: "If they are not comfortable, then you've got to respect that and get them somewhere else or get help." Al's comfort with making decisions on his own did not block his tendency to keep patients in his thoughts during their illnesses, but it did keep him from second-guessing his decisions. He shared that he had been able to deal with death reasonably well, primarily because:

> I always feel like I'm doing my best, and those are my intentions. I don't really look back and say I should have done it differently. I'm not right all the time, that's for sure, but the process is usually the right process.

Like Reginald, Al was comfortable using the right process even if he did not always have control over the outcome. Al had secured his internal commitments sufficiently to deal with the risks involved in his work.

Al's work, however, was not stress free. He found working with insurance companies frustrating, particularly when he had to work with representatives who were not physicians to get approval to order tests and medications that he felt his patients needed. This "administrative nightmare" took precious time away from his working with patients and made it more difficult for him to do what was best for them. His practice group also decided to stop delivering babies because of liability and insurance issues. Al was disappointed as this was his main entrée to acquiring families for his practice, yet by his late thirties, he appreciated not having to carry a pager and get up in the middle of the night. Al had mixed feelings about his career by his late thirties:

> Would I start over and do it again? Probably not. With all the things we have to deal with now, it's probably not worth going through everything I went through to get here. But as far as jobs go, I think it's one of the better jobs I could have. It's still a job. Some people say they get up and they can't wait to get to work. It's nothing like that. I would retire if I could, but I still look at it as I'm very lucky to have the job I have and thankful that I could make the money I make and do what I do, and I'm not out in the cold laying bricks. I've done a lot of other things in my life to know there's a lot harder jobs than what I'm doing. But it's not something I'm crazy to do every day. A lot of that is

because of all the hoops you have to jump through. I think that kind of makes it less enjoyable.

Although Al was disappointed in the nature of medical practice, particularly given what he had sacrificed to become a physician, he was aware that the benefits of practicing medicine outweighed the administrative hassles. It still met his priorities of helping others and living out his principles, and he realized that relative to alternatives, it was a good line of work. Securing his internal commitments enabled him to make the best of his career situation and not get worked up about it.

Al also took on volunteer roles at the hospital. He had served as chief of family practice and secretary of the medical staff and was preparing to serve a year as chief of the medical staff. He did not seek out these roles but accepted them, "because it's a small town and you got to keep a hospital running. The hospital's depending on the people, and they're depending on the hospital." So even though Al was in a private practice and preferred to spend his time taking care of his patients, he served in these roles because it matched his internal commitments. He was aware that his background in consulting and business and his subsequent talent for this kind of work was part of why people kept nominating him for these roles.

Al never hesitated to perform his role as a citizen. He had a long history of volunteer work dating back to college when he was a Big Brother in Big Brothers Big Sisters of America, a youth mentoring organization. He was also considering how to teach his two children to be global citizens. He was unsure how to proceed and somewhat frustrated about it:

> They act like spoiled rotten kids and that just frustrates me to death. I just don't think they can understand the concept of how much they really have yet, and sometimes I'm too hard on them about that. We sponsor a child in Tanzania. They know that we send money to her and that she lives in a mud house, but they don't really grasp that she can't just go to Wal-Mart and get something. I don't think they're at the age to do it yet, but at some point I think it would be worth going to Tanzania and visiting. Say, "here's how they live," and live like that for a week. Then they'd come home, maybe they'd appreciate it. I don't know.

Al and his wife also modeled citizenship through their involvement in church, and Al's wife was heavily involved in civic activities. Although his medical practice was not as fulfilling as he had originally hoped,

Al had secured internal commitments for his life that made accepting his disappointments with medicine palatable. Because his medical decision making had become second nature to him, he could devote energy to serving in other ways and focusing on big-picture issues of parenting such as how to teach his children to be empathetic.

Phillip's Story: Making his Own Music

Phillip dreamed of going into broadcasting and making music after college graduation. After a brief stint back home where there were few opportunities, he moved to the East Coast to follow his dreams. One job led to another, and eventually he became a studio coordinator where he made tapes for blind people. Although he still dreamed of going into music production, he felt the work he was doing was meaningful and would help him meet his goals. Processing his experiences, he adjusted his goals as he learned about himself and those around him and reported that he "got a sense of what is good for me."[6] He spent considerable energy reflecting on his experiences, sorting out his priorities, trusting his own voice, and developing an optimistic approach to life. Upon turning 30, he experienced some setbacks but was determined to press on:

> If I had my druthers, I would be married by now and have plans to start a family. I can't control that. I'm of the ilk that I want to [marry] once. I'll wait until that happens. . . . I'm continuing what I set out to do. Things shake me up, and there will be more—don't get any release from it. Best thing you can do is to make lemonade out of lemons. Until the big break comes, that's what I gotta do. . . . I have chosen to just not let—even though it is hard, and sometimes I need to recoup—but try to show the world that I can rise above. I'm not going to buckle or equivocate or succumb. I do the best I can with what I have. I find that some folks my age tune out problems they face. For me, I'd just rather face them head on and work on them. They aren't going away.

Phillip was determined to succeed in life and relationships despite the setbacks he had encountered. He knew what he wanted, and he was willing to wait and work to get it. He controlled what he could and made the best of circumstances beyond his control.

Phillip found solace in his music, which he produced in a recording studio in his home. His caution in relationships finally paid off in his mid-thirties when he met and married his wife. At that same time, he bought a recording studio of his own and focused on doing voice over work. Although owning his own business had its ups and downs, Phillip trusted himself enough to give up security for flexibility and opportunity. And, as always, he was working to make the most of that opportunity.

During our twentieth interview, he shared that his son's birth changed his life. There was no doubt as we talked that Phillip was thrilled with the transformations that had occurred in his life. In addition to being blessed with a wife and healthy new baby, he appreciated the internal commitments he had secured to guide his life. At the same time, there were many challenges on the horizon, as he explained:

> My poor father was just diagnosed with Alzheimer's. He turns 76 today. This happened about the same time my mom was diagnosed with breast cancer. She made it through chemo and the operation, but that really frightened my dad. Now I'm the adult—a couple years ago, before marriage, I was a freewheeling guy, devil may care, cast my fate to the wind. Now I'm the daddy, the husband, the mortgage, mouths to feed, and responsibilities. Now I'm really faced with my parents' mortality. I'm helping to usher in a new life, trying to figure out 574 miles away from my parents, how will I help with Dad's transition? It is inevitable, and I have absolutely no control over it. That big realization—at this stage—pushing 40 here [laughs], pretty much halfway through my life, and the people who raised me since I was a baby are working their way toward shuffling off the earth. My wife and I have to figure out how often we can visit them, what is possible. I'm glad we had James when we did— even with a struggling business. Dad has an heir apparent—a grandson. He can hold his grandson. By the time James gets older, I don't know if Dad will have a brain left—how am I going to deal with that? How to tell my son what is happening to Grandpa?

Reflecting on how the combination of realized dreams and unexpected responsibilities affected his sense of himself, Phillip said:

> I'm still a work in progress—the old me is shedding skin. I've never had an irresponsible time in my life! Maybe I should have been more irresponsible in my twenties! Too late now. Despite all the responsibility and pressures, I can't really roll up into a ball and the world would go away. I have to face these

things as they come up, do the best I can, be a husband, raise my son the best way I can.

All the internal work Phillip did in his twenties to trust his voice and build an internal foundation paid off in helping him define and move toward his dreams. Securing his internal commitments also offered a basis for approaching the challenges that lay ahead.

THE ROLE OF THE INTERNAL VOICE
IN FACING ADULT CHALLENGES

Collectively these stories illustrate the range of challenges adults face in their twenties and thirties. These challenges require figuring out what you believe and value, how to define yourself, and how you relate to others. In their twenties, some interviewees were pre-occupied with what others expected and thought of them. Barb's "main misery" is an excellent example. As they tried to follow the *external formulas* offered by others to achieve success, tensions arose between their own developing priorities and others' expectations. These tensions led to the *crossroads,* a place where interviewees wavered between listening to others and listening to themselves. To move through the crossroads, they had to *listen to and cultivate their internal voices.* Those who found support for doing so were able to move through the crossroads into *self-authorship*—the ability to use their internal voices to guide their lives. For example, Reginald had support for learning to *trust his internal voice* and was eventually able to use it to work with the authorities in the church, whereas Genesse had insufficient support to trust her internal voice. Anne was able to *build an internal foundation* to guide her life decisions and cope with hardships as they arose. Al and Phillip *secured their internal commitments* to manage their multiple life roles. Despite taking various routes, some of which were more direct than others, most interviewees began to trust their internal voices to guide career and life decisions, build an internal foundation upon which to manage life's challenges, and eventually secure these commitments.

The overarching challenge interviewees faced in their thirties was to integrate their beliefs, values, identities, and relationships into an internal voice and an internal foundation to ground them when confronting the unpredictability or the chaos of their daily lives. As the stories in this chapter reveal, pressures abounded and support for developing trust in their internal voices, let alone for building a solid internal foundation and securing internal commitments, varied. Those who were fortunate enough to have opportunities and support for developing their internal voices were able to withstand the challenges they encountered with greater resilience than those who had fewer opportunities and support for developing their internal voices. The stronger their internal voices had become when major crises arose, the better participants were able to hold on to their own voices than to have them drowned out. Likewise, those who had built strong internal foundations were more comfortable dealing with the uncertainties that accompanied times of turmoil when major crises arose.

The detailed stories in the chapters that follow illustrate how participants moved through this journey to develop their internal voices and how central this was to their success in meeting the challenges of adult life. Reading their stories will hopefully give you ideas about how you can develop your internal voice.

CHAPTER 2

DAWN'S STORY—BRINGING OUT THE TRUTH IN A CHARACTER

DAWN WAS ALWAYS CURIOUS ABOUT THE MEANING OF LIFE and her own sense of self, evident in a conversation she had with herself in the middle of college about her life course. She reported having this internal conversation about taking "the road of integrity rather than weaseling your way through life" while walking in a nature preserve. Dawn referred to this experience in many subsequent interviews and saw it as a defining moment in her life. Her decision to take responsibility for her future led her to improve her grades and get off academic probation. According to her report, after changing her major "five hundred times" (including pre-med and English), she settled on history and theater in her junior year because she liked both.

A self-described tumbleweed, Dawn wandered from job to job and city to city in her twenties in search of a career in theater. Acquiring an internship in theater upon graduation heightened her optimism about making a career in the field. Theater was a context that fed her natural curiosity:

> I have had opportunities to play more than one type of character. The thing that's involved in that is exploring different parts of yourself, learning about how many different types of people you are within yourself and being able to apply that to a script that someone has written. And along with your imagination, you create these different personas. As far as the character

aspect—I think there's a lot of self-learning that goes on continually. And that's one of the things that I think that always
fascinates me about this business is you never stand still.
You're always progressing; you're always moving forward,
learning new things about yourself, learning new ways to present your ideas to a group of people. . . . The technique comes in
as transferring all that is within you to this character, your
abilities to speak the character's truth from, probably, your
truth.[1]

Playing different characters helped Dawn explore parts of herself
and access her internal voice. This was important to her development because gaining confidence in one's internal voice is the key
element in developing self-authorship. Her interest in finding that
voice, her truth, led her first to Australia, a trip intended to "allow
for self-realization and growth and freedom from insecurities I've
had before. Getting to know myself so I know I can access things
when I'm doing a character, feeling safe doing that." Her belief that
"any artist worth her or his weight will be on a path of continual self-
discovery"[2] led her next to Africa, where she climbed Mount
Kilimanjaro. These experiences helped her tap into her internal
voice and hear it more clearly when the noise of daily life was set
aside. The challenge of surviving on her own in a foreign country and
of climbing a mountain helped her hear and test her internal voice.

    Through acting and traveling, Dawn became a good observer
of herself and how she interacted with others. This helped her begin
to develop the self-knowledge that is so crucial in developing self-
authorship. Between self-exploration adventures and traveling,
Dawn worked in theater, mostly in unpaid venues such as her first
internship or independent plays. She waited tables on the side to
earn money and became increasingly involved in restaurant work
over the next few years. At one point, she attended a Stage Combat
Workshop where she met a potential partner. A few months later, an
opportunity to write a play for a theater and to develop the new
relationship prompted her to move across the country, where she
landed a job as a line cook. Three weeks later, the executive chef
quit, and because she did not want to adjust to a new chef, she
asked for the job. She viewed it initially as a way to take responsibility for her financial security so that she could do the things she
wanted to do in theater. Cooking professionally turned out to be
another venue for her creativity and a chance to learn more about

herself. Unknown to her at the time, it would become a central part of her future.

DAWN'S JOURNEY

In her early twenties, Dawn found an outlet for her proclivity for self-exploration in theater. Explaining that she combined herself with the script to bring a character to life on stage, she said, "To bring out the truth in a character, I think you have to have an immense understanding of all the little truths within yourself."[3] The self-discovery inherent in her theater work enabled her to move through the crossroads toward self-authorship. The map of Dawn's journey shows the paths she took to self-authorship and the partners she had along the way.

Moving Through the Crossroads Toward Self-Authorship

Dawn described the effects of self-discovery:

> The more you discover about yourself, the more you can become secure with it. And that obviously leads to greater self-confidence because you become comfortable with who you really are. My confidence level is so much better than it ever has been. I'm more willing to express my ideas and take chances expressing my ideas. . . . When you're confident, you are more willing to say: "This is my opinion; this is why I hold this opinion. You may agree with it or not, but this is what—with my mind I have formulated this opinion and that's how I think and feel." I'm not as afraid to be willing to say that because of what I am this is how I feel. . . . And I think self-awareness too, because you realize that it doesn't really matter if other people agree with you or not. You can think and formulate ideas for yourself, and ultimately that's what's important. You have a mind and you can use it. That's probably the most important thing, regardless of the content of what your thoughts and opinions are. . . . It's the fact that you can form an opinion that's more important than the opinion itself. . . . So it's kind of a self-confidence and self-awareness thing.[4]

Dawn's discovery of aspects of her identity heightened her confidence and lessened her concern about what other people thought of her. This led her to express her ideas and to recognize the value of being able to formulate ideas for herself. Although she recognized her ability and power to use her own mind to create her beliefs and identity, she would need to undertake significant soul-searching to live out that ability. She spoke freely about this soul-searching period as it occurred in her twenties and thirties. I always looked forward to these conversations, as Dawn dove directly into the core of her thinking processes.

Entering the Crossroads: Listening to the Internal Voice. Dawn actively pursued listening to her internal voice, which she referred to as her spiritual self, during her twenties—a quest that prompted her three-month solo backpacking trip across Australia and her trip to Africa to climb Mount Kilimanjaro. One aspect of her internal voice that she was struggling to listen to concerned her sexual orientation. She first introduced this dynamic in our tenth interview:

> One of the biggest things—it hasn't come up in any of our conversations before—was accepting the fact that my sexual orientation is out of the mainstream. It was a big thing for me. It started for me when I was in school. You finally get to a point where you can feel comfortable enough that you don't care what people think about you. The turning point was in the last couple of years. It brought out interesting things in me. It has taken me probably five years to feel solid. Now, I don't care if you know if I'm gay and what you think. It doesn't matter, and this is who I am. Dealing with that with family—I told my parents three years ago.[5]

Although Dawn was aware of this aspect of her internal voice during college, her turning point in cultivating it came a few years after college. Her parents accepted her sexual orientation just as they had accepted her spontaneous approach to life after college. When I asked why this had not entered our previous conversations, Dawn replied:

> It wasn't that I couldn't talk about it; [it] becomes a personal thing. Now I am at that point that I am comfortable—it doesn't bother me. A big thing in the last couple years in my life. That has contributed a great deal to how I see things and how I think. Getting to where I am now, the confidence thing; you know you have the inner strength to stand apart from the mainstream. I don't have to be a duck in a row, following what everyone else is doing. Whether it has to do with being gay or

not. The best way I can explain it is learning to walk. You get stronger and finally run. It is a release, where you are willing to let go of clutter that people throw at you.[6]

Dawn clearly articulated letting go of external formulas about sexual orientation and other matters in favor of strengthening her internal voice. The length of time this took reveals how arduous working through the crossroads can be.

In our twelfth interview, as Dawn neared 30, she tried to explain her spirituality and how it related to her everyday life. Making it clear that she was not religious but rather spiritual, she offered this perspective:

> I believe that there are forces in this world that are more powerful than we are, and there are some we can readily acknowledge and others that I think we cultivate over time. It's, I mean, I would say one of those [that we cultivate] would be intuition— well actually it could fall into both [categories]. It is readily available, but it takes time to cultivate as far as trusting your intuition and trusting that voice that says, "This is where I need to be." To the point where I think it almost takes on psychic proportions. That is all part of spirituality—mine anyway. . . .[7]

Dawn's comment foreshadows the evolution of the journey through listening to, cultivating, and eventually trusting one's internal voice. She described intuition as "listening to the voice inside of you" and noted that, "Your intuition is the central processing unit."[8] Although she labels this spirituality, she seems to be talking about the internal voice and generating general principles for living. In response to my confusion about how she reconciled cultivating intuition with her belief in powerful forces beyond her, she explained they interacted and how she tried to apply this to her everyday life:

> It is a real fine line. To find that balancing point, that ability of saying I really want to do this. Put the thought out in the universe that I can bring this into my life, somehow I will make this happen. Doing that, and allowing the universe to work its magic and bring it to you. It happens, I've done it! I'm trying to understand how that works. The brain cannot process that on a linear level, but the heart and soul can, because it knows what's going on. That is the big clarity that happens when I travel. I get myself to a point—and I'm trying to figure out how to translate this into my daily life—I get myself to a point where I can just strip away—oh, balance my checkbook, the time clock, fight

traffic—you lose all of that. It is a complete simplification of what your reality is at the very moment. Like climbing the mountain. So in the moment, what is past and ahead doesn't matter because you are so consumed by what is going on at that time. That, too, is clarity. . . . Then again, as time goes by, the noise filters back in. Something I am having to learn how to do— coming back to [the] whole spiritual self thing, maybe I've gathered enough insight that I'll know what to do. Whether it is stare out the window for 15 minutes a day or live in the moment. Because, barring deciding to take every day off for life and travel, I have to find a way to function in the noise.[9]

Staying in touch with her internal voice required shutting out the noise of daily life to get to that point of clarity. Much of this noise stemmed from external sources. Because her internal voice was not yet loud enough, she needed to tune out the external noise to be able to hear it.

One context in which external noise drowned out Dawn's voice was a significant relationship. Her partner broke off their relationship, much to Dawn's surprise. In retrospect, Dawn realized that she had lost sight of herself in this relationship, saying, "A lot of it is not listening to myself and not trusting myself." Dawn met a new person at a stage combat workshop she attended and subsequently moved across the country to pursue that relationship. She also created the opportunity to direct one of her favorite plays (Jean Paul Sartre's *No Exit*). When Dawn was able to block out external noise, she was able to listen to herself. In those moments, she recognized and took advantage of opportunities that would help her reach her goals (such as directing the play).

Traversing the Crossroads: Cultivating the Internal Voice. Dawn was challenged to cultivate her internal voice when she was diagnosed with multiple sclerosis (MS) at age 33. The diagnosis accelerated her quest for self-discovery, as she reported in our sixteenth interview just two weeks after her diagnosis:

There is so much processing going on, what I do on a daily basis, trying to fit all the pieces of the puzzle together. I think I'm definitely at a point where I am really defining a lot about my life. Not that it is discovering new things—I'm sure I am— but bringing everything that I've ever thought and believed into a much clearer focus for myself. I'm in very deep thought about evaluating what is important, what is not so important, what gives me comfort, emotionally, mentally, discovering these things. Specifying these things that accomplish these things for me. . . . If you are very specific in your frame of mind in how you approach and handle things, that makes it much simpler. The whole thought process of just taking stock of where you are in your life. It's like putting your life through a sieve, getting the big awkward chunks out of your life, getting the nice finely sifted residue—it is kind of sorting it all out. What is the essence of you and what isn't? What is important to the essence of you and what isn't? . . . You have to decide what it is that you want and don't want. Little by little, things take a much more specific shape. Who is to say, tomorrow I might wake up and have something that occurs in my day that sets me on a completely different road, so there I am again sifting and rebuilding with all this new information that I have. I don't suppose it happens that rapidly. I think I'll be on this path for a while until it is time to go in another direction.[10]

Dawn's processing reflected a shift from listening to her internal voice to cultivating it to make decisions about the essence of her identity. Using all that she previously thought and believed, she sorted and sifted to get to the essence of who she wanted to be. Although this was largely internal work, Dawn enjoyed the support of family and friends as she engaged in this processing. Simultaneously, she was using her internal voice to make decisions about the essence of her relationship to the world:

You take in information and see how it feels given your accumulation of life experiences to that point. If it feels right you keep it; if it doesn't, you let it go. As far as thinking how that relates to like deeper issues, um, I think a lot of it also has to relate to the self, how you view yourself. If you respect yourself, if you have confidence in your ability, that changes your whole perspective. If you respect yourself, it is pretty much a given that you will respect others. Treating others with compassion and understanding can only happen when you've achieved a certain level of that yourself. Just thinking about the energy of the world and how we treat each other and how—that is a big defining thing for me right now. Stepping into that realm of not judging people, treating them with compassion, acting in my life without judging and with compassion. That is a step that I'm trying to take for myself right now; relates to the karma idea—you get back exactly what you give. If you are always putting forth things that are positive in the world, you get things that are positive right back at you. That is how the world works; it may not come back immediately. It is a simpler, more peaceful way of living. That right there eliminates a lot of daily stresses and makes the day much more pleasant. It contributes to you as an individual being a better person and getting more out of life.[11]

This sorting and sifting enabled Dawn to cultivate her internal voice sufficiently to begin self-authoring her life. I was shocked to hear of her MS diagnosis, but her resilience in response to it did not surprise me. This resilience stemmed from her careful attention to sorting and sifting to refine her knowledge about herself.

Self-Authorship: Trusting the Internal Voice

Dawn's new view of relating to others required continued work on cultivating her spiritual core, the essence of herself:

For quite a long time I've been introspective, pursuing that knowledge of self, sense of self, spiritual centeredness—this has evolved over time, but the MS diagnosis accelerated it even more. I think it is fulfilling something that I've always wanted; never thought I'd get it quite this way. You follow the Tao of life, Zen moment, go with the flow, take on whatever comes your way—I always wanted that and I'm finally getting it. There are days when I don't have it, but for the most part I do. I'm trying to make something better out of myself and make the world a better place with me in it. I feel more deeply connected to my spiritual center than I ever have before in my life.[12]

Having heavily invested in cultivating this philosophy, Dawn was determined to use it in handling her MS:

My illness, well not an illness, a condition—it will not control my life. I have way too much to do and accomplish to let it get in my way. It challenges me. And I'm okay to give it that much leeway. I've maintained since the beginning that this is definitely a gift. It can be viewed as unfortunate, but at the same time it has gotten me into this way of thinking, exploring my world, that is different. I go deeper within myself. When you face that you can't do something, the door opens to something you can do. Enjoy yourself and immerse yourself in that. I do control it; it will not control me.[13]

She described herself as "more malleable around obstacles" and added that "obstacles are not a hard blockade, but rather you can shift and move with that energy around them, and they solve themselves." She called this the "art of controlling without controlling":

> Finding the balance between [going with the flow] and me saying I have control over myself, not letting this condition get the best of me. Knowing how to make things happen and let things happen. When you find the balance between those things, life is spectacular. That is kind of a trust thing—trusting that you know yourself enough to dance that line. Know when to make something happen and when to let it happen. Trusting yourself that you know that space. I don't quite know myself enough to trust that yet. I'm working on it. I'm getting close. That deepest self-knowledge to know you can stay there at that middle point and have that balance. That is a constant process for me. To be able to say this is my life and it's on my terms; I love that.[14]

Trusting her internal voice, her spiritual core, seemed to be a prerequisite for her internal voice functioning as the internal foundation for her life. Dawn's MS diagnosis brought home a realization she was already working on: that she could control her reaction to reality but she could not control reality. Her decision to focus on what she could control and to move around obstacles helped her learn to find the balance between reality and her reactions to it. This balance guided her in knowing when to make things happen versus when to let them happen.

Knowing herself deeply enough to trust knowing when to make things happen versus when to let them happen was an ongoing quest. Dawn clarified that the quest was not one of straightforward, steady progress. She noted that she was not always spiritually centered:

> I went through this phase where I questioned everything. I questioned what I believed; I questioned every spiritual principle that I'd ever thought was true; I felt very lost. . . . I always felt like I was fighting to get back on track and I just couldn't and that lasted for a couple of months where I just felt like I was just tumbling around in space with no sense of direction or anything to cling to and I was just out there lost. And I don't know if I can pull it to one defining moment where everything came right back together for me. I think probably sometime in the early spring it started to gel again, and now I feel like I'm at the complete opposite end of the

spectrum because I know, have such a clarity over what I think, what I believe, spiritual purpose, which is kind of an interesting journey. You don't stay in the light all the time. I mean there are times when you go to the shadow lands and I don't know if that was teaching me something? I haven't really sat down and put the pieces together, but it has just led me to this point where I feel so grounded and so connected with myself and the world in which I live, and it has brought clarity, I think, to me about my health, about who I am, where I want to go.

This period of questioning and confusion that Dawn called the shadow lands suggests that Dawn's internal voice faded out temporarily, perhaps because she did not yet completely trust it. The following year, Dawn reported another stint in the shadow lands. She was not rehired after a year as an executive chef, a blessing in some ways due to the stress restaurant management put on her health. She did odd jobs until her relationship dissolved and then decided to move across the country again to help a friend start a café. The café fell through, but "out of the blue," she was hired as a private chef. Two interrelated crises occurred in her life that called for continued work on the internal voice: a decline of her physical health and another relationship break-up. After her MS diagnosis, she had taken up cycling to maintain her physical health and had persisted in doing so for three years. Then things unraveled:

And curiously enough, when I got into this relationship, I kind of forgot about all of that. Like my focus went to the relationship and not me. And all last winter I didn't really exercise. I put on weight—not a lot of weight, just normal, I think, for the winter, not really doing anything. And I started to have problems with my balance, it's just like I started to go on this downward slide. And I think what happened just before the break-up was I was out in [city] to see my doctor, and her consensus was . . . "Well, I think you've gotten worse." And I think all I needed to hear was that. It was just like, "Hell no, I haven't gotten worse." Now whether it's true or not, we're still kind of determining that. That scared me a lot to hear that. Because I guess as can happen with this disease, you can start to go downhill and that can be it. I guess from the beginning I've been like all right, fine. I understand that I have this disease, but it's not going to rule my world. And then I kind of lost sight of that until that moment, "You're getting worse." I'm like, "No, I'm not." And it's kicked me into high gear.

Her doctor's assessment made Dawn aware that she had veered too far toward "letting things happen." She was not "making things happen" because she was not bringing her internal voice into managing her health and contributing to this relationship. She had inadvertently abdicated the front seat of the bike. She elaborated:

> It was even more propelled by the relationship break-up. I couldn't necessarily take care of myself emotionally because I was just completely unraveling, which was okay. That needed to happen, but I had to do something to try to take care of myself, and that was when I started riding even more, 15 to 20 miles a day. I think just the fact that I wasn't taking care of myself and that my health was appearing to be on the decline a little bit, my balance wasn't good and I was running into stuff and falling down. And I noticed that that was happening, but I really wasn't taking any steps to correct it. It was really frustrating me, making me angry, and some of that came out in our relationship. It wasn't necessarily directed at her, but I would just be really frustrated, and I didn't really know why. I stopped approaching myself as someone with a disease or condition that I need to take care of myself. Out of the break-up has just come a lot of self-awareness. It's just like, "Wow, I really have to take care of myself." It happened before, during and after the break-up that this whole turnaround has happened. I've educated myself about a lot of things that I didn't even know were caused by the MS. I've suddenly gotten on this whole educational kick about, OK, what can this do to me? What can potentially happen? Well, I know what can potentially happen, but it's just like, OK, I have this problem. Is that just because I have this problem with my health, or is it because of the MS and, it's just kind of coming back to myself. And I mean that's just been a huge thing. I totally lost it in this relationship and that was a big reason too why it didn't work. You got to be yourself. You got to bring yourself to the relationship, and I just kind of stopped doing that and I'm not really exactly sure why. I'm still working that one out.

This time of losing sight of herself also played out in her spiritual dimension:

> Spiritually I've gone up and down. The last time we spoke when I said it was the most spiritually connected I've ever felt, it went on a tremendous roller coaster ride from there because I've gone from feeling that to feeling absolutely not spiritual at all, feeling no spiritual connection to anything. And now it's

kind of coming back, I feel like I'm kind of touching base again
in that. It's not that you're ever not spiritually connected.
Maybe you just don't always see how you are.

Touching base again with her spiritual core came with the awareness of work she needed to do for her health and to construct
healthy relationships. She recognized the power of her internal
voice in maintaining her health and relationships. She trusted her
internal voice sufficiently to set about the business of building an
internal foundation for herself. Not only was she riding her own
bicycle 15 to 20 miles a day, she was also back on the front seat of
the tandem bike for good.

Self-Authorship: Building an Internal Foundation

Trusting her internal voice enabled Dawn to acknowledge and
accept her personal talents. She explained:

> It's now been three years since the MS diagnosis, and my focus
> is really on taking care of myself, and how can I use this broad
> range of talent that I have to take care of myself physically but
> also to take care of myself career-wise? You know as much as I
> love theater, and I'm not ruling any sort of theatrical activity
> out of my life. It has taken me this long to really settle with the
> idea that I'm very gifted in the kitchen, and, believe it or not, it
> took me a long time to even say that because I have this whole
> modesty complex. Well, I'm kicking that out the door, you
> know? I have a gift and I should be very proud of and not hide
> the fact that I have a gift. And so there's been a remarkable
> amount of self-discovery and self-awareness that has taken
> place in the last couple of years for me.

Acknowledging and accepting her personal talents was a building
block for focusing on her purpose. She began to think more long-
term than she had in the past, turning her focus toward creating
both an internal and physical foundation for her life:

> I started to look at what I'm good at and how to take those
> things, and particularly with the cooking, it's just like, "No, I
> am tired of working for somebody else's vision." I have my own
> ideas. I have my creativity. I have my own style in the kitchen.
> Why can't I start working for my own vision and make that a
> success, and make a living off of that? And I think in the past year
> is when I really focused in on the long term and settling down a

little bit 'cause, I mean we've talked since I was a freshman in college basically. You've gotten a pretty good idea over the last, say, five to ten years of what kind of a gypsy I've been . . . just kind of goin' and doin' whatever, wherever, however. And I think in the past year I've really started to bring the focus of my life into a more specific area and having a place to call my own. But I love the flexibility that I have now 'cause I don't work every day and now I'm focusing in on getting my own place to call home, and building this whole network and infrastructure for myself. So then I use that to kind of launch myself into all these directions that I want to go and things I want to do, but when I come back, it's like I know I have this framework in which to exist, and that's made a big difference. And I don't know if part of that is because of the MS or not. I think it is because the precarious nature of my health, although I'm doing everything I can to keep it from being precarious, and that certainly is working, I think I need a framework or some stability there just so I know that I've got a solid place to be no matter what happens in my life.

Dawn's focus on her internal identity had routinely overshadowed any concern about a physical infrastructure such as a home or stable job to support her life. Yet her deepening understanding of her MS and herself has provided her with the confidence necessary to structure her external environment in a way that best fits her needs and interests. Shifting from her gypsy past to a more stable future, she now uses her own voice and vision to create a framework for her life. Whereas the structure others created for her had been confining, her own self-made structure is freeing. Beginning to feel both internally and physically grounded, Dawn moved closer to her core as she accepted and celebrated her talents and started to incorporate them into her identity:

I work magic in the kitchen, and my therapist would be so happy to hear me speaking in such really incredible terms about myself. Now I'm realizing, too, that what I've held onto all along is that it is very much a creative and artistic outlet for me, which is why I started cooking professionally in the first place because my theater work wasn't making me a lot of money and I had to support myself. I started cooking, and it's just like a huge opening to all of the wonderful things in life that I am. Also, opening to myself, being a wonderful person, and enough of this downplaying it. Life is short. You've got to celebrate every moment that you have. Part of that also has been like this acceptance, even three years into it, of the whole MS thing. Just the whole concept of really accepting . . . I mean I'm sure I denied it a little bit, but just accepting that it is a part of me. It does not have to rule my life in any stretch of my imagination. It will not rule my life. I just feel such a complete sense of settling into myself and everything about me. This is the most peaceful I have felt, I think, in a very, very long time, if ever, you know? And I just feel like I'm landing in who I am and what it is I'm meant to do, and where, all these things that I can do and all these tools that I have available to me, and I know how to use them. And it's like OK, the extraordinary life has begun. I mean it has always been so, but it's just like now you're completely aware of it. I opened this door, and there is no going back. I have all this energy now and this excitement about where I'm going and what I'm doing and how I'm going to do it. But it had to be my willingness to change that, to stop the downplaying, to really just kind of embrace myself for all the amazing things that I can do. Even celebrating the little things that may not be necessarily categorized by some people as amazing but . . . like the fact that I get up every morning and ride 15 miles on my bike. That's pretty amazing in its own right. So there's been a big shift in that approach to myself and my life.

Dawn's refining of her internal foundation by embracing her talents, her MS, and the things she could do fueled her quest for her spiritual core:

I want a greater relationship with the powers that move this world and the people in it. I think that's a big basis of my spiritual ideology. I think about how things work and the energy, how forces work, and higher powers, and bigger powers than we are . . . I'm like, what is the meaning of life? I want to know that answer. If there is that answer to be had, and that's how I function because I believe that there is always more; therefore, we just have to open ourselves to it and go get it. And it's a very conscious quest for me. I think that's one of the things that gives me this strength that I seem to have. I'm learning a lot about strength right now. Coming out of this break-up, I've had to go to places in my heart that I could never really willingly dive into and be vulnerable and just be emotionally torn apart in order to put myself back together again. There is a definite spiritual aspect of all of that. Learning how being that vulnerable is not weakness but rather strength, and being willing to dive into that and know that you're going to come out of it and be even stronger and even more grounded. Three months ago you couldn't have convinced me of that, but now it's just like, okay. It's been a journey into the deepest part of myself that has really, um, it's almost, I just feel so solid—like I know me better than I have ever known myself at this point in time in my entire life. I seem to come to those big conclusions when I talk to you. This is the most spiritual I've ever felt. This is the most peaceful I've ever felt. I know me more than I've ever known myself in my entire life. But I guess that's me. I mean that is my process, and that is how I function in this world. Now I guess I have this greater awareness of all of that.

Dawn's conscious quest for more meaning helped her continually build her internal foundation with her therapist as a good partner through this process. By opening herself to that something more, by going to get it, she developed strength even through painful explorations. Each journey to the shadow lands made her stronger because she emerged each time with a stronger understanding of her spiritual core. I came to have great respect for her courage in self-exploration. The continual deepening of her sense of self led to a transformation from knowledge to wisdom that she described in our next interview.

Self-Authorship: Securing Internal Commitments

In the process of implementing her decisions about her career, health, and relationships, many of the strands of her previous introspection came together. She reported:

I feel like I'm in this situation where I'm learning a whole new side of me that I suspected might have existed before, but I never had the opportunity to get to know it or put it into practice. How resourceful I am and how strong I am and resilient I am and smart I am and just all these new facets of me that are starting to come to light. I'm very much enjoying the whole process of getting to know that. It's almost another level. It's not to say that I didn't see those things before. It's just maybe a deepening of all of that, a maturing of all of that.

Intrigued, I asked Dawn to elaborate. She explained her transformation from knowledge to wisdom:

It's starting to feel—more like wisdom than knowledge. To me, knowledge is an awareness of when you know things. You

> know them as facts; they are there in front of you. When you
> possess the wisdom, you've lived those facts, that information,
> so fully that it takes on a whole different aspect than just
> knowing. It is like you absorbed that information into your
> entire being. Not just that you know things. It is something
> deeper. Knowledge is brain—wisdom comes from a different
> place I feel like. Something deeper connecting with your brain
> so that you have something different to draw from. A point
> where knowing you are going to do something. The knowledge
> has a deeper level—internal, intuitive, centered in entire
> being, the essential part of you that just—makes the basic
> knowledge pale by comparison.[15]

Dawn's description suggests that wisdom emerges when knowledge
merges with sense of self as a result of living the facts. She offered
two examples in which she relied on this internal, intuitive wisdom.
She reported that her cooking was so intuitive that she often thought
about other things while she cooked, rarely used recipes, and knew
how ingredients would taste together even in dishes that she did not
personally like. She explained, "There is just a sense that these elements will all go together—I know it." The second example was riding in the MS 150 in the summer heat. She knew instinctively that
she was able to ride 150 miles despite the physical challenge it
entailed. She never doubted her ability to finish the journey.

Her efforts to merge her knowledge of MS with her sense of
self led her to a workshop for individuals with chronic diseases. She
shared an important insight she had gained:

> There was an exercise that we did . . . it was picking an element
> of our body symptom and what that meant and all of a sudden
> this whole warrior character came out in me. And then we had
> to pick another . . . something else and how that made me feel,
> and it was much softer and much more thoughtful and much
> more relaxed. So, the upshot of it was, you have the warrior but
> then you also have this other side of you that's waiting to come
> out. It was an amazing time. I felt like I was on my way to that
> destination before I took the workshop, but that just kind of set
> everything up. It's a very creative approach to psychology that
> I have really gravitated toward, and it's been fantastic. Under-
> standing that . . . I didn't have to carry all the armor; I didn't
> have to carry the warrior tools anymore; I could set those down
> and just be a much softer, much more loving person toward
> myself and other people and toward the MS, and the same with
> the MS toward me.

Dawn reflected that the warrior had been her process for dealing with MS initially. She described it as "strong, bold, brave, conquer to keep myself going forward." Discovering another, softer side enabled her to reframe her sense of self with MS. She came to see it as "a friend that helps guide me, [to] give me information on how to best proceed on my path. . . . I know how hard to push myself, know when to say stop."[16] She had adopted her own health problems as a partner on her journey. She gleaned another insight from an exercise where she was asked to walk from point A to point B to map out how her body symptoms made her feel. She reported what happened:

> It was in a conference room, so there were a bunch of people in the way. So I constantly had to weave in and out of the people 'cause I picked my spot where I wanted to walk to. When I stopped and turned around to look, I just started laughing because that's how I walk! Maybe it was a little bit more exaggerated than how I walk normally, but I don't walk a straight line. I kind of weave, and it was just really starting to understand how my body does work. It's like by not walking a straight line, I cover more territory and I see more things, looking at it that way. So that's been kind of a shift for me.

Dawn's insights about her body and her health reveal that she was open to finding new parts of herself and thinking in new ways about the role MS played in her life. As was typical of our conversations, the discussion turned to how crossing over into wisdom related to spiritual matters. Dawn offered:

> I have a tremendous will, but what does that mean exactly? I mean is this what some people call like their deepest soul? Is this a higher power? What is this? And you know, maybe that's where I am right now, now that I've gotten to this new level, and I don't really know how to explain it. And it's just a feeling of completeness. I feel like I could point my finger at something and raise it up and lower it. I don't know what it is and why is it traveling in a lot of my life, yet in some places not so much? Not that it's selective, but I think that's when experience comes in. I have a lot of experience in the kitchen, so therefore, I have a lot of confidence in the kitchen. I have a lot of experiences as an athlete, so when I ride my bike, therefore, I have a lot of confidence as an athlete and on my bike. Personally, not even in terms of dating relationships, but in friendships, I'm a little shyer and, hmm, maybe not as confident as the rest of my life would indicate. So maybe that's somehow tied to the amount of

experience one has and how it contributes to one's confidence. But I don't know what it is, and I do feel like I'm in this moment of trying to really kind of put my finger on it and see if I can find that answer.

Dawn's will, her wisdom about herself, was stronger in her work and cycling than it was in relationships, a theme that would resurface in more detail the following year. Her confidence in herself and her feeling of completeness, however, did initiate a shift in her spiritual perspective:

I think it's definitely very spiritual. I think maybe even my perspective on that is changing a bit in just that this is . . . I would say this is very spiritual but not necessarily in the ways that I thought it would have been say a year ago. Can I explain that? I don't know. It's just um . . . I guess because it feels much more free form, not as concrete as I guess I would have maybe said some things were spiritually in the past. This feels much more amoeba-like and not as well defined, but yet comfortable and very much a part of me. I think that's the best way I can say it. I mean . . . OK, so now do I get to the point in my life where like everything becomes undefined and not really vague, but indefinable? It just becomes something that you *know,* but you can't really describe it? I mean what's that about? You start to shift over into information or feelings or intuitions or senses . . . that aren't necessarily tangible, but you almost pick them up by osmosis. When it starts to become that sort of a thing, that to me is crossing over into wisdom.

Dawn seemed to be communicating that the deeper her knowledge of herself becomes (or as it becomes second nature), the more intangible, flexible, and free her core sense of herself becomes. She *knows* more firmly, yet in less concrete ways. This wisdom led simultaneously to a greater sense of freedom and a greater sense of certainty. Dawn realized that the freedom she had always craved did not preclude having a physical infrastructure of a home and stable job; in fact, she realized that a stable physical infrastructure for her life allowed her to exercise her freedom in more powerful ways. Dawn's merger of the physical infrastructure of her life with her internal foundation reflected her ability to shape her external environment rather than to be shaped by it, which resulted in a new degree of balance for her:

I want to be able to balance that absolute freedom, that fly-by-the-seat-of-my-pants with a settled, comfortable living. I want that financial security to know that my bases are covered, but then I can go ahead and be that fly-by-the-seat-of-my-pants kind of girl when I want to be. It's like creating a structure that I can float around in or on or above, but I always have that structure. It's just a whole different definition of freedom in a sense, and I really enjoy it. To say that I enjoy it more than, you know, just being able to take off and do whatever I want . . . it's just different. And much more grounded and much more solid and, in some ways much more powerful.

After I asked her to explain what "more powerful" meant, Dawn continued:

Well, it kind of goes back to that whole superhero thing I was telling you about. . . . It's in that confidence. Not that I wasn't confident because I think you have to be confident to take off to Australia for three months by yourself. But it's different. Where that might have been a little more powerful in a youthful, whimsical sort of way, this is just . . . there's certainty. That was, "I am throwing myself into the great beyond and I don't know what I'm going to come up against. I am just putting my faith in the fact that everything's going to be fine because I'm not really entertaining any other ideas." This is just . . . it's just a certainty . . . as certain as I was when I got on my bike to ride 150 miles. It's like, I absolutely know this to be true, and while we don't know what each day's going to bring for us, there's just a connected . . . and I think that's where the spirituality ties in again . . . there's a connectedness and it's just not so much casting yourself into the great beyond and whatever happens, happens. Now it's just like, well, let me do this, and then I'm going to watch what happens. It's more engaged and okay, now I'm going to do this, and I'm going to watch what happens. That's a very conscious way of expressing it, but you know, I think it does become more unconscious when you're actually proceeding through each day.

Dawn's greater sense of certainty stems from the internal wisdom that prompts her to know she can do what she sets her mind to and adjust to unknowns that the next day brings. These external uncertainties do not shake her internal certainty. This grounded, more solid, and more powerful internal core yields a different form of freedom that is more substantive than the physical freedom to spontaneously decide to travel. This well-developed internal foundation allows her the freedom to act, watch what happens, and be confident that she can make something positive take place. She is living the commitments she has developed. Just as Dawn describes using this internal foundation—what she calls wisdom—as a source of freedom, she uses her newly constructed physical infrastructure to support this way of life.

Dawn's comments reflect greater confidence than she had earlier when she talked about putting something out into the world and having it come back to her. Now that she has cultivated what she earlier called intuition into a solid internal foundation based on her deep understanding of herself, she consciously acts on her internal commitments and waits to see the result. Her actions are calculated rather than exploratory because she knows what she wants and trusts that she can influence the outcome to achieve her goals.

The following year, Dawn was applying her wisdom about herself in a new relationship and in starting a private chef business. She was starting to act on the decisions she had been making in previous years. The most difficult area for her was relationships, an area in which she expressed less confidence in earlier years. She was taking the risks to share her internal self with another person. She described what it was like to act on this commitment:

> I know what I want in a partner and what I need to bring to the table. These are the things that I need to work on. I still am discovering how. Within myself I have been . . . safe. But then, when you have to deal with someone else and knowing that that's something that you want, I definitely would love to be in a long-term relationship, a very caring, open, nurturing, communicative relationship with someone. When you find someone who is that and you're not, it's like, okay, I got some work to do here. I'm pushed up against some big edges and, it's like, okay, you have a choice. You either stay here and be miserable or you can cross over and yes, it's scary, and yes, it's risky, but what's on the other side would be absolutely blissful. And so risk taking has also been a big, big part of the last couple of months. It's like every big decision that I've made in the past couple of months has all led to other decisions, big decisions to be made and a lot of other things connecting. Once you decide to move the boulder, it's going to start rolling; that's the choice you made. You took the risk; you pushed it. . . . Everything that comes along with it, you just have to be there for. Getting specific about some very big things—my business and this relationship, moving. Making these big decisions has all just kind of created this . . . this chaos but it's a wonderful chaos. I'm just

kind of moving through it seeing how everything's going to kind of settle down into place and it's great.

Dawn's desire for an infrastructure for her life and a loving, long-term relationship led her to big decisions and significant risks. As she described earlier, she actively engaged in watching what would happen and was eager to see how it would all settle into place. Despite her certainty that it would settle into a good place, she described yet another level of self-exploration she experienced:

> I've really kind of had to open up part of me that I've kept closed off for a really long time. Not closed off, but protected, very protected, and not wanting to step out there, not wanting to take risks and, you know what? I'm okay where I am by myself on my own, but then discovering oh, I want so much more. It's like okay, but to get more this is what you're going to have to do. You're going to have to take those risks. And I have taken some very big risks particularly around this relationship. I did something that I've never ever done before in my life and made up my mind. It's like this is what I want and to the point where I made a move with her stating that. It's like, you know what? Here I am. This is what I want. I think this has a lot of potential. In a very bold way to say let's see what happens. Which I've never done that before—ever. It paid off. Suddenly . . . all these things I'm starting to get a clear vision of in opening myself back up to the world.

As Dawn developed her internal foundation, she had focused primarily on understanding herself. In earlier relationships that did not work out for her, she had lost herself in the process of trying to please her partner. Processing these experiences led her to realize that she needed to apply the honesty she had gained within herself to her relationships with others. So, she returned to build her internal foundation in this arena. Opening herself back up to the world, however, meant facing the emotional barrier she had built up over time:

> I think it has just taken time to come to the surface to get me to pay attention to it. I've never been one to be really open and vulnerable. I'm feeling like currently that's what's getting the most immediate attention and response is that it's like, okay, to get what you want, there's going to have to be a certain element of that. So yes, that has been something that I've never dealt with really head on is like being really open and being really honest emotionally and accessible emotionally. I'm a very strong person.

With the whole MS . . . there is an emotional component to it that
has really kind of thrown me for a loop—having a short fuse or
being overly emotional, crying or things upsetting me that really
don't make sense to upset anybody. In dealing with all of that, I
think it's made me want to pursue it even more and knowing
that I want a relationship and what I want from my relationship
and to get that you're going to have to go here. You're going to
have to face up to this emotional side and really start uncover-
ing a lot of it. Those two things have really brought it closer to
the surface in the last couple years. I feel like I'm more ready to
take on that challenge now than I ever have been before. Maybe
having more inner strength and more courage to say okay, this
part of me can be exposed. It's okay. I'm not going to keel over
dead, you know.

The inner strength Dawn had amassed in building her cognitive
and intrapersonal internal foundation offered sufficient security to
engage in yet another level of exploration and vulnerability in the
interpersonal realm of development. Despite her strong sense of self
and her conviction of bringing herself to the table in the relationship, it was still a struggle:

I was still processing that a lot 'cause a lot is going on right now
around the whole MS disclosure, not with her but with some
other people. I got a little fearful, um, how are you going to handle this? What are you going to think about all this? Because this
is huge. I mean this is a big part of who I am and . . . did I wait
too long? Probably. But it was all fine, and it really opened up a
lot of communication with us, but . . . I felt like in a sense I kind
of stepped back a few steps 'cause I was so bound and determined to do everything differently this time and, you know, new
resolve. Everything's coming together, like we had talked about.
And it's like I feel strong, I feel powerful, and then I got to that
and it's like [moan]. And I just took like three steps back and I'm
like, "no, you can't take three steps back. You have to stay with
this. You have to be open and honest and pursue this."

As Dawn predicted, the boulder continued to roll. Once she was honest with her partner about the MS, her partner reciprocated the
honesty in observing that Dawn was neglecting the condition.
Although it was hard to hear, Dawn owned up to it. She explained:

I'm back in a phase of discovery with myself—with myself,
with my MS, and I really didn't anticipate that because I've
been so . . . felt so great and I've been doing all these things. I'm

not staying on top of it, that's come out recently and I'm like, wow, okay, I have really, really put a lot of things aside that I'm now having to deal with. I haven't really been on top of maintaining a relationship with a neurologist, probably because I didn't have health insurance, and now I do, so it's time to get that ball rolling. I mean it really has to be a daily maintenance. Okay, where am I today? I had done that workshop, and that was all part of the maintenance, and then I got really comfortable. It's just become a coping situation like, well yeah, my balance is a little off, so I just compensate for it rather than saying, yeah, my balance is a little off. What can I do to fix it? And that's a bit of a wake-up call too, so um . . . yeah, there's a lot going on right now and it's all very big and I mean it's fine. Ultimately, sitting here talking to you I'm in a very comfortable space and I can say, you know what? It's fine. It's going to be scary. It's going to be uncomfortable and yeah, I'm okay with that because it's just things I have to deal with and I have to work through. And knowing that I don't have to do it all by myself, you know, I think I can kind of lose that, too. I definitely do that. I'm like, you know what? I can handle this. This is my deal. I can handle it. I don't have to do that anymore. And being okay with that, too. So, it's all very risky right now, and it's great! I can honestly say that.

Although Dawn had uncovered the warrior part of herself in that workshop a year earlier, she had not completely let go of it. It was her default reaction to challenges in her life. At this point, her inner strength was allowing her more flexibility to acknowledge the requirements of managing MS and also to accept help from others in doing so. She described this as trying to be more human:

I'm on a mission to bring back the humanity to myself. You know what? You are human. You don't have to be Hercules about the issues that come up in your world and how well you can handle them and how much weight you can carry on your shoulders. You can be . . . huh, interesting—I was just going to say you can be normal. Well, because that's an issue that's come up. I think a lot of the things that I have done regarding myself physically is to prove to myself and everybody else that I am normal. I don't have this thing that . . . or yes, I have it but it's not, you know, it's still normal; it's still functioning. Rather than, the normalcy in it all is that, there are going to be good days and there are going to be bad days, and you are a person with all of this going on, and it's okay if you're not having your A game today.

Dawn was still trying to set aside the warrior part of herself. Accepting a new normal for herself was all part of the ongoing quest to know herself more deeply. As was the case in the crossroads, trusting her internal voice, and building her internal foundation, securing her internal commitments was an ongoing process. She enjoyed the support of her new partner in this process.

A Glimpse of Authenticity: Moving from Self-Authorship to Self-Transformation

Dawn's quest to know herself more deeply opened the door to moving beyond self-authorship:

> That pursuit of wisdom, that pursuit of something deeper, knowing yourself. That's always been prevalent with me, and I think I'm entering a very big new phase of all of that, and at the core of my being I'm like, well, this is what you want. This is part of your mission in life is to plumb the depths, seeking something more and seeking that wisdom. So, this is just a whole new way of doing that. I just didn't know it was going to happen in every facet of my life, but that's how it happened, so . . .

Dawn's ability to enter this big new phase hinged on the work she had done all along in getting to know her essential self. Wisdom about what she was capable of in cooking and what her body was capable of with MS offered an infrastructure from which she could be vulnerable to explore further. She attributed her ability to act on the wake-up call with MS and the challenge of an honest relationship to her essential self:

> I mean that's what's at the core. Every now and then, I get glimpses of what that is and how powerful it is and . . . I mean, it's the authenticity of who and what I am and I think it does lie underneath everything. When I do have moments of being so completely in that space of that essential self, I mean it's like that's what got me into all of this, this month anyway. I mean it really is because I just made a choice to do something very big and bold and powerful, and it came from there. I have no doubt that that's exactly where it came from, and I was really existing in that space for several days. I haven't quite mastered how to . . . how you go in and out of that because now

I feel . . . there are moments when I feel like I have actually gone backwards and I'm in an old space that I used to be in before I discovered that, and it's like, ooh, okay, how do I navigate all of this? It lies underneath all of this, and I think within that lies how to deal with some of these issues that have come up, really being yourself and how to, I think that's just going to help foster all the positives that are going on. I mean it's definitely going to contribute to the well being of my relationship, . . . of my business, . . . of my person, my body. I would like to get back to that or get closer to it or know how to go to it for information on what I'm doing. But I definitely think that at the core there is just that essential self. It is who I am; it's what I am; it's how I do things; it's what I dream about; it's what I want out of my life. But you know, more than just like, ooh, I want to go to Europe or ooh, I want to have my own business. It's the structure around that—how I make those things happen, the gifts that I give in those things or it's just, I guess, my method of living. I've just had little glimpses of it, so the picture is not really clear, but I think it just . . . it has to do with being open . . . sounds kind of grandiose, but being open to your truth. What is the truth of me? I have a pretty clear sense of that. It's just that there's power, there's discovery, there's . . . you know, it's always a journey. And I think if I look at everything that way, that's a big part of how to navigate it because that comes from . . . that starts to incorporate all the things that I am and all the things that I want. I want to be wise, grounded, centered, connected to myself and everything around me.

The essential self that Dawn described struck me as her internal foundation. Her ability to catch a glimpse of it and to be aware that she existed in it for several days indicated that she was beginning to stand apart from it in order to be able to reflect on it. Her ability to identify an "old space" she was in earlier and to reflect on it shows this movement. In the midst of developing self-authorship (or any other phase of development for that matter), we are "caught up" in it, just as we find ourselves caught up in the immediacy of daily situations. Once we have the chance to stand back to reflect on daily situations, we have an increased ability to interpret our experiences and figure out what they mean for us. The ability to "stand back" from our view of ourselves to reflect on it marks another phase of development in which we can gain the potential to transform the self we have authored. Considering how to navigate that essential self, or that internal foundation, opened the door to further growth.

Dawn's observation that knowing the authentic self is always a journey captures the story of her twenties and thirties. Constantly plumbing the depths moved her closer to her essential self, and she in turn used that wisdom to act on what she wanted in life. At the same time, it continually opened new doors for further exploration and growth. One of the consistent themes of Dawn's story is that the journey toward the truth of oneself is like a roller coaster ride. Times of great clarity were often followed by a lack of clarity, perhaps related to attempts to live out her authentic self. With wisdom came the certainty of knowing her self and the freedom associated with being grounded, centered, and connected to self and others. Yet being able to exist in that space, to navigate it in everyday life, remained a challenge.

Dawn's Story Line

Dawn, like her peers, faced three major questions in her twenties: (1) How do I know? (2) Who am I? and (3) What kind of relationships do I want to construct with others?[17] The who am I? question was in the foreground for Dawn in her twenties and thirties. To move toward self-authorship in considering these questions, Dawn initially needed to work through the crossroads, learning to listen to her internal voice, then actively cultivating it, and finally moving to self-authorship by trusting it. She began listening to her internal voice through her theater work and her self-discovery trips. Her MS diagnosis at age 33 accelerated her work on cultivating this internal voice to make choices about her identity and her life. The sorting and sifting she engaged in as a result led her to respect herself and to treat others with compassion. Her ability to distinguish when to make things happen versus let things happen enabled her to achieve the Tao of life that she desired. This was an indication that she had developed her internal voice sufficiently to guide what to believe, who to become, and how to relate to others—to self-author her life. Trusting her voice then allowed her to build an internal foundation. Dawn foresaw this internal foundation during our twelfth interview; subsequent interviews revealed, however, that it took further development of self-authorship to build an enduring internal foundation.[18]

Dawn built an enduring internal foundation by accepting her talents and strengths and making decisions to incorporate these into her identity. She accepted her talent for cooking and incorporated it into how she thought about herself. She refined and strengthened her identity through her willingness to explore her sense of self even when it was painful or risky. She worked through her continual challenge to figure out what role MS played in her life. She had the most difficulty building an internal foundation in the interpersonal arena because she did not have as much confidence there as in other areas. Her strong internal foundation in the intrapersonal arena helped her gather the courage to do the emotional work required for honest relationships. She emerged from each journey into the shadow lands stronger and more focused.

Her continual self-exploration yielded an integration of Dawn's internal foundation in all arenas of her life and enabled her to secure her internal commitments. When this internal foundation became the center of her being, it became second nature to her. Her ability to "live" what she knew about the world, herself, and others yielded freedom and certainty simultaneously. It enabled her to merge physical and mental infrastructures to create the space to balance making things happen with allowing things to happen. Crossing over into wisdom enabled Dawn to define normal in the context of her internally generated constructions of how to know, who to be, and how to relate to the world.

Yet Dawn still struggled to implement this wisdom in her relationship with her partner. She knew cognitively and interpersonally the kind of relationship she wanted and how she would need to function intrapersonally to achieve it. She possessed these capacities but was not always able to use them consistently, which was evident in her process of achieving clarity, losing it, and regaining it. Dawn was able to see and articulate times when she was not using these capacities, when she felt as if she was in an "old space" that she had occupied earlier. As Dawn constructed her internal voice, she played it out in various contexts and put pieces of the puzzle together. When she had enough experience with and confidence in these aspects of herself, they became ingrained to the point that she described them as wisdom. This wisdom led her to the awareness that she had not yet achieved wisdom fully in interpersonal relationships.

Dawn's penchant for self-exploration and her progress on building an internal foundation and securing internal commitments heightened her resilience in facing the challenges of life in her thirties and encouraged her to continue pursuing her truth.

CHAPTER 3

MARK'S STORY—DEVELOPING A SPIRITUAL PHILOSOPHY OF LIFE

ONE OF THE FIRST CHARACTERISTICS I NOTICED ABOUT Mark was his inquisitive mind, a characteristic he attributed to attending an innovative grade school and cultural events he attended with his parents. He viewed the world through a rational, intellectual, analytical lens and avoided feelings because of the hurt of his parents' divorce when he was a young child. As a result, he relished the intellectual climate of college and excelled academically. In his late teens and early twenties, he enjoyed a positive relationship with his long-time girlfriend and moved seemingly effortlessly toward his goals. Because he was clear on his career goal of becoming an attorney, he carefully calculated the best path to attain it. He actively pursued his interests, attracted mentors, and used university systems to his advantage. He reported interviewing college professors to ascertain their politics before taking their classes— an approach that contributed to his academic success. At the same time he learned he could interact more effectively with his peers if he was less antagonistic, and so he modified his initial tendency to take extreme positions and undercut the positions of his peers to instead seek common ground and consensus.[1] He honed his inquisitiveness and his abilities to analyze multiple perspectives, judge evidence, and choose what to believe accordingly. His plans gained him admission to the Ivy League law school of his choice.

During college, Mark's interests and conventional social expectations of success coincided. At law school, for the first time, his interests and the legal culture's map for success conflicted. The emptiness Mark encountered after reaching what he considered the pinnacle of success, his law school admission, precipitated his paying attention to his internal voice. Mark had always subscribed to the notion of being true to himself and often acted in ways that drew disapproval from his peers, the most prominent example being his long-time interracial relationship with the African American woman who would eventually become his wife. Mark reflected that in high school and college he was able to act in ways that he thought were personally authentic and still follow society's expectations. As his career goals and personal life began to intersect more tangibly during law school, Mark encountered conflict between his happiness and external definitions of success. He identified pain as a call to address his own responsibility for his beliefs and identity:

> You learn it from just being at a point of great pain and trying to solve the pain. I think that is where most people learn their greatest lessons—through some kind of pain. The lesson is made much more real and brought home, and it's one you don't forget. I think you can learn through quieter pain, and that would be an example of attaining a goal you thought would kind of be an end-all and be-all, and then when you get there it doesn't bring you the kind of satisfaction you thought it would. Or the satisfaction it does bring you is ultimately pretty empty.

Solving this pain set Mark on the road to refining what it really meant to be true to himself, to moving toward self-authorship. Mark's map shows the paths he took and partners he had along the way.

MARK'S JOURNEY

Mark had always been interested in the question, "what is the good life?" His disappointment with law school prompted a new exploration of the characteristics of the good life.

Moving Through the Crossroads Toward Self-Authorship

Mark approached law school with the same calculation that had helped him excel in college. He began to follow what he called the legal culture's map for success—get to know influential professors to get a good clerkship, get on the law journal, and write papers to publish. He was taken aback when he found this external formula unfulfilling:

> I said, "Is this map of success given to me by the legal culture really a map at all to success?" And it depends upon your definition of success. A great résumé or accolades, yeah, that's the chart to a sign of prestige, that's the way to go. But I realized that I couldn't be a person who sacrificed happiness to that goal of prestige. . . . I never <u>dreamed</u> that I would be unhappy working on the law journal. I didn't think it would be as tedious and boring as I found it. That never figured in. There was no way law school and its classes could be as big a turnoff as they were.[2]

Entering the Crossroads: Listening to the Internal Voice. Mark's reaction to his work and his questions about the map to success led to a long period of reflection and a change of heart:

> It was a tough decision. I came here thinking about a Supreme Court clerkship. Now I'm not even trying for it. And it doesn't bother me that I'm not. I'm going in other directions that are more fruitful, I think. That kind of careerist perspective can get you in a place in ten years where you really don't want to be because you didn't listen to your internal feelings. . . . But, more importantly, the internal cues, which I never used to listen to and which in the classroom I never listened to. I had to go to the internal cues because I'm getting to a point in my life where I could get locked into a situation and say inside I'm miserable even though objectively from the outside I've been quite a success.[3]

Mark was no longer able to silence the internal cues and worried that moving ahead with the plan for success would leave him miserable. So he opted, for the first time in his early twenties, to listen to these internal cues. Although he was letting go of external formulas for law school success, he would spend considerable time in his twenties listening to and cultivating his internal voice.

For Mark, as well as for many of his peers, pain and dissatisfaction were a signal that external expectations were drowning out his internal voice. The need to solve the pain led him to pay attention to internal cues and listen to his own voice.

Traversing the Crossroads: Cultivating the Internal Voice. In cultivating his internal voice, Mark drew on a variety of partners. He noted the value of advice he had acquired from his mother: "A phrase that my mom used to tell me, but I think is the best advice I've ever gotten is above all else 'to thine own self be true.' I think that that is really a key to who I am, definitely."[4] He also came across the tapes and books of Tony Robbins, a life coach and motivational speaker. While Mark was somewhat suspicious of Robbins' qualifications, he found his ideas helpful:

> One thing Tony Robbins talks about is you can choose and you can install certain beliefs in your belief system and become more productive for it. For instance, one belief he would say that would be good is the past does not equal the future. So what you've done in the past, what's happened to you, that doesn't necessarily constrain you. And my own take on that is whether or not that is true, having that belief is what can catapult you into a future you really, really like. Now maybe, in fact, the past does dictate some of your future. But by installing that belief, you're rationally manipulating your mind and your systems in such a way that you're going to succeed. But manipulating your own beliefs, I think that's really interesting stuff. I mean, making yourself into something, not what other people say or not just kind of floating along in life, but, you know, you're in some sense a piece of clay. And, of course, you've been formed into different things, but that doesn't mean you can't go back on the potter's wheel and instead of somebody else's hands building you and molding you, [you use] your own, and in a fundamental sense change your values and beliefs. I certainly believe that's possible and I think it's really important that people believe they can do that.[5]

Mark adopted this perspective that he could go back to the potter's wheel and mold himself. He actively tried to do just that, as he explained:

> I think everybody has enough bad things going on in their life that if they focus on those, heck, you can feel bad very easily. Now I also believe that people have enough good things that if they focus on that and dwell on that that they'll feel pretty good about life. So the other thing is change my mental focus. And all these things are rational calculations I make to manipulate my emotions to make me feel good. And I do those kinds of things on a daily basis. Even like getting up in the morning or when I'm driving to work and saying, "What am I grateful for today?" Or if I don't feel particularly grateful, "What could I feel grateful about today if I wanted to?" When

you ask your mind that question, there's a whole laundry list of things that can pop out of why you should feel grateful: grateful to your parents for helping you through school, grateful to your wife or spouse for, you know, blah, blah, blah. And so you ask yourself questions like that in the morning. So those are two examples of things I do on a daily basis or almost daily basis to manipulate emotion. The author of the work I read has particular gestures that he uses or that are common to him. I'd still bring myself to it and I'd still make up my own techniques, too. So, anyway, I think it really increases your quality of life to do things like that because the bottom line is are you happy? And if you can take control of yourself in such a way that you can be happy in many different environments, that's wonderful. You've got a tremendous advantage.[6]

Mark's quest to make himself happy led him to take advantage of any resource that he found useful. I have to admit being surprised that he used some of these resources given his standards for credibility. Yet he made it clear that he was bringing himself to this task. His aim was to take control of himself in order to be happy. Fortunately, he had a long-time partner in Michele to support him through this process.

Self-Authorship: Trusting the Internal Voice

In addition to these daily mental adjustments, Mark began taking control of himself in more substantive ways by using his internal voice to guide important life decisions about his identity and relationships. He explained:

It was a slow process. The most significant decision I made during the process between moving from a very planned life and thinking about goals as a useful way to plan years into the future, was the decision to propose to Michele. That was definitely a turning point because in the year before that, I thought of how getting married to her would compromise my career goals. By the end of that year—we broke up the summer before my second year (of law school)—the reason I decided to propose was that she took my life to another level on a daily basis with her personality, outlook, attitude, and perceptions. That made me happier on a day-to-day basis than anything I could glean from any work or academic environment I had been in. Once I made that decision, then I made some other decisions that led me toward happiness and away from extensive thinking and goal planning. For example, I decided not to attempt to join the law journal [a credential], some others in terms of classes and clinics— academic course decisions that led me down a path of enjoying day to day rather than deferred gratification.

Cultivating this internal voice sufficiently to trust it took time, as Mark articulated:

> Coming to an answer takes years; ask the question over and over to get to the bottom of it. The key to the question of what makes me happy is how I answer it. I reflect on it more; it seems that I get different answers or conflicting answers. Keep pushing; ultimately it comes down to judgment and experience. I have faith in myself and my decision-making processes. I'm comfortable in making decisions and acting on them. I'm very thoughtful. I'm confident once I've made a choice, but not to the point of blindness, I can revisit it.[7]

Mark's track record of reflectiveness and of making good judgments and decisions gave him faith in himself. His continual self-exploration further reinforced his growing confidence that he could adopt a particular belief that would make him happy in his life. Trusting his internal voice enabled him to move from thinking about this concept to internalizing it:

> Whatever I am in my life right now is primarily the product of decisions I made. I feel like I am able to do it; if I need help, I'm not afraid to ask for it. People pick up values from parents, the environment, and never go through them to decide which ones make sense. My point is you are in charge of adopting that value; it might destroy you if you have adopted the wrong one. This is solely utilitarian. This may have been something I believed before, but it wasn't a core belief, not internalized [until recent years]. It has made a tremendous difference— impacted every area of my life: spiritual, politically, socially in relationships, career. I believe I am the author of my life. I can make decisions right now that can change it in any direction. [That's a] tremendous amount of power; external influence pales in comparison. As a child and young man, I felt much more at the whim of fate and am still at the mercy of fate, but I interpret fate, decide what it is going to mean to me, and take action in my environment. My parents divorced [during my childhood], and there was nothing I could do. As an adult, if I hear devastating information, I can say, "Okay, I can control my response and it won't affect other areas of my life. If it does,

that is my choice." It's a radical responsibility in a way—authoring your own life. In another way, it is a radical freedom. You can construe it as either—I use freedom.[8]

This struck me as the same realization Dawn expressed about controlling her reaction to reality rather than controlling reality. Mark clearly explained that it was his choice whether to allow reality to affect him. Although Mark internalized this way of thinking, he was still on the quest he had started years earlier of understanding the nature of the good life and his own personal happiness. By his late twenties, he was shifting his attention away from his emphasis on the intellect and logic. He explained what prompted this shift:

I really had to expand beyond the intellect when I got more into the real world. Intellect is no longer my god; I used to think I could solve anything by thinking. I don't know if it defrauded me or not, but it didn't lead to an understanding of who I really am. I decided to study more deeply emotions and spirituality. Have to go beyond intellect to understand those things, have to turn the intellect off.[9]

At this point in his life, Mark had the internal capacity to define his beliefs, identity, and social relations. He used his intellect to manage external events and forces and shape his view of the world and himself. Yet, he still had the sense that there was something else to explore, some way to deepen and refine his understanding. This conscious effort led to building an internal foundation.

Self-Authorship: Building an Internal Foundation

In his exploration of how to live a good life and address the problems of the real world, Mark began reading Chinese philosophy books. At the outset of our eleventh interview, he reported that he was able to "step into Taoism, for example, and look at life through those lenses and learn some information about how to live a good or rewarding life." This meant exploring a whole new side of himself:

I'm engaged in the development of a personal philosophy that goes beyond surface level understanding. For me, I am gaining knowledge in a way I never have before: by not thinking. It's completely an alien way of me understanding a way of life. In college, I believed you had to analyze it. I believe there is a

truer way to understand than through analysis. Forms of meditation. Turning your mind off. Then gaining an understanding
of who you are and what this is around you, the world, without
mental effort. I could read a text at college or law school and
could say this is a feminist critique of this text, then whip on
the other pair of glasses. I found conservative lenses in law
school. I could figure out what various kinds of people would
think. With Taoist philosophy, I've gotten closer to understanding what my own pair of eyes internally and externally is seeing. It is more fundamentally true to my human nature than
political critiques. Getting toward more important questions
than what is a critique of this movie—getting to what it means
to be a human being with a soul.[10]

This did not sound like the person with whom I had been talking for
the past eleven years. This new lens seemed to eclipse Mark's focus
on intellect and rationality. In response to my inquiry about that, he
offered:

I'm not sure it is essential in knowing self. Who you are is as
close as the tip of your nose. I can come to an understanding of
that through silence, quieting of mind and body. That has no
need for rational thought. Rational thought can act as a barrier
between one's understanding and internal nature. I am less
stressed at work than I would have been because regardless of
what happens in any environment, there is a part of me that
remains untouched by it. It has ripple effects throughout my
life. In relationship with my spouse, I am less concerned about
things that may undermine marriage, like finances—because
ultimately that is a mere piece of straw in one's existence. . . .
I have thought my whole life; it is shocking to read not to think,
but at the same time I had a feeling of scales falling from my
eyes. No bright light flashed, but it carried a lot of intuitive
power to it. Maybe if I shut off idle chatter in my head about
relationships, careers, and future, I would feel better about self
and have a fuller understanding. It is a paradigm shift, no
doubt about it. I haven't gotten to a point with it—it is evolving,
a work in progress.[11]

Mark was now working Taoist principles into his growing philosophy of life. The paradigm shift Mark described struck me as the
development of his identity that heretofore had been overshadowed
by the way he viewed and interpreted the world. Just as his capacity for making judgments at the end of college eclipsed listening to
his internal voice early in law school, his facility with the intellect

and rational thought interfered with understanding himself and his relationships. Yet with his confidence from his intellect, he began building an internal foundation and was able to "put on" the new lenses discovered through his reading to see and understand these parts of himself. He noted that when something had intuitive power, he paid attention to it.

Mark viewed part of this shift as spiritual and stated, "Now I have an understanding that there is always a spiritual part of me present."[12] He began framing the good life as "a spiritually informed life, a life of understanding not born from or dictated by rationality. It comes from experience of one's self and one's true nature, and the ability to access that nature." In an effort to describe what he meant by the word *spiritual,* Mark offered:

> It has nothing to do with religion, and everything to do with one's soul. A part of you is a spirit, an intimate word. Not apart from you, an intimate part of who you are, have been, will be, after leaving [your] physical body. . . . It comes from getting closer to [my] own spirit—not an overarching deity—a part of me that knows me better than I consciously know myself; it knows right for me. This is not a denial of responsibility for one's decisions; it is assuming one's responsibilities. I arrive at answers differently. I am still the author of my own life. No abdication of control over one's life. I could make a host of decisions to be different. I've found a truer identity that leads to understanding and informs important life decisions.[13]

This truer identity seemed to be the integration of Mark's way of viewing the world, himself, and his relationships. As this integration became more complete, his internal foundation grew more solid. Accessing his spirit, his true nature, required putting rationality into a new perspective:

> I can see it [rationality, intellect] as a tool, a really sharp knife I can use to slice some things that are of importance to me. If you are using it constantly, 100 percent, you are cutting yourself off from yourself; you don't really understand who you are, and then you can't relate to others except the intellectual. That is not the way to relate to other people. One of the ways in which I brought the spiritual and emotional into daily life, and removed intellectual, is with arguments I have with Michele. Being intellectually right means nothing! First of all, the relationship is the most important thing, and how can you extricate yourself from this without damaging that relationship?

Hopefully, it is through sympathy, understanding, a kind of detachment—I use this in just about any situation—when I am having a difficult time. Oftentimes, it manifests itself in detaching from intellect—it is chirping in my ear about career, money—those things don't matter emotionally or spiritually. There is no way to be at peace with yourself, and often with others, unless you turn the intellect off. It's like a waterfall of thoughts cascading down; you need to step behind that waterfall, no longer in the water, can see it go by, but at a point of stillness. Not thinking. Letting thoughts just pass right through. It took me a long time. . . . Spirituality is the core—most important. Thoughts give rise to emotion. Intellect is not my master. I can turn it off. I was not like this when younger, before I learned meditative skills, and before I understood who I am. I [can] let the knife of intellect slip from my hand.[14]

Previously intellect defined Mark. Listening to it constantly created stress in his work and personal life because it created negative emotions for him. Now, it has become a tool he can use in appropriate contexts yet turn off in other contexts where it interferes with his happiness. As parts of his internal foundation came together, he was grounded enough to put down the knife of intellect and open himself up more fully emotionally and spiritually. Michele continued to be a valuable partner in Mark's journey.

Understanding who he was and trusting this spiritual core led Mark to distinguish between making things happen and letting them happen, the same idea we heard from Dawn in chapter 2. He stood ready to accompany his wife, a medical student, to her choice of residencies, even though he would have to retake the bar exam and find another position. As he noted, this was a work in progress, and the tension between controlling with the intellect and going with the realities of life remained:

I aspire to—I don't have it—a lightness of touch in life that makes you graceful. Ummm . . . I mean, not turning the canoe around and fighting the current. I'm going with the current in life. By graceful I mean I'm engaged in a dance with realities that I run into. Quietly accepting it and moving with it. It is tough to tell who is leading. I'm leading in defining my reaction to what life gives me. I'm leading to different areas on the dance floor, or steering the canoe in certain directions, but I'm not fighting reality. That leads to being graceful. People who trip in this dance are those who fight with their partner—a fight with life; they are left with nothing sometimes.

As Mark approached 30, he was determined to live by this philosophy even though it was still under construction. He was on the front seat of the bike but knew there were realities he would have to navigate as the journey continued.

Mark's work as an attorney continued to be a source of frustration, while his marriage and a year off to write a novel were the sustenance of his early thirties. He often observed what he saw as abuses of the law, as he reported, "I just hate being in the midst of that morass." Although he noted that he was responsible for creating negative feelings through his interpretation of events, the work itself still triggered negative emotions in him. He dealt with this by immersing himself in studying philosophy daily. He offered further explanation of the philosophy he was refining:

> There are two basic schools [of thought] out there that I've found attractive. One is a completely agnostic or more atheistic program of keeping one happy. And that's kind of a psychological approach. You learn a few things about human psychology and your own psychology, and then you can really understand that you are the one creating your own happiness. It's not some external circumstance. Understanding how your thinking creates emotion. The more spiritual perspective says you are a soul in a body, and who you are is an eternal being. You're going to live on long beyond when your physical body dies. So you should live more in this material world from the perspective of your soul or your spirit. In that way, you detach from the world, and by detaching, you detach from emotions and thoughts and see things in a much, much broader perspective. And things don't worry you because the fact of the matter is, you're eternal. That's a more spiritual perspective. What I try to do is use both techniques and combine them. The various authors I've read, much of the text will be very similar in approach. But then there is a break between, you know, one has God enter into the text, the other doesn't.

As was his practice, Mark took parts of various perspectives that he judged useful and incorporated them into his philosophy. Mark used this philosophy to face challenges in everyday life, one of which was his reaction to the events of September 11, 2001. Explaining how it played out, he said:

> Well, number one, would be detachment. You can't get warped into the emotion of the moment. Now that said, it's incredibly emotional. And it [September 11] was emotional for me and

affected me and made it very difficult for me to go to work on a daily basis because I was upset by it. I felt like work was the equivalent of arranging deck chairs on the Titanic within the week or two after September 11. I mean it just didn't matter. I felt like geez, this doofus on the other side won't give me a dis- covery response under oath. I mean, what's that matter? [laughs] It doesn't. Stupidity. So, I went on a lot of long walks during lunch to try to reconcile and work with what had hap- pened on September 11th and also just getting distance on work I thought was meaningless in the wake of that. But ultimately there has to be some detachment there. Put September 11th in the context of the Holocaust, it's nothing. If your philosophy is big enough to contextualize the Holocaust and reconcile reli- gious or spiritual beliefs with the existence of the Holocaust, it's big enough to embrace September 11th. Or the car wreck you see on the way to work. So, I think my philosophy is big enough to do that. But, it doesn't make it easy, and it does in fact make me uneasy that a philosophy has to be big enough to embrace that kind of horror. It's a tremendous challenge. It cast kind of a low-grade depression over me for two or three weeks. I was very interested in it from a political, cultural, "what are we going to do about this?" perspective. So, I'd watch a lot of news about it, which sometimes drove me into more depression. But, ultimately I didn't feel like I could just close my eyes to it.

This perspective reveals that having an internal foundation does not eliminate the challenges of life. It does, however, offer a context through which to process them. Doing so led Mark to living his phi- losophy in even more substantive ways.

Self-authorship: Securing Internal Commitments

Mark emphasized the importance of a foundational philosophy to deal with life's realities in our seventeenth interview as he dis- cussed the upcoming birth of his first child. Explaining his perspec- tive that most aspects of life are beyond one's control, he felt that "it's either get a philosophy that's going to be able to provide a foun- dation or undergirding for what could happen in your life, or when it does hit, you're going to be lost."

Mark reflected on the history of his philosophy, the foundation he was relying on in preparation for the arrival of his son. He described it as a combination of personal experiences, such as his parents' divorce, and others' history from which he had learned how to accept life's realities. One example was his study of Victor Frankel's writings:

> I remember a quote in a book I was reading about, essentially, trying to be happy in life, and there was a quote from Victor Frankel about the last of human freedoms is to create one's own life in any given set of circumstances. That's pretty close to a quote. . . . that quote kind of put a hook in me. And I knew he had come out of a concentration camp. And I'm like, well, how do you do that?

Mark continued to refine his notion that detachment from the immediate circumstances of a dilemma, or taking a broad perspective, was valuable in accepting life's realities:

> I'm as guilty as the next person about getting too emotional or angry about this or that. I prefer—the best me doesn't get worked up about much of anything—keeping a perspective on things, keeping a certain distance or detachment over things, or even if you look at it from a temporal sense, out of the immediate moment. Next week, it's not going to matter whether something got filed or not or whether [a case] was won or lost. It's a much bigger process than that that you're involved in. And I think that when you get so focused down on the stakes of something out there in the real world, whether this happens or that happens, you lose a broader perspective that can lead to a calm, rational decision.

Mark worked hard at getting "the best me" to come out in all arenas of his life as part of his on-going commitment to living a good life. He articulated that this philosophy was ever-evolving:

> Once you get the philosophy kind of set, and to a certain extent it evolves a little bit over time, or it becomes more clear, but once the philosophy gets set, it builds upon itself in daily decisions and actions. More broadly in the bigger annual or career decisions, or family decisions that you have to make. And then, that becomes your life, that trail that's behind you of all these decisions and choices you've made. So, that's where I am right now. But, hopefully, over time, mine will set a consistent pattern according to the philosophy that I have. . . . I mean there is a difference between thinking about something like this and actually living it. And it takes a certain amount of courage to live according to one's convictions. If you understand a set of convictions that's one thing, and you can admire them. But, to live it, there are real life costs to doing that. And, that's a difficult

bridge to cross. But, I mean, you get to a point where you just don't have any choice. You have to live them. You know, just like you have to breathe. You have to live them. When there's enough dissonance in your life that you're completely unhappy.

Although Mark had been living these convictions, whether handling his dissatisfaction with his law work or supporting his wife emotionally during her medical residency, their necessity hit him with full force with the birth of their son, Nate. His ability to live his convictions at this point was, as he had predicted, crucial. In our eighteenth interview, Mark shared the story of how, after a long unsuccessful labor, Michele had a Caesarian section delivery. As doctors prepared her for the surgery, Mark sat outside the operating room and felt uncertain about what was happening with his "whole life, the most important part of it." Fortunately, Michele and Nate came through the delivery fine, but challenges remained when they discovered within the first few months that Nate had a serious health problem. Uncertainty again set in. As Mark discussed how he approached this situation, I gained a better understanding of the meaning of his use of detachment, a notion that I had struggled to understand in previous conversations about detaching from intellect, detaching from emotions, and detaching from immediate stakes in a situation. He recounted the story:

> The health of the child is completely beyond your control. He had a serious medical issue—essentially his intestines twisted and, yeah, kids can die from that. On the first emergency room trip, I was out of town, so Michele and her folks went. And the second one, the next night, I was back, so I went and was there until 3:00 or 4:00 a.m. when it got kind of corrected. Michele and I got him to the car, and we went to the hospital, and Michele knows the way around the hospital pretty well, got to the pediatric ER. I just took a book along with me. There's a certain process that you go through in whatever kind of situation or emergency. For me, at the hospital he's getting the best medical treatment he could. Michele's there. She's a physician. It's completely out of my hands at that point. She was much more emotional than I was about it. I just couldn't see how I could do anything productively by getting incredibly emotionally worked up. So, I was just there and ready to help in any way possible. Michele would go talk to docs and another doctor would come in. I'd hold Nate down while they stuck him with various things and pried, and that was very tough for me to see

him in pain and not be able to alleviate the pain. That wasn't a pleasant experience at all. He could have died, and I knew that Michele told me that and I couldn't . . . I was just going to take it moment by moment, not lean to, "Okay, we're going to dig a grave." So, I just kind of took it moment by moment and thought things would resolve, and they did, and he's fine, and he's happy and healthy.

The key to Mark's ability to "take it moment by moment" and detach from his emotions about the potential of losing his son was what he called "complete acknowledgment of it being out of my control." A combination of trusting his wife's ability to work with the doctors, turning off the intellectual knowledge of a potentially bad outcome, and believing that things would resolve themselves enabled him to work through this reality rather than fight it. He was not avoiding the reality of a negative outcome but chose not to deal with it unless it actually materialized. It appeared that he had achieved the grace in the dance with reality that he aspired to earlier. I marveled that he was able to bring his "best me" forward in this circumstance.

Mark's philosophy of going with the flow and accepting how situations would resolve themselves played out in a career change, as well. Unhappy with law, Mark had decided to look for a teaching job after a three-month stay at home with Michele and Nate. During that time, he regularly visited with a law client who ran a business in the same building where the law firm was located. Mark had become friends with this client and found conversations with him intriguing. During one visit, the man offered him the job of director of operations of his company. Mark recounted his reaction:

> He told me this on Friday, and I did tell him it sounded interesting. So, I researched the company a little bit—it's privately held, but I looked at his Web site. I grew more and more excited about the possibility over the weekend. When I talked to him on Monday, we chatted about it more and then decided on salary and benefits, had a handshake and that was that. He wanted me to start the next day, and I was like, "No, I'm not starting until Michele goes back to work."

Despite hearing the "go with the flow" philosophy in recent interviews, the spontaneity of Mark's decision surprised me, particularly in light of his having a new baby. When I asked about how quickly he appeared to make this decision, he said:

My sense was, well, this is a unique opportunity, number one.
Number two, it's just worth exploring and giving it a shot. When
something lands out of the blue like that in your lap, you're not
invested in it. You're like, "Okay, I'll give this a shot and see
what happens." But director of operations, well, it's not that big
a leap from labor and employment law because I interacted with
a lot of directors of operations, especially when their company
was being sued or when their managers had screwed up.

Mark's confidence that he could succeed in this job was part of the
decision, as was his continuing commitment toward not planning
too far ahead:

The older I get, the less interested I am in the future. Now,
maybe part of that means it's a real realization that I have less
control than I ever thought I had over how things actually
unfold. Sometimes, I just feel like a ball—you don't know
where the next bounce is going to be—just kind of roll with
that. And then when you hit the ground or the wall, you just
kind of make your adjustments. I'd say there's more of the illu-
sion of control in certain situations in my life. Things outside of
my control dictate a certain flow. They don't dictate my reaction
to it. But certainly with Nate, I'm interested in the future and
providing good solid foundations for him, but to a certain
extent, life can just bore the hell out of me. I prefer life being
unpredictable at this stage. It's boring to me if I know exactly
where I'm going to be a year or six months or three months
from now. But when I was talking to you when I was eighteen,
nineteen, twenty, there was a path, and it was laid out, and I
knew where I wanted to be in five years, and I was going to
focus on this and bup, bup, bup, bup, bup, bup to get to a place
like [institution] law school. So, that kind of organization and
focus, I don't know, maybe it's because I do like certain things
about my life so much now that I don't need to have any outside goal like that anymore. I'm just not interested.

Solving the pain of his dissatisfaction with law, dealing with realities such as September 11 and his son's health, experiencing a certain level of boredom, and making the commitment to maintain the
good life he had thus far enjoyed enabled him to give this new director of operations role a chance. He "knew" that he could do it.

Another component of Mark's ability to go with the flow was
the internal foundation that he had been building for some time:

At various times when I've talked to you over the years,
maybe I would have described myself as an agnostic. I don't

think I would have ever described myself as an atheist, but I will say this: that at least for me a lot of the solace that comes from having a foundation, returning to a foundation inside that maybe has always existed but that you didn't perceive clearly. It does have to do with faith, spirituality issues, and they can be a tremendous strength and allow the kind of philosophy that we've described to exist. I don't think it's a necessary component, but I've found it a crucial one for me certainly.

The personal philosophy Mark had begun work on some years earlier had evolved over time to serve as his internal foundation. Living his convictions yielded the consistent pattern he had predicted would emerge.

The following year, Mark reflected on the transition he and Michele had experienced the previous year and elaborated on how faith had been important to getting through it:

The sea is a lot more settled right now. That was a particularly tumultuous time— job transition, life transition with the child, Michele finishing up a very long and trying residency. There was a host of issues going on then that caught up to us at the same time. Part of getting through that kind of thing is endurance, trust, kind of faith, not only some faith in higher powers or spiritual matters, but faith that things do resolve for the better. There's also a certain amount of grit and determination one needs to sustain oneself through these various stormy seas of life, and even when you know you're not doing as well as you'd like to, you still try to do the best you can. If you persevere, the problems and issues do resolve themselves. Others will come down the track that you can't even see, and what you try to avoid is making some kind of ultimate final mistake or decision. You know, you just proceed more on a day-to-day course. It's faith, it's trust, it's love that kind of gets you through some of these things. Also, there's a growing responsibility that keeps one, I think, ultimately on track. Other roles come up that demand new creativity and a kind of new thinking and procedure, and whether that's the growing and evolving role as husband or the new growing and developing role as father or, on a career front, you know, a growing and developing role in career, not only director of operations, but then I was promoted in June of 2004 to executive director, which took on a few more responsibilities. So, I mean life will keep you growing and evolving if you're going to stay on the playing field of it.

Mark's new roles as father and executive director kept him grow-ing, but he maintained his internal philosophy in how to manage them. When I asked how he managed decisions in his work, he offered:

> I run the day-to-day operations and rely on the president of the company for his advice and consultation. We talk things through, but I'm in charge, whether it's how many paper clips to purchase or whether we're going to buy another company. Plus, I'm a lawyer, so any litigation, it's on me to solve. But I do like the job a lot. I'm pleased because normally a position like this would be 80 to 90 hours a week. I just won't do that to myself or my family, to my wife or my son, and he understands that and respects it and that's why I'm still here . . . I get all the major stuff done. Other china that I see falling off the shelf, I'm quick enough to snatch before it hits. Other things I let slide, but anyone who's been trained in a major law firm, you constantly see you're at the brink of malpractice on so many cases 'cause you're so swamped with work. So, you deal with that as an attorney, all the multitasking and prioritizing, and then it's just similar issues in the business world, but a lot of my decision making is exceptionally fast. So, it's over and done and not much twiddling of thumbs. I go a lot more by feel. I've taken hundreds of depositions, so I know what questions I want to ask. I know when people are being evasive. If they are, how to get an answer out of them, and not in an antagonistic way. It's good to be the ultimate authority. I've always liked that. When you're executive director of the company and the president gives you plenty of authority and room and just wants to be con-sulted, you've got an open field to run across in a lot of ways. And there's a lot of responsibility with that, plus stress, but it's just lightning fast decision making then, and you move on.

While Mark used his legal training to multitask, prioritize, and get reliable information, more importantly, he was using the internal foundation that had become second nature to him. The freedom and certainty that comes from feeling secure about his values and phi-losophy (his internal commitments) enabled him to balance his intu-ition with his intellect and to go by feel, despite the enormous consequences some of his decisions entailed. He enjoyed the chal-lenges of this role, while at the same time making it secondary to his family.

Mark's wife initiated another major decision during this time. She found a house in a good neighborhood that she wanted to buy. His boss encouraged the purchase, but Mark hesitated about the million-dollar price tag. He described how he processed the situation:

> There's a certain flow to it, and you go with that flow. [Buying]
> the house has to do with faith and trust and how life works
> out . . . faith and trust in your spouse, faith and trust in your
> boss in my case, and respecting others' opinions. My initial
> reaction was I didn't think it was necessarily the smartest
> thing to do, but it's a complex issue because you have to
> respect and prioritize what your spouse values. When I was
> moving forward with this house, it was with a decision made
> in my own mind that six months after we buy it we could be
> bankrupt. Well that's not going to feel too good, but I'm will-
> ing to make that risk, to take that risk. Once I made the click
> in my mind, okay, well, if you go forward, you have to accept
> in six months you might be bankrupt, then I didn't lose any
> sleep over it 'cause I'd already accepted that could happen.
> I've done some different things with our finances, using every
> skill I have with those to make sure we stay afloat, but I didn't
> necessarily think it was a particularly good decision, that's for
> sure. And the other thing is, I know within 20 seconds
> whether I'm interested in a place when I open the door. It's
> just emotional, boom. And this place, in five to ten I knew I
> was in trouble. It was too good. And I knew Michele was over
> the moon about it. So . . . but that's the other kind of compli-
> cating factor in terms of, was I right or wrong from a financial
> perspective. So you go forward with faith and trust, and you
> try to line up as many correct chess pieces in their place, then
> what if you lose? Well, that'll be one heck of a challenge. I
> have a habit of always looking at worst-case scenarios. That's
> my own psychological default position I've always had, only
> accentuated, of course, by legal training. So that's just an
> unfortunate mental issue I have.

Concluding that "life comes down to more of a feeling than anything else," Mark reiterated that faith, love, trust, and respect were more important factors in arriving at a decision than an intellectual calculus. His internal wisdom enabled him to integrate his intellectual analysis with his intuition. Yet he acknowledged that he still had to work against his default, worst-case scenario instincts:

> I'm a worst-case scenario guy. I don't like that. I don't think that
> is the way to live. You end up living in fear of some things that
> could happen that won't happen. The closest literary analogy to
> that comes out of a short story I was assigned [in college] in

English lit. "The Beast in the Jungle" is the story, and the protagonist is John Marcher. He spends his whole life waiting for this beast to leap into his life in some way, and he loses the ultimate love of his life, realizes that, and at the end of the story he throws himself on her grave. I've gone back to that story a few times in my life and . . . somewhat of a depressing tale, but I do think that at my worst I end up being John Marcher. You're thinking that something's going to happen, and you're waiting for it, and you're planning and you're plotting and then you miss the joy of the particular moment. A certain part of me in the back of my mind lives that way, but when you look at the choices I've exercised, I have made choices, some of them maybe quite bold in the world, and stuck with certain things. And you think about marriage. You think about family. You think about the really big decisions. And so I'm able to defeat some of those impulses that distract me from the present moment or where I'll miss an opportunity that may never come again. So luckily, I'm not John Marcher. It's just at my worst I sometimes think like that guy. How can I deal emotionally with certain things? That's always where my John Marcher calculus kicks in.

As Mark became increasingly comfortable with operating on faith, love, trust and respect—and as he kept his John Marcher inclination in check—he was also open to altering his long-standing critique of organized religion. The implications of raising his son sparked this shift:

This feeling has ebb and flow to it, depending on the particular part of my life, but certainly faith in a higher power, faith in God that I gain sustenance from. I'd say over the course of years, it's certainly something that when you build a family . . . I was raised Catholic. Michele was born into a Christian tradition, went to church. We met at a Catholic school. And you want to raise your kids with morals. I think children of atheists and agnostics can be raised with plenty good morals, no question about it. I also think that one great way to learn ethics and morals is from spiritual training and guidance and religion in someone's life and that the younger that starts the better. Michele and I looked for a church when she was pregnant. We joined the church, and Nate was baptized there. So, there's a whole faith in a higher power there. I'd say it's given me great support at different points in my life, even since the last discussion we had. There's also something that's not necessarily tied to religion or spirituality, just a faith that life works out. Good things happen. A trust and faith in yourself that you'll be able to surmount certain obstacles. A trust and faith in your spouse that she'll be able to and that you as a couple in a marriage can get through certain things. So, some of the faith is more supernatural, others decidedly natural in every way and earthbound in every way.

The security afforded by Mark's internal foundation opened him to the idea of joining Michele in church activity and led to his subsequently developing new facets of himself. Because this notion of a supernatural faith was new in our conversations, I asked how it related to the theme of freedom to construct your view of the world and self that he had articulated over the years. He responded:

I think we're on a pathway to some form of spiritual development in this existence that we have and . . . but as part of that, you make particular choices, and you do have freedom of choice. I believe in that completely. There is freedom of choice. You can do or not do anything in the context of your life. And so I don't think there's some predestination that, you know, God makes you do this, that, or the other. I do think that things that go on in this world, as horrific as they are—if you want to think about things like the Holocaust. It's hard to wrap your mind around it frankly. When bad things happen, things we judge as bad, faith sustains us through that, and bad things have to happen for a reason. Even if you're a person of no faith, an atheist can understand that some of the best things that have come into their lives have come through getting through difficult and challenging circumstances, and there is a strength that comes from that. But I think that life has meaning. I mean, life is not just pushing a rock up a hill, and parenthood helped me understand that, too, because it's a relationship where there's a lot of giving and a lot of love and support. But for me, there's no question of predestination and free will. It's all free will, and you exercise it and . . . but I mean God puts certain opportunities before you, but it's your choice whether you take path A, B or C. . . . you have to be able to mediate it and understand what it means to you to exercise A, B and C. Now, your decision may not be objectively the correct one, but there may not be an objectively correct one. But you decide the level of meaning you give certain events.

While Mark found some solace in there being some larger reason for horrific events, he firmly held to individual choice. This struck me as consistent with his philosophy of life. Mark's belief in free will mediated his parenting philosophy. He described his approach:

My instinct is if the kid falls, unless he hits his head, I'm not flinching, not moving toward him. I'm not reacting that it is a serious event or that he should cry. If he does cry, I'm there with unconditional love. You really have to let your kid experience consequences, even if they suck. He sleeps at night because we used tough love putting him down. He had to cry, and we didn't go in there. We knew he was safe; he had to learn to console himself.

Similarly, Mark allowed his son freedom on the playground to interact with other children and work out problems. Mark was always present and intervened when he thought it was necessary, but he wanted his son to learn to deal with things on his own. He elaborated:

I'm hoping my son doesn't necessarily pick up the worst-case scenario issue. I prefer he'd see life in some way as conspiring to help him out. When he looks at life optimistically and moves forward on his own, that events conspire to help him out regardless of . . . whether he views a specific event or happening as good or bad, he can't really see the full context of it, so his own individual judgment doesn't really matter. He's just got to move forward with his own program, and then other people will assist along the way. You'll just be a happier person in your life and this world more if you go through life believing events and people conspire to help you. At the same time, if you're really going to take full advantage of that, you just can't be a toad on the couch, somewhere expecting life to blow in the door to help you out. You have to be out there confidently moving forward, and when you slip and fall, you pick yourself back up. I mean, you call upon help when you need it, but the fact is, if you're out there putting one foot in front of the other, you can find and attract people who will help you out and become your mentor and that kind of thing. In my own mind, these are not inconsistent. The first point is he is part of the world himself. So, if he picks himself up, the world's helped him. And the second thing is more utilitarian, the best outlook to have.

Mark attempted to interact with Nate in ways that fostered this outlook. The blending of giving his son responsibility and unconditional support was Mark's way of living his convictions. He wanted Nate to believe that things work out, that the world will help you. Yet, he wanted him to exercise his free will in shaping his life. What might appear risky to other parents (e.g., allowing the child to fall) was not risky in Mark's eyes because he was moving forward with faith and trust that things would work out. He was more interested in how Nate came to view the world than whether he incurred a few scrapes and bruises.

Mark blended free will and unconditional support in his vision of his marriage as well:

> There is a point where spouses have to allow the other one individuality. I respect that position and won't interfere with you following it, but I have my own track. If it is a life of love and respect that you are going for, those things have to be minimized. Listen to perspective, come to understand opinion, then there is a mutual respect to allow the other spouse to not go with it. Come to mutual agreement to respect one another's choices.[15]

Mark seemed to convey here that he and his wife each had their own internal foundation that they brought to their relationship. Inherent in their respect for each other's choices was a commitment to share their intentions clearly and provide support for each other. Mark elaborated:

> You have a life partner. You've got to discuss with them what you're thinking, what you want to do, what your hopes and dreams are, what you're looking to accomplish. And I think the responsibility comes in with that communication of what you want to do, why you want to do it. A spouse is entitled to know that, and you've got to be clear and be there and talk about that kind of thing on a daily basis. But in terms of the ultimate choice and decision, I think what you have to do is ideally be the kind of spouse you want them to be. And what I mean by that is when you are going to make a decision, or let's say when your spouse is going to make a decision, you want to be able to support them unconditionally. And so, when there are times when you have to make a decision for yourself about what you want to do and how you want to do it, then hopefully they'll support you in that same kind of unconditional way. And that said, some of these kind of value issues you've got to work out before you get married. You've got to understand the other person pretty darn well beforehand and be real clear and honest about who you are and what you want to do. . . . I mean it's ultimately a commitment to the partnership. That's what it ultimately comes down to. And you know, from the minute Michele and I started dating and before we started dating, I always had a great deal of respect for her and who she was, and that's never wavered. I've always respected her a lot, so it would be extremely difficult for me . . . I don't know if I ever could, especially after this

long a time, but I don't know if I could ever change that. She's got my everlasting respect, I'd say. That makes it easier to continue in dialogue, even one I find unpleasant.

Mark unconditionally supported Michele through medical school and residency. Because he prioritized her values in analyzing decisions, he moved ahead with the house she wanted. In return, she supported his stopping work to write a novel, leaving his law firm, and eventually quitting work to stay home when they were expecting their second child. Because of their mutual respect for each other's internal foundations, they were each able to exercise free will and enjoy the other's support. His internal commitments were secure enough to afford the flexibility he demonstrated in interacting with his wife and son.

In our twentieth interview, Mark announced that he had quit his job as executive director. The reasons he gave were giving priority of family over career and disillusionment at work. Speaking to the first issue, Mark said:

> Michele and I are still doing wonderfully together. Marriage has been probably the best thing about my adult life. Next month, she gives birth to our daughter. But in terms of the significance that three human beings, including my wife, put on me in my roles as husband and father, and luckily Michele's in an economic position where I don't have to work. So when you look at the demands of running a national company and the demands of your family, which are most important? Which are you going to get the most out of and reward from and have the most ethical and moral duty to? It's all family-based for me, and that's clear. I did not want to miss out in helping my family through this transition. I didn't want to miss the opportunity to make that as strong a foundation as possible, and luckily I have found the rewards of fatherhood to be just incredible. . . . So, the career decision was actually a pretty easy one, just like getting engaged clarified career decisions for me back in law school. So, I think that's a long-term value that I've tried to work through throughout my life—family over career. So, it's been an easy transition for me to not be working. I set things up well enough financially before I left work to make sure that . . . I mean any issues of bankruptcy have long left the forefront.

Mark's second reason was his growing disappointment with his boss—who he had initially respected but later learned had lied about a number of issues—that only reinforced his decision to quit this job to maintain his convictions. He explained the situation:

> Punting on this particular career was really ultimately a no-brainer. I remember dropping off Nate at a childcare facility because school was out, and everybody was working, so I had to go to a new one. . . . Dropping your child, a three-year-old, in the middle of a room where he doesn't know anybody and just seeing the look on his face as he kind of looks around, for me was heartbreaking. I related it to my boss, the president of the company, because I'd just come into work and I was a little late. I just did this, "Boy, it really kills me to do this," and he was like, "Well, I had to do it with my kids. Tough shit, you know, they'll learn." I was like, what? We're not on the same plane in terms of values here. That kind of outlook really offended me, quite frankly, so I knew the relationship would not last long. And he knew I took a great deal of time off when Michele first had Nate, and he was like, "That's impossible here." I was like, I'm going to make my own choice, get out on my own terms. As I was leaving, things were coming to a head at work. He wanted me saddled into this house so I couldn't leave him. Our mortgage and financial commitments would be so large that I could not leave. We'd be so wrapped up in this house that Michele couldn't even look for a job elsewhere in the country. We'd be entrenched. That was his game. He got really angry and embittered at the end. He always had an agenda, and he would do a little bit of lying, cheating, and stealing, and when I saw that, I was just offended. I finally was able to scratch beneath the surface of what he'd always tell everybody. It was a tremendous disappointment. He had done kind of a snaky sales job on me on a few things, and that was just kind of repugnant, left a very bad taste in my mouth. That said, you've got to try to look for the good in it, and you know, that job was a sustaining factor for Michele and I through over three years.

This career decision is another example of Mark living his values. As soon as Mark realized that his boss did not genuinely support his commitment to his family, he began to look more critically at what was taking place. Because of his enduring belief in prioritizing his family first and solid sense of what constitutes ethical behavior, it was not even a dilemma for him to leave this position. Interestingly, he was able to suppress his John Marcher inclination.

Mark's Story Line

Mark's self-authorship evolved through the quieter form of pain—disillusionment with the career for which he had prepared most of his life. His realization at law school that he had been ignoring his internal cues led him to recognize that he had avoided feelings in college. He initially used his intellect, his forte and default mode of operating, to listen to his internal cues and cultivate his internal voice. He went on to identify values and beliefs that he integrated into his philosophy of life as a means to achieve his vision of the good life and happiness, and he did so both in daily living and in larger decisions. He first developed his internal voice with his intellect leading the way.

Although Mark trusted his internal voice, he began to experience the shortcomings of a purely intellectual approach to life. Working through life's realities and his relationship with his wife, Mark yearned for some additional source of understanding beyond the intellect. He built and refined his internal foundation through exploring Chinese philosophy to find a truer identity beyond the intellect. This growth in his intrapersonal dimension helped him acknowledge that he could not control external circumstances and should dance with reality rather than fight it. It also led to his ability to detach from intellect and emotion, and not worry about things he could not control in challenging situations.

Using his evolving internal foundation to guide his everyday life yielded increased flexibility and comfort with going with the flow of life. His true identity, his spiritual self, came to the forefront as the consistent anchor of his life. With this foundation, he merged how he came to know with his sense of self. He was able to live his convictions in handling his son's health crisis and in his various work environments. He was also able to live his convictions by quitting work at various times to care for his children. He was able to move forward with faith and trust in all arenas of his life. He exercised his free will in his career decisions and lived his internal foundation in his relationship with Michele and Nate. Mark enacted the philosophy he hoped his children would adopt: Move forward with your own program, and the world will conspire to help you out. Mark trusted that if he stayed on the front seat of the bike, willing and helpful partners would jump on the back as they were needed.

CHAPTER 4

KURT'S STORY—BEING TRUE TO THE MAN IN THE GLASS

KURT HAD A PENCHANT FOR INTERACTING WITH PEOPLE. His experience as a Little League baseball coach and summer camp counselor came in handy in his active involvement in college activities, including joining a student service foundation and co-chairing the annual bike race. He reported that he "absolutely loved giving campus tours" because he felt like he was serving people. His communications major seemed a natural fit. Upon college graduation, Kurt took a job as a legal assistant in a large law firm in a major city. He sensed that "being a lawyer would be good because I would get acceptance."[1] His reason for taking this position was to see if attending law school was what he really wanted to do. He observed that the attorneys spent the majority of their time doing paperwork and were highly achievement oriented. He did not see how his love for interacting with and serving people could play out in this setting. He also began to think that being happy in his work might be more important than making money.

Kurt wanted to make a daily difference in people's lives. He noted that he would be a teacher "if there was more of a career" to it. Describing himself as a "nature boy in the truest sense," Kurt had always considered moving out West but hesitated to leave his family. When his father announced that Kurt's parents might move to Florida, Kurt realized that he needed to decide for himself what he wanted to do. A year later, Kurt and a college friend moved out West. He spent the first year there working in a youth activity center. Kurt commented that after leaving the law firm he was "living for the day."

In contrast to college where he had goals for what to accomplish next, his biggest goal at this point was to ski every ski run on the mountain in a year. Although he enjoyed the job and the community, he missed his family. When his brother moved to another western state a year later, Kurt joined him, despite feeling like he was casting his fate to the wind in moving with no job. He landed a job at a YMCA youth camp for the summer and then accepted a fulltime retail job at a hardware store. He shared that he would like to be making as much money as his brother, but he also thought there was something to be learned from making $5.50 an hour. He began to feel the need to reestablish his goals and return to the question of what to do for a career.

Kurt spent the next year and a half searching for a career. His manager at the sporting goods store asked him to introduce a preschool class to camping. He reported that it was the first thing he had been excited about for a long time. This, along with his prior experiences with kids, prompted him to consider teaching. He returned to school to prepare to become a math teacher. While taking classes, he worked the night shift as a machine operator at a manufacturing company.

During these years, Kurt reported that he was engaged in a lot of self-reflection as he tried to figure out his career path. It seemed that whenever he achieved success, he became bored and feared that continuing would not keep his interest over the long term. He noted that this had happened as early as elementary school when he was in baseball. He started playing in third grade, and reported, "By fifth grade I was a star, then in sixth grade I wanted to give it up." He repeated this pattern in high school. After excelling as a track star, he lost interest in track. In college, he did not seek the presidency of the student organization that ran the annual bike race although it was the natural next step for him. He was also continually trying to find and maintain his own voice in his work. That would become a theme of his twenties and thirties. Kurt's map shows the paths he pursued in his journey toward self-authorship and the partners he had along the way.

Kurt's Journey

In his early twenties, Kurt attended a couple of workshops through which he became aware that he relied on others' perceptions to validate his sense of self-worth. Recognizing the problem, he said:

The power of choice is mine; I have a choice of how I want to perceive each and every situation in my life. . . . Obviously I'm not to that point yet because I choose to make myself happy and make myself sad on what other people are thinking. But I think I'd like to someday get to a point where I can say, "Okay, that's your perception. I am not dependent on you for my happiness or my sadness." And I think that would be a very strong, very spiritual place to be.[2]

As he reported at age 30, he spent most of his twenties trying to get to that point. I found his reflections on relinquishing external formulas and working through the crossroads quite enlightening.

Moving Through the Crossroads Toward Self-Authorship

Kurt combined his insights from the workshops with those he gained working as a legal assistant. Recognizing the need to depend on himself for his happiness or sadness, Kurt set out to listen to his internal voice.

Entering the Crossroads: Listening to the Internal Voice. Kurt described the experience of his early twenties:

It has been like my own personal spiritual path—exploring, trying to understand why I am here, what I have to contribute to life on earth. I am motivated by personal satisfaction, I kind of abandoned [external reassurance]—[I have] more of a self-acceptance rather than external. I'm letting go of external influence to a large extent. I've done personality assessments, and one of the tenets of self [for me] is gaining acceptance through pleasing other people, sometimes sacrificing my own needs. I'm letting go of that to become more in tune with who I am and what makes me happy. I would not have imagined working for a hardware store three years after college. I came to an acceptance of what is in life, rather than changing externals. It's a great job, and I have fun doing it. Self-acceptance, being able to say, "Yes, this is my choice, and I'm happy with it." By doing what I want, I have abandoned [self-sacrifice] but fall back into it sometimes. Learning is a process, slow and steady. It is still hard to stand up for my needs and too easy to meet others'.[3]

Despite working to let go of external validation, Kurt was aware that he still had to work at abandoning his tendency for self-sacrifice.

Traversing the Crossroads: Cultivating the Internal Voice. By his mid-twenties, Kurt returned to school to become a math teacher and worked nights at a factory. He was still working on listening to and cultivating his internal voice and drew the distinction between talking about it and living it:

> My philosophy, what I'm looking for out of life, is the same: the ability to influence the world around me in a positive way. What has changed is that it has further unfolded in my life—two years ago I was talking about it; now I'm living it. That's a totally huge difference. I probably thought I was living it then. What is inside impacts what is outside, but it comes from inside. The inside is not influenced by others. You have to learn that it does come from inside. For a while, you think others can make decisions; you learn in the end that it comes down to you. There is a poem, something like "Man in the Glass." It talks about going through life, but the only person you answer to is the man in the glass—the mirror, looking at yourself. I can't remember the exact lines, but one is that the most important person is the person in the glass. My parents have instilled that a lot. They never gave answers, just said, "You get out on your own, and we'll support you." My experience with the law firm set me on the road to where I am now. I thought it would bring me happiness. I tried to live society's plan for me. No way! Then it was like, "Okay, I don't think there is any self-actualization in what society has planned." In order to self-actualize yourself, you have to look inside yourself.[4]

Kurt's parents had introduced him to the poem *The Man in the Glass* (see http://www.theguyintheglass.com). The first verse of the poem reads:

> When you get what you want in your struggle for self
> And the world makes you king for a day,
> Just go to a mirror and look at yourself
> And see what THAT man has to say.
> For it isn't your father or mother or wife
> Whose judgment upon you must pass,
> The fellow whose verdict counts most in your life
> Is the one staring back from the glass.

Although Kurt could not remember the exact lines of the poem, he was convinced that looking inside was the way to go, and he was better able to stand up for his needs as a result. His parents were good partners for him as he worked through the crossroads portion of his journey.

Self-Authorship: Trusting the Internal Voice

By his late twenties, Kurt abandoned his plan to become a high school math teacher. He reflected that it was "fulfilling a martyr role; doing what is righteous," yet "limiting myself, not giving [my]self its fullest expression." He participated in a committee of machine operators that developed a training program and found this very fulfilling. He decided to commit himself to the manufacturing company to see what might come of it. This commitment led to Kurt moving into a supervisory position on the sunrise shift. Kurt commented that he was still hard at work cultivating his internal sense of self:

> I'm not as far as I want to be in identifying my values, goals, and then the actual things to achieve them. . . . [At work], we were thinking about posting another supervisor position for the day shift. Working on the sunrise shift is difficult. I always feel tired, so I thought about trying to get the day shift position. But then something is not right there for me. It doesn't feel right—not where I am needed right now. . . . I don't know if I feel there are greater things to do on the sunrise shift. I'm trying to get inside that a bit to figure out what isn't right. I don't want to abandon my shift, so part of it is what I can commit to people. For me, it goes back to the head and heart thing. In my head, it makes sense; in my heart, I'm not quite there—I don't know what is there—have to honor that. I couldn't, being true to myself, couldn't go into [the new position]. I could succeed, enjoy it, but it would be making a mistake.[5]

Despite his lack of clarity about what his heart was telling him, he knew there was something about applying for the day shift position that did not sit well. Kurt had a sense of loyalty to his shift that struck him as more important than following his personal interests. Concluding that failing to honor that internal feeling would be a mistake, he did not apply for the position.

Kurt was aware of his struggle to place his personal satisfaction above his commitment to others' satisfaction:

> One thing I recognize . . . is that I have a tendency to over commit myself to things. I go around committing to everyone who needs something and then see what is left for Kurt. Sometimes, there is something left, sometimes not. I have to start cutting out some before I can give to Kurt. For me, balance is not a conscious thing—it just happens when I am following what feels right and what doesn't. If I go out to try to get balance, you can bet I won't get it. The act of consciously trying to do it

> eliminates the possibility of achieving it. I don't know why that is. For me, if I want balance, I have to be balanced. If I want peace, I have to be [at] peace. If I go out and look for it, it is elusive—it's outside. I have stopped looking for it outside myself.[6]

Kurt's struggle to balance his needs with those of others remained. When he found himself shortchanging his own interests or seeking outside approval, he lost the balance and peace of mind he desired. Although determined to stop craving outside validation, his strong interests in maintaining relationships often pulled him in that direction. This interest seemed to stem from his interest in serving others, a loyalty to his work, and a residual desire for others' approval. He needed continually to cultivate his voice to avoid over committing to others at his own expense, often finding himself back at the crossroads to self-authorship. As evident here in his decisions about his work, he had learned to trust his inner voice enough to act on it.

Self-Authorship: Building an Internal Foundation

Once established in his supervisory position, Kurt was ready for a change. He shared what happened when he acted on his internal voice:

> I had accomplished what I wanted—turned around the sunrise shift. I told my boss that I'd like to be a key player—he said, "No, I need you where you are." I insisted that I wanted to start learning, that I was ready for challenge. [There were] two others who'd been with the company longer than me, who were much older than me, and I was hired. In four years, I have become the boss of the guy who hired me. But for the first time I'm concerned about getting fired about results. I always felt sheltered in other positions. I wasn't the one setting the course, or planning; I was always under someone else's umbrella. Now I'm holding it. I can't let people get wet, or I might lose my job. I have to show results, prove [my] worth. I never had to do that before. I'm my own worst enemy, critic, with that.

Kurt got what he wanted but reported that the job was highly stressful and overwhelming. Despite positive feedback from his boss, he worried that he was not improving productivity and felt he was constantly behind on decisions that needed to be made "five minutes ago." He reported that the "perception of my boss is what I'm getting done, mine is what I haven't done." He was also concerned about losing who he was in this role. He wanted to be of service to others and to give his employees the benefit of the doubt. His boss was more focused on results than on people. This made Kurt worry about his ability to apply the basic principles he had developed in this job. In talking through this, Kurt turned to spirituality:

> Spirituality is a driving, motivating thing; spirituality is who I am. [It is] certain kinds of universal principles that I've adopted as beliefs, cornerstones in my life—[you] just get different circumstances to apply those same principles to. It is an escalating spiral; everything is an expression of love or call for love. Back when I had less responsibility, that was easy to apply. It was easy to send and give love. When I became a supervisor, it was a little more difficult with people screaming at you. I learned how to apply those same principles. Now with this new job, it's a whole new opportunity. Be accepting, supportive, respectful. Spirituality is still who I am—other things are just what I do. The way I do my job is related to these principles. Rather than trying to control external circumstances, I am controlling reactions. That is my spirituality.

Kurt trusted his internal voice enough to accept reality and control his reactions just as Dawn and Mark described in earlier chapters. Kurt's idea of sending and giving love stemmed in part from his study of the book *A Course in Miracles*. He adapted the book's notion of operating from a space of love to believing in others, being honest with them, respecting them and reinforcing positive behavior. Kurt had been refining these core principles during his twenties and now embraced them as central components of his identity. Their importance to who he was contributed to his concern over applying them in this new role. He found it hard to give love when employees reacted negatively to what he believed was a positive philosophy.

When I asked Kurt about when he had arrived at this notion of controlling his reactions rather than the circumstances themselves, he replied:

> Recently. I was aware of it as early as college. I could talk about it, even before college, but it never meant anything until four months or so ago. It was in my head; now it is in my heart. I never had to make choices like I have to make now.

Kurt's explanation helped me understand why I had interpreted his comments in earlier interviews as an internal foundation. He had intellectually articulated this belief about controlling his reactions, yet he was not yet able to live it until he had to make difficult decisions. This forced him to embrace this internal foundation in his heart—as an embodiment of who he was rather than an aspiration of who he wanted to be. He explained how he was using his internal foundation to frame external influence on his behavior:

> It is not that you get to control the circumstances of events happening to you; I've tried to stop that and [instead] control how I think about it. I had hoped I would have a family by age 31—but I'm not dwelling on it. I couldn't work the hours I work right now if I had that. It is nice to have the flexibility to do that. I try to control events less and control my perception of them more. What other people think is still a motivating thing for me. There are times when I am extremely confident, and then what people think doesn't matter. It is the power of my conviction. At that time, I am going to do it, it is going to happen. In the mode I am in right now, I am concerned about what other people think but not to gain approval for myself. It is more where I am in a whole learning process. I have a great relationship with my boss. A lot of times I'll ask him how he'd play something. I want to know what he thinks. But it's not who I am; I'm not basing my identity off it. It is not for gaining self-worth, just for getting resources. What makes our relationship solid is that we have an understanding—he'll come to me with the same thing. We ask what each other thinks. It is a positive mutual understanding. We aren't looking for each other's approval. My boss is not concerned about what other people think—he doesn't define his worth on that. I take a lot of that from him—he's a positive role model.[7]

Kurt was making progress achieving the power of choice he had imagined years earlier, yet his comments reveal that it was hard to maintain this outlook consistently. When he trusted his internal voice, he had "the power of his convictions" to act on it; however, when he was less confident, he had to return to developing his internal voice and building his internal foundation. His boss provided a positive environment in which Kurt could join him in mutual decision making without concern about others' approval; as such, his boss was a crucial partner for Kurt. Kurt would continue around this cycle of working to trust his voice, building his internal foundation, and living his convictions in the coming years.

Kurt's progress was fortunate in light of the challenges on the horizon. The political dynamics in his workplace created an extremely challenging context in which to continue to apply his principles to his work. As Kurt was trying to grow into his new role as a manager, frustration among the employees led them to express significant dissatisfaction. Kurt reported how this affected him:

> It was a very difficult thing for me in my role as manager. I just had turned thirty-one and did not have a whole lot of credibility with my role. People perceived that I was somebody that would work hard, but at the same time, I didn't really have anything to back that up. So, they put another person who had been with the company a long time, but who had less education than I did, over me. That was certainly a big pill to swallow for me. Some real hard feedback came my way because here I was thinking I was, in my best effort, doing everything that I felt I needed to do. I was being asked to do many things that ended up upsetting the manufacturing personnel.

Kurt's loyalty to his superiors led him to carrying out their plans. When the employees complained, the company promoted a person whom the employees trusted to be Kurt's supervisor. Kurt struggled with this undermining of his credibility, and the negative feedback shook his confidence. Kurt understood the company's decision, and his commitment to the success of the company helped him "swallow" this pill; however, it complicated his work in a number of ways, as he described:

> It was incredibly difficult for me because I was still performing in the same role. It was just now that I wasn't the point person for it, and that was frustrating. I always will, and I always have, maintain that I am here to support my boss. It is my number one priority and my number one responsibility to make our boss successful. So, I kept on gritting my teeth and saying okay, even when I was being asked to do things that were clearly his responsibility. I held on to that belief because I had really nothing else to hold on to. That, okay, I am doing the right thing, and when the time is right, people will recognize the values and my contributions to this whole process, even if it appears that the credit's being given to him. He's always appreciated my work. It's not that he has never acknowledged my contribution to the whole thing. But, I was always concerned about how other people were perceiving my contribution.

Kurt's values drove him to support his boss. He made a commitment to others' success, yet felt torn when it came at his personal expense.

On the one hand, he told himself that eventually others would recognize his contribution. On the other hand, given his sense that he lacked credibility in his role, he continued to worry about whether his contribution would be recognized. This situation got increasingly complicated when the company merged with another company, and leaders saw the duplication of roles as inefficient. They moved Kurt to a different managerial position. Despite Kurt's assessment that he was more qualified than the other person for the original managerial position, he took this move in stride and chose to perceive it as a great opportunity rather than be angry about the move. Kurt did well in his new position and had mixed feelings a year later when the vice president approached him about moving back to the position he had held earlier. Kurt explained his hesitation:

> He talked to me about flip-flopping roles with [the other person]. He said, "What I have right now is I have two people in the wrong positions. You clearly need to be the one that is managing the entire organization." I said, "Of course I'll embrace any kind of opportunity that you see me benefiting the organization." I expressed to him that I am not being fully utilized in my role. I'm intentionally not doing everything that I could be doing simply out of respect for my boss. So, then there's a lot of fear with it, too, because here I am being put back in the position that I seemingly failed in initially. I feel like I learned a great deal from that failure, and I've worked hard to become a much more respected individual by the more than one hundred individuals that are working around the production floor. And at the same time, though, to me there is almost only failure that could be realized from this. The factory is running well, so it's going to be difficult for me to make the sale [for] why we're doing it this way. That's a concern. Because I'm carrying with me that my perception that, in other people's eyes that I might have failed at what I was doing initially.

Kurt stood ready to do what was needed and felt that he could offer more than he could in his current role. His loyalty to the company came first, but he did draw attention to his need to be fully utilized. At the same time, his sense of having previously failed in this role left him wondering how he would persuade the employees that this was a good decision. When I asked why he perceived that he failed initially, Kurt responded:

> The failure is that I probably could have done things differently the first time through, so that the complaints never even came

up. Maybe I'm taking too much ownership for that whole process because truly I was just putting in place policies, procedures, practices that were being asked of me to put in place. If I would have had a little bit clearer picture of what was going on, it was my role or responsibility to go back to him and say, no, this is not a good idea to do. It was some feedback that I got, in terms of not being approachable, even to the clothes that I wore. I purposely have dressed down. That's difficult, because I'm not doing me a service by not being who I truly am in a lot of different roles or responsibilities or functions.

In the unfamiliar circumstances of his first managerial role, Kurt had leaned toward carrying out the vice president's wishes. He found himself in a dilemma when doing so gave rise to negative feedback from the employees. At that point, his internal voice was not strong enough to question his superiors or to maintain his sense of self in the face of the employees' criticisms. In opting to support the company and his boss, he had ignored his sense of self and expertise, and even gone to the lengths of changing the way he dressed. He was pulled between supporting the company, expressing himself, and gaining the respect of employees. Keeping his internal self in clear sight was difficult in these circumstances.

Upon being thrust back into the position from which he had been removed, Kurt again faced reconciling his bosses' and the employees' points of view. He described how he was trying to approach the dilemma differently this time:

> One thing that I'm trying to do, from a management perspective, is get people to do things that I want them to do and allow them to feel like they are the ones making the decisions. Anybody can go tell somebody what to do. That is something that marked how I was working before. Now, I've really worked to use my communication skills and abilities to lead people to the outcome that I want to see, only allow them to think that it's the outcome they came up with. I'm a little concerned about it in terms of the honesty and integrity piece of it, but at the same time, a successful manager is someone who gets things done without other people knowing that they've been managed. The managers reporting to me right now have been with the company for years. It's been this real interesting experience trying to gain their respect, getting them to do the things that are being asked of me from the groups that they manage. I've been able to get more out of the people that I work with since I've really taken that as a way to approach things. I think they feel

better about what they're doing too. You really encourage people to come to you with ideas and do much more than saying, okay, this is how it's going to be.

Kurt knew he needed a new philosophy of management. He struggled a bit to build this new element of his role. Kurt allowed his employees to feel that they were generating the ideas because he felt it was more palatable for them than telling them what to do; however, he wondered whether he was being honest since he knew what he wanted them to do. He was trying to balance success both in terms of productivity and results (and supporting his boss) and in terms of keeping employees happy. Rather than move back and forth between support of one or the other, Kurt was trying to reconcile these two perceptions of success, particularly when they conflicted. This balancing act made it difficult for him to apply his principles consistently.

Kurt was doing a balancing act in a larger sense as well, as he tried to balance work with other aspects of life. He had attempted to develop other personal interests, including officiating high school basketball, to achieve contentment. Kurt reported feeling that what he was looking for was continually getting clearer. His relationship with a management coach, something he had begun during his initial difficulties with employees, was helping him identify what he enjoyed. He attributed some of the positive developments in his life to this increased clarity:

> I always look to do things from the inside out. I don't look for opportunities to provide me with the internal state of mind; I first concentrate on that internal state of mind. Lynn Grabhorn wrote a book called *Excuse Me, Your Life is Waiting*. It talks about being clear with what you want, and then when it happens, experiences come in to support that because you attract those things to you. I'm clear on what I want and what I want to feel, then these experiences develop and come my way. I attribute the plant manager position to this. I didn't go asking for this. To me, it is like the important piece is to begin with the end in mind. What do I want to accomplish with the situation I'm in? It is even larger in how do I want to live my life, how my marriage will turn out? It is not conscious. Something presents itself to me and this is the next logical step.
>
> Dating my fiancée falls into this process. The situation kept coming back for me. For three or four years, we were friends. She asked me to go skiing, I asked her to a movie one time; she said sorry. Working with her it was difficult—me as a

manager wanted to be conscious of harassment. We are told over and over again, it is okay to ask once but not more. The timing wasn't right. Then I thought, it is here, it is here for a reason, available to you. See what might come from it.[8]

Kurt's continual looking inside helped him make the best of many situations. As he was focused on what he could learn and how to make himself happy, opportunities presented themselves.

Like Dawn and Mark in previous chapters, Kurt had developed a philosophy to guide his life. Kurt's efforts to look inside echo Dawn's sorting and sifting to get to the essence of who she was and Mark's going back on the potter's wheel to mold his own beliefs and values. Kurt's experience confirms Mark's advice that a philosophy is essential to face life's challenges. Refining their beliefs and values, along with the realization that they could control their reactions to reality helped all three build internal foundations. The security of those foundations then helped them recognize opportunities as they arose.

Asked how Kurt knew that he wanted to marry his fiancée, he responded:

> One thing that is very apparent to me—I spent the entire decade of my twenties getting in touch with who I was and what is important to me. From the time we started dating, there weren't any questions. It got to a point of—it was weird. We went into the relationship with a totally different set of goals and objectives [than in earlier relationships]. To the extent that we could, more than any other relationship I've had, we entered into it as complete people. We weren't lacking for anything, weren't needing affirmation, or needing each other to give us something to complete us. From a perspective of infatuation, I have never had that with her—have had it with other women—but it's the pendulum thing again. Always been in the middle with her; wonderful thing of us sharing our lives with each other, we both have a similar set of beliefs, allowing me to be that whole person that I already am, not having to put on an act. I haven't felt the whole infatuation thing, just an even keel kind of thing. That has allowed me to feel great about making the commitment. The support from her— the beautiful thing about that—I don't need to change a single thing and still be loved as much or more than I was this morning. Hopefully, that is the environment I create for her as well. Accepted, respected and loved by me. That's how it has come to be and how I've been able to commit to that and feel great about it.[9]

Kurt's internal foundation allowed him to be whole and authentic entering into this relationship. He was able to apply his principles of manifesting love in this relationship without having to balance competing interests. As a result, he acquired a new partner to accompany him on his developmental journey.

The following year, Kurt reported his surprise that this relationship was even better after he and his wife were married. Kurt noted that the symbolic nature of getting married took their dedication and commitment to each other to a different level. He also felt this in decisions he made at work because Jan worked in the company that Kurt managed. He was sometimes placed in an awkward position in terms of sharing sensitive information with her in her dual role as wife and employee. Yet, they were able to talk openly about it. I was intrigued that Kurt appeared much more comfortable handling dilemmas in his marriage than he did with his employees. Asked what he attributed this to, he said:

> I think that it is the fact that both Jan and I are whole and complete where we are, and so there isn't a huge overreliance on the other individual. There isn't a huge dependence upon the other individual. It truly comes from a place of being totally happy for that individual, where they are, and, more importantly, recognizing, okay, with that being said, what is the best way that I can support you in terms of you doing or being exactly who you want to be?

In this relationship, Kurt was whole and complete and didn't second-guess his interactions with his wife. Being able to be totally authentic, he was also able to engage her help in balancing his responsibility for the company and his responsibility to her as his wife. This contrasted with his relationships with employees in which he often felt he had to modify his expression of himself to achieve success. Jan's ability to be a good partner supported Kurt's development as well as their relationship.

While Kurt was deepening his relationship with Jan, he was developing a new type of relationship with his employees at work. A few days prior to his marriage, and only a year after Kurt's move back to his original managerial position, he was promoted again. This marked the beginning of Kurt's shift from management to leadership:

> I've always appreciated that opportunity and excelled at recognizing what my boss's needs were and exceeding those. We have a site general manager who is, in effect, my boss, and at

the same time, though, it's a different scenario now that I'm in charge of all of the manufacturing for this facility, as well as the health and stability of our entire site. I needed to adopt more of a leadership position. I've had to step out of my comfort zone. If I don't think that something is right or best for the organization, I was never really the one having to get up on the soapbox and communicate that. I could always feed the information to my boss and have him take it to the organization and communicate the reasons why we don't think it's the best decision. Now all of a sudden the spotlight was on me, and I was needing to take information and direction from the other individuals on the operations team and clearly communicate those to the rest of the organization. So, it's something that I'm still working through. I don't want to always be perceived as a naysayer or an obstacle to something getting done, and at the same time I need to balance the need for me to be true to myself, and if I really don't think that something is in our best interest, then I need to find a way in which to communicate that. It's been a change of perspective that I've had to go through in terms of how I approach my day-to-day job and get much more out of the day-to-day management and more into the week-to-week, season-to-season leadership of the position.

Kurt was now the boss he had always fed information to and supported. Kurt realized that he would need to develop this new leader part of himself and find a way to live his convictions in this role. He observed that the tension between being himself and being perceived positively by others was magnified by this new role:

For the first two to three months, I was always second-guessing myself. Should I have communicated this way? It would take me fifteen to twenty minutes just to send out a run-of-the-mill e-mail because I was always trying to second-guess how the other person was going to perceive it. Finally I'm just like, "I am who I am, and I'm just going to go forward and do what I do and be who I am, and if at the end of the day that's not the person that [the company] wants in this position, then I'm okay with that." Not to say that I don't want to continue to work on the things that I need to be working on to make myself a better employee, better communicator, better leader. As far as me being who I am, I've transitioned from trying to change a lot of the core foundation of Kurt. I've accepted that and said, okay, I certainly want to be open to learning more. I certainly want to constantly be reinventing myself, but at the same time, I'm taking [others' perceptions] for what they're worth.

Despite Kurt's temporary return to concern about others' perceptions, he now trusted his internal foundation enough to maintain his true self and to use others' feedback in that context. Having just had a very positive performance review, he described how he was processing the critical information he received:

> The feedback is coming from individuals that don't want their comfort zone to be pushed. I could be more effective in communicating goals to everyone, so that they know the rationale behind it, rather than me just doing what I want to do. And at the same time, though, it is tough to hear . . . and I have to be careful with it. If they really saw the big picture, then I wouldn't have gotten any kind of negative feedback. But then, at the same time, I need to own it a hundred percent and say, okay, why aren't they seeing the big picture and is it something that I could be doing different before I conclude it's something outside of me. A lot of who I define myself as is . . . I gain an identity from being successful in my role and being good at what I do and take a lot of comfort in that, and that's certainly a motivator for me. When you're going to put in that time and energy and then you get the feedback that that's not working the way that you had planned it to work, that just makes things a little bit difficult at times.

Kurt's sense that things were not working the way he had planned hinged on his employees not understanding the rationale for his pushing their comfort zones. Kurt's struggle with this feedback, despite the overall positive nature of the appraisal, was colored by the overall stress of this new position. He described what he thought was the source of this anxiety:

> The majority of my stress comes from the fact that I'm having to abandon what has made me successful to this point and embark upon a new set of rules or responsibilities in order to be successful in my new role. One thing that I continually come back to is the difference between managing and leading. This is the first role that I've had that has a higher reliance on the leadership piece and less of a reliance on the management piece. Maybe I was overstating that I have to abandon all of those, but I think I do have to abandon the day-to-day management. Everyone saw that I was successful at managing, so that's still kind of the expectation. They're still like, "Take it to Kurt and he'll get it done." What I'm trying to do is put more of that managing role on to all of the individuals on my team on a daily basis. I'm trying to have that be embraced by all of the

other individuals of the team so that I can head off in a different direction and identify opportunities to further improve our
effectiveness and our success.

Kurt's bosses and his employees had always rewarded him for getting things done. As he attempted to give his employees more
responsibility and push their comfort zones, some of them saw him
as arrogant and felt he was avoiding being labeled the bad guy by
challenging them through their supervisors instead of directly. His
respect for his supervisors prevented him from going around them
to interact directly with employees. Once again, Kurt found himself
struggling to apply his principles in a new set of circumstances. He
was quite aware of these tensions:

> As I hear myself talking, I want to be very careful not to attach
> my identity to those things. And I even heard myself a little bit
> in the conversation earlier attaching some of my identity to the
> success that I have within my role, and I need to be careful
> with that. I know from an intrinsic perspective that that's not
> necessarily the case, but in terms of where I'm living my life
> right now, . . . [that's] one of those lessons that still needs to be
> learned, that I'm not fully through that one yet. I go back to
> some of those universal truths that I believe on a spiritual
> level. Have my circumstances changed to the point where I
> have to try to apply these same things to a different set of
> circumstances? Absolutely, yes. I'm probably just in the begin-
> ning stages of being able to apply those things. As I'm thinking
> through it all right now, I'm still in the learning stages of this
> position. Based upon whatever my external environment is giv-
> ing me at the time, so, learning how to be a husband, learning
> how to be a plant manager, learning how to be on the executive
> team of our company, pretty soon learning how to be a father.
> I'm not necessarily real comfortable with that new set of
> circumstances and how I can maintain who I am, or not neces-
> sarily maintain who I am, but fully express who I am with that
> new set of circumstances.

Kurt's experience suggests that although his principles were intact,
each new context challenged him to maintain these core values. The
less comfortable he was in each new role, the more he was tempted to
pay attention to others' perceptions of how he was doing. Happily,
being aware of this, he was able to reflect on how to keep true to himself in each new context. As he refined his core values by applying them
in new contexts, he moved closer to being able to live them consistently.

Self-Authorship: Securing Internal Commitments

Kurt continued to grow in his transition from management to leadership. After two years in this role, he was able to clearly articulate what became of his earlier notion of encouraging his employees to develop their ideas:

> The majority of my direct reports have been with the company since it was founded. They're certainly pros in their positions, and I'm trying to steer the ship in the direction that I think it needs to go, and sometimes in contrast to the direction that they are comfortable taking it. There have been some unique opportunities and interesting challenges along those lines. I've been required to change my leadership approach depending on who I'm working with and what we're trying to accomplish. I've tried to drive the decision-making process down to the individuals that are actually having the ability to impact the decisions or having the people that are going to be executing the decisions making the decisions. And that has proven to be very successful—a lot of our people are engaged in the process. It's been reflected in our performance, so I feel very good about that. I certainly think that's something I've helped to instill and have reaped a lot of the rewards from that paradigm shift that we've been able to make.

The paradigm shift that the company underwent was, in large part, a result of a shift in Kurt's thinking. When he initially took on this position, he had focused on getting employees to think they were making the decisions, and you will recall that he felt conflicted about whether this was completely honest. When he shifted his focus from succeeding as a manager to achieving success for the company through his leadership, he genuinely wanted the employees to make the decisions. He shared how this shift in his thinking took place:

> It's been a very challenging six months really for me personally and the rest of the organization. I was getting pretty discouraged with it because it felt like I was needing to carry a lot of the burden. I have a couple star performers. But a lot of other people were content to just sit and watch me work 13-hour days, and if I needed anything, I would go to them, but they certainly weren't going to initiate anything. A couple things slipped through the cracks, things that we should have, would have, could have caught, we didn't. I made a conscious decision to take a step back, set the expectation, and allow the individuals to really run with the stuff. I feel like now I've

regained my necessary role within the organization. It's engaged other individuals in terms of their productivity and their output for the organization. The day-to-day control I do feel like I'm giving up, but it's primarily by necessity, in terms of me being able to do the work that I need to do.

Recognizing that he could not be effective if he was doing work that should have been delegated, Kurt consciously reassigned his and his reports' responsibilities. Although he made these changes out of necessity, his ability to do so hinged on his trusting himself enough to let go of control and accept the uncertainty that might ensue. He also had engaged in some internal reflection about his earlier approach when he was first promoted:

I was probably more involved in a lot of decisions that I shouldn't have been involved in at that time. Part of me needed to be involved with that only because . . . I'll make an excuse for it right now, and I don't know if I'll let myself keep it or not, but the excuse is that having not really been involved directly in a lot of the areas, I didn't have a background or any kind of framework or foundation from which to ask questions, determine where there were opportunities, what we're doing well, and where we need to improve. Now, is that me trying to micromanage and me not having confidence in the people that work for me? Yes, I think that there's a little bit of smoke there. I've gotten better with knowing what to pursue and what not to pursue. I was so naïve and ambitious that I felt that probably everything needed to be pursued. I've recognized that that's not always the best case or what is required in the moment. At the time, I was very much struggling with needing to develop my own way. I didn't feel that I had the respect of the people that I was working with. One of the critical components of my job is interacting with the people. I certainly was feeling less than adequate as far as my own knowledge was concerned. Was I looking at the right things, could I even carry on an intelligent conversation with my new peers, and what did that look like? I think I've been able to learn those things over time, and so now I feel very comfortable. I was able to ingrain in myself the fundamental belief that people truly do try to make a positive difference and try to do the best that they can with what they have available to them. It was a real paradigm shift for me.

Adopting the belief that people would try to do their best helped him trust his employees; however, there was more to this equation. Kurt had learned to trust himself as well:

I had to realize that I wasn't going to be all things to all people. I remember talking to our human resource director. I said, "I am who I am. Granted, there are some things that are great about me, and there are some things that are probably less than great about me, but I can't continually modify who I am to try to be all things to all people." I'm thirty-six now, and I feel good about who I am and where I am. [It was] like a public demonstration or proclamation of this is who I am, and it is more important for me to be who I am and maintain that than it is to continually modify that to be held in high regard with other individuals.

Kurt had finally completed a process he'd been engaged in for years: fully separating his sense of self from others' perceptions. His internal sense of self was solid enough and he trusted it enough that he could maintain his commitment to his inner self despite the opinions of others. This enabled him to achieve the same sense of "whole self" he had established in his marriage, and enabled him to develop relationships of mutual interdependence with his employees. His paradigm shift was rewarding:

I really believe in engaging as many people as possible in the process. When I can help create an environment where people are engaged and they're finding value and satisfaction, there are a lot of auxiliary benefits. It really has transformed our work force to a more cohesive unit and helped us accomplish a lot of things. In terms of producing a consumer packaged good, we want consistency. Now that we've engaged everybody, it's amazing because we are doing very well in that area. It's something that everyone has identified themselves and seen the intrinsic value, and they're actually having a much greater impact than I could have ever have had. The other component that I think is pretty important is I set up the organization so that we're giving feedback to the executors on a very regular basis. It's happening every shift, where almost immediately the production operators are getting feedback on their performance. The feedback component has been extremely beneficial in further engaging individuals into the process.

Kurt's personal paradigm shift enabled him to take up his leadership role effectively and to apply his principles to this new set of circumstances. Maintaining his internal foundation enabled him to enjoy mutually reinforcing relationships with his employees and enhance the company's success, two goals that had often been in tension with each other in earlier years. His employees were becoming good partners on his developmental journey.

As he grew into his leadership role, Kurt was also growing into the new role of father:

> It's allowed me to more fully express who I am. Part of me is surprised at how much value I place on being a father. Work has always been very important to me, but anything that relates to being a father immediately takes precedence.

Kurt also saw fatherhood as an opportunity to manifest the principles of his identity that he had worked on for so long. Although he recognized that his son would eventually choose his own values, he felt responsible for getting him started:

> My every intention is to pass on that set of values to Terry. I've never felt that it was my place to impose my values or beliefs onto others, and almost by default, I get to do that with Terry. Like I've now been given permission . . . it reinforces it for me having to work with Terry. Something that's very important for me is to reinforce the positive, reinforce the behavior that you want to see more of. Having a twenty-month-old baby at home that knows the word "no" now and is very much establishing his own presence, I have more situations in my life to put those beliefs into practice.

Up to this point, Kurt's primary opportunities to express his values had been in his work. Now, he had a new line of work, fatherhood, in which he was responsible along with his spouse for shaping his son's perspectives. Kurt was happy to have his principles in place to bring to this task. He readily lived his convictions.

With all this success in growing into new roles, it surprised me when Kurt shared that he was feeling as if he was stagnating. Asked to elaborate, he said:

> I feel comfortable, successful where I am right now, but I might be ready for the next challenge. I need to kind of create the environment or create the opportunity for something like that to take place. It's funny because you work so long and hard to try to get comfortable someplace, and then the moment that you're comfortable someplace you're like, it's kind of nice to be comfortable, but it was just more dynamic when I've actually felt that I was working toward something as opposed to having arrived at that spot.

Kurt had been so focused on constructing himself and his purpose that he had not considered what to do when he accomplished these tasks. His drive for growth left him feeling that he should be achieving more.

A year later Kurt found another opportunity to apply his life principles to a new situation when his daughter was born. He explained:

> At the core of my beliefs is how can we see this differently. It's what I'm doing at work; it's what I do in my own personal life, in my relationship with my wife. Rather than always just reacting to that first, your patterned response, pausing that minute and [asking yourself], okay, how could I see this differently. I know that I'll play that game with Terry and Theresa 'cause to me it's always been so powerful. I'm already starting to do that with Terry, who is four and a half. How could you do that differently or what else could this look like? Let's look at this upside down and see what we think that we see.

Kurt also maintained his focus on reinforcing success:

> The other piece I am applying in parenting right now is reinforcing the positive, building up on the behaviors and the actions that we want to see more of, letting them know that I value their decision. Some of it is manipulative in the sense that [you're] setting the situation so that he can be successful and really reinforcing that success. Another one of my personal beliefs is: that which you focus on, you get more of. So let's be focusing on where we're having success. So, I absolutely know that this will transfer over into how we raise Terry and Theresa and any kids that we have after that.

As Kurt noted, his parenting philosophy stemmed from an overall philosophy about the value of seeing things differently. He explained this in terms of a model he liked:

> S + R = O; situation plus response equals outcome. Again, you can't control the situation. The situation is given, and you can define what you want the outcome to be, but in order to make that equation balance, you have to assign an appropriate response. It's not perfect, it's not infallible, but at least it provides us with an explanation of where we are, why we are where we are.

Kurt and his wife used this model to think about their personal life and Kurt also used it in his work life.

At the time of our twentieth interview, Kurt again reported he had been promoted. This promotion came as a surprise because he hadn't anticipated it so soon. The general manager was leaving the company, and the search for his replacement had been unsuccessful. Two days before the general manager's departure, the chief executive officer came to Kurt's office and asked him to take the job. He was promoted to acting general manager and once again promoted to lead others who had been his peers. Kurt did not hesitate to support his company, yet he was acutely aware of his ignorance of certain areas:

> Now, I'm overseeing areas that I know little to nothing about. I've come up through the operations group. Now, I need to interact with and oversee our marketing department and our sales team. I know very little of what it is that makes them successful in their roles and what challenges and opportunities that they face. I have some knowledge, but it's more just my intuition than anything else in terms of being able to guide, direct, oversee, question, challenge, as we go through that process.

In contrast to earlier years when Kurt had worried about his lack of knowledge, now Kurt's internal wisdom allowed him to rely comfortably on his intuition. I asked Kurt how he planned to approach this challenging position. He explained:

> I still have the same philosophy that it's my job to remove obstacles for them, or it's my responsibility to find opportunities for people to do things more efficiently. It's a very bottom-up rather than top-down approach, and so, I said, "What is crucial to our working together very closely, which is what I expect us to do, is that I have to have implicit or inherent trust in you." We need to be aligned, that we're both looking out for the same thing, which is what's in the best interest for this company and how are we going to go about accomplishing that. That's where it starts in terms of working with individuals to which I have very little frame of reference. The consequences are much, much more significant now to this new role. It's more the interconnectedness of it all, and once I can get clear on that in my mind, then things seem to logically fall into place as it relates to questions that I should ask or areas we should be focused on. Going back to overseeing those groups, developing very close interpersonal relationships with the people that I'm working with, looking to really add value to what it is that

they're doing each and every day and then really trying to better understand, not necessarily the specifics but more the relative relations between the various levers that they have available to them to influence the business, and then trying to connect all those pieces together somehow.

Kurt saw his role as one of connecting disparate pieces of the business to accomplish company goals. He relied on his colleagues to help him understand their parts so that he could engage them in exploring how to think differently. In response to my request for more detail on how he thought about this process, he offered:

I'm trying to better understand how [employees] draw the various conclusions that they have. And when I understand how they drew their conclusion, that's when I find that I can add a lot of value because then what I like to focus on is how do we look at that differently. That's the conclusion that you came to based upon the assumptions that you made, but what other conclusion could we come to? I want to know what's going on and what is out there that's potentially going to come up and bite us. If I better understand how it was that people came to the conclusions and what assumptions they made in order to be able to come to those conclusions, then I can, in my own thinking or with them, go through and say, okay, is there any risk that this assumption might not come true, or how does this dynamic change if this assumption changes? Then, you can steer it down different paths. What are the potential risks out there? What [do] we need to be putting in place, a contingency or action plan, just in case one of our assumptions gets turned upside down? We want to be aware of that, see it coming, put in place plans to counteract it if it's going to have an impact in terms of how our business performs.

Kurt believed that exploring assumptions helped his colleagues shape responses to get the outcomes they desired. He used this process to identify risks and opportunities. He viewed the capacity to think differently as the key to success and thus stressed this in his interactions with his colleagues:

How can we look at this differently? Let's have a real open, stimulating debate. Let's challenge each other. Let's find a different way, or let's challenge all the assumptions that we have. That's the piece that I think is very powerful. To me, whenever there's a paradigm shift, it's extremely stimulating. That's when everything comes together. I'm always challenging to see if we can come up with a paradigm shift, pushing the envelope a little bit further, further, further. What would it look like if we did this or, going forward we need to be looking at it from this perspective and, how will that affect us? It's amazing when you see [paradigm shifts] because all of a sudden you've truly made something out of nothing. It's very empowering for the people that are doing it, and that starts to breed an exciting culture. Tying a couple of pieces together, understanding how it was that people drew the conclusions that they drew, and then going into each one of those assumptions. That's really where you can start to get some of these paradigm shifts is looking at all of the assumptions that you're making and see if you can spin an assumption a different way and get a totally different result. That's the only way I think you can come to different conclusions.

Kurt's ability to question assumptions and see systems differently, combined with his trust in his internal foundation, enabled him to create the contexts for paradigm shifts to occur. Kurt was also pushing the envelope of his own thinking and spinning assumptions to come to different conclusions about his career. He described the perspective with which he accepted the promotion to acting general manager:

I had to operate from the perspective of okay, if I take this position and say things don't work out. Say my philosophy can't turn the trick, and they need to bring in somebody with a lot more experience . . . again, I was thinking this job was for me four years from now, and that was with a whole lot of active development on my part in order to prepare myself for that. I don't know that there's necessarily a job for me to go back to, then that might mean that I have to find a job someplace else. If I don't get tied up into the specifics of it and thinking that it's got to be a certain way, then I think that there are always going to be those opportunities to apply what I want to a different set of circumstances. I'm okay if the form changes. I'm not so tied up into the form now. There was a time back in the beginning of my career at [company] where I was, like, I'm here for thirty years. That was the ultimate goal and objective was positioning it so that I could stay with [this company] for my entire career. Now, that's not the ultimate goal and objective for me. The ultimate goal and objective would be more the continued development, continuing to evolve in my understanding of life, of business, of interpersonal relationships. It's just kind of allowing that spiral to continue to expand.

I had the sense that Kurt's internal foundation had become second nature to him and made uncertainty less challenging. His recognition of not being so tied to "the form" suggests that he was able to reflect on his internal foundation. Intrigued by this change of perspective, I asked Kurt how he had come to see his ultimate goal differently. He replied:

> I got clearer on what was driving what or what was providing me (pause) all the things that I want to have in my life. It wasn't working at [company]. That was a big piece of it, and at the time, I thought that that was the cause to all of the effects that I was realizing in my life. . . . it's really having the drive toward self-actualization. And then all of the other kind of tangible or intangible benefits are just details that are reinforcing the fact that I'm on track. In my life right now, the fact that there is harmony in many areas leads me to believe that I'm on track, that I'm pursuing what I need to be pursuing, that my actions are in alignment with my focus and I'm moving in the direction that I want to be moving in. If there was not harmony in all the areas of my life, then I would use that as an opportunity to assess what is [it] that's not providing it and what is it that's keeping me from that harmony and trying to address that in any way that I could.

Harmony in many areas seemed to stem from Kurt's integration of his beliefs, identity, and social relations into one internal foundation that sustained all parts of his life. One event that stood out in Kurt's mind as important in this shift was the departure of the company president. Kurt respected this president and viewed him as highly successful. He was somewhat surprised when the president announced that he would like to pursue other endeavors. Kurt described what this meant to him:

> It sent me a message to say, wow, it's okay to take those risks. It might be fun to take those risks 'cause I want to see what might happen. That was a paradigm shift for me. I'm like, wow, that was a way of looking at things significantly different than what I had looked at them for quite some time. It's actually a quite liberating place to be because, in terms of this current role, I mean I'm acting like I can't fail because really from a lot of perspectives I don't think that I can, you know? If that's the way that I choose to define this game, or if those are the rules that I want to apply to the game that I'm playing, then it's all going to be okay.

This paradigm shift liberated Kurt from his earlier definitions of success. Because his new ultimate goal was his own continued development, it was no longer tied to his present position and company. He was heavily invested in succeeding in his new role as acting general manager because he was committed to his company's success, yet he was also aware that he might not have the experience to do so. He was able to frame the possibility of not succeeding in this role as another form of opportunity. Just as he was constantly pushing his coworkers to examine their assumptions to enable new conclusions, he was pushing himself to do the same.

Kurt's Story Line

Kurt's journey toward continual self-transformation—where he consistently pushed himself and others to probe deeply held assumptions—began with two very powerful insights about himself that he gained shortly after college. The first insight was that he had a tendency to define his worth through pleasing others. The second insight was that doing so was problematic. In his early twenties, he recognized his own power to choose what would make him happy. He just was not able to implement it immediately. The fact that Kurt was aware of his reliance on others was the key to cultivating his inner voice and traversing the crossroads. He began looking inside himself for what to believe, how to craft his identity, and how to relate to others. Articulating the importance of his internal voice was easier than using it consistently. Kurt reported that he spent most of the decade of his twenties developing his internal voice.

By age thirty, Kurt had enough trust in his internal voice to act on it. He described this as controlling his perceptions rather than his circumstances. Kurt noted that he was aware of and could talk about this notion during college but was unable to "live" it until he was faced with hard decisions in his first promotion to management. He made the distinction that it was in his head earlier, but now in his heart. Kurt was beginning to build an internal foundation from the beliefs he had self-authored in earlier years. Bringing this idea of controlling perceptions into his heart meant that he was integrating components of his identity. Once Kurt began to build this internal foundation, he was able to recognize opportunities that he wanted to pursue, one of which was a relationship with the woman who would eventually become his wife. Because they were both whole when they entered the relationship, Kurt was able to be authentic and express himself fully. He never worried about her reaction because he trusted himself and their relationship. Their partnership was an optimal context for Kurt to live his internal foundation.

Kurt's internal foundation also enabled him to attract opportunities in his work; he reported that he felt opportunities for promotion came to him because he was focused on applying his internal principles instead of seeking out promotions. His first promotion was a struggle because it came in the early phases of his building his internal foundation, and he still struggled to reconcile competing loyalties. He was intent on applying his principles of service and love but found this difficult, as he felt caught between his boss and his employees. Carrying out his boss's directives, which he identified as being of service, led the employees to feel dissatisfaction instead of appreciation. As he worked through that situation, Kurt recognized the tension between implementing his boss's vision and being true to himself. Kurt was able to use his internal foundation and his ability to control his perceptions by looking at his move out of this management position as an opportunity for growth. Yet Kurt continued to struggle throughout his promotions with keeping others' perceptions in perspective. As each new promotion came along, he worried about whether he had the respect of his colleagues and whether they would recognize his contributions. The constant tension between success of the company and satisfaction of the employees made applying his principles consistently difficult.

When Kurt was promoted to a senior management position at age thirty-six, he immediately felt the pressure of others' reactions to his management. This time, though, he quickly shifted to being true to himself, to the point of publicly declaring that the company would have to accept him as he was. Kurt reported another powerful insight at this juncture—an awareness of his tendency to tie his identity to success at work. Just as his earlier insight about pleasing others was a springboard for growth, this new insight provided a springboard for Kurt to move beyond it. He was able to reflect on his earlier management approach and understand that it had been constrained by his concern over his lack of knowledge and wish to earn the respect of his peers. At this point, he trusted himself completely and thus was able to place trust in his employees and make what he called the paradigm shift from manager to leader. At age thirty-nine, when Kurt was promoted to acting general manager, while he admitted that he did not have the knowledge he would have liked to have had for this position, he did not concern himself with his colleagues' perceptions. He was confident that he would use his philosophy to do his best to succeed. He also accepted the possibility that his philosophy and experience level might be insufficient and that he might have to leave the company if that were the case. Risks began to look interesting rather than frightening, an attitude that grew out of his confidence in his internal foundation. His mantra had become "how can we look at this differently?" He applied this in his work, in parenting, and in his relationship with his wife. Openness to altering his perceptions to envision new outcomes in all aspects of his life reflected the freedom that came from the grounding of his internal foundation as well as his drive for self-actualization.

Self-Transformation

Shadow lands

Building Internal
Commitments

LIBRARY

Shadow lands

Trusting
Internal
Voice

Self-Authorship

Shadow lands

Self-
Authorship

Shadow lands

Listening to
Internal
Voice

Cultivating
Internal Voice

Good
Partnership

Good
Partnership

Crossroads

Voices
EXTERNAL
INTERNAL

PAIN

External Formula

SANDRA'S JOURNEY

CHAPTER 5

SANDRA'S STORY—LIVING HER FAITH

SANDRA ENTERED COLLEGE WITH A CALLING TO SERVE OTHERS as a key tenet of her Catholic faith. She majored in psychology and attributed her interest in the helping professions to an experience with a high school friend who went through alcohol treatment. Through her volunteer work, she found a position in an adolescent chemical dependency unit at a local hospital during her senior year. She continued to work at the hospital after graduation but found that the basic beliefs she had developed about how patients should be treated were not reflected in this unit's practice. She returned temporarily to work at a hardware store where she had worked summers during college before pursuing a master's degree in social work. By the time she returned to school, she accepted a part-time counseling position in another chemical dependency unit. For the next three years, she balanced working part-time, graduate school, and a field placement doing long-term counseling with adults in a mental health center. During this time, she gained practical experience, compared her academic learning with her experience to judge its validity, and began crafting her professional identity. I sensed that she had a clear vision of her values and beliefs.

Asked to describe the source of her values and beliefs, Sandra said: "My belief system is strongly based in my faith. Learned from parents early on, then you get out in world and have to make your own decisions." Sandra's sense of her call to serve stemmed from her

Catholic faith, her attributing surviving childhood medical problems as a sign of support from God, and her friend's experience with alcohol treatment. Having heard Sandra talk about her frustrations with the emotional intensity of her work, I asked whether her faith was steady over time. She replied:

> Yes. There have been times when I've been confused, but it has always been a framework that never changed. My steady faith brought me though all of things thrown at me. When I was younger I had a lot of hip surgery, body casts; it was really a hard time. Even then, I can look back and see, being very young and not having it very developed, but having my faith— believed in strongly by my family—I remember praying going into surgery. One of the most important people in my life as I grew up was my orthopedic surgeon. I can see some of the faith things even in him. He performed the first surgery on my hip when I was three. He died when I was twenty-four or twenty- five. Through that whole time, there were lots of hip surgeries. He would say, "Well, not quite as good of a job as God could do, but pretty damn close don't you think?" (Laughs)

Sandra's faith and her intention to live it via the call to serve set the stage for the nature of her developmental journey in her late twenties and thirties. Her map shows the paths she took toward self-authorship and the partners she had on the journey.

SANDRA'S JOURNEY

During her twenties, Sandra developed confidence as a counseling professional, defined boundaries with her patients, and acted on her values. She forged honest relationships with her supervisors and sought their feedback to refine her effectiveness. She trusted her professional internal voice enough to define what was right for patients in various circumstances and to challenge her supervisors when she disagreed with their approach. Her professional life offered a context in which she began to move through the crossroads toward self-authorship.

Moving Through the Crossroads Toward Self-Authorship

Sandra devoted most of her energy in her mid to late twenties to her professional development as a counselor.

Entering the Crossroads: Listening to the Internal Voice. As she pursued her graduate studies in social work, she routinely compared what she was learning with her prior work experience in chemical dependency units. She was critical of new perspectives when they were inconsistent with her experience. Upon obtaining her master's degree, she worked with a supervisor who helped her hone her own decision-making skills. She described what happened:

> [My supervisor] was terrific. He built my confidence; he trusted me, never second-guessed me. He forced me to explain my reasons. That trained me to do this for myself. I had to think about it, so I got better at it. I knew he would ask. He trained me to do it on my own; thus, I made better decisions. He had confidence in me, so I did too. It was a precious gift.[1]

Sandra gained sufficient confidence through this supervisory partnership to begin to trust her own internal voice. Yet, she trusted it more in some contexts than others, as she described in working with her colleagues:

> There are a lot of good people on staff. We have peer review meetings for two hours every week. We discuss cases. The team perspective, ideas about what to try, is really terrific. I rely more on them than on my supervisor. If I have a lot of experience, I make my own decisions; that is part of gaining confidence as a therapist. I don't ask about chemical dependency issues because I have a good base of knowledge and can make good decisions. If it is new ground, I'll ask a colleague who has more experience for their opinion. Usually I say, "Here is what I was thinking about doing, what do you think?" to see if it sounds like a good clinical decision.[2]

Sandra trusted her internal voice in areas where she had sufficient knowledge; in others, she consulted peers to check out the validity of her plan. She reported shifting from asking others for advice on what to do to asking their opinion on a decision or perspective she had already reached. She noted that receiving her advanced social work license also heightened her confidence. This license, the fruit of two years of supervision and passing a state test, certified her for private practice.

Traversing the Crossroads: Cultivating the Internal Voice. The following year Sandra shared that her confidence level was "up" but that she found it hard to hang onto consistently, owing to the emotionally depressing nature of her work. I asked whether the dips in confidence she mentioned were significant. She replied:

> It depends—sometimes they are. I struggle with depression every once in a while and it is all connected. I have systems to bring that back up, things to do. I bounce back. I know who I can count on at my job and say help. Sometimes I need an outside view. I'm still the source of the final decision, definitely. I have been told I'm stubborn, and it is pretty accurate! I feel like I have a strong sense of what I think is right to do in a certain situation; it is a gut level thing, values that I fall back on, and I deal with things in those boundaries. I ask for input, look at things from different angles. Sometimes, I am too close to something; others could stand back and see it differently. Sometimes, I can incorporate those views. Usually they fit together. There have been times when I go with my own decision regardless.

Sandra trusted her internal voice most when she had experienced the situations before and had developed her solutions to them. When she felt unsure, she consulted others but did not always take their advice. She was careful to reach beyond her particular perspective to make better judgments, yet trusted her gut instinct in specific cases. She was aware of the role depression played in her lapses of confidence—something that would continue to haunt her in the years to come. She was making progress on cultivating her professional internal voice.

At the outset of her career, her faith and her sense that she had a calling as a counselor aligned with her professional development. As she encountered the complex dynamics of her patients' lives, she felt the need to explore her faith further to resolve questions about why children were abused or to make sense of alcoholism. Despite a steady faith, Sandra continued to find social work draining. The long hours, taking paperwork home at night, and the emotional intensity of the work had already led her to consider changing careers. Yet, Sandra felt she had invested too much time and energy in preparing for counseling, and she still viewed it as her life calling. This tension would continue well into her thirties. Sandra's twenties were a time of developing her voice as a therapist, reconciling her faith with her attending to her patients' realities, and dealing with the tension between her increasing stress and living her calling through service in social work. It was also a time to work on separating her sense of self from her role as a social worker.

Self-Authorship: Trusting the Internal Voice

Near age thirty, Sandra left her job doing short-term counseling and took a new social work position in a medical unit. Describing her reasons for the change, she said:

> I've been counseling for a long time. After so many years, I found myself saying, "I don't want to be this involved in people's lives. I want to have my own family and friends and be in their lives. I don't want all this responsibility." The job ate up your life if you allowed it to. It drained you emotionally, trying to be there for people. [I was] on call a week at a time. The caseload was enormous. In order to feel good about myself, I had to give 100%; I was just shot. I can't reconcile this for myself; it is eating up my whole life. So I quit.

Recognizing that the job had taken over her life, Sandra was working to separate who she was from her professional role:

> I have a clearer vision of what I really want to do. I have a stronger image of who I am. I'm not so wrapped up in being a counselor. I'm being Sandra. I have a clearer vision of Sandra and the different things that make up who I am. I went from "I am a counselor" to "I do some social work."[3]

Sandra's work had taken over her life and left little energy for anything else. Understanding as a counselor that she needed to maintain her sense of self to help others, she was determined to subsume her work to her sense of identity. Changing positions was one way she hoped to support this shift.

Sandra's stronger sense of identity proved useful a year later when the company for which she worked became a for-profit. She disagreed with some of the company's policies, and described standing up for her beliefs with the administration:

> I am not afraid to say what I believe in and stand for it. I don't make reckless decisions that hurt my lifestyle or self—like quitting my job—but I am able to say, "This is how it is." . . . I've never been one to be pushed around. To help others, you have to maintain self. Now that I'm out of my old job, I recognize the point where I began to lose myself. If it happens again, I see it and don't do it. I don't worry much. I'm confident that I do a good job; I know this. If others disagree, they can find someone else. I have a lot of feedback that I trust is the truth. I've taken charge and [I] get things done. I am more confident. I am able to recognize signs more quickly now. It sounds nonchalant, but that is how I feel.[4]

Referring to herself as a "stubborn bullhead," Sandra attributed not being one to be pushed around to her father and her grandmother, a "fiery redhead"; however, it was clear that her confidence in her work and in her self-image were strong factors here. Her awareness of when she began to lose herself in her previous position helped her identify boundaries beyond which her integrity would be compromised. This outlook struck me, as I reported in *Making Their Own Way*, as an internal foundation. Sandra was clear in what she believed, confident enough to act on it, yet careful to weigh the consequences. As I would learn in subsequent interviews, this internal foundation was limited to Sandra's professional role as a counselor. It was not yet strong enough to withstand the intensity of her social work and not yet integrated with her personal identity. Because she was just beginning to separate her personal identity from her professional identity, she had not yet listened to her internal voice in other arenas of her life.

Despite Sandra's strong professional self-image and confidence, she felt that her medical social work position was beginning to challenge her, in part because of problems with some of the patients. One patient, who had a history of domestic violence, threatened the staff. Sandra was torn about it:

> I knew this man. I knew his psychiatric history, and he was in a lot of pain. It's not that he was a bad person. He had terrible life circumstances. I wouldn't have wanted to be in his shoes either.

Because they worried about the safety of their staff, Sandra and her supervisor arranged to have this patient treated at a full-service hospital where security was available. They did so out of empathy for him and out of the moral belief that he should receive the best treatment possible. In dealing with such patients, Sandra drew on her confidence to challenge the physicians to do what she thought was right. This experience led Sandra to volunteer to open a new unit in a different part of the city. On the one hand, she wanted to stay with her patients and the supervisor with whom she had a great partnership. On the other hand, she knew she needed a sane environment. Leaving this unit meant breaking emotional attachments to her patients and leaving support systems. Yet, Sandra again acted on her sense that her job was taking over her life. She described how this challenged her faith and her beliefs, and how she dealt with the issue:

> I've always been pretty entrenched in Catholicism, and I was involved in a special group, Cursillo, that is very supportive. I talked with my grandmother quite a bit to try to help make sense of things, and I talked with our priest. It challenged my faith because I thought we're doing the best that we can here. The entire staff really did work hard to make it comfortable [and] treat everybody equally. When this comes up, it was a challenge for me because it makes you mad. It's like I have bent over backwards for you. I've done everything I can to help you. Then he threatens us. It's like, I'm so glad I've spent all this effort. So, that's how it challenged it a bit. It did help to talk with Father. He helped frame things for me but he also was supportive.

Sandra struggled to maintain her faith in the face of her patient's lack of appreciation for her and the staff's efforts. Tensions between her faith and dealing with the realities of her patients' lives had surfaced earlier in her counseling career but not to this level of intensity. This experience was a crisis of sorts that called her faith and her call to serve into question, and it eroded her confidence to the point that she had to rely heavily on others to work through it. She drew strength from partners she trusted—her supervisor, her grandmother, friends, and her priest. These partners helped her replenish the energy she lost from constantly giving to patients. During the next few years, however, the constant giving to patients left her emotionally exhausted. She was beginning to feel that the responsibility she felt for everyone else was eroding her responsibility to herself:

> It's a drain as far as everybody's always asking you for something or demanding something. Life is challenging enough for myself to keep everything in line and then to have ninety more people . . . they all depend on me and expect for me to handle all this stuff for them. I've had a caseload for fifteen years, people that I'm responsible for. How about they're responsible for themselves? I think Sandra's going to be responsible for Sandra for a while and only her, not have a hundred other people to worry about.

Sandra put a lot of energy into serving her patients; she worried about their welfare. She succeeded in drawing physical boundaries for what she would and would not do for them, but her emotional boundaries with patients were becoming blurred. Her objective to worry less and take more responsibility for her own life was reinforced by a death in her family:

> Part of that, too, is it's been over a year since my grandmother passed away. I don't know how to put it, but kind of a slap in the face like, everything could be over. And I really had to sit back and take inventory. . . . Was I spending enough time with my family, who were the most important people to me? Was I doing enough for them, or was I spending all my time and energy to where I was zapped at night doing stuff for the patients? I have a clear set of boundaries for dealing with the patients. There are things that I will do for them and things that I will not because if you don't have those boundaries, they'll just suck you dry. I do have that, and I feel like that's pretty healthy, but when Grandma died, I really had to sit back and say, "Did I spend as much time as I wanted to spend with my grandmother?" You have to think about what's the most important thing in your life, and that my life could be up any time, too.

Sandra had always said that she had clear boundaries with her patients; however, her grandmother's death prompted a period of questioning about whether she had gone beyond those boundaries. It struck me from the intensity of her feelings in this conversation that her patients had, in fact, sucked her dry. Perhaps her boundaries were well established in her head but not yet in her heart. She was so focused on her professional life that she had not attended to listening to her internal voice regarding her personal life.

Sandra's quest to be responsible for herself led her to attend to some other aspects of her life. One was the important task of replacing her orthopedic surgeon, who had died when she was twenty-four. Based on her own medical history and her social work experience, she had a sense of what she wanted in a physician. She wanted a surgeon who respected her, listened to her opinions, and considered her individual circumstances in determining her medical treatment. She wanted to develop a trust with her doctor so they could mutually manage her health. She visited and rejected more than one doctor before finding one who met her criteria. She was also in search of another kind of partnership that was more elusive, saying: "I would really like to find myself a husband. I don't know about kids, but I really would like to share my life with somebody." Sandra combined opportunities to meet new people with her call to serve by taking a citizen's police class. She explained her choice:

> That was more of a 'be involved in your community' type thing, meet new people, and branch out. That was the best decision I have made in years. It is a citizen's class, but you get the inside look at what they have to deal with. I met so many neat people who just really want to be involved, care about other people, I just was so glad I had the opportunity for an inside look. They really invited us into the inner circle. Now, I have lasting friendships from that. It really opens your eyes into other people's lives and what it means to protect and serve. It was a chance to learn more about other professions, meet all kinds of new people. This was a real opportunity for service work.

Sandra acquired new friends and new insights into the inner workings of the police department. She also acquired the insight that she could not see herself as a police officer. Sandra continued to struggle with career options; she wanted to serve yet also wanted a job that was less emotionally draining than what she had done for the past decade.

Self-Authorship: Building an Internal Foundation

Sorting through various values and beliefs, Sandra decided to become a paralegal. She explained why:

> It is similar to social work in a lot of ways. I wouldn't have a caseload. To learn more about the legal system, and be—still somewhat of a social work role—out there on front lines for people who need the help but aren't educated about how the law would work for them. It would be a chance to choose who I work for. If I work for a lawyer, I can pick one that I think is ethical, or if I want to work for a corporation, I'll pick a corporation I feel is in line with my belief system.

Sandra was able to frame paralegal work as an acceptable way to live her faith and maintain her call to serve. She also anticipated being able to choose workplaces that were consistent with her values. This showed she was maintaining and building her internal foundation in her professional life. Changing careers was taking on increasing urgency as she became increasingly frustrated at work.

The decision to make a change had been long and complex. Sandra described how she had gone about it:

> It took me years to make the decision. I went to the library, did research, and got the *What Color Is Your Parachute?* book. Talk to family about it, talk to friends, and write down what my strengths and weaknesses are. Got all kinds of vocational books, got on the Web. I had gone down to the university and done personality testing. Computerized programs that tell you what you'll be good at—kind of funny—it said I would be a good social worker. I said, "I already know that—I'm looking for something else!" I did a lot of praying about it too because I don't want to feel like I wasted all that time. I know it is not a waste. I've used my degrees for years, and everything else about education that goes with it, experiences. But still, I'm only thirty-four, and I want to switch. I was stuck there for a few years, thinking I shouldn't switch. Finally I thought, but I'm not happy. So, who cares? It seemed to fit with my talents as a person. I talked to several people who are paralegals, my lawyer friends; they all had great things to say about it.

During these years of exploration, Sandra had tried to listen to and trust her own internal voice. The arena in which she was confident in her internal voice, her professional life, had steadily deteriorated and emotionally drained her. She trusted her voice about what was right for patients and, to some extent, about what was right for her in an instrumental sense (e.g., what kind of doctor she wanted); however, in making career decisions, her internal voice was overshadowed by the "shoulds" that she adopted from her environment—that her education should support her calling to serve. She had not developed her internal voice outside of these contexts and, thus, was not confident even as she made the decision to pursue paralegal classes.

Another factor holding her back was fear that she wouldn't like this either, another indication that she did not trust her internal voice:

> Fear of, okay, now a psychology degree, a social work degree, been doing this stuff for thirteen, fourteen years, and really don't like it—a lot of fear of—what if I don't like that either? I met with my financial adviser about the cost of this. I'm a social worker here. She said, "If you think about staying in social work until you retire in twenty-five years, what is the first

thought that comes to your head?" I said, "Finding a bridge to jump off of!" (Laughs). She said: "Go back to school! So, if you go back and go through whole thing [and don't like it], then you have more education, met new people, have new experiences in life." So at least [I would be] preoccupied from looking for the bridge!

Sandra had really wanted to just tweak her career to find a less intense role but still use her training. Talking with her financial adviser at least clarified that staying in social work was not a viable option.

Another major hurdle that complicated Sandra's decision was the strong relationships she had with her parents and grandparents. As an only child who had frequently undergone surgery through her childhood, Sandra had come to rely heavily on her parents and grandparents. They had sacrificed a great deal to help her through her medical problems, and she wanted to make them proud of her accomplishments. They did not understand why she had chosen social work. She described how their opinions affected her:

My parents have never been that excited that I've been in social work. My dad wants me to make money. Doesn't want me dealing with crazy people. We had a cancer scare with him—he had surgery last October. Some reflecting came from it—then I started to think well, what they think means more with that scare. It was like God, my dad could be gone. He is fine now, and the cancer is gone, thank goodness, but that really turned my life upside down. But now, really only those four [people]; they have the bite. They have the opportunity to say something. I really don't care what other people think. I think I made the best decision I could at the time.

Sandra cared deeply what these important people in her life thought of her, even when she disagreed with them. Intellectually, she was sure she had made the best decision she could at the time; emotionally, she was still hurt by their disappointment. Sandra also cared deeply about fulfilling her call to serve. I asked her to talk more about how praying contributed to making this decision. She explained:

Feeling like I need to live my faith, part of that is helping other people, which was a big snag for me leaving social work because that is how I've been living my faith. So much more time is spent at work, and you have to try to balance family, friends, social, health—now, if I take away where I'm not doing as much service, where am I going to fit it in? Then, I sort of came around to a different viewpoint of it. I'm still going to be living the faith, still going to be doing service work, just in a different manner. That is part of the reason I kept getting that silly book—*What Color is your Parachute?*—because the author says how even an artist can be serving the Lord with their talent. He gives examples and goes through quite a few different vocations. That book really helped. I don't have to be out there in trenches doing this stuff. I can still be an example of my faith and be helpful to people in a different way, showing my light.

Sandra originally believed that social work was the only way to use her education and the only way to sufficiently live her faith. This conviction had for years been her major sticking point. *What Color is Your Parachute?* offered Sandra another way to frame service, but she still wanted confirmation from God that she was moving in the right direction. As always, when she was not confident, she consulted others. She explained how she sought this guidance:

Praying. How can I still use my talents to where I feel like it will be pleasing to the Lord? [sighs] I did a lot of talking with a friend about that. It is hard to know, is this just what I want? Or is this what I should be doing? Is this the Lord's will for me? Always end my prayers with "your will be done." Is this his or mine? If they are the same that's cool, but if they're not, I'll feel it pretty quickly and it won't be good! (Laughs). I went through quite a few questions for myself: Is this a fair request? Is this still in line with the belief system that you have? Is it a good risk? Is it about financial gain? Is it in line with your morals? For a long time I would look for signs, look for changes in the way I felt, or the way things were going. I would think maybe I'm supposed to stay. Then, other times I would think I'm not supposed to stay.

A lot of Sandra's hesitation stemmed from concern that she was doing this for herself instead of for the Lord. She briefly acknowledged that it was possible His will and hers were the same, but she framed most of her thinking around the two being divergent. She struggled to determine whether what she wanted was what she should be doing, whether it was legitimate for her to want a change, and whether this violated God's will for her. Some hints of an internal foundation were present in her consideration of whether this was in line with her beliefs and morals, yet she was not confident about the decision because of her concern about God's will. She continued to debate this with friends:

> I talked to a close friend, and he said: "You are so unhappy. I don't think any plan the Lord has for you includes that. You can't use your talents if you are that unhappy. You start to close up as a person." That is what I was doing. It just got to the point where I couldn't take it. I did some reading of the Bible; all of a sudden, things just started popping up where I thought, I'm making the right decision. And they were subtle, I was looking more for—I always say I want to ask God for a banner— because I have no idea! Otherwise, I just go round and round in my head. I'm trying to make it fit, or is this how it is supposed to be? My friend also said to step away from that, don't make it so linear. Could be that God said choices A, B, and C are all fine. Now you pick. Just don't pick D. So, finally I said, "Okay let's go with A." Things have been falling into place, so I think well, this is okay. Some of it is financial security because if I could, I would just quit. The big hang-up there is medical insurance with my hip problems. I have to hold on to good coverage. For as long as I can remember I've worked and gone to school. Or then I had such a draining job, where it just completely took over my life. I deserve a break. If I can have some little fun job, do school, and enjoy school, hey I deserve it! It has taken me a long time to get to that point too. That's where my work ethic comes in. You can't quit; you can't give up social work until you're finished with school. Why not?

Sandra was working against a lot of internalized "shoulds" and external constraints. Her story about her career decisions revealed that she was consciously working on how she framed these issues. She was trying to convince herself, with her friend's help, that God approved of this change. She was trying to accept that it was time to take a risk and that she deserved a break after all of her emotionally draining work. She was also consciously working on her sense of self in relation to others. Turning to relationships, she offered:

> Sometimes I think, oh, I'm never going to find anybody—usually when I'm on my pity pot. Most of the time, I'm rather independent. It really is going to take somebody different to fit with me. Somebody who has a strong sense of self because I do my own thing, and if they can walk beside me that's good, but if

they want me to walk behind or in front, forget it. If I could just find a good man.

Sandra's independence was primarily instrumental—she managed her house, her finances, and her health. Sandra also started working with a personal trainer, in part to maintain her hip joint and in part to work against the stress she was experiencing in her work. It became a good partnership:

> I've been working on trying to bring up my self-esteem. I lost ten pounds. I set up an appointment to talk with my trainer. I changed my eating habits, and I really feel it now if I don't go work out. I know I'm strengthening my bones with weight exercising. I've felt so much better about myself, aside from having more energy. I'd come home from work and be zapped. I was getting to a point of getting depressed. The job took its toll. The unit where I am right now is difficult. The staff is so not supportive of each other or me. Very backbiting—the ground is unsure, you never know where you stand. I'm thinking, what am I doing this for? It grates on your self-esteem. Give, give, give and don't get back. I have a wonderful support system outside of work. I really do feel better. I sleep better. It was depression coming on with the job. I felt like I took control. Everything was starting to spin. I picked one piece, got to get a hold of something here. I've gotten ahold of some other pieces since then. For a while, I felt like I was in the centrifuge here!

This conversation revealed that her work had eroded the internal foundation she had originally built as a professional counselor. Her depression surfaced again, and she knew she had to control some piece of her life. She chose physical health first, given her medical history, her understanding of depression, and the urgent need to manage stress. She then took up the career piece. As Sandra prepared to start paralegal classes, reduce her work to two ten-hour days, and shift patients to other social workers, she reported:

> I feel like I'm rounding the bend, taking my risk here. A lot of it was the police class—I grew a lot with that. I faced some issues that were very difficult, like my dad's cancer. I feel like I've come out on the other side. I don't know if I can put into words how much that makes you look in, and look around, prioritize. It really hit me like a ton of bricks. I learned a lot from it. Even though I did social work for a lot of years, I learned more about grief and how to be there for other people, family

members, or friends that I would find out later who had family members who had cancer. You don't have the inside view until you've felt those feelings. I learned even more—a lot about grief with my grandma passing away. Felt pretty proud that I held everything together, kept working, didn't let it interfere. I really felt like I came out on the other side a much stronger person and with a much stronger relationship with my dad. He didn't treat me like I was a little girl. He treated me like I was still his daughter but on the same level.

Sandra had had her share of painful experiences, but she felt she was learning from each one. Living through her father's cancer and her grandmother's death revealed a rift between Sandra's professional self and her personal self. She was able to handle illness and death with her patients. When it came to her father and grandmother, it felt different. She needed to dig deeper to cope with these issues when they hit her firsthand in her own life. Coming out the other side of these experiences heightened Sandra's self-confidence in her personal life, something she was continuously trying to build. The fact that her father accepted her as an adult with skills relevant to his condition during his illness was a major shift in their relationship that also helped Sandra's confidence. She was working consciously on maintaining her health and her self-esteem and taking the long-considered risk to begin a new career.

Sandra's paralegal studies were short-lived. She found the material boring and learned about aspects of the job that didn't sound attractive. By the second course, she knew it was not for her. She took a third course at the director's urging, but said "I should have trusted my gut, but now I can say I gave it a fair shake." Sandra quit the program because she instinctively knew that it was not right, yet her lack of trust in her internal voice led her to take the program director's advice to take one more class. Or perhaps it was the fallout she knew would come from the decision that led her to take the third course. Making that decision again brought to the fore her long-standing concern about what her parents thought. Despite the change in her relationship with her father during his cancer treatment, Sandra still worried about her parents' reactions:

I'm still their daughter, even though I'm thirty-five. All I can do is change the way I think and feel about it. There was a lot of, "What do you mean, you're not going to continue classes? I thought that was what you wanted to do?" Well, yeah. So did I.

I sent out some pretty clear messages that it was not okay for them to criticize the fact that I was quitting. I'm an only child. I have a double whammy because I'm an only grandchild, too, on my mom's side. So, it's like having four parents. They all think they know what's best. And, sometimes, they do. In the past couple years, we've had some difficulty because I say, I'm thirty-five, I'm an adult, and if I want to make this decision I'm going to. I've done a lot of work on—it's my life; it's not theirs— a lot of work on not feeling like I'm not letting them down some- how because, I think about it, in the end, why am I trying to make everybody else happy? If it comes to that last moment of my life, who cares!

Sandra was intellectually claiming her life as her own, as she had done for some time. She always acted on her beliefs and values but had a hard time when she felt her folks were disappointed in her. She actively worked to change how she responded to their reac- tions. This is another area in which Sandra had convictions in her head but had a hard time playing them out in her heart. This meant using journaling and talking with friends to process her feel- ings. Sandra was not yet able to distance herself from her parents' and grandparents' reactions, so she didn't engage them, and instead turned to others for support. Sandra called a friend who had been through a similar experience. She helped Sandra reframe her thinking:

I said, "Now I've started this paralegal thing, and I can't quit." She said: "You changed your mind. You're not quitting; you sim- ply changed your mind. Woman's prerogative." It was just the words. I'm not quitting. I can't quit. I changed my mind. It really made a difference. I have no idea why. I think it was wiring from when I was a kid. "We don't quit."

On the one hand, Sandra "knew" that she should quit the paralegal program. On the other hand, she could not see around the "we don't quit" philosophy with which she had grown up. Her friend gave her another way to look at it, and the words that resolved this tension. Reworking how she framed her thinking, Sandra returned to work- ing with a career counselor to rethink how she could serve others and still maintain her sanity. She continued working twenty hours a week at the medical unit because she felt that increasing her hours would add to her stress level. Instead, she volunteered at the police department for another twenty hours a week and started applying for dispatch jobs. I asked her how she sustained the hope that she would make it out of this stressful situation. She replied:

> I'm always involved in the Catholic Cursillo. I did another weekend for them in February. I was kind of in a strange place spiritually because I had been praying for so long. It was like, please, I have to get out of here, please. I don't know what I'm doing wrong. I feel like I'm spinning my wheels because it's not like I'm not doing anything to try to make the change. My friend's mom was the team leader for this past weekend. She calls me up, [saying] "I'm creating this next team, and I've been praying a lot about it and the Lord said your name." I thought, "What? [laughs] He did not!" She's like, "Yeah, I really feel like he was calling you." When I experienced my own weekend for the Cursillo, I had been going through a really bad time of depression, and it was a spiritual experience. I was cured for a few years. I didn't have depression. I've done teams before, and I felt so connected to the Lord spiritually and bright with hope. So I joined this team. I didn't feel connected this time. I was like, is this over? [laughs] It was like, hello . . . I'm down here getting depressed again, still stuck in this same job. Are You listening? [laughs] That's what I do to try to keep from going under: mostly faith-based stuff and talking to friends. I try to eat right, exercise, try new things, new challenges outside of work, meet some new people, do some new stuff. But I'm running out of ideas. Plow along.

Sandra continued to make efforts to improve her life. She focused mainly on the instrumental aspects of maintaining her health, trying new experiences, and meeting new people. Although she asked God for help, she seemed to be waiting for signals instead of really listening to her internal voice.

The following year, Sandra reported that she had finally been hired as a dispatcher and left her social work position. Although she was glad to finally be out of that highly stressful position, she reported being overwhelmed in her dispatch role. She was still in training and frustrated that she wasn't picking up on all of the information as quickly as she had hoped. This led to a pivotal conversation with a friend about Sandra's relationship with God:

> I've had my crisis periods, especially when I was about two weeks into the new job and I thought, duh, what have I done? There have been some periods where I just couldn't even focus to pray. . . . A friend of mine said to me, "Well, you're praying

too hard." 'Cause, I keep praying about this stuff and I'm not getting answers, and I'm feeling more and more wound up about it and I'm miserable. She said, "You're asking, asking, asking, praying, praying, praying. And God's thinking, 'You know what? If you have all the answers, then you go ahead and do what you're doing, and as soon as you let go of it a little bit and let me steer, then you'll get your answers if you want. But for right now, you're hanging onto that steering wheel and you're just going, Which way do I go?' " She said, "So, if you can let go a little bit, I think it'd be better. Back off of it some." I've been struggling with that because she said, "Let go and let God." And I said, "I don't know what that means." It goes back to the same . . . I take care of everything, you know? How do I let go?

I found it difficult to connect Sandra's notion of self-reliance (with her house, finances, jobs) with letting God steer. To understand how those two things interacted, I asked her, "What does it mean when you say things are good with your faith versus times when you're rocky? How do you put together relying on God for direction, answers, and relying on yourself for the same things?" She explained:

I think that the times that it's rocky is when I'm trying to steer. I'm praying, but I'm grabbing the steering wheel, and I'm trying to make it go my way 'cause I'll have something in my head that I think should be happening, like I should be getting this dispatch job. Or I should be getting out of what I'm doing now because it's been a miserable four years. How long do I have to be miserable? So, I would get wound up to the point where I thought, "I'm just going to break apart in a million pieces. I have got to do something." So, then I would start questioning, "Okay, I'm listening." Am I praying about this in the wrong manner, or have I switched channels? What's going on? God's been in charge, and it gets rough when I don't like the timing because I keep telling myself, "Okay, well, in God's time," and I'll do my reading in the Bible. It'll become clear because it's God's timetable, not mine. If I want it now, well . . . so? I try and let Him be in control, and I think that when I allow myself to get miserable and try to take too much of the control back, that's when things fall apart. I think the pain level rises to a point where I have to let go. He's probably out there, shaking his head, [saying,] "If you would stop grabbing the steering wheel, everything would be good." (Laughing) People say, "Let go and let God." What does that mean exactly, versus "God helps those who help themselves"? Am I just supposed to sit back and not look for another job? If I just sit on my butt, well, He's not going to like that either. How do I let go but still put some effort into this? 'Cause if I just give up on it completely, well, nothing's going to just fall out of the sky into my lap. Sometimes I'll have the clarity where I think, "Oh, this is what I'm supposed to do." And other times I think "This is what I'm doing; I don't know if it's right." But, you know, I can exhaust myself pretty quickly running that in my head.

Sandra was torn between giving God control of her opportunities and trying to make them happen herself. She was not clear on how to balance making an effort to influence her life and taking too much control away from God. Clarity came at some points, but it was elusive. As had been true for her for a long time, she trusted her internal voice when she thought she knew what was right; when she was unsure, she wanted assurance, usually from God. Her soul-searching led her to make a distinction between self-reliance and self-confidence:

> I am learning a lot of lessons about self-reliance versus, I guess, self-confidence. You know, not making my worth be part of what I choose to do for a living. I'm a worthy person, even if I decide that this isn't what I want to do, or I'm allowed to change my mind, or I'm allowed to make my own decisions. I guess self-reliance has always been hooked into my self-confidence. So I thought, well, I made a bad decision, or I made a mistake or . . . then I would beat myself up. But because I had that mindset of I have to do everything, I can't make a really big mistake. What if this [the dispatch job] is a big mistake?

Being self-reliant as a single woman who required good medical insurance made Sandra fearful of making a big mistake. This view of herself as self-reliant translated into questioning her worth when she made mistakes. Early in her social work career, she was both self-reliant and self-confident. Years earlier, she had become aware that she needed to make her work secondary to her personal life. Now, she was realizing that she needed to build confidence in an internal voice unconnected from what she did for a career. This explained her protracted struggle to see herself as a worthy person if she quit social work. In the course of this conversation, she said: "I'm working on it, yes. It's not all the way there yet, but working on it, I'm working on self-confidence basically. What people think doesn't matter." When I asked if it mattered in the past, she replied: "Yeah, a lot. I think it has. I tried to tell myself it didn't, but . . ." This line of conversation raised a question I had been struggling with for some time related to Sandra's assertiveness in her professional life and her concern about her parents' and grandparents' opinions. My question yielded this response:

> I don't know if I would say smaller decisions. . . . If I think it's the right thing to do, I go ahead. I don't care what other people think. But I guess if it's a big decision that's going to impact my life in lots of different ways, then I think maybe I do care. Is everybody going to look at me and think, is she job hopping now? But then the other part of me says, "Who cares what they think?" 'Cause it's not that important.

This response suggested that Sandra was confident in her beliefs when she knew what was right and when the decision was not about her personal life. In other words, her professional identity development had surpassed her personal identity development. Professionally, she had come to trust her internal voice, built an internal foundation with it, and knew instinctively what was right. Yet in her personal life, she had worked long and hard to convince herself that she had the right to make her own decisions as an adult. As we continued to talk, I asked how her internal "shoulds" played out in this notion of what others might think. She concluded:

> It's me. I mean that's something that I've been struggling with because I am such a perfectionist and I am my own worst enemy. Some things are cycling through—they kind of come back when I feel unsure about situations, and then they go away, and I work through it. I guess right now I'm thinking about a lot of stuff because this whole new situation, and I basically flipped my life upside down. I'd like a break, you know? I wanted a break from feeling so rotten for so long, and now I'm feeling rotten for different reasons. Now I'm feeling overwhelmed and thinking, oh my God, there's no end in sight of trying to learn all this.

As much as social work had been emotionally draining, Sandra was confident in doing it. As she noted, much of her self-worth was tied up in what she did for a living. Now that she had flipped her life upside down, her confidence was eroded, and she faced what appeared to be an uphill battle to learn all that was necessary to be an effective dispatcher. Sandra's insight about things cycling through captures much of the turmoil of her thirties. Because she was unsure of herself and her relationships outside of her professional role, she had no internal foundation to ground her as she started this new life. Despite years of making life and death decisions in social work, the stress of dispatch work was overwhelming.

Sandra stayed five months in the dispatch job. Despite positive feedback on her performance from her trainers and their pleading with her to stay, her stress level felt unbearable, and she finally quit. Her internal 'shoulds' came forward full force:

> I beat myself up heavily about, "I should have been able to handle it . . . I should this; I should that—should, should, should, should, should." My grandparents said, "We're glad you left." I called my friend that I used to work with at the medical unit. She said all the things that I needed to hear like, "You went out and tried it, and I'm so proud of you" and then she said: "Look at it this way. We're women. We have the prerogative to change our minds, and that's what you did. You didn't give up. You changed your mind." That helped so much, I just couldn't believe, just reframing it.

Sandra's reaction revealed that she still had work to do on self-confidence. Her internal voice was not strong enough to withstand her own critique and her sense that her parents probably thought she should have known better. She needed the perspective provided by her grandparents and her friend. She worked to reframe her decision as not quitting. She had been applying to local libraries, a job she perceived as fun and less stressful, and finally got in at one of the libraries. For the first time in as long as she could remember, she had a job she loved:

> The main difference, well, aside from stress level . . . nobody's going to die if I make a mistake at the library, whereas somebody could have died if I made a mistake in my other job. It's not the helping profession, although I still feel like I help people . . . you help with education, with research, just talking to people and giving them access to information and entertainment. There are people who come in who just want to talk to somebody. I don't have a caseload, thank God. I don't have anybody depending on me for life or death circumstances or getting their medicine that they absolutely have to have or getting their food or getting their heat for the winter. I don't get yelled at. The people I work with are wonderful. Everybody's friends

and works together as a team, and if you need help, you don't even have to ask. Somebody will notice and come over and help you. I tell them all the time, "[Sigh] you guys are the greatest, you know? Where have you been all my life?"

Sandra was finally relieved of her burden of responsibility for life-and-death decisions. Although she had appeared confident in handling social work decisions in earlier years, it was likely that a large portion of her emotional stress and depression stemmed from taking too much ownership of this intense level of responsibility. Having reported early on that she needed to give 100% to feel good about herself suggested that her self-worth was too closely linked to this responsibility.

Moving to a role in which she was not emotionally linked to her clients and in which coworkers were supportive lightened Sandra's load considerably. She recognized the impact her prior roles had on her, saying: "I'm not depressed. I was very depressed for—close to ten years probably." She was able to conceptualize her role at the library as one of service, and at the same time, undertook volunteer activities that helped her live her faith in the ways she had earlier tried to do in her work. She realized, though, that it had to be a small part of her life, instead of her whole life, if she was going to escape depression.

I asked Sandra how she thought our earlier discussion about God's guidance and grabbing the steering wheel had played out in this change of her circumstances. She said:

> I'm not sure about the role it played 'cause sometimes I think to myself, "Did I finally learn the lesson that I was supposed to learn so that I could move on?" Possibly, the lesson would be that it's my life and my decisions. I handle whatever comes from my decisions, and what others think doesn't really matter. I don't want my parents to be disappointed in me, but I think, possibly, the lesson was you do what is right for your life. You make the decisions for your life. Others don't. I don't know if that's the lesson, but I just kept thinking there must be some lesson that I'm not getting because I'm stuck, stuck, stuck. And then suddenly it all opened up. The call from the library was the beginning of things just opening up—the drain opened and there I went. (Laughing). I did a lot of work just trying to trust myself and take credit if it was due. I've spent a lot of work on that in the past two years probably. Part of that was because I felt like I had an opportunity to work with

a whole new set of people and an opportunity to make new friends and change my life into something that I wanted. So, I thought, well, if you're going to do it, then you better start doing something for yourself. So, I did do a lot of work on that—a lot of prayer work, a lot of talking about it and . . . So, I'm getting there.

All this work Sandra had been doing on self-reliance, self-confidence and trusting herself enabled her to start building an internal foundation for her life that was unrelated to her work role. It enabled her to develop the notion that it was her life, not her parents'. Although she had constructed that idea earlier, she had not been able to live it. More importantly, perhaps, trusting her internal voice enabled her to discern the connection between God's will for her and her own happiness. She was able to take risks and move forward in ways that she had been unable to do in previous years. Not understanding the nature of prayer work, I asked for clarification. Sandra explained:

> A lot of my prayer tends to be grateful thank you, thank you, thank you. Before, it was a lot of imploring and, asking, asking, asking. When I do prayer work, I do more of the "please give me guidance. I'm going to shut up and listen." Just try to have conscious contact and just shut up, so that if there's going to be some kind of message or something I should learn, that I won't jabber through it. I do a lot of Bible reading, too, where I would either look up in the index . . . try to find . . . if I was struggling with something in particular, passages on that particular thing, or pray and then just open the Bible and see where I was. (Laughs). And I would consciously work at trying to get the message that I was supposed to be getting, so that's what I mean when I say "prayer work." I use the Bible a lot. I have one of those New Living Bibles. It's a study Bible. And I always got hung up on the fact that the one I used to have, I could read it and not know. But it was okayed by the Catholic Church. This one is not okayed by the Catholic Church, but I get it.

Earlier, when Sandra was trying to find answers, she relied on the church-approved Bible. Now that she was working to figure out issues, she was not concerned whether the church approved her Bible. I shared with Sandra that I was intrigued about the combination of her thinking there was some lesson she was supposed to get and her notion about doing what she needed to do with her life.

In response to my question of how those two things go together, she said:

> I just believe that in order for me to really be happy, I have to do what's right for my life, which then puts me in harmony with what the Lord wants for me. So, it's like we're walking together instead of I'm over here and He's going, "Yoo hoo, come back this way." That's something I struggled with probably my whole life was that I felt called to do counseling. But it was making me absolutely miserable. So, then I had to rethink. Does the calling change (laugh), or was I wrong or what? And that was something I talked about with my grandma for a while, and we decided, not that we were right, but we came up with the calling can change, and that if you're miserable in your job, you're not really helping people. Because you have to help yourself first in order to be able to help people. I think that if I'm on the path that I'm supposed to be on, then I'm doing things in my life that I'm supposed to be doing and I'm serving God, and I'm happier. I don't think that He says, "Well, not this job, but this job." It's more general than that, but I do think that some of it is maybe learning through suffering.

We joked about how much she had learned through suffering. Part of her suffering was having to rebuild her initial internal foundation when it became clear that her professional foundation would not sustain her personally. Ironically, Sandra had articulated the notion that you have to help yourself before you are able to help others almost ten years earlier. No doubt this came from her psychology and social work training; yet, it took years for her to accept that helping herself was indeed part of what God wanted for her. The lesson she extracted once she "let go and let God" was that His will and hers were, in fact, the same thing. Once she accepted that it was okay to do what was right for her life, to make her own decisions regardless of her fear of disappointing her parents, she was able to begin to trust her internal voice about how to frame her identity and her relationships. She was able to reframe her relationship with God from asking for an answer to walking together in harmony. Self-authoring her life enabled her to bring her voice to her relationship with God.

Sandra's Story Line

Sandra explored the driving questions of her twenties with her faith as her foundation. She committed to serving the Lord in college, and that commitment never wavered. She followed the call to serve in terms of who she should become and how she should relate to others. Traveling the crossroads, she blended what she learned from her experiential and formal educational experiences to listen to and cultivate her voice as a counselor. She integrated insights from patients, colleagues, and supervisors in refining her counseling work and establishing rapport with patients while establishing appropriate boundaries for these relationships. During her twenties, she also learned something about her own limits in an intense, emotionally draining line of work. This was the beginning of a long process to reconcile this professional internal voice with her personal internal voice.

As she neared thirty, Sandra listened to her internal voice to seek a clearer vision of herself as she moved into medical social work. She trusted her ability to serve patients effectively, had a clear sense of what was right in her work, and stood up for it when her supervisors worked in ways contrary to what she believed. She acted with integrity and trusted that she would find other work if this created conflict with her employment. It appeared, at this point, that Sandra was well on her way to establishing a firm internal foundation. Her confidence in her professional life, however, exceeded her confidence in her personal life. Sandra experienced a prolonged conflict with aspects of her inner voice. She was committed to serving the Lord through using her education in the counseling and social work arena, yet she also recognized that she could not continue this emotionally draining line of work forever. Despite the move into medical social work, the nonprofit company that aligned with her values became a for-profit company a year after she began work there. The patient load increased, as did the paperwork and focus on insurance, rather than patient care. Her work continued to drain her emotionally, in part because she felt responsible for life-and-death decisions for her patients. Her confidence was eroded by the lack of support in her work environment and her lack of a vision for how to fulfill her call to serve without staying in social work. She became depressed, and despite praying regularly, felt she was not getting the guidance she sought from God.

Her grandmother's death and her father's cancer called into question whether she had maintained appropriate boundaries at work. It appeared that patients' needs had depleted her energy beyond what was acceptable. This reinforced her notion that she had to find a new way to serve. Her increasing stress level and her depression added urgency. She turned to her faith and her support systems for help in reframing the idea of serving the Lord.

Sandra's friends and her grandmother were good partners who encouraged her to think differently about her service and to include her own happiness in the equation. She found this difficult because she had not developed her internal voice in the intrapersonal and interpersonal dimensions of her life. Despite articulating on an intellectual level that she was an adult and should make her own decisions, she cared so much about what her parents thought and disappointing them that she did not trust her voice. Even when she acted on her decisions, she worried about her parents' reactions. The intensity of the stress of her work and the depression that accompanied it magnified her reaction to others' criticisms and led to feelings of failure.

Depression also muddled Sandra's thinking about her relationship with God. It made it difficult to sort through questions such as: Do I deserve happiness? Am I called to serve through social work? Is there a lesson I'm supposed to be learning, and will I remain stuck until I learn it? Thinking God's will and her will were two separate entities, she spent years praying to learn what his will for her was. She felt that she should be doing something to help herself and prided herself on being self-reliant, yet she wanted a clear sign from God about His plan for her. Her vision of herself as self-reliant prompted her to try to take control from God to solve her problems. She reported, in retrospect, that she was stuck for an extended period of time because she tried to take control from God. A friend suggested that she let go, but she found it extremely hard to do.

After much conscious work on trying to trust herself and to figure out the relationship of self-reliance and self-confidence, Sandra began to trust her internal voice in terms of her identity and relationships. Although she was not yet at a point of trusting it enough to act on it, she was at a point of desperation in terms of stress and depression. She "let go" in terms of quitting her job and accepting a job at the library, and she "let go" with God. Her depression lifted as she shed her burden for life-and-death decisions, and she found a supportive work environment. These signals led her to believe that she should trust her own voice. She was able to discern the lesson she had been pursuing for so long with God: Doing what was right for her life was God's will for her.

It was not until her understanding of the Lord's lesson that she accepted making decisions, regardless of who might disagree. Bringing her internal voice into her relationship with God brought her into harmony with Him. It remained to be seen whether she could do the same with her parents.

LYDIA'S JOURNEY

CHAPTER 6

LYDIA'S STORY—EXTERNAL CHAOS; INTERNAL STABILITY

LYDIA WAS VERY SHY UPON ENTERING COLLEGE. She reported that she was not shy upon leaving high school because "I did a lot of things, and I was on the top of the heap." Entering college, she viewed herself as "at the bottom of the mix again." Another aspect of going to college that frightened her was the realization that she was on her own:

> Through coming here and not knowing a soul, and all of a sudden you realize you have to do it on your own. You can't fall back on anyone. At home, my parents taught in the same school district that I went to, so they were always there. I mean, always there. And here I was on my own. And I wanted to prove myself.

Lydia's life had been somewhat predictable, and during college, she followed her parents' footsteps into education. She majored in computer science education, with a second specialization in teaching mathematics.

Lydia proved herself during college by succeeding in acquiring two teaching certificates and being actively involved in college life. Looking back, she speculated that she learned more in her campus activities—which included a social sorority, two service organizations, a university-sponsored and two national organizations for math teachers, and broomball—than she did in her coursework. Of her work in her sorority, she said:

> It's taught me how to handle certain people under certain conditions, how to approach them, to use the right wording to get

what you want across to them as being a positive experience, how to get up and speak on your feet and come across like you know what you're talking about.[1]

She gained confidence speaking on her feet through student teaching her senior year, a time when she also reported that the reality of making her own decisions about her future hit home. Lydia was aware of the need to use her inner voice to make these decisions but realized she had not yet fully developed it. Her confidence in and use of her inner voice would grow as she navigated future challenges. She landed a teaching job in a district not far from her college town and within reasonable distance of her family. A year later, Lydia married her fiancé, who was in the U.S. Navy. This marked the end of the predictable portion of Lydia's life. The transitions that followed became the driving force of Lydia's development through her twenties and thirties. Her map shows the pathways she took toward self-authorship and the partners who accompanied her on her journey.

LYDIA'S JOURNEY

Soon after she married, Lydia moved to another state where her husband was stationed. This thrust Lydia into a whole new life of change and resilience.

Moving Through the Crossroads Toward Self-Authorship

Upon moving out of her home state for the first time, Lydia found herself in a crime-ridden city where she initially knew no one, and she was on her own for months at a time while her spouse was at sea. She commented on how her perspective on military life had changed rather quickly:

> I used to think that there was no way I could ever do this, that I couldn't stand to have him gone, I couldn't make all these decisions by myself, I couldn't do those kinds of things. And especially if we ever had a family that I would have to be a single parent for three months at a time. But I see other people around me do it, other people whose children are grown up, and they've done it, and they've coped and they've survived it. And it was part of their lifestyle. And I thought, "Well, if they can do it, I can do it." So, I don't fight it. I know he's happy

doing what he's doing, so I'm not going to try to talk him out of it because I'm not miserable. It's just different from other people's lifestyles.

Seeing others succeeding in this lifestyle enabled Lydia to envision herself succeeding in it.

Entering the Crossroads: Listening to the Internal Voice. Lydia's spouse was not sure that the military would be his career, but Lydia knew that was a possibility when they married. She reported the effect of having to make a lot of decisions in his absence:

> When I lived by myself [last year], I would just make a decision, boom, and that was it. Now I think about it more; I think about, "What do I think?" and then I try to think about it from his point of view as best I can and see if I think that that would be still a good decision or a wise decision. So, I guess I don't [decide on a] whim as much; I think more about what I'm doing on difficult decisions.

One of her difficult decisions was whether to notify her husband of his grandmother's death while he was at sea. Her mother-in-law wanted to wait. Lydia considered what she thought, then drew on her own understanding of her husband's point of view and decided to notify him. She used the same process handling the theft of their car. She gained experience listening to her own voice, in part, because she was unable to communicate with her spouse except through the Red Cross and regular mail, which she received at two-week intervals. She was also forbidden to share his itinerary with people she did not know or over the telephone. She kept busy teaching adult computer classes at a community college and interacting with other Navy wives. She enjoyed learning about their Navy experiences and getting to know them socially. She joked that her sorority skills got her elected to an office in the wives' organization.

Traversing the Crossroads: Cultivating the Internal Voice. The community college's emphasis on financial over educational priorities led Lydia to change to teaching at technical college the following year; however, it wasn't long until financial issues muddied that job as well:

> If I could just keep in my little room, I would be fine, and I would really enjoy it. But it's when you have to deal with the

rest of the administration, and they're telling you to do things that you know educationally that's not what I should be doing, and it's going against things that I was taught and things that I believe to do in education, then you have a problem, a conflict within yourself. Which do you do, something you were taught, something you believe in, or something that they're telling you to do because it's going to save them a couple of dollars?

Having taught for two years at this point, Lydia had integrated what she learned in college with her classroom experience to form beliefs about good educational practice. When she was asked to operate in ways contrary to these beliefs, she felt conflicted. She confronted her administrators about these issues. She requested up-to-date computer software and equipment, registered her frustration when equipment was not repaired in time for her class sessions, talked to her supervisor about the dilemma of teaching without the proper equipment for her students, and offered proposals for improvement. Unfortunately, because of budget constraints, these issues were never resolved. Because she could not find another teaching job, she persevered until the following year when her husband began an overseas tour.

Self-Authorship: Trusting the Internal Voice

For their next move, Lydia and her husband were given a choice of and received the overseas tour they wanted. Lydia worked in accounting for the first seven months. She then returned to teaching math at a private school for the remaining year and a half. She talked about how the experience changed her:

> It has made me more independent of what I know—more willing to try new experiences and not be so hesitant about it. I was so shy when I started college—not anymore! Because if there is one thing that living in an area that is not yours teaches you, it is that you have to get out there and speak up for what you believe in and what is right, to not let others roll you over to their ideas and roll you over to their ways.[2]

Lydia and her husband traveled extensively during this time, and she also had to understand the local culture to be effective in her teaching. She learned to express herself and her beliefs, and she had opportunities to cultivate her own voice. The experience also opened her mind to new experiences. She described them as allow-ing her to reinvent herself:

> It was a fabulous experience. I did things I never would have thought I would do. It makes you feel small; there are so many other people out there! If you have experienced this much, how much more is out there? I have a thirst for more. If you stay in the same place, you get in a rut. It is so exciting! You don't know what you are capable of; you reinvent yourself as you gain new experiences. We had earthquakes; we got used to it. We had [electrical] power-sharing there. There were six months when between two and four hours a day you had no power. It is fun to teach when the power goes out; eighty-five degrees—it gets overwhelming. It got to be a joke. Everybody accepted it. Here, the power goes out, and people are beside themselves. I learned to be more flexible. When you experience other things and see other people deal with things, it puts your life into perspective. The more people you know and more experiences you hear about, you get stronger. I am a strong person now; we move and redo everything. I'm fortunate; I've stumbled onto things. I'm like a cat; land on my feet. Life is too short to be bothered by little things like moving and being uprooted from job and friends. There are other jobs and friends.[3]

Experiencing how others lived enabled Lydia to put life in perspec-tive. She was able to see moving, changing jobs, leaving relationships and building new ones as "little things" instead of crises. The strength she was gaining from these experiences was an internal strength—a trust in her own voice that she could take with her no matter where they moved. This internal sense of self helped her frame military life as an opportunity rather than a stressful experi-ence. Lydia's husband was a strong partner for her during this process; his steady presence on the back of the bike helped her nav-igate these challenges successfully.

Lydia was ready to support her husband's military career as long as he was happy doing it. Lydia reported that she made deci-sions based on what made both her and her husband happy, rather than on what other people thought. In reply to my question regard-ing how this came about, she said:

> It was when we decided to move [overseas]. We didn't make very many people happy. A lot of our friends just thought we were crazy. It was kind of like, now we're going to do this. It's going to be an adventure. It's going to be fun, and I'm not

going to care that you're not happy and that you're all concerned about it. I'm going to do it because that's what's best for us to do, and it's the right time in our lives to do it. I'm going to do what I want to do—what's best for my family and what's best for my happiness—'cause it's my life. I only get one shot at it. That was a big change point for us. It turned out to be a fabulous experience, such a growth for me as a person . . . my husband and I as a couple . . . that it was so the right thing to do.

Lydia's mother was among those who questioned this decision. Lydia realized at that point that she and her husband had to focus on their lives and what they were doing. She noted, "You can't always be a pleaser." This experience marked the foregrounding of Lydia's internal voice in terms of how she made meaning of the world. Although she recognized the external influences in her life, she considered them in the context of doing what she thought best. Having a good partner to support shifting external influences to the background was crucial.

After two years in their overseas assignment, Lydia and her husband returned to the states to an unfamiliar city on the West Coast. Lydia took another teaching position and began work on her master's degree in educational technology. She also became pregnant right before her spouse left for another sea tour. Juggling all of this prompted her to reevaluate her priorities:

I've had a lot of struggle since starting my graduate degree— time management, where are priorities, focus, how to spend my time where I want to or on activities that in the long run don't match my priority system. I read the seven habits book— here are roles, priorities, time—it should match. I looked at mine—they didn't match. What is the higher priority, grading 150 papers or writing my paper? That is where I struggle. My classes are Saturday and Sunday, ten hours each day, one weekend a month. Get up Monday morning and keep working— no down time. It's a twelve-day week. On the second week, my students don't get my best. At first, I thought one weekend a month, no big deal. But then all the work that goes along with it—how to fit in a schedule that is already packed. Some part of my life is different from other parts; military people don't know work people—two separate social groups that don't mix. How do you split your time? Then class people, another chunk that doesn't know the other circles. Maintaining circles, I don't know if I'm doing a good job at any of them—there are so many. Which to let go? There are really none to let go. Especially in the last three months since my husband left [for military deployment], it is a huge problem because everyone thinks I have nothing to do. My schedule is so packed, I have no time to recover before the next day is up and running. It is the biggest inner turmoil. I became a teacher to help other students—that is the core of why I teach. If I've lost that, then what difference does anything else make as far as the profession? The degree is a professional step—am I taking away from part of the profession because I am trying to grow professionally? . . . Too many irons in the fire—some are burning and some are underdone. I'm not doing anything well because I'm doing everything. It is coming to a head—I'm pregnant, so what good am I doing myself and child—exhausted and not taking care of myself. Where are my priorities? What to accomplish this year? I don't know that there is any answer to time and priority questions. I'm due in June—we are moving in June. Full plate! It has been a huge inner battle. I feel it because I see light at the end of the tunnel—sometimes an oncoming train, sometimes the sun.[4]

Although by this time, Lydia was accomplished at juggling multiple responsibilities independently, pursuing all her priorities at once led to internal conflict. Lydia's priority to become a better teacher by taking classes conflicted with her priority to teach effectively. Her priority to complete her degree prior to the next move and birth of her child conflicted with having sufficient time to devote to teaching. Taking care of her health for the benefit of her baby conflicted with her workload and her interest in involvement in the various support circles in which she participated. She had taken on so many priorities that there was not sufficient room to pursue them all. Recognizing that it was all coming to a head, Lydia knew that she needed to sort out her priorities. Doing so helped her build an internal foundation to guide her decisions.

Self-Authorship: Building an Internal Foundation

Fortunately, there was light at the end of the tunnel because Lydia and her husband would be moving to a new assignment the following year, and Lydia was accustomed to using her internal voice to reinvent her life, to construct a "new normal." She attributed this to military life. Talking about all she had done between ages twenty and thirty, she felt her lifestyle had completely shaped who she was:

> When I first walked on to the college campus, it was hard for me to relate to that. I was so shy, so nervous; my hands would sweat when I talked to anyone. I couldn't look at you straight in the face; I had a hard time talking on the phone. Once I knew a person, I was fine, but I was so very shy about getting to know anyone. Now, I walk into a new school, none of that happens. I'm at my neighbor's classroom introducing myself, asking questions about what they teach. It is almost like I have a repertoire of things to say. What is there to be nervous about? People are fascinated with what I have done. I am very much more independent. People who've known me the whole time have just seen it—how much it has changed and brought out things in me. I never dreamt of going anywhere by myself that involved being with other people, couldn't go to a meeting myself. Now, no big deal. I think that is what the military has brought to me, a gift it has given to me. I've come out of my shell. This is who I am. If you like it, fine; if not, I don't worry about it.

Although she had committed to too many priorities, her confidence in her ability to resolve the situation enabled her to see beyond her momentary frustrations. Reflection helped her make decisions for the future:

> Next year will be a huge personal life adjustment . . . I'm getting a master's degree but not going to work next year—crazy. I'm going from a place where I know so many people, so engrossed, then have a baby and move across the country and know no one. It will be a complete switch of what defines me and who I am. My husband will be home all the time, which is good, but an adjustment—a huge life swing. I have felt I was who I was through success at work. Who are you? A teacher. Now I'm going to be a parent. It will be a different focus on who I am and what my purpose is. Lydia the wife, with a son, but my independence will still be there. I know that will still be part of me. I will still be so organized that it will drive people crazy. Those things are still the same. I don't want to be defined as so-and-so's mom or so-and-so's wife; I need my own identity. Getting my master's degree is rolled in there—I need to do something for myself. That's why I waited to have children; I wanted to teach and didn't want to give that up. I can't do both well. I don't know that I'll teach for several years, or ever full

time again—that is a real possibility. I'll also adjust pretty well to new situations. I haven't had a bad job since graduating from college, except one. I could pick good jobs, sense if I belong there, if it is a place I can give something. I think that will stick with me, I'll do that when I go back.[5]

Lydia initially said this would entail a switch of identity but then clarified that it would be a change of focus for her identity. She planned to carry her internal sense of identity, the one she had crafted through her success at teaching, with her into the new role of parent. Just as she was able to choose good jobs where she could contribute, she was confident she'd be able to nurture her child. She was confident, yet flexible, about what the future would bring. Lydia's knowledge of herself and her ability to manage situations led her to the light at the end of the tunnel. She completed her teaching contract but missed her finals because her baby came early. Her husband returned shortly before the birth. She had the baby, made up her finals, and two weeks later, they moved to another West Coast state for their next assignment. Lydia had learned to be a good partner for herself while her husband was away.

In their new assignment, Lydia's husband was home regularly because he was taking classes full time for his master's degree. Despite not having to manage everything on her own as she was accustomed to doing, she felt some trepidation:

> I have to say it was really scary. I remember the plane flight and thinking, oh my gosh, what am I doing? And getting [there] and just feeling like this little lost soul. I remember my in-laws were there to help us move in, and I still remember dropping them off at the airport and getting back in the car with Luke, and David was at school. So, I remember just turning and saying to Luke, "It's you and me, kid." That's all I knew. And I didn't even know what I was doing there very well. But I was really fortunate. [City] has a lot of great programs for young mothers, so within ten days I started going to a program that basically were all women who were stay-at-home mothers who had babies within eight weeks of Luke's age. So, we were all in the same boat. We weren't working outside of the home. We were just trying to figure out what was going on inside of the home, and that group of women pretty much saved my bacon because they kept me focused. And when I was having a bad time of it or something wasn't going right, I had like twelve other people who had gone through or were going through something

similar, so you had that sympathetic ear. And that's what's kind of scary when you move is that you lose all of those friendships and those sympathetic ears, and so you get to a new place and it's not the first thing you want to do is meet someone and say, "Geez, and I had the worst day yesterday. Yadda, yadda, yadda." You just want to keep it positive and the right foot forward until you cement the relationship enough . . . but in that case it seemed to work really well.

Because Lydia was embarking on motherhood rather than teaching, her normal confidence was shaken. As was typical when she started a new venture in a new place, she sought out a support group quickly and landed on her feet, but it was still challenging:

> I think I was up at least twice every night. I occasionally got like four hours of sleep in a row. When he started sleeping through the night I was, like, I feel like a person. I have a brain. I can think. Wow. I was barely functioning doing what I was trying to do, so I guess that kind of plays into my . . . surrendering to motherhood. Just letting it happen and doing what you needed to do for your child and putting yourself second fiddle, which is fine. I was first fiddle for a long time. I think it's a blessing that we waited as long as we did to have a child because it got it all out of my system, wanting to work and wanting to do my own thing.

Lydia's surrendering to motherhood reflects the notion of finding the balance between making things happen and letting things happen. She also appreciated having her husband home on a regular basis to share their son's early life and to relieve her of his constant care. With the support of her partners—her husband and the mothers' group—she was able to maintain her balance.

The next move, two years later to the East Coast, was easier because Lydia was settled into her role as a mother. Noting that she could identify the children she had taught who had stay-at-home parents, and that both her own and her husband's mother had stayed home until they went to school, she was committed to being a stay-at-home mother, too:

> I do what makes me happy and that's [staying at home] truly what makes me happy. When I taught, teaching made me happy. There were many days when it drove me crazy because I wanted to do so much but I didn't have enough hours to get it all done, and that's one reason why I know I can't teach and raise Luke and do them both the way I want to do them. So, you

pick the more important of the two, which is obviously raising Luke, and so the other one can always come back at another time. I feel very blessed and very fortunate that I can do what I want to do, that we have that life that can support that.

Lydia and her husband were both doing what made them happy, but they foresaw future complications due to the complexity of military life. Lydia anticipated that they would struggle to balance career and family now that they had a son:

> The next job is going to be the hardest one because it's going to pretty much make a decision on how long he's staying in the Navy and is he going to . . . it's bad to say, but . . . sacrifice the career for the family. It wavers back and forth. And it's really hard now because of Luke and he'd be eleven or twelve when David retired; that's sixth grade, so you're getting to when it's tough to be moving them around, in my opinion. And having been a teacher seeing military kids move, they all have the name of military brat. There's a reason for that. Also, knowing his personality and how shy he is and how new situations are difficult for him and not to say he'll always be that way. He's two, but he probably is not going to be a very good mover. That'll make a difference, too, and also probably the health of our parents and what they're doing. You have to factor it all in. Usually, you get to a point where there are a couple jobs that'd be okay to go into, and so then you pretty much pick by location where you wanted to go. We knew this time, when he was leaving the West Coast, that we really wanted to go back to the East Coast. Take a great job, but take it on the East Coast. Who knows what we'll do after this?

Lydia valued their experiences in military life, yet balancing family and career needs were superseding the days of the Navy being an adventure. She noted that the economy and government policy were changing the patterns of Navy life and would probably result in David having to go back to sea sooner than they anticipated.

Despite her awareness of this likelihood, Lydia was settled in her life—in her sense of self, her marriage, and her role as mother. She reported that her sense of what made her happy had become a part of her personality:

> I probably don't think about it that much anymore because it's become a part of who I am. Whereas before it was, "No, that's all right. I'm going to do that." It was more conscious, I guess,

that it was happening. And now it's just more . . . I guess I don't think about, "Oh well, that might make that person uncomfortable." It's not even a conscious thought. It's just, "Well, that's of course what I'm going to do."

Lydia described how she adopted a positive attitude:

> You have to make the situation what you want it to be, and if you're miserable, it's because you made yourself miserable. You didn't go out and do what you needed to do. So, maybe a little more proactive toward making it happen the way I wanted it to happen instead of kind of sitting back and letting it happen. But you only have so much time when you live in a certain area, so you can't sit back and let it happen or it'll never happen. I've become more like David's family. And very positive.

This attitude began when Lydia and her husband framed the overseas tour as an adventure. She learned through her many moves to "make things happen," yet she also knew when to let things happen. Gaining an in-depth knowledge of and confidence in herself resulted in her knowing what she wanted to do naturally. Her ability to align her circumstances with her values and beliefs became second nature to her. This set the stage for her to secure these internal commitments.

SELF-AUTHORSHIP: SECURING INTERNAL COMMITMENTS

For the next few years, Lydia's husband had shore duty. They bought their own home and became settled in a community. She began occasionally teaching evening classes after her son turned two; however, she was still primarily focused on parenting. She described parenting as the "best job":

> It's so wonderful to be with him all the time and to feel like you're not missing anything, to watch all the changes and all the growth development, and also to feel that you're part of that, that you helped make that next step happen. Sure, there's some moments that you're thinking to yourself, "Gosh, this is not exactly what I want to do today," but when you think about the overall picture and when I sit back at nine o'clock and think about my overall day, it's full of highlights. It's not that one time when he wanted that and I wasn't going to give it to him,

so we had a mini little meltdown in the middle of the floor. But he also has a temperament that very much matches mine, and in a lot of ways that's very good because, not that we don't butt heads sometimes, but I can see where it's coming from, and you know how to defuse it because it's your own. And so that makes it an easy at-home situation. I love it.

Lydia's positive attitude led her to focus on the highlights of the day instead of the hassles. Seeing her own personality in her son, she was adept at interacting effectively with him. Asked how she made decisions about child rearing, she said:

I usually read one or two or three different sources to get different points of view. And then you kind of shake it in with . . . David and I talk about it, and I talk to other moms about what they think, and then you think about your own child's temperament. So, it's just one thing that you're adding to the box of knowledge to figure out what's going to be the best solution or the best way to handle it. So, it just depends on the situation, how much you really take whatever's being said. One thing that I've really noticed [is] that I've become an advocate for Luke. If there's a doctor that I don't agree with, I don't just walk out of the office upset that they didn't do whatever test I thought they needed to do. I pretty much stand up and say: "Look, I think you should do this and this is why. Now tell me why we shouldn't." Sometimes that changes them and they go ahead and do what I'm asking them to do. And sometimes they say, "No, we're not going to do it because of this." And then I understand it, and I'm okay with that. Whereas I would have thought that I would have been more of the pushover. And I think part of that is just because I'm older. I'm not the twenty-two-year-old mom; I'm the thirty-three-year-old mom. And that makes a difference.

Lydia's internal foundation gave her the confidence to analyze information and perspectives in light of her child's temperament and any given situation to choose a course of action she deemed to be appropriate. Her analysis at physicians' offices prompted her, with no apparent hesitation, to push for what she thought was right. Although she attributed this to age, it was more likely a result of her securing her internal commitments and, thus, having the ability to live out her convictions even in the face of uncertainty or doubt.

Lydia was secure enough to also listen to her child as part of her parenting philosophy. She described a time when she reevaluated how many activities to schedule for Luke when he indicated that he wanted to stay home more often:

> One day he just looked at me and he said, "I need more time to stay home and do my projects." And I said, "Well, what projects do you need to do?" And he started listing them. So that's when I said to myself: "Oh my gosh, what have I done to my poor kid? He feels like he has no time at home." So, this summer we've scaled back, and now we have two things that we do a week where he socially interacts with other children, and the rest of the time it's just the two of us. So, somewhere you need to find a mix where it works.

Lydia's goal to expose Luke to different perspectives through socialization reached an extreme that made him feel overwhelmed. Listening to him carefully, she altered their activity schedule to accommodate his needs. Yet, she also continued to listen to her own needs:

> It's more of a challenge to be a mom who stays home than it is to be a mom who has a full activity [schedule] for her children because the isolation is more when you stay at home. You're getting social stimulation, as well. Because if you drop them off at a class, you're talking with the other moms, or if you're all there together, the kids are playing and you're talking, . . . so sometimes you have to sit back and say to yourself, "Am I doing this activity because *I* enjoy it or because he is getting a good thing out of it?" So, that's sometimes hard to look at it and say, "Oh, I need to drop that activity even though I really like those people, or I really enjoy doing that with him, but he's not getting out of it what he needs out of it." So, it just depends. And I think that was one reason why I did go back to work 'cause I felt for two years I had devoted almost every hour of every day to him. And whereas I didn't regret any of it, I also thought I can't do that my entire life because then he's eighteen and he leaves. And then where am I? I mean there is a point at which you smother, so I can't do that all the time. You do need to figure out where it works. There's some times where we have a play date with someone, and I know that it's not his favorite child to play with, but I may do it just because I really want to see that mom, and that's the only time I can see her. It's one day out of fifty, an hour out of the day, but most of the time, most of the activities are totally "how is this benefiting Luke?" I actually sit back a lot of times at his activities and just kind of watch him interact to see if this is a good thing. You try to be

the best parent that you can, and you know that you're not doing everything right, but you're doing the best you can, and that's all you can do. He's well loved. He's well cared for. I don't think he's doing too badly.

Lydia appeared comfortable balancing what was best for Luke and what was best for her. Her comfort with not doing everything reflected her faith and certainty that things would work out.

During our conversations in the years that Lydia's husband had shore duty, she often said she was waiting for the bubble to burst. After nearly four years, it did. Her husband was redeployed to sea four months after the birth of their second son. Lydia described her reaction:

> The Navy has taught me well. (Laughing) I was never this resilient in college. Some of these things I needed when I was in college. With age comes some wisdom, or some stubbornness. I don't know which it is. I know that I very much control everything as much as I can, and I just think that's because there's so much I can't control that what I can control I really try to control as best I can. And I pretty much can sense or know when I'm getting in over my head, and then I pull back the reins and take control again. I have to do that. That's my survival because I tell everybody else at six o'clock in a lot of households someone else walks through the door. In my household, the dynamic doesn't change. And that's good in some regards. Alex was never fussy at six o'clock when everyone says, oh the baby's so fussy. Well, the dynamic never changed, so he didn't sense any change, so there was no change in his demeanor. So, in that regard, it was good, but in the same regard, if I'd had a really lousy day, at six o'clock I was just continuing with that lousy day, and no one was coming to take the baby or take the four- or five-year-old that was driving you nuts. (Laughs) You just have to be patient. A lot of that teaching junior high has come back, that whole, okay, dig deep; you do have patience for that child.

Lydia was aware of her limits; she could see when she was getting in over her head. Yet, she was accomplished at controlling what she could. This was the first time Lydia had to manage two children alone. She marshaled her internal strength and her positive attitude to meet the challenge. Near the end of the sea tour, her husband called while she was out of town visiting her in-laws to break the news that the tour was being extended. Her in-laws expressed surprise that she was not angry. She shared what happened:

> I like to think that I'm taking it in stride. . . . How can you be angry? It's not his fault. That's the way of the job, and you just have to roll with it. Things I can control and change, I do, and things I can't, I just roll with and let go of because I can't sit and get mad about it. It's wasteful of my energies. Even when David was going to deploy, I accepted it a lot faster than he did. He had a really hard time, and he didn't want to believe that it was going to happen. I just went straight to, okay, what am I going to do? I just leaped over the hurdle of this is going to happen 'cause I couldn't do anything about it, and if I can't do anything about it, I'm not going to fret about it. So, I like to think I'm rolling with it just fine.

Lydia did not have energy to waste on worrying about things that were beyond her control. She "rolled" with uncertainty and focused on what she could do, shaping her reaction to reality. As I marveled at Lydia's resilience in this situation, she continued:

> I don't want people to have pity on me or to . . . There's so many other people in the world who have far more difficult situations than I have. That's one thing that's kept me going. I think about all those people who died in the World Trade Center and all those families that were left without that person. My husband is out there. I e-mail with him every day. He is supporting me. He loves me, and he's going to come back home. I do not have that bad of a situation. Whereas there are millions of people who have much more difficult situations than I do, and that's just how I choose to look at it. I know that there are lots of other people who are in my same situation who don't choose to look at it that way, and that's their choice. But to me, this is just a temporary bump in the road of life, and it's not going to last forever. I know it's helping me just to get through every day and every moment the best that I can. I've also learned to say, that's the best I can do right now. I hardly ever used to say that, so that's the best I can do right now, and that's how it's going to have to be.

Lydia's choice to frame her situation in the way that she did helped her cope and appreciate that her husband was safe. It was clear that having her husband as a partner continued to be an important factor. Although she recognized that some in her situation chose to frame these circumstances differently, she was committed to framing it positively based on her conviction that this was best for everyone. She also was realistic about what she could do. Understanding those limits framed another decision she and her husband had to make because, even when his ship returned, he would still be three hours away from home. She described the decision about whether she and the children would move:

> While he's still in [city], we will be here. Originally, we had thought that maybe we would move in August, and then I started thinking about the logistics of moving by myself—even when the ship was supposed to come back in August—to be ready for the start of school, and I decided that the logistics of that were just a little more challenging than I wanted to deal with. We decided together. The support system was here. Moving to [city] really puts us further away from our family, and during this time, I didn't need that extra three-hour drive if I did want to go see them. And to try to start new . . . there were enough challenges and changes without starting fresh with not knowing anyone in the neighborhood or anyone really to help you. When push comes to shove, needing help, you'd like to know someone that can help you. And having just moved somewhere and then having him leave like that, and with the new baby, it was just enough.

Considering her own needs for seeing her family and getting help with the children and their needs, Lydia and her husband decided that she would not move. She shared that sorting through things together to ascertain what was best for everyone came naturally to her and her spouse:

> I think that's one thing that the military has done, is really cemented our relationship because it's sent us to some bizarre places where we didn't know a soul. All we knew were each other, and it really takes you to a next level . . . you have to have complete faith and trust in that person because that's all you have. And that has served us very well . . . over the three ships and the overseas tour. And to think, I grew up in [state], never left the house. My parents lived in that house for almost thirty years.

I asked how going through this together affected how they maintained their relationship. Lydia replied:

> We never worry about each other's relationships. We know it's fine, and the one that we worry about is the children's. And

Luke's because he knows David, and you want him to continue to know that. I probably worry more about Alex than David does just because I know Alex more as a person. When David left, Alex was slightly expressive. And I've just watched him blossom. The hardest thing for me about this is when something really cool happens with the kids, I just want to be able to have him come home and say, "Watch this. Do it again." Instead, I'm taking up some machine [video camera], and it's just not the same for him, and it's not the same for me to share it with him that way. But I am grateful. It's not like Alex is the first baby or the only baby. He did get to see all these firsts with Luke, so he won't see them with Alex, but at least he has seen them with a child. And we just kind of flip-flopped it. He wasn't there when I was pregnant with Luke, and he was here when I was pregnant with Alex. So, he got to be there for the pregnant part of this one and the first year of the other one. So, in all, he got one whole kid.

Lydia was so grounded in her marital relationship that she never worried about it. She was able to express, and act on, her own needs, yet she was also able to hold her husband's needs in the foreground of their relationship. She had mixed feelings when their needs differed:

The only time I ever worry about him is when they're in port. I really don't like it when they pull into port. I'm glad for him. He needs to get off the ship. He needs to feel some earth under his feet, but at the same time, the incident of the *Cole* just rings in your head. I remember where I was when I heard of the *Cole*. It just shook me to the core because that could have been my husband. And that it was somebody's husband, and that was somebody's wife. That bothers me. But as long as they're steaming out in the middle of the ocean somewhere, I know they're fine. I always thought I couldn't be married to a Marine; I couldn't be married to an Army guy.

Lydia's fear for her husband's safety was heightened by the bombing of the *U.S.S. Cole* in the port of Aden, Yemen, that killed seventeen sailors. Yet, she knew he needed time in port. She was in tune with her spouse because of their complete trust in each other. Yet, she also described that they were open to learning:

Any married couple looks at functional relationships and relationships that are not functional. You want to look at the ones that are functional and say, okay, what can I draw from that?

What's going to make that work? I think it's the same with parenting. You know great parents and you know dysfunctional parents; you look at that, and you try to draw from those great parents. Okay, what are they doing? What's their magical equation? And it works for them because their kid's like that. My kid's not like that, so that wouldn't work for me. You draw from those people, and you learn from those people, and then you try to make it work as best you can in your life. Sometimes, it works, and sometimes, it's just not your personality or it's not something you're comfortable with, and it's not going to work.

Lydia gathered insights from other couples and parents but applied them in the context of her relationship and her children. She and her husband took a similar approach as they combined their individual insights into one coherent parenting philosophy:

Sometimes I'll do something, and then I will e-mail David and say, "Now, what do you think?" or "I'm thinking I need to change this somehow. Do you have any ideas?" So, I still ask for his support. It'll be interesting to see what's going to happen when he works back into the mix. We've always in the moment backed each other up. Then, after the kids are in bed, "You know, maybe we should have handled that differently." But never in front of them! They never know that we weren't this iron curtain in front of them. So, it'll be interesting to see how Luke reacts to it all. Alex won't know too much of that yet. What'll be interesting for him is when he's two and Dad comes home to stay. He'll be like, "What happened? You come home every day now?"

Lydia and David processed their handling of situations after the fact and were open to considering alternatives. Perhaps some of their flexibility in this regard stemmed from the constant readjustment to David's presence and absence. Most likely, some of it also stemmed from Lydia's faith in her internal foundation and her internal commitments and the strength of her partnership with her husband.

Despite being accustomed to Navy life and understanding that the mission always comes first, Lydia still marveled sometimes at how world events such as September 11 and policy decisions about when troops would come home affected her daily life. If the ambiguity of complex international issues was not enough, she also learned to embrace uncertainty and instability when her second child developed significant health problems while David was at sea.

She described what would be a two-year ordeal of understanding the problem and a long-term ordeal in handling it:

> Alex was vomiting five to seven times a day for about seven weeks. You could tell it never reached his stomach because you could go through it and say this is what he ate today, and you could see it in what he gave back to you. And I kept telling the doctors, "It's like it never even gets to his stomach." And they're telling you, "Well, are you giving him too big of bites?" I did at one point call my mother-in-law to come down. I'm like, "I need you to come down and make sure I'm not losing my mind here. This kid is really doing this." I mean, the doctors all just kept looking at me like, "Please, he's fine. Look at him." And they're watching his weight, and they're watching his height, and "Oh, he's fine." And I was like, "I'm sorry, this is not fine." So, again it's advocating for your child. I must have gone to every pediatrician in our office, trying to get them to refer me to somebody, anybody, to see what was wrong. They all know me up at Walter Reed.

Lydia kept pushing doctors to figure out what was going on. At one point, they did a surgical procedure intended to remedy the problem. Unfortunately, Alex's problems continued after the procedure. Lydia kept on at the doctors to solve Alex's problems. Shortly after David returned from his sea tour, Lydia took Alex in for more tests, and they finally obtained a diagnosis:

> He has something where lesions grow in his esophagus, and then food gets stuck in the esophagus and can't make it down into the stomach. So, then it became the, okay, well, that's fine. What do we do? 'Cause the kid's got to eat, and what's causing all of that to grow in there? We found out that he has many food allergies. He's allergic to wheat, dairy, eggs, tree nuts, peanuts, fish, and shellfish. So, then it became trying to figure out how to cook him anything that did not have any of those products in it. It was the craziest thing because we weren't even cohesive back as a family unit yet from being apart for that long. It was like you were in a dream or reading it in a book. It wasn't like it was actually you that was having all of this happen. It wasn't like you envisioned his homecoming. But you get through it, and you move on, and we're none the worse for wear.

Lydia's typical approach to accepting a problem and directly taking action to address it held true in this situation, even with the stress of having a sick child. Her confidence in herself and her trust that things would work out positively kept her moving ahead. She reported what she did next:

> So, it became educating yourself, not only on what is this disease because it's only been diagnosed in the last seven years, now that it's even been given a name. So, it's try to figure out what's out there. Rarely do you find someone who's ever heard of it besides have knowledge of it, and the doctors don't really know very much about it, especially in children that were as young as Alex. The research is done on kids over three. So, it's been learning what all of this is, right along with the doctors who are trying to help you as best they can. At the same time, trying to understand his illness but also trying to cook on this brand new diet for him. It has been an extreme challenge.

Part of the challenge was understanding this disease. An equally complex challenge was managing the food intake of a three-year old. Lydia described what this entailed:

> He eats a lot of rice products and soy products and vegan cheeses. He can't do any soy cheese because it has a milk protein in it. He can't even eat deli meat because of the way they baste the meat with a butter or cheese or some kind of topping, something wheat. So, you can't go through the slicer, so you make a whole ham or turkey and cut it. It's taken me back to, "Oh, this is how people used to cook before we had all these convenience foods." I prepare everything. There's some baked goods that I can buy that are safe for him to eat—as safe as I can figure out. The whole legislation that has come up with listing the allergens on the box has really . . . and having it just in English, "This product contains wheat," because wheat can be listed . . . there's like thirty different words that mean wheat. And so to have eight different categories that have thirty words apiece in your head can get pretty mind-boggling. It makes me thankful that I'm an organized person.

Lydia spent considerable time learning what Alex could eat, shopping at five different groceries to find the products she could use safely, and preparing food for him to eat at home and everywhere he went, including preschool. As always, she controlled what she could and recognized that there were aspects of this she could not control. As was the case with earlier challenges in parenting, Lydia did not hesitate to involve Alex in helping manage his food intake, and she automatically sought out the support of an allergy network. She described efforts she was making in that regard:

You have to start learning to trust other people that they're not going to go over the boundary of what he's allowed. We also have to keep educating Alex as to asking if he can have that or saying no if somebody hands him something that he doesn't know about. That's a lot to take on when you've just turned three. So he's learning. He understands that there are certain foods that he can't have, and they make him sick, and that's just what we say. There's a network that deals with allergies that I am a member of, and if there's one thing that they just keep saying in that newsletter, it's that you have to educate your child because you cannot be with them twenty-four hours a day, seven days a week. They're going to be with themselves. So, I spend a lot of time thinking about that, how to make it so that he can know to say, "No, I can't have that," or "What's in that?" or "Did my Mom send that?" He could outgrow some of the allergies, but he won't outgrow them all, so it's just a matter of he's going to have to deal with this at some level his whole life unfortunately. I don't think there's going to be anybody waving a magic wand to get rid of it.

Even with all these precautions, Alex still had regular episodes of getting food stuck. Sometimes, he was able to dislodge it, and sometimes, Lydia took him to the emergency room to have it removed. She relied on the internal foundation that had become so much the core of who she was to manage her everyday life:

Over the years, I've learned more to depend upon myself than anyone else. I feel like I have a really strong inner strength, kind of that pull-yourself-up-by-your-bootstraps and keep going. I look down the road probably more than I ever did just at where are we going with this. It used to be look to the next tour, and now we look more down to the next five years, as far as the children go and Alex's illness. I thought that I had gotten used to Alex's getting food stuck, and then about ten days ago when one happened, I thought, "I don't think I'll ever get used to this." You kind of go through . . . I don't know . . . a panic almost, or you thought you were on the bright side of it. And then you just get fearful, and not fearful for the moment because you know the moment's okay. You'll get through the moment, and you know where to go and what to do to get through the moment, but fearful for the long term of it, and where is it going to be and how is he going to handle it when he's sixteen, eighteen, twenty-five, goes to college? Is he going to stay away from beer 'cause he's allergic to wheat? Okay.

(Laughing) You look at all of that. I'll worm in there somewhere and figure that out.

Lydia's inner strength and her adeptness at handling crises made handling each incident manageable. It also stood at the foundation of her ability to trust her children and other support networks to help her manage the unmanageable. Yet, this was the first time in our twenty years of conversation I had ever heard Lydia use the word fear other than related to her husband's safety. Having children, particularly one with a challenging illness, was mediating her outlook on the future. Still, she knew instinctively that she would figure it out. She used her planning skills to do the best she could, but she did have support from others as well:

> David and I talk about it a lot and that helps, so we're on the same page and going the same place. I do have a girlfriend down the street, and her son was in the hospital for many, many long months, but it helps because she's been there with a sick child. So, it's one of those things that I know if I call her, she's going to be like, "Whatever you need," 'cause she understands that side of the coin. But you figure it out. You have plans in your head. There's that planner thing! I do that when David's deployed. You have a plan if something happens what you're going to do. You have to.

Planning had always been a survival skill for Lydia as she moved and adjusted to new communities. Over time, it became a matter of planning for uncertainty, particularly as she handled Alex's health. She maintained this same flexibility with regard to Navy life. David had returned from his two-year sea assignment, and his assignment to the Pentagon meant they all lived in the same house again. Lydia knew, however, that change was on the horizon:

> He will probably leave there by the end of another year. It won't be that long, and there is something now that's happening with everything that's going on in Iraq and Afghanistan. They have assignments that are called Individual Augmentations; they take people from shore places or ships that are not deploying and put them over in that region to do certain jobs. David has been on the short list for that several times, so it does make us wonder when his number's going to come up. A couple times, when he was assigned to the ship, he managed to dodge those. And he's probably had twice since he's been at the Pentagon where the piece of paper's come in, and somebody

else has volunteered to go. Some of them are in a combat zone, and that's quite a different Navy from what I've experienced. Now, I'm used to the "you're on this gray ship and it's out in the ocean." Life's good in the middle of the ocean. (Laughing) But sitting at a desk in your bulletproof jacket and walking to your barracks and then walking back to the office. That's not something that either one of us wants him to face. But we know people who have done it one, two times already, so if he stays in long enough, the time will come. It's just when is that going to be? There aren't enough bodies, and it's always the mission first, so that's one thing that if you're a military wife you have to understand. The mission first. It's not like he's selecting it.

Lydia could handle this level of uncertainty because her internal foundation was second nature to her. In light of Lydia's concern for her children and the strong possibility that David would get an assignment very different than what they had grown accustomed to, I asked Lydia what their plans were for his remaining in the Navy. She replied:

You never know. We know that he'll do this until he has twenty years in, and he's almost to 16, so it's four more years for sure 'cause you're not going to walk away at sixteen years unless they tell you to. But it's what do you want to do, and it was interesting when he got back from this deployment to watch that change because before it had been the two of us, and it was not a big deal. And now it's a big deal. He's not there for six months; he's missed a lot. Especially when he left and Alex was four months old, and he comes back and he's eleven months old. There's a big difference there. I know that he will probably deploy probably one more time I would think before twenty, if not more than that. And so that, I think, will really make his decision pretty clear 'cause not only will it be how well he works through it, but how well do the children handle it. Luke is just not a kid of change, and it worries us both when we actually move from this place 'cause we've been here so long—the boys and I have—and Alex doesn't really remember anything else, anywhere else. I don't know where it's going to go from there.

And so the uncertainty of the future continues, complicated now by their concern for their children. Lydia's wisdom—her inner strength, her ability to accept any change, from her son's illness to her husband's possible assignment to a combat zone, as normal, and her confidence in "figuring it out"—sustains her and her family.

Lydia's Story Line

Lydia's transformation from a shy and intimidated college student to a resilient adult is striking. She gained confidence throughout college but still thought in her early twenties that she could not adapt to Navy life and make decisions by herself. Moving with her husband to their first military assignment threw Lydia head first into a life of constant uncertainty—and the crossroads. She began moving toward self-authorship out of necessity. She learned how to make decisions on her own because she had to; there was no one else around to rely on. She made decisions for herself, and in her husband's absence, intuitively knowing what his preferences would be when she could not contact him. Simultaneously, Lydia was forced into building relationships with strangers, primarily the wives of other sailors. She began to appreciate multiple perspectives as she encountered other women who lived the Navy life. Surviving this new life boosted her self-confidence and helped her to increasingly trust her own voice. The confidence and trust she developed in listening to her internal voice helped her make the most of the overseas tour.

Her husband's first overseas tour promoted Lydia's personal development and her marital partnership. Living and working in another country, as well as traveling widely, Lydia had to negotiate new cultures. She learned to express herself and respect other cultural norms. Seeing alternative ways of living helped her put her life in perspective, appreciate it, and yearn to learn more about the world. Because she and her husband had only each other in moving to the other side of the world, they came to trust and have faith in each other. She described the tour as an opportunity to reinvent herself, to enrich and deepen her identity and belief system. She would use this capacity over and over again during her twenties and thirties. By the time she returned to the states, Lydia had reinvented herself by moving her internal voice to the foreground of how she saw the world, her identity, and her social relations. She was ready to develop that voice further to make decisions for her future.

Lydia developed her internal voice in her professional life by pursuing professional development opportunities in her teaching career and enrolling in graduate school. Her intrapersonal and interpersonal growth continued, as she constantly joined new communities and sought out new relationships in each one. Her relationship with her husband deepened as they learned to communicate long distance and make the most of any time they had together. Developing an enduring trust in her internal voice, Lydia was ready to begin building an internal foundation that would sustain her through the uncertainty associated with supporting her husband's military career and raising her two young children.

By the time her first child was born, Lydia knew without a doubt that she would put her professional life on hold to fully commit to motherhood. Despite her initial uneasiness about how to raise an infant, she never regretted the choice and immediately found a new mothers' network in a new city. Despite her growth in trusting herself and handling uncertainty, Lydia recognized the value of networking with others who shared her life circumstances and noted that the women in the mothers' network "saved her bacon" during the transition to motherhood.

A couple of years into motherhood, Lydia was internally settled with herself. She knew who she was, what made her happy, and how to achieve that happiness. This knowledge of herself, which she labeled wisdom, was such an ingrained part of her that she no longer consciously thought about it. Her relationship with her husband was so strong that she never worried about it despite their extended periods of being apart. This wisdom—the securing her internal commitments—made her life seem settled, even when externally it was constantly changing. Her husband's deployment shortly after their second child's birth and illness would have been perceived as crises by many, but Lydia took these events in stride and indicated she and her family "were none the worse for wear." She spent little time lamenting about these realities; instead, she chose to be thankful that her life was easier than many others and moved quickly to figuring out how to handle her circumstances. Obtaining the information she needed, building relationships for support, engaging in mutual relationships with her husband and children, and mustering her inner strength came naturally for her, even when she was uncertain about what the future would bring. Her ability to accept the ongoing uncertainty of her family's life was no doubt grounded in the internal foundation and commitments she had acquired. Through this life of constant change and of reinventing herself, Lydia was indeed like a cat—always landing on her feet no matter what.

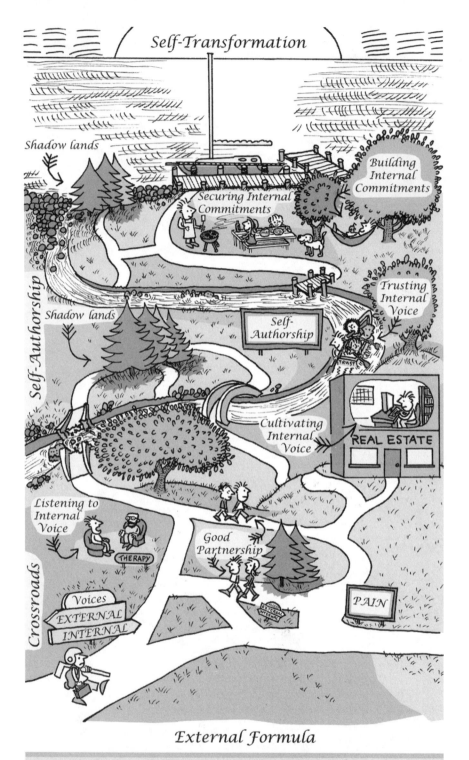

EVAN'S JOURNEY

CHAPTER 7

EVAN'S STORY—BEING THE BEST YOU CAN BE

EVAN WAS NOT VERY FOCUSED ON A CAREER PATH IN COLLEGE. He majored in political science for no particular reason, and later switched to English. He joined a fraternity and lived in his fraternity house his sophomore year because he found living in the residence halls too restrictive. He developed close friendships with his fraternity brothers but recognized that he was spending more time socializing than studying. Evan decided that this lifestyle was not a fit for him personally or conducive to his college success, so he transferred at the end of his sophomore year to a university near his hometown. When he transferred, he switched his major to communication with a concentration in public relations. Evan moved back in with his parents and worked two jobs in addition to finishing school. Reflecting on college, he said:

> Just the experience of four years is catastrophic on the way you were before. You're just a lot more wise to what's going on. It amazes me when I think back to just a year before. I just had no clue, and you think you know a lot. And you really don't. That's why I always try and keep an open mind about things because you really need to experience stuff to learn it. I look at things completely different, too. When you're in school, there's a time limit on things. The semester ends at a certain date. You know where you're going to be; you know what's going to happen. And now it's like you're floating in space. There's no time limit, and you don't know when things are going to end. The world becomes a bigger place. So does, I guess, your brain.

189

Keeping his mind open to learning would be a driving force throughout Evan's twenties and thirties.

By his senior year Evan had already acquired a job in commercial real estate. He created a position for himself at the real estate company after graduation, but he did not initially envision this as a long-term career. He excelled at the communication aspect of this work and intended to return to school to learn more about the financial side of it. Evan married a year later at his fiancée's urging. He described his decision to get married as logical because they "weren't running away from each other."[1] He also wanted a stable life, so he "wasn't against" marriage. They had already lived together, so Evan did not view it as a big deal. He and his wife moved in with Evan's parents to get started financially. He took up managing a hockey league because he loved hockey. He worked hard at his job because of his work ethic and his love of learning. He was busy organizing his life, yet he did not have a clear vision of what he wanted his life to be.

EVAN'S JOURNEY

Evan's map shows the paths he took toward self-authorship and the partners who accompanied him on his journey.

Moving Through the Crossroads Toward Self-Authorship

As parts of his adult life seemed to fall easily into place, Evan continued to approach life with his penchant for organizing everything to keep his life in order and his tendency to do whatever he took on to perfection. His mid-twenties required some realignment of this approach.

Entering the Crossroads: Listening to the Internal Voice. In our seventh interview, Evan reported that seeking perfection had created some problems:

> I overworked myself last spring. Every spring, I run this hockey league. I didn't realize I was getting into the state I was in, and by June, I had totally burned myself out. I walked around like a zombie, and I was really depressed. I had worked on two really hard deals right before that, in addition to running that league. It took its toll without me really realizing it. I always thought I was superman and could handle it. I did

handle it, but I paid the price. That put things in perspective for me. I was placing too much importance on things that I really shouldn't have. Now, I take it easier than I did. The world doesn't rise or fall on how I come through at work. I'm not a superhero, so I still do my best, but if something doesn't go through, I'm not going to be crushed. . . . I'm really glad it happened now because I've been able to do a lot of heavy thinking and just see what's important to me and what direction I want to take. One thing I did decide was that I really don't appreciate the industry that I'm in. Sure, I make a lot of money, but if I could get into something that I would enjoy and I made less money, it wouldn't matter.[2]

This bout with depression landed Evan in the crossroads and led to a realignment of his priorities. He began to listen to his own voice about what was important to him and what direction he should take. He had an important partner in a counselor he sought out to help him with this challenge.

Traversing the Crossroads: Cultivating the Internal Voice. Despite his lack of appreciation for the industry he was in, as he cultivated his own voice, he all the same decided to make his career in it. A year later, he explained how his attitude about work had changed over the previous year:

My liking this was a gradual thing; probably happened when I left the company I started with and went into a situation where I was not challenged. I grew to really enjoy this when I was asked back to my company, made an officer, and allowed to become heavily involved. I realized I had learned a lot, proven that I can function in this environment. That gave me confidence to do well—I look forward to going to work. It is less of a chore and more my life. It has become what I am.[3]

Evan's growing enjoyment of his work stemmed from recognizing that he liked the challenges. The challenges increased when his company merged with another:

Earlier this year, I and four people from my company were "sold" in the merger to another company in the city. Now, I take the train every day. It is a wild ride. I'm getting settled in—I like it a lot. I was thrown into a brand-new environment— Madison Avenue—playing with the big boys. It is not a new job but tripled the responsibility for me. I didn't go unwillingly, but not by choice; I am in the river, and that is where it flowed. I'm grateful for it, there are no problems, but I had feared it. It is a big pond. It amazes me at how big it is. If you think about it too often, it is overwhelming. I'm used to the suburbs, five minutes from the office, not wearing a suit. Now, it is high theatrics. If you are going to advance, you have to go to the city.[4]

Although Evan did not initiate this change, he saw going with the flow of the river as an opportunity to learn more. His approach paid off, as he explained:

When my company merged with this company, they planned to ditch me at the earliest opportunity. I dug my heels in and rolled up my sleeves down there. Now, the whole staff that worked on properties was reduced to me. I am organized to a point that is maniacal—which they like. I got a raise. They saw how I did this; they gave me more properties. The company has continued to grow. For right now, I still have much to learn. I like to learn hard things. It is beyond my control, but in a way I'm comfortable with it. I am given the time and space to learn on my own without being forced to do it one way or another. I've done it my own way. I've made lots of mistakes, learn not to do it again. I obsess about it until I solve it, or adjust that this is the situation now and I can't change it.[5]

Evan secured his place in the company by demonstrating his worth, but his primary goal was learning and doing his best. He particularly valued the opportunity to learn on his own and work his own way. He was not afraid to make and learn from mistakes. He was willing to go with the flow because he made things happen when he could and accepted it when he could not.

Self-Authorship: Trusting the Internal Voice

The level of autonomy Evan experienced at work and his constant focus on working to improve his performance enabled him to come to an awareness of how his mind worked:

I told you about this feeling that I had once I became "aware." That is the best word that I can use to describe the difference between how I view my intellectual level now versus how I felt prior to "noticing" my surroundings and my relationship with the world around me. It was like I woke up one day and things just clicked in my brain and things became clear to me for the first time. The most dramatic difference between before and after was my ability to think and the subsequent confidence in my abilities and trust in my decisions. I have developed my own approach to solving problems, one that has proven to me to be a good one, and one that has proven to be a good teacher. When it becomes apparent to me that I have relied on this ability, I often try to remember what I did before I began to understand how *my mind* worked.[6]

Evan's drive to overcome challenges in combination with his growing ability for self-reflection enabled him to develop his own problem-solving approach and ability to think. He had come to trust his own mind to think through problems. His epiphany about how his mind worked emerged from self-reflection and became a building block for future growth. This self-authorship in how he came to know something was also spreading to other dimensions of his life:

As my personality and sense of self have really begun to develop and become more refined, my ability to direct my life accordingly has become increasingly confident. As I realize who I am, and what is important to me, it becomes easier for me to establish my priorities. Identifying and arranging my priorities has helped me to develop a "road map" for reaching short- and long-term goals. Don't get me wrong. I am not trying to predict the future, and I by no means know exactly what I want, but I have developed a general idea and use my knowledge as a guide.[7]

His work on sorting out what was important to him led to refining his sense of self, which in turn helped him refine priorities without being overdeterminative about what the future might hold. He was using this new knowledge about his mind and his identity in reframing relationships with others:

I find that I am constantly rebalancing my identity in relationship to others. With my parents' divorce two years ago and the purchase of my home, I am becoming a central figure in the extended family and have left behind my "youth"-oriented identity. At work, my identity continues to grow almost as fast as my personal identity. Since I began with the current crew 2 1/2 years ago, I have been titled asset manager, senior asset manager, assistant vice president, and now vice president. My identity within the group has changed very much. I owe this to my abilities in being aware of how my mind works and dealing with my personal set of realities.[8]

Evan was comfortable with his ever-growing responsibilities because he was able to refine his identity in these contexts. Evan's "personal set of realities" posed their own challenges; however, because he possessed this awareness of how his mind worked and who he was, he was able to work his way through both work and personal challenges. It was still difficult sometimes, particularly in a major difference Evan had with his wife:

> I find comfort in organizing things. My wife is the complete oppo-
> site. I'm at my wit's end with her sometimes because of her
> habits around the house. Everything I own, I know where it is at
> all times. Her car is a disgrace—it is an extension of her closet;
> my stuff is in my trunk in an Eddie Bauer bag in compartments.
> Every once in awhile it comes to a head; never gets resolved.
> Then other stuff occurs, and you stop focusing on it. I've learned
> that criticism doesn't help. I don't worry about it. We have our
> own rooms where we can go where the other isn't forbidden, but
> we keep our stuff there and respect that. That's one way of deal-
> ing with it. When it becomes a problem, it becomes a problem. It
> is not easy to be married. There's no way to describe how I han-
> dle it; I do what is most right or convenient at the moment. I'm
> more focused on myself than on partnership problems. I have
> enough to contend with during the day; personal stuff builds up
> in the week. I can't deal with it. Whatever happens, happens.[9]

At work, Evan reported that he either obsessed about a problem until he solved it or accepted that he couldn't change the situation. The latter seemed to be his sense of his and his wife's difference in organization. Despite this difference, she was a steady partner in his life at a time when other partners were dealing with their own diffi-culties. He also reported that he was backing away from his ten-dency toward perfection. Having experienced depression a couple of years earlier, he was worried that it might recur as he changed jobs, his parents divorced and sold their house, and he changed lifestyles. He was able to weather these transitions without a recur-rence of his depression, in part because of his change of perspective:

> More with personal stuff than with the job, I get the attitude that
> you do what you can. In the past, I always tried to keep things
> perfect. It is a waste of time. Expect things to go wrong, and you'll
> be better prepared. Things were going good for me—the power
> went to my head—I felt like I was in more control than I was.
> Now, I'm at the attitude of screw it, but I'm not irresponsible.[10]

Although Evan was willing to make some compromise in his drive for perfection, it didn't reduce his sense of responsibility. Evan had come to terms with what he could control and what was beyond his control. He took active responsibility for what he could control, yet he changed from expecting everything to be perfect to accepting things might go wrong. Knowing how his mind worked and refining his sense of himself gave him confidence to direct his life.

Self-Authorship: Building an Internal Foundation

As Evan continued to refine his work, his identity, and his priorities in his personal life, he reduced work to one part of his identity as opposed to allowing it to define it, as he had earlier. He explained:

> My work role doesn't define me. I take the train in every day, for three years now. Taking the train is a physical separation between work and personal life. I transform from one thing to the other: two separate lives. The train ride is 30 minutes—I sleep through some of it. I wake up a different person, transformed, my game face on, uniform, do what you got to do. When done, go back on the train, reverse transformation, and I'm out. I don't give it another thought. I never dream about work, never discuss it with my wife. I've come to enjoy the activities that define life as how I like to view it. I like work; I would keep working if I won the lottery. I like coming in and being involved. I shut it off, go do my thing. I still play hockey every week—as I've done for 27 years![11]

Evan had used his sense of priorities to put his work in perspective. These priorities also helped him set clear boundaries, which in turn allowed him to successfully balance professional and personal commitments. He still took work seriously, however:

> I give anything my best effort I can, whether I enjoy it or not. Once I get to my office, I take it seriously. Not so seriously where it stresses me. No point in that. When I was younger, I let it get to me. When I was inexperienced. No matter what, the sun always comes up the next day. Very rarely is my work a life-or-death situation. There was a time when I was depressed. I took a lot from that, use that as a guidepost. It was good to get it out of the way early! Now, let's get on with things.

Evan had learned how to frame work as an opportunity for building his knowledge and skills:

> I thought I was doing well last year, but I look back, and realize I knew so little. It continues that way each year. I'm glad; it is humbling. My dad used to tell me when I was a kid,

"There is always somebody bigger than you that will kick your butt." I keep that in mind. I try to improve what I already know, so I can move on to the next level. At the same time keeping prior responsibility, taking it with me, adding, building onto that.[12]

Evan was acquiring more and more responsibility, yet he seemed less pressured than he had been before, primarily due to the internal foundation he was building. Confident in himself and his ability to deal with things he could not control, he was taking on additional responsibility in his extended family:

I have accepted a role in my extended family, not the leader, but it seems to be getting to that. I'm not ready to start my own family with kids. That is not something that I want; not now, don't know if I ever want it. When the time comes, it will be like everything else. If the time comes, fine. I got married early enough; I learned not to rush into things. Not everybody in my family has a house, so people have functions here. That's thrown me. I am the oldest. My family split apart; my parents divorced. Dad isn't around. I've stepped up in that area. My grandmother passed away in December; my grandfather is still around, but they are no longer the "king and queen." With my grandmother gone, we've had to step up taking care of my grandfather. The rules are up for grabs. My brother is not around. I'm the hub of communication for things. I don't mind it.

Evan noted that he was still processing all these changes and still finding out how they affected him. He missed having his brother around as default company to hang out with and to feed his animals; however, his main concern was to maintain awareness of how all this was affecting him to make sure his depression did not return. These life changes, in the context of what he had learned about himself through his experience with depression and the refining of his identity, led Evan to commit to the outlook on life he had started to articulate a couple of years earlier:

Now, we just kind of accept these things; nothing ever stays the same. If you expect it, it is easier. A lot of things I am incredibly inflexible about. As far as other people and other things, I don't try to control. I've gradually gotten that way. The only way is to experience this and to see what happens when you don't take that route. The experience you accumulate can be painful but necessary. It adds to your repertoire of being able to deal with things in the future: been through it, lived, know what is coming next. It is less frightening, less mysterious.[13]

What Evan was actually adding to his repertoire was refining how he faced his personal realities, his identity, and his relations with others. He was solidifying his internal foundation to the point that he could deal with uncertainty.

In our twelfth interview, Evan volunteered another piece of information about the upheaval his extended family had undergone in recent years, which had no doubt contributed to his developing sense that things do go wrong:

> My dad is still in jail; I visit him once a month. The trial was two years ago. At first, it was a real drag; it costs me $300 a month to support him. That stinks. I'm really the only one that takes care of his business. My brother moved away and doesn't participate in it. Luckily, I make enough money that it doesn't affect me. He is appealing, so it will probably be a couple more years. I am not going to fund his appeal; I'll support him in other ways. I buy his cigarettes, but I told him I wouldn't throw money away on attorneys. I don't want to be in control of that. Nonproductive for me to be over involved. My parents divorced before that, so mom doesn't have to deal with it.[14]

Evan seemed surprised when I mentioned that he had never introduced this topic in our conversations during those years. It fell into the category of things he could not change, so he had accepted it and made the best of it.

Another event Evan accepted and made the best of was his wife's pregnancy. As he told the story, he made it sound as if it was totally his wife's doing:

> Pregnancy was not planned! If I had to plan it, it never would have happened! It's giving in a little bit to growing up; there's no going back after that! I take it seriously—once you are locked into something like that, that's it. I'm enjoying it. It took me a little bit of time to accept that this was happening— however right or wrong that may sound. Once I was able to come to terms with that, it really didn't affect my thinking that much—I already had a whole bunch of mouths to feed, so it was not that much of an adjustment. People who don't have animals might not grasp the concept of what I'm trying to say. It is not that far off from raising a puppy—on a schedule, responsibility for making sure a person is taken care of. It's a little bit more expensive! It was a matter of time for just

realizing there is no getting out of this. Eventually, in back of
my head, I guess, it was exciting. It was something that really
frightened me for a long time. I don't know why. It is such a
serious thing—being responsible for somebody forever. It was
different than getting married; if that was not right, you could
get out of it, if push came to shove. Only a semi-permanent
thing, realistically. Once this went into effect, you can't undo
it. Once a child is born, you are attached to another person
through the child. Permanence, responsibility, always played
a part in my willingness to go through with it. I knew if my
wife didn't just force me, I would never do it. I needed that
shove. She just did it—I don't ask, I don't even want to
know![15]

Once his wife provided this shove, Evan worked to come to terms
with it. His internal foundation helped him reconcile himself to this
new responsibility. Solidifying his internal foundation also helped
him accept how he differed from his wife and to appreciate their
relationship:

We still have a lot of differences. Yes, it used to cause a lot of
problems, but now it doesn't. We came close to calling it quits a
couple times, but not that close. She does her part, works hard.
I don't know too many other people who would put up with
hockey and my family. I am not the easiest person to live with.
We do our own things and don't get worked up about it.[16]

Evan did not ignore or avoid conflict. He knew himself well enough
to manage stress and work through conflict. "Not getting worked up
about it" was a major accomplishment for Evan during his twenties.

Self-Authorship: Securing Internal Commitments

By age thirty, Evan had become comfortable with himself. He was
confident he could live through new experiences and approached life
as a learning experience. He was increasingly aware of what he did
not know:

When you're a kid, you think you are developed, but you aren't.
At this age, you realize you aren't. Experience level helps you
to become comfortable with yourself—realize you have lived
through certain events and either have taken it on the chin or
given in, but you're still here and still going. You realize you
can live through certain things. . . . I open my mind to learn;
you never know what is coming down. I call it floating on the

waves. I kind of imagine myself in the water, a Cancerian thing to do, going with the direction of the ocean, going up and down with the waves, knowing that there are times at the top; other times the waves are above your head. I don't try to control it; it is impossible. Taking that into account allows me to relax and deal with things. You can't control things that happen to you, but there is no reason why I shouldn't control what I can. I'm not ashamed to organize. Why shouldn't your house look the way you want it?[17]

Floating on the waves was Evan's way of acknowledging that certain aspects of life were beyond his control. His internal foundation was strong enough that he could adjust to external circumstances and accept them. I was eager to hear how the floating-on-the-waves philosophy would play out in parenting. In our next interview, Evan reported that he was enjoying it so much that he tried to get out of work on time to get home. He felt that having a child had brought him and his wife closer, and he was satisfied that they were managing things successfully:

We may not have the biggest household, but there's a lot of stuff to manage and keep it running smoothly, and that's more my job than my wife's job. I can always find something to do. I mess around on the computer a lot, mostly just on different hobbies. And I can do that, or clean up, or play with my daughter, or play with my dog. There's always something tugging at my time. We've never sat down and officially divided our responsibilities, but we realize who's better at doing what and have leaned toward those responsibilities and let the other one do the chores that do not interest us.

Things were "running smoothly" at work, as well:

Because I've repeated the same processes over and over for the past twelve years, there's a lot of skills or knowledge that I've acquired that are second nature at this point. When I do have to take on a task that I might not have taken on before, or one that's more difficult, I can process it much quicker than I used to. My blood pressure doesn't rise up above normal. Not a lot of things frighten me anymore, and I'm very patient when it comes to taking on something new. There's nothing hidden behind the curtain that I don't understand. I know the pieces of the puzzle are there, and I have the skills necessary to deal with them. So, it's not as hard as it once was. Over the years, taking the train into the city, I geared up, and taking the train home, I let it go. I very rarely think about work when I'm not there. Very seldom do I find myself daydreaming about problem solving at work. Once I'm done, I shut it off. While I'm there, I give it 110%. Once I'm home, my mind is elsewhere.

With work and personal life going well, Evan was still as interested as ever in self-improvement and personal growth. Like everything else, he pursued it on his own terms:

I always joke with people that my brother and I are literally polar opposites. He is hooked on self-improvement books, tapes, videos, and you couldn't force me at gunpoint to watch that stuff. Not because I don't feel that I could use some self-improvement, but because I prefer to do it my way than to have somebody tell me how they did it themselves. I know how to rewind my gears and tighten my bolts. No one knows better than me, I might be lazy about doing it at times, but I eventually get there and deal with it myself. I feel very strongly about that type of quote unquote improvement. I know when I suck at something, or if I'm not pulling my weight at something. I have to look at myself in the mirror every day, and I do not stick my head in the sand when I have to deal with my shortcomings. But, I deal with it in my own way.

Evan was aware of his areas for improvement, did not ignore them, and felt he knew better than anyone else how to rewind his own gears. In response to my question about how he knew what his shortcomings were, he replied:

I think I'm my absolute meanest and worst critic. Anything that I do that is good, I still can manage to find fault with myself or something that I didn't do, or something that's not perfect, and while I don't necessarily strive for perfection, I'm a glass-is-half-empty kind of person. I can always do something better. I'm just not satisfied with anything that I ever do. I think it's absolute sin to be satisfied with where you are or what you do. I think that if you're not always trying to improve or do something better, then you're lost.

I was confused about how this notion of never being satisfied with oneself coexisted with Evan's notion of floating on the waves and not obsessing about things he could not control. He clarified:

Well, I look at them as two completely different things. One is negative, and one is positive. If I were to obsess on something like credit or how much money I owe, that's a negative.

I'm worrying about it; I'm wasting energy on it. Worrying does not solve the problem. So, rather than just freaking out about it, if I think about a way to improve upon it, and then that's a positive. For example, every time I referee a hockey game, I'm always trying to go for a perfect job. I know there's no such thing as a perfect job, but I try to do the best possible job that I can, and if I make a mistake, I can't let it affect me for the rest of the game. I've got to let it go; it happens. I will just take that mistake, learn from it, record that experience and try not to get put in that situation again, and just build upon that. Rather than obsess and worry about it, I just let it go. I will remember it, but I won't play it over and over in my head.

Evan clarified that he viewed the critic as a positive because he was always looking to do something better, but at the same time, he didn't beat himself up about mistakes. Evan's ability to rewind his gears and tighten his bolts as needed kept his life running smoothly. He saw his challenges as opportunities to grow. Evan did not fear uncertainty because he trusted his internal foundation to work through whatever came his way. He kept problematic experiences in perspective, as he did with his father's ongoing incarceration:

I never mention that to anybody, not that I'm embarrassed of it. It's just that I don't want to waste any type of energy on it. I visit probably once every other month. He's in year five now and, when you're in prison, time stands still. He works, he takes a lot of classes and works in the library and works on his case, but when he's talking about his appeal with me, I'm just like, (whistle) my mind goes somewhere else, and I'm nodding my head, but I'm not really listening. I don't give it any thought during the day unless he calls or I get something in the mail, then I toss it in a file box that I keep. I'll glance through it. I know it's kind of harsh to say, but it doesn't really interest me at all. I can't afford to waste money to contribute to an appeal. I've completely detached myself from it. I deal with it on a reactive basis. It's one of those things where I have absolutely no control over the outcome, and I can spin my wheels forever doing what he wants, but I have my own life and things to do that are much more productive and much more beneficial to my family than his incarceration.

I marveled at Evan's ability to take this situation in stride and stay focused on his own priorities. He commented on how he had grown in this regard during the previous ten years:

I've gotten considerably better at it as time's gone by. I can remember when I was twenty-one, twenty-two, I used to get really upset by things. If something went wrong, or something didn't go the way I wanted it, I wouldn't cry, but it would bother me. Now, it's wave it away and fly. Now, with a birth of a child and the experience of having dealt with problems in the past, problems are not as big to address. If something messes up, oh well, I'll fix it. Once it's happened, it's happened. You know the saying, don't cry over spilled milk. I live by that simplicity every day. I try to do what I can. If I can't get to it today, then that's too bad. I guess my motto would be the sun is still going to come up tomorrow; deal with it then. That's not to say that I put things aside and ignore them, not at all. It's just that if something occurs that is beyond my control I just change my method of attack and go on from there, or go to plan B.

The contrast between his perfectionist "superhero" approach of his early twenties and his floating-on-the-waves approach in his early thirties was striking. Trusting his internal foundation had become second nature to him. Because he was secure in his internal commitments, he was able to face the additional external challenges that arose in his life.

A month after our fifteenth interview, Evan was in his Manhattan office when planes hit the World Trade Center a few blocks away. Knowing he worked in Manhattan, I sent an e-mail to check in with him. He replied that he was safe, but that it felt like being in a movie, only it was really happening. In our annual interview a year later, we discussed his reaction:

Well, I wasn't too close to the Towers. I was right where I am as we speak, but I could see parts of it happening. It's not something that I would want to go through again. It took me a long time to get myself together after that day. For weeks afterwards, I ran through it in my head and was constantly thinking of ways to be prepared in case something else happened, and what I had to do at work and at my house so that I didn't get caught in a situation like that again. And it took its toll. I wasn't scared to come to work, but now I keep a backpack with a change of clothes and sneakers here, emergency supplies in case I have to walk home from work. But it was pretty stressful. It took quite a while to find out who I knew that got killed, and I was still finding out more people months and months later. No one in my immediate family got killed, but a lot of acquaintances that I knew through hockey, or husbands or wives or daughters or brothers of people that I'm friends with died. I wound up working in one fundraiser as a referee for a local adult hockey team that I ref games for. They lost three guys. That was pretty sad. But even as late as six or seven months afterwards, I was still learning of people that got killed that I kind of knew or I didn't realize that I knew right away. So, it's pretty tough.

I asked Evan how this event had affected him. He replied:

It's a pretty radical change of the view on the world when you go through an event like that. You definitely rearrange your priorities. Most people are somewhat over it, but around New York, it's still a pretty sore subject. I was building a philosophy before 9/11, but that kind of solidified my thinking on a lot of different things, and a lot of things become less important after that. I don't quite take so much as seriously, and, on the other hand, I don't take a lot for granted anymore either. I appreciate a lot more things now, not that I didn't before, but I place a higher value on certain things as opposed to others. I had discovered that path before this, so it wasn't that much of a radical change, but uh (long pause) it did, for a few weeks, it did really shake me up. I actually came down to work the next day. I came down just to see what was going on in the streets and clean up my office. What else was I going to do? Sit home and watch them replay it on the TV minute by minute? So, it wasn't like I was scared to go on living or doing anything, but I was shook up, though, for sure.

Evan's strong sense of himself and his priorities helped him cope with this tragedy. Because he had, for some time, been identifying his priorities, this solidified his thinking rather than changing it radically. Yet, he allowed himself to experience the sadness of losing friends and colleagues and recognized that it did affect him. An avid reader, Evan reported that he normally read a thousand pages a month, but after 9/11, he could not concentrate to read for eight months. He allowed himself time to process his emotions.

In the midst of this time, Evan's younger brother had a heart attack at age thirty-two. Evan's ability to float on the waves helped him work through this experience, as he explained:

He had some kind of blood condition that caused a blockage in his arteries. They had to rush him in to surgery and do an angioplasty. You should have seen the way everybody was on my case. "Oh, you have to go in right away." I was like, "Okay, everyone relax. I am fine. You will find out that I am fine, trust me." I didn't think of it as being a big deal because he lived, and I knew he would be fine. It scared my mom, and my wife was all over me. He had the heart attack on Wednesday, and the previous Sunday, we had refereed three games in a row, so we were on the ice for 6 ½ hours straight, and he was fine. I don't even think he was out of breath. We were joking around.

Evan saw no point in getting worked up about this because his brother survived. He did go for tests, and they confirmed that he did not share his brother's condition.

Refereeing hockey, something Evan and his brother often did together, was a mainstay in Evan's life at this point and had been a thread in his life for a long time. It started at his first college when, after having been in a couple of fights, he became a referee to avoid being suspended. He continued after transferring colleges but recognized that he did not have the maturity for it. After being out of it for ten years, he was invited to do it again, accepted, and "quickly rose through the ranks." Evan recognized now that his maturity was a major factor in his success:

> I very rarely have problems, like somebody getting on me for a call that I made. I know what's a right call and what's not a right call, and I also know when somebody's being a jerk because they're angry that their team is losing or if I really messed up. And I'm not perfect, but I try to keep my mistakes small. I'm pretty conscientious about calling a good game because I'm a fan as well, so I don't want to see a bad game. I have a pretty good attitude when I'm out there. I basically let the teams play, and then I adjust the game when necessary. It's more about them playing and having a good time. It's not about me showing up, being the ref, or being the center of attention. I take a position where I'm there to manage the game, rather than necessarily control it. I'm there to make sure it runs smoothly and that everybody enjoys themselves, and no one gets hurt. I think that's a better way to look at things. There are times when I have to hand out some heavy punishment but it's a last resort, and I try not to be heavy handed. So, I've gotten to do some pretty fun games and meet a lot of nice people, and I enjoy it. Most of the time, I get paid for it. I'm just trying to take it as far as it'll go, which is pretty much college. But I want to keep moving up the ranks a little more if I can.

Because Evan was clear on his identity and his priorities, he was able to establish his role as referee in a way that was consistent with his values and yet worked for the players and fans. He attributed part of his success in hockey to his ability to maintain an even keel, yet he also felt he had gained some of that ability through refereeing. He did move up the ranks:

> That is part of the reason that I have excelled so rapidly. I mean it was meteoric, to go from never having done it to *sshhtt,* I mean I tore through the ranks around here, right through the roof. There are hundreds of guys that are better than me, but for around here and my age and my experience level, it was good. When you're refereeing, it's very important to be impartial and calm because the calmness is infectious to others, and you're in a very unique situation where you could go from a game where the two teams are just going through the motions to two teams and fans, parents, and factions that are very emotional and very intense. And you're not the focus of that intensity, but you're in between it, and it's a valuable tool to have, to keep things under control. When I am dealing with people that are emotional or highly charged, it's been very helpful.

Evan was able to function successfully as a buffer for other people's intensity because he was clear on his role as referee, confident that he knew how to do it well, and able to remain calm under any circumstance.

In the course of conversation about highlights of the year, Evan shared that his wife bought him another dog as a tenth wedding anniversary present. Evan had come to appreciate marriage over the years:

> The more I think about marriage, the more it suits me, you know? I'm comfortable in the family setting. I got a good thing going, and I get to develop a lot of the things that I enjoy, where if I was single, I might not be able to do that. I have my house, my dogs, and my daughter. I get to do a lot of different things, and that makes me happy.

Evan was satisfied with most aspects of his life; however, the company he had been with for fourteen years was experiencing some difficulty, and he had considered leaving. An opportunity arose, and he pursued it:

> I left in February of last year, so 2003, and the new job was a perfect fit. They got about 2,000 résumés. I got right to the

front of the line and got right in there. The other company was floundering, and I just had it with the owners. I just wanted a change of scenery, plus I wanted to get out of Manhattan. This job is a lot better. I get paid more. It's a little bit bigger company people-wise, but still small relatively speaking. There are maybe fifteen or twenty people that work there. Much larger, asset-wise. We have about 200 small properties, as opposed to the twelve big properties at the old firm. It is the same type of work and a much easier commute. I'm in the car, and fifteen minutes later I'm at work. It's a very orderly, upscale place, and I don't have to get dressed up. It's very casual. So it's a much, much, cooler place to be.

I asked if Evan felt compelled to change jobs. He reported that he was just ready:

They weren't pushing me out the door by any means. If anything had happened down there, I would have been the last one to turn out the lights, and I never gave them a reason to get rid of me; I did too much for them. No one's indispensable, but I don't make waves. I'd been with them long enough, and they weren't heading in a direction that was very stable. There were two partners, and they fought constantly, and the money situation wasn't good and just being in Manhattan . . . I'd had enough of the train and working downtown. So, I actually wasn't looking to move very hard, but Kristy pulled the job description off of Monster.com on a Monday, and the next morning I just shot my résumé in and got a call . . . that was Tuesday. I had an interview by Wednesday.

Initially this change sounded somewhat spontaneous; however, it is clear that Evan's partners were going in a direction than he questioned, and a number of aspects of the job no longer were consistent with his priorities. One of his professional priorities was to move out of leasing, which the new position allowed:

I concentrate more on construction and the management side, which is the direction that I wanted to go in. It's much less glory in the management department because we only spend money and fix problems rather than bring in new deals and make the money. But that's okay. I don't need recognition. I'm happy to work behind the scenes. I like taking care of things, and this is exactly what I like doing.

When he started in commercial real estate, Evan prided himself on bringing in the money through leasing. Now that he had a solid internal identity of which his career only played a part, he was happy to work behind the scenes. It allowed him to do what he did best: organize and take care of things. Despite moving to a new company and accepting new responsibilities after working at the same company for his entire career, Evan felt settled:

> My life is very stable. . . . The only challenges that I really find myself encountering are ones that I seek out. I don't, knock on wood, have very much hardship, but maybe a combination of part luck and part skill. The types of challenges that I have I consider fortunate challenges. We've been in this house for eight years, and one of our upcoming challenges is to find a bigger house. I am very cognizant of people that don't even have a chance to get a house . . . it's so expensive. The price that we paid for the house that we live in now, you can't even get a co-op in an apartment building for. I've been fortunate in that regard. A lot of the challenges that I've faced in the past few years I've overcome, so now, it's very stable and more concentrating on building on the base that I've created. And that's the way I like it. I've always been that way. I'm lucky in that regard. I found my niche a while ago and stuck to it and found it works.

Evan's comment sparked a conversation about the meaning of his building on the base he had created. It concerned a recurrent thread throughout our interviews about him always trying to learn something new, hone some skill, or figure something out. In response to my question about whether this approach is how he built this base, he said:

> Yes, exactly. The challenges that I face at work, I don't even consider them challenges at this point because it's just learning new things and increasing my capabilities in areas where I have already learned basic skills. I don't even think about it as challenging myself anymore because it's just so natural. A couple of philosophies that I've taken to heart over the years when facing challenges . . . if one person can do it, you can, too. You can learn anything if you just take the time and focus and you want to learn it. I don't think that there's anything that I could not do. It's just a matter of time and somebody to explain it or help me. Some of the stuff that I've done in hockey I'm like, "Why can't I do that?" No one dies doing it . . . you may not feel that comfortable at first, but you hold on. You do it as well as you can. And if other people have survived, you sure can, too, and that's what I think has

enabled me to excel. Also my ability to remain even-tempered. I don't think that I am difficult to work with or be around. I like to keep things on an even keel and go with the flow. I definitely think that's helped me. And, as I've said before . . . consistency. (Laughs) If I am one thing, it's very consistent.

Learning new skills and increasing his capacities were so ingrained in Evan's approach to life that they were just natural parts of his existence. His internal foundation had become deep and broad enough to allow him to routinely take risks, ask for help, and work through the discomfort of learning new things. The combination of his confidence that he could do anything he invested in and his ability to float on the waves made challenges appear routine rather than major issues. I observed that he didn't get worked up about much of anything anymore. He replied:

Exactly. My blood pressure does not ever go up, which is a good thing. It's very hard to get me worked up, and my actions and behavior may appear effortless and at times it is, but it's an art form. I really do work on trying to be like that, and I think about it. I make an effort about it. I'm aware of it. And I don't go around preaching to people or try to be Tony Robbins and teach people self-improvement. Rather than rely on what's worked for other people, I've kept to what's worked for me. I don't try to force that on others, but I keep what I think is worthy and useful, and I don't dwell on things that are not helpful or useful or unimportant. I've got enough things to think about, so I don't dwell upon those types of things. I do work at it.

Thus, although growth and pursuing growth opportunities had become natural for Evan, he still worked at it. He consciously thought about what worked for him and incorporated it to build upon the base he had created for himself. He also found growth opportunities in refereeing hockey:

The reffing has taught me some very helpful lessons, too. I went to school for hockey at the Olympic Training Center in Lake Placid. That was the first time I was back in class in I can't remember how long, and it was very intensive. It was unexpected because I thought it would be more about hockey and less about life, and it was more about teaching others and expressing yourself to students and public speaking. So, it was a good lesson in those areas.

Although Evan always sought to grow in his role as a referee, his advancement surprised him:

> Advancing in refereeing, this will only be my sixth year, but that's continued to grow, much to my amazement. I really thought that the farthest I would go would be to do high school teams, which I was perfectly happy to do. Every year, I've had more opportunity to advance in that, which has been shocking to me because I thought I was too old to move on. The first big area was to move into doing college level games, which I did not actively pursue. It just kind of came to me, so I went with it, and this'll be my third year in that. And they've increased my schedule each year, doing men and women's hockey.

Because learning was a natural part of Evan's identity, the lines between his professional work, hockey, and personal life were blurred. He reported that he applied the public speaking instruction from the Olympic Training School to doing a humorous "shtick" as the best man at his brother's wedding. He noted: "It was like my own little HBO Special. I destroyed the crowd! It was like being a rock star." Evan also integrated lessons from hockey into his approach to parenting. He enrolled his daughter in a full-year hockey clinic, but he also enrolled her in ballet to help with balance and movement. Hockey was an arena where Evan could continue to build on his capacities and implement his parenting philosophy simultaneously. In our twentieth interview, he shared:

> I still learn. I still look for things to improve upon. I went to skating instruction over the summer just to work on my skating. People raise their eyebrows when they hear me say that. I tell them that even professionals have to work at it. I went to a camp with Kerry as well. I still read up and try to improve my performance as much as possible because it moves me to the next level. I never stop trying to improve. What's the point of doing something if you're not going to try to get better at it? I do not advocate complacency. I limit myself though. I have my hand involved in a lot of different things, but I'll focus on things that I can do really well.

Taking skating instruction after thirty-plus years on the ice and refereeing an average of six games a week captured Evan's commitment to improvement. He also took up scuba diving and kayaked across Long Island Sound. Explaining why he took on these pursuits, he said:

I just dream these things up to see if I can really do them. Also, Kerry likes it, too. If I do it for anybody, it's for Kerry, to show her you can do this. When we were in Galapagos, we had a kayak on the boat. The two spots where we could kayak, the captain was going out on the kayak and Kerry's like, "Can I go with you?" And he was like, "Yeah," and he was shocked. Kerry could paddle with him and he was psyched that an eight-year-old is holding her own. So, it seems to be working, doing what I want it to do.

It was no accident that Evan was involving Kerry in his quests for conquering new challenges. It was part of his parenting philosophy. When I asked what he hoped to accomplish, he said:

I just want her to be a good person and be well adjusted and well rounded. I don't set a lot of rules for her. She goes to bed when she wants, so the rules I set are: Do your homework. Go to practice. You make a commitment, you keep it. You're respectful to everybody, and you're well mannered, and we'll have no problems. I explained, "A lot of these things that you get, other little kids don't get, and they can disappear real fast." And she knows that. I never get calls from school, and I don't have problems that a lot of the other parents have that protect their kids too much. I let her do a lot of stuff that other kids her age don't do, and I think that prepares her better than other little kids. And you can tell. I mean she doesn't carry herself like most of the kids in her grade. There are still kids that are kind of babyish, and I think that's all gone with her. But she's still a kid. I don't force her to grow up anymore. I just want her to be more prepared.

Evan took Kerry to games he was refereeing and allowed her to sit in the stands by herself at high school games. Evan was pleased that Kerry liked hockey, although they did other things together as well, such as an annual camping trip at the Bronx Zoo. Evan and his wife were, in his opinion, 95% on the same page about their parenting philosophy. They included Kerry in every aspect of their lives and did not hide reality from her. As Evan reported, she was aware of the war and some of its implications:

She asked me if I was going into the Army, and I said, "No." I asked her, "Why?" She said, "I don't want you to." I hadn't thought about that. Some of the guys that work hockey with me are in the military, and some of them leave for overseas. But little kids are definitely more aware than you think. We have to go about work during the day, but they're talking about current events in school, and especially around here, the kids are more aware because every September we have to deal with 9/11. And Kerry's been to Kristy's office, and Kristy's office overlooks the hole at Ground Zero. I haven't been down there. I have no urge to go down and look at the hole. I was down there when it happened. As each year goes by, we unfortunately grow hardened to it. I mean there are kids that I still referee that lost parents, especially locally here. But kids . . . they're definitely aware.

Although Evan and Kristy agreed that they should allow Kerry to be aware of harsh realities such as war, they differed in opinion on more minor points, such as the importance of being organized. Evan described the status of the ongoing issue of organization:

I get home, and these guys are a mess. The girls do not keep the house. What's that old tale where the ants stock up for the winter and then the grasshopper has no food? That's them—no preparation whatsoever. So, I have to get Kerry set for the next day. I take care of my chores; do whatever I have to do; take care of the dogs. It's an assembly line to get out in the morning, so I just try to get everything done in advance. Kerry's got practice once or twice a week. I'm playing on a team this winter for the first time in a few years. I've got a game once a week during the week, so when I finally sit down, it's nine or ten o'clock. I think, can I possibly squeeze in one more thing tonight?

I asked Evan if he thrived on this kind of pace. As is evident in his reply, it was a component of his penchant for keeping everything running smoothly and taking advantage of opportunities:

I wouldn't say that I thrive on it. I don't need to have it. A lot of the time, I'm just trying to squeeze everything in. Some stuff gets sacrificed along the way, but it's not like I'm an action junkie, no. I can take it easy, too, with the best of them. But I don't like to waste time, that's for sure. There's too much stuff that's fun to do.

Evan continued to take life in stride, including losing some important partners in his life:

My grandfather died last year. The same summer, my referee and chief mentor died. So, two World War II–era guys that I talked to pretty much every day, or every couple days, were gone pretty quickly. I still go to dial them on my phone. My referee mentor, all last year his specter hung over the rink. Horton was at all my big games, and I was used to looking at certain spots and seeing him there, and it was difficult to do. Not having him at the rink or not having my grandfather to call . . . it's like all of a sudden, boom, that's it. [My grandfather] was pretty involved with Kerry. At least he got to see Kerry play a couple times, and he lived a full life, so I'm not sad for him, but it was difficult.

When I asked Evan how he was dealing with these losses, he reflected:

I don't think you have a choice. You have to move on. The tough parts were when hockey season started back up again because usually I'm always on the phone with . . . Horton was the guy that passed away. And I'm on the phone with him constantly because of scheduling. With my grandfather it's just more routine . . . come to the games or talk to him about whatever. I was sad. Guys like that you can't really replace. I had kind of outgrown them for advice or assistance, but as far as like enjoying having them around, that was different. So, it was a difficult habit to break for sure. And I still . . . when I have long trips now, and I'm riding home, and it's like man, I wish I could call my grandfather.

Evan's approach to accepting things he could not control continued to serve him well. He maintained his philosophies of always learning and not getting worked up in his workplace. About work, he said:

I enjoy work, but I leave it at work. I've been at it since 1989, so I'm not changing careers anytime soon. I'm kind of tagged in what I'm doing, but the guys that I work with are pretty cool. I work hard while I'm there, but when I leave, they let me do my own thing, so that's pretty important. I still work on new and different things all the time and try to perfect working on them, so in real estate that's the good thing. Something new always comes up, so whatever angles you think you have covered, whatever deal you're working on will find some way to get screwed up that you completely did not imagine at all. There are too many moving pieces to the puzzle, so it never works out the way you really want it to (laughing), and that's fine. That keeps it interesting. I work on over a hundred properties. So, in any given day, I could be working on twenty-five, thirty different files. I only have a finite amount of time to get certain things done, so what I try to do is move each one along a little bit at a time each day, so that they all move along and stay active, and then on days when I have to devote more attention to one, I prioritize that and take care of what I have to. But, in the meantime, I stop trying to make something completely perfect. Accept the fact that this is what I think it'll take to get it done, and then if something comes up, I just deal with it.

Multi-tasking was not an issue for Evan. Keeping up with the moving pieces provided him the challenge he enjoyed, and his attitude of doing as well as he could kept him from overinvesting in work. He not only believed but also enacted the philosophy he had crafted years earlier: "It's futile to try to control every aspect of anything, whether it's work or your life. You have to just roll with it." He still felt he was improving this capacity, often through hockey:

Refereeing . . . there are a lot of good byproducts to that for work and a lot of other situations. You just learn to deal with it, and you learn patience. You learn dealing with people. You learn how to make decisions quickly. You learn how to treat people. You have to hold yourself to a higher standard than everyone else because you're in charge. I definitely think it's helped me at work. Whether it's something like holding my tongue if somebody says something or just dealing with a higher pressure situation, I definitely have developed those types of skills as a byproduct. At the level that I work at, the games are tremendously difficult most of the time. I have to focus on a second-by-second basis a lot of times because there are a lot of things going on, and there's a lot that I'm responsible for. I just try to do my best, stay focused, be fair, and hopefully I'm in position, make all my calls and nothing controversial happens, and I'm happy. I think I've done my job well if no one knows I was there or no one knows my name.

As long as Evan lived up to his own expectations, he was satisfied. All of the aspects of his life had become seamlessly intertwined and all stood squarely on his internal foundation.

Evan's Story Line

Work and marriage fell into place for Evan in his early twenties without much ado. As he pursued his zeal for learning and doing everything to the best of his ability, he found himself burnt out. Working through his depression with the help of a counselor helped Evan start to identify his priorities and move through the crossroads. He listened to his own voice in deciding what was important

in his life, and in doing so, began to reconsider his perfectionist ten-
dencies. Becoming aware that perfectionism had contributed to his
burnout, Evan began to reshape his world by categorizing situations
into things he could control and things he could not. Listening to
and cultivating his internal voice led him to an awareness of how
his mind worked, a refined sense of self, and an adult identity in his
extended family and work community. This helped him succeed at
work without undue stress. He was also able to accept differences
between himself and his wife and come to appreciate the stability
marriage provided. Numerous stressful family events that were
beyond his control occurred in his mid-twenties, yet Evan honed his
ability to accept these events in order to maintain his mental
health. The internal foundation he was building grounded him, as
he chose how to respond to these external situations.

　　Evan's thirties were more settled than his twenties, although
challenges still arose. Evan's commitment to reflection and work at
self-improvement yielded an internal foundation that allowed him
to ride the waves of his life. As he settled into his core sense of self,
he also settled into his work, his marriage, and parenthood. He
learned that he could live through trying experiences, continue
growing, and excel at anything he put his mind to. Securing his
internal commitments, he took reality as it came, chose how to focus
his attention and energy, and elevated not getting worked up to an
art form. He prioritized personal life over work, although he enjoyed
continued success at work because he took it seriously. It became
second nature to the point that he enjoyed the challenges and did
not get worked up about things going wrong. He enjoyed fatherhood
and found reward in involving his daughter in activities he had
enjoyed as a child. He became increasingly involved in hockey, taking up refereeing instead of coaching as he had done in his twenties.
Hockey offered a combination of personal enjoyment (he had played
hockey since early childhood), the challenge of self-improvement,
and an activity he could share with his daughter. Evan also used it
to refine his human relations skills and apply what he learned in
other arenas of his life. He was able to shape his life to his liking
because he finally had a clear vision of what that entailed. The
wisdom he achieved in his thirties grounded his personal and
professional life and allowed him to float on the waves.

CHAPTER 8

HOW TO BE GOOD
COMPANY FOR YOUR
OWN JOURNEY

THE CHALLENGES OF ADULT LIFE ARISE whether you are ready for them or not. The degree of support you have, either within yourself or from others around you, plays a significant role in your ability to face and work through these challenges. All of us become overwhelmed when our challenges far outweigh our support systems. We also become complacent when our support systems outweigh our challenges. When we are challenged, yet have sufficient support to face our challenges, we are able to grow and reframe our beliefs, identities, and relationships in more complex ways. Having an appropriate balance of challenge and support improved the project participants' capacity for trusting their internal voices and building an internal foundation, which in turn led to their ability to successfully navigate their roles and responsibilities as adults. Although challenges were often all too easy to find, support was far less prevalent. This chapter examines the challenges and supports that participants encountered to portray what good company for the journey to and through self-authorship might look like. I look at those aspects of participants' stories that demonstrate how they became good company for themselves, so that you can consider ways to support yourself in this journey.

KEY EXPERIENCES THAT SUPPORT DEVELOPMENT
OF SELF-AUTHORSHIP: PAIN, PERSPECTIVE,
AND PARTNERSHIPS

Despite their varied life experiences, the participants in my study reported a combination of three experiences that prompted the development of their self-authorship:

- Some kind of "pain" or experience of cognitive dissonance that prompted them to reevaluate their lives or beliefs,
- Gaining perspective on the cause of the pain through this reevaluation, and
- Having good partners (or internal support) for thinking through their issues.

These three experiences occurred throughout the journey—at all the phases, whether at the point of beginning to question external formulas, navigating the crossroads, or developing self-authorship.

Although the challenges the study participants faced varied in form and intensity, they all caused enough discomfort to prompt participants to take responsibility for reexamining their beliefs, identities, and relationships. Mark described what prompted his accepting personal responsibility for his beliefs, identity, and relationships:

> You learn it from just being at a point of great pain and trying to solve the pain. I think that is where most people learn their greatest lessons—through some kind of pain. The lesson is made much more real and brought home, and it's one you don't forget. I think you can learn through quieter pain, and that would be an example of attaining a goal you thought would be an end-all and be-all. And then when you get there, it doesn't bring you the kind of satisfaction you thought it would. Or the satisfaction it does bring you is ultimately pretty empty.

In Mark's case, this quiet pain came from realizing that his success at law school, and again later as a practicing attorney, ultimately felt empty. Sandra experienced great pain in the form of stress in her professional work, despite her success as a social worker. Genesse experienced this pain because she could not find meaningful work roles. As I recounted in chapter 1, pain came in numerous contexts: making career choices, dealing with workplace issues, balancing work and personal life, grappling with relationship issues, parenting, and coping with major health crises. Regardless of the nature of the pain, most participants concluded that resolution lay within them.

How do you face this pain? How do you work through it effectively to develop your internal voice and foundation? The stories here reveal a multitude of approaches. Dawn turned inward to self-reflection to face her multiple sclerosis (MS). Mark actively sought written and human resources to reconsider his purpose in life. Kurt worked at using his power of choice to make himself happy. Sandra prayed and conducted extensive research on less stressful careers to live out her call to serve. Lydia and Evan adopted the perspective that everything is a learning experience for dealing with the unexpected upheavals in their lives. Participants engaged in counseling, talked with friends, and used self-reflection to gain perspective on their lives. They engaged in new experiences to explore their values and identities, and some used faith to handle crises in their lives. Different approaches and perspectives worked for different participants. The common thread of these approaches and perspectives, however, was that participants felt the necessity to sort issues out for themselves (although not necessarily *by* themselves; more on this in a moment). Additional stories presented in this chapter explore how participants blended their personal characteristics and their circumstances to gain perspective to be good company for themselves.

As I noted, sorting out how to know, who to be, and how to relate to others does not need to occur in isolation. Good partners are a crucial form of support in facing the challenges of adult life. Kurt and Sandra found good partners in their supervisors. Lydia and Mark found good partners in their spouses. Dawn and Evan found good partners in their therapists. Participants also found good partners in their parents, friends, educators, and community leaders. Chapter 9 includes additional stories that highlight the key characteristics of good partnerships. Recognizing, however, that good partnerships are not always readily available, I turn now to stories about how to be your own good partner.

SUPPORTING YOURSELF

One of the significant challenges of adult life is taking over responsibility for your life from those who guided you to the threshold of adulthood. Initially, this involves managing daily tasks, establishing financial responsibility, living and working independently, or even starting one's own family. Whether the process is smooth or rocky, eventually, the expectation for you to be "in charge" of your life extends beyond the functions themselves to the essence of who you are. Recognizing the value of your internal voice, and learning to trust it to build an internal foundation for your life, is a crucial aspect of moving toward authoring your life. In turn, trusting your voice enables you to build authentic relations with others. Listening to their internal voices helped participants gain perspective on their experiences and enabled them to take charge of their lives.

Lynn's Story: A Change of Perspective

Lynn's initial years after college were a struggle. Unable to land a full-time teaching job after three years of substitute teaching, she reported feeling like a bull waiting for the rodeo gate to open. When it finally did open, she tried to be "super teacher" to show that she could do the job. She ended up exhausted and aware that she needed to "do something to make me happy instead of doing everything for everyone else."[1] Despite her good intentions, circumstances continued to contribute to her unhappiness. Her teaching positions were challenging because of the deprivations the children faced. She reported crying many nights over her sadness at their life circumstances. Each time Lynn settled into a teaching assignment, she faced changing building or grade, or the principal with whom she worked well left. Even after acquiring full-time teaching positions, her work remained a source of stress. In addition, over the course of her twenties, she became increasingly frustrated about not finding a mate. In her late twenties, she reported realizing she needed to adopt a positive attitude. Doing so was difficult. Her increasing misery led her to a turning point:

> It was probably around my thirtieth birthday that I made the big transition as far as what I had to do. That was the year that I quit my other job, took the year, and did what I had to do for me and step away from the classroom. And it was really a big turning time in my life, and it was needed. I was not happy in anything that I was doing. I was not happy in my work. I was not happy in my social life. I was not happy with myself, and it just got to the point of being 100% miserable and saying, okay, I need a change. I need to get it together. It's going to kill me. I was unhealthy. I was not treating my body right, not treating

my brain right, and I knew I was sinking in a hole. I don't know what did it. I just remember sitting down at one point with my parents and saying: "I don't know what to do with myself. I don't like my teaching job. What else can I do?" I went through every profession that I could think of. What can I do to make myself happy? I thought it was all work. But once I stepped away from work and reflected on myself and found out . . . work was part of it, but it wasn't the whole picture, that I had that time away to reflect and have a lot of alone time and figure myself out. I forgot who I was, and I wasn't the bad person I thought I was, and I wasn't the miserable person. I found the good in me, and it came out. I got my act together. I don't know how I did it, but I did, and I'm happy, so I'm pretty content in my life right now and pleased with where it's going. It's been a good year, so I'm just kind of going with the flow. I think it was consuming me, and I was miserable. And I just got to the point of you're either going to lead a miserable life and be an unhappy person and you're not going to have friends or a significant other, or you can go the other way and say it's okay. It's not going to kill you. It's not going to be detrimental that you don't do everything all the time perfectly. So I chose that path.

Lynn allowed the rejections she encountered in her job search and the struggles in her teaching contexts to erode confidence in herself. As she became increasingly miserable, she became increasingly negative. It was not until she stopped teaching and worked in adventure and outdoor education for a year that she had the opportunity to reflect on who she was and recover herself. She enjoyed teaching in this environment, spent significant time alone reflecting on who she was, and talked at length with friends about her concerns. Her parents and friends served as good partners by respecting her thoughts and feelings and helping her sort through her experiences. Being in a positive environment helped her realize that she was not a failure and that she could change the course of her life by making positive choices. Once she brought out the positive in herself, she was able to adopt a new perspective that changed her outlook on the challenges in her life. Trusting her internal voice supported this new perspective. By her mid-thirties, she reported:

I am quite a different person than I was a few years ago. You just have to face the facts that you can't control the world, and it took me a long time to be okay with that. I used to feel like I had to be in control of everything in my life, and it just didn't work. And it made me crazy. You just have to sit back and roll with it, and I happily have learned to do that. Sure, I get upset about things, but then you just have to get over it. Who knows where anything is going to go? I just resign myself to that realization. If I'm single, I'm single. It wasn't where I thought I'd be at thirty-five. It's lonely sometimes. But I'm content. You have to come to the realization and deal with it, or you're going to be miserable and out there looking for "the man." And that's not me. I just have become, over the years, a strong and independent woman that I don't feel that need that at twenty-one, twenty-two, twenty-three, twenty-four I thought was so important. Because that's what society tells you is important. You need to get married. You need to have babies. Not my gig. Not to say that it won't become something in the future. But I'm okay with it now.

The complexity of work and personal life demanded that Lynn find a new way to think about herself and her life. She had learned how to focus on the positive aspects of her personal circumstances rather than hope for something else. I asked Lynn if she could remember the point at which she shifted from focusing on what society wanted from her to what she wanted for herself. She replied:

I knew you'd ask that. I would have to say right around my thirtieth birthday. Turning thirty was rough. I think the older you get and the more alone time you have, the more you figure out one way or the other, that you're okay with it or you're not okay with it. I kept people at arm's length for a long time. Let me feel the waters and see if I can trust you to let you in. Just becoming more confident in myself was a big thing, too. Growing up and facing the real world, so to speak. I'm trying to stay positive and live my life. Live life to the fullest and what happens, happens. You can't really control it. I'm trying to live by that motto of you've just got to live for the day. And that's been the last couple years.

Lynn's increased confidence in her own voice enabled her to build her internal foundation. Her foundation was based on accepting herself, accepting that she could not control external circumstances, and choosing opportunities to keep her life positive. This foundation kept her going when external circumstances did not go the way she desired. In her late thirties, the downsizing that occurred at her school meant changing grade again. While not thrilled about this, she took it in stride. She noted that other people had greater problems than those she faced, and refused to revert to negative thinking.

Although she had some partners along the way, she had learned to be good company for herself to sustain her positive outlook.

Heather's Story: Facing Fears

Heather's life in her twenties had all the markings of success. She succeeded in her business career, married, and reported that she knew herself and was in control of her life. She devoted considerable energy to helping others—her parents who were going through a divorce, a "little sister" she met through volunteer work who was experiencing major problems, and a biological sister who was also encountering major life problems. In the midst of trying to help her family, Heather discovered that she was "externally driven by a weird force telling me to live up to what I thought was right."[2] Faced with figuring out how she felt and what she wanted, Heather reported having no idea. As she began to work through how she felt and what she wanted, her emerging internal voice began to question her marriage, which she described as the merger of two externally defined people. Heather worked with a counselor to define and trust her feelings and salvage her marriage. At age thirty, Heather reported a bout with depression and a period of separation from her husband. Although she came out of the depression and reunited with her husband, they continued to struggle because her husband wanted everything to get back to where it had been before, and she felt that, "having gone through so much change, that just didn't fit for me." Then things became increasingly complicated:

> I thought that I had gotten myself squared around and had my relationship back on track. We got pregnant that fall. Things were going a little rocky for us. The emotion of my first trimester took me back toward depression. I was not getting any support from my husband, but I was still committed to the relationship . . . obviously, I was pregnant. [Then] another relationship entered my life, and the culmination of that was that I really had to face how much I'd been lying to myself about the state of my marriage. The time I separated from my husband earlier and all of the counseling I'd done around my marriage as far as trying to make it work, trying to figure out if I should be there, I never really let myself fully face my fears and fully be honest about where I was. And that [new] relationship really forced me to do that because I felt things

for this person that I knew I'd never felt for my husband, and so I really had to question my marital relationship. And so I pulled back from that [new] relationship and reevaluated everything.

For Heather, the new relationship created enough discomfort, or pain, to prompt her to spend time deeply examining her internal desires and emotions. Her process of questioning and reevaluating her marital relationship and other aspects of her life led her to the following conclusion:

I'd been lying to myself about whether my marriage was successful and I had a lot of fears to face. I wrote down twelve fears that were keeping me in my marriage, the point being even though I thought I'd tried to conquer a lot of that internal/external stuff with what my sisters went through, I still was not giving myself permission to leave my marriage. Now that I've done that, [it] has been the last thing moved to reconquer my life. That's why I never got there. That's why I wasn't there the last time I talked to you because even though I had grown [and] I had come to realize a lot of things, I still would not permit myself to leave my marriage. I would not permit myself that failure. So it's been a real interesting ride for me because I ended up leaving my marriage when I was four months pregnant, which is kind of a bizarre thing. People kind of look at you and say, "Why the hell couldn't you have figured it out before then?" I don't really have anything better than a shoulder shrug for them. So it's been rough.

Despite all her work in counseling, Heather had been lying to herself because she could not allow herself to fail at marriage. Once she articulated the fears that were keeping her in the marriage, she realized that to author her life, she had to face those fears and construct her own internal sense of what marriage meant. Fortunately, her counselor remained a supportive partner by respecting Heather's thoughts and feelings and helping her sort through them as they evolved. Trusting her internal voice and acting on it was difficult, as she explained:

I lost most of my friends. People definitely with a child think you're wrong, so even though inside I knew I was doing the right thing, and that was enough to keep me pushing for it, I still had obviously plenty of guilt, self-doubt, and bad images of myself. I struggled with that plenty and struggled with being a good mom. I did have a couple really good friends that stayed with me, and my family obviously stayed with me, although none of them are physically near me, so that makes it difficult. I knew I was going toward a better place. I knew that I would eventually get there. Some days, I didn't know how I was going to get to the next day, but you just do. You feel yourself acting on instinct, and your head catches up later. It has been frustrating because I was mouthing the words. Just because you've reached a new level of awareness doesn't mean behavior automatically follows. You think: "I'm aware of how things should be now. I should just not get down on myself anymore. I shouldn't doubt myself." It takes time for the behavior to catch up, and that's frustrating. I definitely had days where I didn't know what I was going to do. But for the most part, I still feel pretty lucky. I know that my life is going in the right direction now. I feel lucky that I'm only thirty-three, and I feel like I have a level of awareness that some people aren't fortunate enough to reach at my age. Once you go through a divorce when you're four months pregnant . . . I moved into an apartment on my own when I was eight months pregnant . . . and nursing a baby on your own. If I can do that, and if I don't care what people think about that, and if I can mentally and physically get through it, then I really don't have any excuses for not doing what I want to do with my life.

As hard as she found acting in accordance with her new level of awareness (which I heard as her internal voice), Heather persevered and kept her internal voice in the foreground. She was so sure that she was moving in a good direction that she kept pushing ahead—some days instinctually. The friends who faulted her choices ceased to be good partners because they did not respect her internal voice. She knew that trusting that voice was more important than what others thought of her. This resolved the tension between her two conflicting drives:

Confident, strong, I think you can be that way in a lot of areas of your life . . . work especially I was. I didn't have any of the same problems there as personally, as far as going out on a limb, taking a risk. I feel more consistent. I used to feel like I was two different people inside, and I just thought that's the way I was. That's been a big, big change for me to not feel like I have two competing parts of myself. I had one part that wanted to do it this way, and one part that wanted to do it that way, and they were both true and valid parts, and they just didn't always agree. That's completely gone away, which is a huge weight lifted. I don't think I realized at the time how much energy that took up to have that going on. I thought it was just normal. Now that I don't have that, things just are much more natural. I mean it's just amazing the different energy that I have. I'm not as fretful . . . a much calmer energy.

Having to resolve the competing parts of herself constituted Heather's crossroads. Heather had the sense that her personal self was now in sync with her professional self. Having read *Making Their Own Way*, Heather used it to frame her internal foundation. By her mid-thirties, however, she reported discovering that it was still a work in progress:

> I can walk into a room of senior executives and literally have no nervousness, even if I know that I'm going to say something that might push some buttons. You would think that level of confidence would translate into my private life, but it doesn't directly translate. And so, [I'm] realizing that there's still a struggle there. I've pushed myself to do, in my gut, what feels right, but that doesn't necessarily mean that there's not a lot of churning going on underneath when I'm doing it. I have one of the happiest kids I've ever met, and I will push mothers to take credit for being mothers, but I still struggle to do it myself, struggle to take any credit for my son, still question the parenting decisions I make, and I laugh at myself when I find myself doing it. Getting that internal foundation strong is still just a challenge, and things bump up against it, and you realize that you're not quite there, and you face the fact and you take it head on, but it's still a journey, not an end point yet. It's cleaning away the external noise and clutter and cobwebs. I think you can hear it. I'm in a much better place. I'm just much more stable emotionally, much more sure of myself. A lot of that is just clearing stuff away and then also having the courage to be myself, which . . . it's still just a tough thing to do sometimes—put yourself out there.

Heather's story reveals the energy it takes to trust the internal voice and to act on it consistently. Although few people stayed with her through this journey, she stayed true to herself. When she faced up to her feelings for another person and her fears about leaving her marriage, she felt compelled to follow her internal voice. Over time, her relationship with her son and her relief at maintaining her internal consistency kept her focused on following her internal voice and building her foundation. She found solace in the courage to be herself.

Kelly's Story: Grounded in Faith

Kelly gained in confidence through her early twenties because of her success as an elementary school teacher. Learning that her preconceived notion that her life would be "set by twenty-five" was untrue, she opened herself to taking life as it came. This realization was sparked, in part, by a relationship she broke off because she felt she was losing herself in it, and, in part, by a union action at her school that put her in an awkward position as a new teacher. She began to explore her faith in her mid-twenties. Growing up in a Presbyterian home where faith was not discussed openly, Kelly reported that she had been "going through the motions" without really thinking about her faith. A conversation with a friend led her to listen to Christian radio, talk at length with her aunt about faith, and read the Bible regularly to address doubts she was experiencing. She reported a transformation in her mid-twenties:

> I discovered where God fit in my life and that started to give me the confidence to stand up to myself, or stand up for myself. Once I did that a few times, and I found out that it really was important what was internally happening, as far as my decisions and how I felt about my decisions, that's much better than trying to wait for somebody else to give you the positive strokes. It's much better emotionally and mentally to know yourself and be confident in yourself.

Kelly's faith helped her develop her internal voice over the course of her twenties. She reported at thirty-three what this meant for a significant relationship:

> It was one of the first relationships where I didn't have to second-guess what I said. With him, I could just say anything, and he wouldn't care. He'd just take it and accept me for absolutely 110% who I am. We've always been extremely bluntly honest with each other because we'd rather deal with ramifications from honesty than ramifications from dishonesty. I'm thirty-three and he's thirty. When you're twenty-two, twenty-three, twenty-four, even twenty-five, you're still learning about yourself. We were already over those bridges. We were very comfortable in our own skins, and we didn't have to get through any of that muck. So, it just kind of flew. This relationship was different than anything I'd ever experienced before. There wasn't any of this second guessing on either side that you get sometimes when you're not real sure in a relationship. It was just rock solid right from the get-go.

Kelly's trust of her internal voice led her to trust this relationship and her decision to marry. She embarked on married life with her philosophy that "there is hope" and that hope is a gift from God. She explained how this connected to her faith in God:

> When you have faith in a greater being and a greater plan, it gives you peace, and then when you have that peace, it makes it easier to focus on the inner self because you're not worried about the world around you. You can focus on your inner self and the decisions that you make on a day-to-day basis. It gives you the confidence to stand up for yourself and what you believe and the decisions that you make. And you know that they're not sporadic decisions. They're decisions based on the plan. They're decisions made with a reason. So, when you make decisions that way and you make life choices that way, it's a lot easier to be confident in yourself and stand up for yourself and not worry about what other people think. I have a lot of respect for people that have different views and ideologies, but I know that what I do is right for me, and it doesn't bother me if someone believes something different because, frankly, I don't have to live their life.

I was curious about the relationship between focusing on the inner self and God's plan in decision making. Kelly offered her take on it:

> I think probably either way you go is okay as long as you're okay with it internally, and you've thought about the ramifications. I think God has a plan. Frankly, it's hard for me to think that God knows what choices I'm going to make, but I think He does, but yet He still does give us the choice. That's hard for me. That's an issue that I've not solved yet. The plan is created with the love of God, and even though God might know what choice we're going to make, it doesn't prevent us from making the choice. It doesn't prevent us from being in control. I just see it as a loving figure who knows which way I'm going to go and will support me either way and love me either way. It's very complicated . . . I think a lot of people, frankly, have trouble with that aspect of God because they see it as taking their power away, and I don't see it as that.

Kelly felt that the love of God would be with her as she made decisions that she was comfortable with internally. In that sense, God served as a good partner who respected her thoughts. Kelly's understanding of her relationship with God was also shaped by serving as a moderator on the deacon's board at her church and attending the National

Prayer Breakfast. Through these experiences, her interactions with diverse others led her to see the complexity of people's beliefs and the uniqueness of each person's relationship with God. Thus, she was able to construct a relationship with God that blended belief in a greater plan with her own internal authority. She also noted that:

> Faith grows and changes and comes and goes. Sometimes it's great and wonderful and high, and other times it's kind of dark, but you know it's there. And that's the incredible thing about a faith in a higher being is the knowledge and trust that even if it's dark, it's still there, and that there will be another time when you're up at the top of the roller coaster ride.

Unbeknownst to Kelly, the roller coaster ride was about to begin. She had her first child, who was born prematurely after a difficult pregnancy, two days prior to September 11, 2001. While Kelly and her husband David lived far from the terrorist attacks, David was in the National Guard. During the next two years, he narrowly avoided deployment numerous times. A long bed rest and a significant health problem on the child's part complicated Kelly's second pregnancy. Fortunately, the immediate health concern was remedied, but four months later, David left for an 18-month deployment in Iraq. Kelly tried to express her feelings through her tears:

> I've been amazed at how roller coaster my emotions have been. I am a pretty happy-go-lucky, down-to-earth, don't-get-mad, very easy kind of woman. I have had a deep, dark anger against the Army for this whole thing. It's a feeling of being controlled by the Army. I don't know when I'll see him again. The sense of touching somebody who loves you is gone. It was just a huge emptiness right away. The evenings are hard. They're empty. They're lonely. It's painful. One positive thing is we've realized how strong we are. We've realized how deep our love is because we've realized how dedicated we are to each other, and if we can get through this, when we get through this, we can get through anything. I know our marriage is sure and strong, and our dedication to each other is unbelievable. It's going to be emotional. I feel like I'm in a constant state of prayer about David's safety.

Kelly's anger surprised me, given her complex relationship with God. I asked Kelly what role faith played in her coping with this situation. She replied:

> It's hard to say it's been a source of strength because I still feel so weak, but I think I'd probably be weaker if I didn't have it.

I'd probably be more lost if I didn't have it. I've been really struggling. People say, "Kelly, just give it up to God and trust God." For the first time I'm really struggling with the whole control issue because I'm feeling so controlled by the Army. It is hard for me just to give everything up. So, I just pray a lot. When I start to break down, I get somebody over here and I go for a walk, or I just throw the kids in the stroller and we go for a walk. David's supportive, too. It's amazing. He's over there in the middle of it, and I feel like he is my rock. I'm almost embarrassed to say that 'cause here I am sitting in the middle of Midwestern Americana, and I can't be the rock for my husband, although I think I am. But I'm relying on him more than I thought I would have to as far as keeping me centered in my faith. I've typed up some phrases from the Bible, and I've taped those on my mirror in my bathroom so I can just read those, about being strong, trusting God to hold you up when you can't hold yourself up.

Prior to this experience, Kelly had been able to hold her own and exercise her free will in her relationship with God. Now, constricted by military decisions that were beyond her control, she needed more help. Despite having good partners in God and her husband, the stress was still overwhelming. A year later, eagerly anticipating David's imminent return home, Kelly reported that she didn't know how she would have survived without her faith as her anchor. She shared that during long walks she alternatively cried and repeated the phrase "I can do all things through He who gives me strength." Kelly's internal foundation, of which her faith was a part, helped her be good company for herself as she coped with David's absence, her fear for his safety, and the general uncertainty his service brought to their lives.

The readjustment was difficult as well. Kelly reported that David exhibited anger that he had never previously displayed, to the extent that she sometimes wondered, "Who is this guy?" She also developed a hyperactive thyroid, believed to be the result of stress. She reported that although she thought they had gotten back onto the same page, there was a new form of stress:

He's safe, he's home, it's great. Then you feel guilty when you get mad at him or disagree. Any negative emotion, your mind is saying let's try to be thankful, everything should be perfectly wonderful. And life is not perfectly wonderful. I was talking to David over the summer, when I was trying to understand why

I wasn't spontaneous, free-spirited, have fun, do whatever—free and easy—where did that girl go? What happened to her? It was a lot more stressful than I expected it to be. That doesn't even include extra stressful things we've had to deal with. I was under the misperception that because I had been an early childhood teacher, parenting would be a breeze. What I failed to realize is that school kids leave at three and don't come back until the next day! Parenting is such a twenty-four-hour job—physically and mentally exhausting.

Kelly intentionally started to carve out time for herself with the goal of reducing her stress:

If I can't take care of myself, I can't take care of family. Who else is going to? That's where I am right now, trying to overcome that. It's weird at thirty-eight, still all these things you are dealing with and trying to learn—does anybody ever get there? I don't know.

Kelly trusted her internal voice and had built a substantial foundation with faith as a cornerstone. It helped her through two difficult pregnancies and her husband's deployment to a battle zone. Yet, she recognized that she needed to continue to be good company for herself if she was to maintain that foundation.

Alice's Story: A Life Blessed

Alice described her life in her twenties as "pretty fairy tale:"

You want to go to college, great. You do that. You get good grades. Want a master's? Fine. You do that. You want to get a professional license? Great. You want to find a great guy and get married. Wonderful. You want to buy a nice house. No problem. You want a beautiful baby? Fine. No fertility issues. I mean I had not really had any speed bumps.

Alice acquired a master's degree in counseling, became a licensed therapist, and had managed to work out an ideal balance of career and parenting as a result of flexibility at her workplace. As a therapist, she had engaged in self-reflection in her professional preparation that helped her cultivate and trust her internal voice. Her Christian faith, a mainstay in her life, led her to view herself as fortunate, gifted at helping others, and able to guide her own life. This faith became one of the cornerstones of the internal foundation she built as she defined boundaries with her clients, sorted out career and parenting priorities, and identified her internal values and beliefs during her twenties. She enjoyed good partners at work and in her personal life. Then the fairy tale came to an abrupt halt during her second pregnancy when she contracted Guillain-Barré syndrome. She described the situation:

> At its worst, I was totally paralyzed. They did catch it early enough and started some blood treatments before I was totally incapacitated. But it's very humbling not to be able to do anything for yourself. The other thing that goes with Guillain-Barré is excruciating pain because essentially your nerves are raw because the myelin sheath has deteriorated and so everything hurts. Trying to lay in one position was very painful, and yet because I was paralyzed, I couldn't move myself, and so I had to rely on someone just to move me to a different position. I can remember one night in the hospital looking at my husband, and he was just beat. He had finally fallen asleep in the chair. He was all slumped over, and [I was] just looking at him thinking, "Well, do I lay here in pain or do I wake him up to move me?" Whose need is greater right now, his for sleep or mine for relief? Those were probably the hardest things, other than not being able to take care of Faith and having her be so confused because she would put her arms up and say "Mommy." I just couldn't respond to her. I couldn't even smile. I couldn't even blink. I mean I looked like a stroke victim. My face just hung. So, I couldn't give her any . . . even any nonverbal [reaction] . . . and she was afraid of me at times, which was very hard.

In the midst of this frightening situation, Alice was confident that she would recover. She attributed this to her faith. She described an experience that validated the role of her faith in her recovery:

> I was very, very fortunate that my recovery has been near a hundred percent. I did the whole thing, from being in the hospital for a month and then rehabilitation and going from the wheelchair to a walker to a cane and trying to take care of a toddler and give birth. So, it was just a real wild time for us. Once I got to the point that I could walk, I knew that the physical strength was coming. It was a gradual flow, painstaking, but it was coming. The pain was unrelenting to the point that even while pregnant, I was doing IV morphine. It was just ugly. I thought, "This is the piece that's going to be debilitating, not being able to care for my children and being in this much pain." I guess it was several different times I just felt very assured that once I delivered that the pain would go away and I would

be able to care for my kids. I just had such a peace about it: "Let's get this baby out of here 'cause I'm going to be okay." I delivered three weeks early, he was fine, and the part to me that is so validating is that at the time that I delivered him, and I mean really at the moment of delivery, the pain left. I mean it was just gone. I went from IV morphine to nothing. I know in my heart—I knew then and I know now—that that was a gift from God. I know what it was, but as I described it to my OB, my neurologist, there was no medical explanation given as to why that would happen and just the fact that it happened so immediate. That's not how things happen medically. I do strongly believe that my recovery was swifter and maybe more complete because of that.

Alice's internal foundation helped her view her cure in the light of her faith, particularly since there was no medical explanation for her immediate release from pain. Her belief in this gift from God helped Alice recover and return to work part time. She enjoyed therapy and believed her illness had made her a better counselor because it had deepened her empathy for people in situations they could not control. The internal foundation Alice had built through her professional training enabled her to be good emotional company for herself during her illness and recovery.

During her thirties, Alice continued to secure her internal commitments, which involved actively cultivating her relationship with Christ. That relationship was her anchor in grieving her mother's death from an eleven-year battle with breast cancer, as well as for dealing with parenting and everyday life. I asked her to explain how she perceived this relationship. She offered:

My anchor is my relationship with Christ. It's who I am in Him. It's the recognition of what that relationship is and the peace that comes from that that just kind of surpasses . . . the rest of it in my mind is just like static. There's a clear channel. There's a clear reception. There's a clear voice. There's a true north. The rest is static. You view it as such, and it just is not that derailing. I'm not trying to say that I don't cry or I don't get mad or I don't have a bad day. I'm not trying to paint any kind of unrealistic picture, but at the end of the day, none of those things get me too upset. The best way I can describe it is it's more like an . . . internal need, an internal drive that brings about such peace and happiness that it's certainly not a burden to develop it any more than if you're starving it would be a burden to eat.

What Alice was describing was her internal foundation, framed through her relationship with Christ, which enabled her to find peace. I, of course, wanted to know more about how Alice cultivated this relationship that brought her peace in the midst of pain. She was happy to explain:

> Sometimes, it's just as simple as reading my Bible. Sometimes, it's just being prayerful throughout the day, being very aware of God in the little details. To show you an example, a lot of things could be chalked up as coincidence and maybe some of them are, but I guess I always view things through the lens of how my life is blessed, how I'm taken care of, how things are okay. Last week, I had a cancellation of an appointment. The person who came in right before that was a person incredibly in crisis, a person for whom the standard fifty-minute clinical hour was not going to suffice, and I just look at that and go, mmhmm, the next hour's free. I can just give this person more time. I look at that as God providing. He needs me to minister to this person. Those would be those kinds of God-in-the-details things. And that's not to say that when the coincidence happens and I'm on the short end of the stick that I think that's God mad at me today. I don't view it that way at all.

Alice emphasized that her relationship with Christ was not based on anything that she did, but on whether she listened for the clear communication:

> I see a direct correlation between the choices that I make on an individual level to cultivate my relationship with God and the choices that I see my husband make on an individual level to cultivate his relationship with God. That's an act of our own will. That's an act of my choice. There are times when that's not an easy choice. So, that is a discipline. It's sometimes a sacrificing of my own stubborn will. But I see a direct correlation between that and the sense of peace and contentment and happiness and connectedness that I feel in my marriage and in my home and personally and relationally. I don't believe it's a doing. I think it's there. It's freely available. It's whether I avail myself of it or not, whether I choose to put myself in position to receive. When I don't do that, the static gets louder, and I can get distracted by the competitive nature of the schools, or, oh gee, are my kids going to be okay? Or gee, I don't have a marketing plan, a business plan; what if my practice dries up? I just don't go there. And that's why I say it's more of an internal desire; it's an internal hunger. It's kind of like if you're going to

eat junk food all week, and you really know you need vegetable soup. It's that same feeling; it's that same internal desire.

Alice seemed to have an internal compass that helped her alleviate the stress of everyday life. Her internal commitments, one of which was choosing to put herself in position to receive, helped her maintain her free will and be at peace.

Alice and her husband were thrilled when their daughter chose at age eight to accept Christ and be baptized. Alice explained how this affected their parenting practices:

> With our faith system, it's really left to the individual whether they choose to accept Christ to be baptized. Our role as her parent is to teach her, to guide her, but ultimately that's her choice and her responsibility. She made the choice to do that, and so my husband and I together baptized her. Now, in parenting there are many power struggles that I can take myself out of because she has put herself accountable to a higher power, and so it doesn't have to be me and her going head-to-head. It'll be: "Let's talk about that from the standpoint of what God wants for you. How does God define your beauty and what's that got to do with what you're wearing today?" Many times, my encouragement to her will be, "I would like to ask you to spend some time talking to God about that." I'll see her make choices then on that level, and I don't have to butt heads with her as much. I don't take it on from the standpoint that I abdicate my responsibility. I don't at all. But I trust that it's going on because I see the evidence of it. For instance, I will see her go to her room, shut the door, come out, and approach her brother with an apology, and I didn't hold her feet to the fire and say, "You have to tell him you're sorry." When I see that happening, that does give me confidence that there is something real happening there. But now do I say, "You can wear whatever you want to school as long as you and God have talked about it"? No. (Laughing) I will talk with her about what defines our beauty, and what's the true source of our beauty. There's nothing wrong with wanting to look nice and do your hair. I do that, too. But we're not going to do that to the point that that's our only definition.

Alice was confident in handling issues with her daughter, in part, because her daughter was developing her relationship with Christ and, in part, because Alice had a clear sense of the boundaries of responsibility. Just as Alice had worked out appropriate professional boundaries with her clients, she merged her personal beliefs and faith to work out her sense of parent-child boundaries that would help her children develop responsibility for themselves. Alice's development of her own professional and personal identities, and the combined strength of her internal foundation and her relationship with Christ, led to the outlook that "my life is blessed." This outlook helped her manage her private therapy practice and the trials and tribulations of parenting.

Cara's Story: Step by Step

Cara pursued her dreams through advanced education during her twenties. She usually found herself with little support in male-dominated environments. Cara articulated reaching what she called a "snapping point" during her doctoral work in her twenties. The stress of a professor expressing a romantic interest in her was a stimulus for her realization that she had to stop letting what others wanted control her. As she reported at the outset of chapter 1, she became aware of the invisible force she'd been pushing against, and she decided to listen to her own intuition. She decided it was time to take the front seat of the bicycle. She found support over the next couple of years in two places—her husband and one of her faculty members:

> Patricia has a quote on her desk: "Care too much about others' opinions and you'll be their prisoner." I obsess about what others think. I think about that, and say to myself, "don't go there." My husband said the same thing to me, but I discounted it. Of course he is going to say that, he's married to me.[3]

Success in her graduate work and completing her dissertation helped her trust her internal voice and build her professional internal identity. She also came to appreciate the way her husband perceived her. She noted that: "When someone loves you unconditionally, it is healing. It changed my perception of myself."[4] His way of seeing her helped her see herself in a new way, as did her parents' readiness to embrace her as an adult. These partners' respect for her thoughts and feelings helped her gain respect for herself. She also took up kickboxing to build her confidence. Collectively, these events helped her strengthen her internal foundation as she neared thirty.

Accepting a faculty position upon her graduation offered Cara a context for continued professional success. Despite the typical apprehensions about teaching effectively and publishing enough to achieve tenure, Cara excelled in academic life, as did her academic spouse. She sometimes worried that she was too friendly with students who were near her age; however, she held students accountable. She refused to budge in one case when a student challenged his grade. Despite university officials encouraging her to just change it, she refused, even when he threatened her and other students. Professionally, she did not allow external pressure to interfere with what she thought was right.

Yet, external pressure surfaced again in a stronger form in Cara's personal life. At thirty-three, she reported a struggle with the issue of having children:

> I'm thirty-three, so I'm a little panicked. Yet, if I had more time, I probably would really be taking more time, and maybe I do. I just don't know. A lot of career academics don't have children. I have other friends that just cannot wait to have babies and are obsessed, in my mind . . . they probably think I'm not obsessed enough . . . with having a kid. It honestly is the sole source of conversation with a lot of people I know when they see me. "When are you having a baby?" And, "Oh, that's so sad that you don't have kids yet." It's almost like you don't want to have a baby just to be perverse. Yes, I know, like some weird, bad personality trait.

Cara and her spouse were trying to have children, but she was not totally convinced she was ready. Part of Cara's struggle about whether she wanted children was internal. She explained her conflict:

> I don't want to wake up when I'm forty-five and think, "I wish we would have had kids." It really worries me that that will happen. Or we could adopt—that sounds like a really good idea to me— yet when I talk to other people who really want kids, if they couldn't have kids, they would need therapy. I'll think why am I not like that? Why don't I have that urge? I don't feel like I have it like they do, and I'm not sure why that is. There are other women close to my age that I've met now in the academic community, so we're all kind of the same like that, and I wonder why. Is it like the job that's made us like this? I just got a Ph.D. I worked all this time and maybe it's a selfish thing, but the idea of giving up some of that freedom sounds awful to me. But it seems so natural compared to the reaction of society, and that bothers me. Like, my God, do I have, like, any female hormones in me? That's been something I've been thinking about a lot.

These thoughts reveal that Cara's concern was why she did not feel the urge to have her own children like her friends. Although she was comparing herself to others, her focus was really on understanding the internal feelings she had. At the same time, however, some of her concern was related to external expectations. Her resistance to others' expectations (i.e., not having a baby because others wanted her to) stemmed in part from her resolve to not revert to swaying to external influence as she had reported doing during most of her twenties. I asked to what extent her use of the words *unnatural* or *awful* related to others' constructions of having children. She agreed that she was affected by others' perceptions, particularly those of her family:

> My parents really want a baby, and I'm the only child, so I'm the only one they're going to get. When I talk about adoption, they just look crushed. I talked to them the other night and said: "Look, to have a baby we might have to go all the way to in vitro, which I just don't know if I'm willing to do. I'm not that desperate for a baby." And they look at me like, "Well, it can work. We know lots of success stories," not really hearing what I'm saying.

In this instance, Cara's parents were too invested in a grandchild to respect her thoughts and feelings. She had no one except her spouse with whom to discuss the career implications of having children. I asked Cara how her struggle related to our earlier conversations about emancipating herself from external expectations. Her spontaneous reaction revealed her difficulty of maintaining her internal foundation:

> Oh no! I'm back, aren't I?! It's really true. Professionally, I feel really competent or at least confident in what I'm doing. I don't know why I don't have that same confidence about this. I want to say, "Oh, it's because I have Catholic parents"—like the guilt and the only grandchild—but I'm sure it's deeper than that. I do think part of it's a need or a desire to really connect with other people. I do feel uneasy when I don't have that kind of connection, and this is one way [to connect]. I have two really good friends from college, and one of those friends I knew also in high school. And we are just so close, and I'm the godmother of one of those kids. I have two grandmothers that are alive still and . . . my grandfather died last October, and one of the oddest reactions I had was I felt so sad that we hadn't had a baby by then for him to meet. And I got in this panic where I

was like, "Okay, we have to have a baby so [the grandmothers] can meet him or her." Well, when I thought this out, having a child for your grandparents? Because this would make them so happy? I get the sense from my parents that they're hoping that that happens, too, which is really nutty. I realize it's nutty, but yet at the same time, I can still feel that kind of pressure to make them happy.

Cara could reflect on her desire to make her parents and grandparents happy while simultaneously realizing that this consideration was "nutty" in terms of decision making. Asked how she thought she would work through all of this, she replied with a sigh:

I have no idea. I really don't know. This phrase keeps coming to my mind, which is something my grandmother always says, which is "step by step." Usually, if I think about all these issues at once, I am frozen. It's just too much. First, see if we're going to have kids—there's no baby. If we end up adopting, it's going to cause some waves in the old familia, but [we'll] have to deal with it when it comes. I don't know if I'm in denial or . . . but usually that's the way that I would tend to handle things like this. Step by step. But I'm kind of clinging right now to wanting things to be like they were, even though I'm not who I am, and [my friends] are not who they are anymore.

Cara had reconstructed herself through her graduate program and professional work. This left her feeling disconnected from her friends, and heightened the struggle about having children. She recognized that she was not who she used to be, but her longing for connection and reluctance to leave behind who she had been left her torn and disconnected from her earlier support systems.

The intensity of the struggle to maintain her internal voice intensified a year later after she was diagnosed with endometriosis, had surgery, became pregnant unexpectedly, and had a miscarriage. She reported that while her academic work had been helpful in keeping her from becoming really depressed, she was still depressed. Asked how these events contributed to depression, she offered:

I don't even know. I just feel like I don't know what I want to do. I don't know if I want to have children or not. I feel like I have to now make that decision because of my age, and now that it's an option. It's interesting, too, about the kid. We did three ultrasounds before the miscarriage. If you see it, you really connect with this thing. I still am really pro choice. It's

not a small issue for me; it's pretty big. You see the ultrasound
and you're like, "Oh." It's really weird because I'm connecting,
yet I would still argue this now, but especially in the past, but
it's not a baby. But then you're grieving for something, but
really at the stage that I had the miscarriage, it was still really
small, I mean an inch. Really it's a huge sense of loss. You
almost feel kind of hypocritical, for in the past, people would
say, "It's a baby," you know, "How can you get rid of a baby?" I'm
like, "It's not a baby." And then now that was me. But it's also
different; I wasn't making a choice. The other thing was that
we did tell some people. And everyone was so happy, this huge
deal in our families, huge celebration, and then all my girl-
friends that have children that I told . . . just really happy and
wanted to talk to me all the time. And I realized . . . this goes
back to the connection thing . . . how much more in common I
suddenly had with them. It was just like this big celebrating
time, and then how crushed my family was when I had the miscarriage. So, it's getting in the way of my knowing what I want
because I feel like so much pressure that part of me wants to
react to that and say, "I'm not having children," almost in a
reaction—you can't push me into doing this. So, it's childish.
It's a huge issue. What kind of decision-making is that?
But there's always so much noise around me that I'm having a
hard . . . which is something I think I've always struggled
with . . . like pushing that out to see what I really want. So, I
mean it's the same struggle I've had, but now it's in this situation.
And then I'm mad that it's even an issue, you know? It irritates
me that this is taking up so much of my time and my worry.

The external noise became so loud that Cara struggled to hear her
internal voice. She was not, as she feared, pulled back to the crossroads because she could see, separate out, and reflect on all of these
competing notions. But her desire to connect, and the difficulty of
connecting with other women who shared her professional identity,
combined to make hearing and trusting her own voice a major
struggle well into her thirties.

   Cara proceeded, step by step, to build her internal foundation.
Another miscarriage further complicated the choice of biological
childbirth or adoption. The risks of pregnancy outweighed their interest in a genetic connection, so they chose adoption. She described the
effect of this choice on her relationship with her parents:

   It was a very huge growing-up process for us, even though we
   were thirty-six. It was kind of a separation from them that was

probably needed, like we are doing this. You are either on board or you're not, which we've really never done before firmly.

Cara and Jack were good partners for each other, each respecting the other's internal voices to stand up to external pressure. At the age of thirty-six, Cara and her husband brought their new eleven-month-old daughter home from China. The transition was complicated. The baby initially gravitated toward Cara's husband, and they had difficulty setting boundaries with grandparents during the child's transition. Despite these challenges, Cara found the adoption and the baby to be an amazing experience that altered her perspective:

> [Before,] anything at work could just send me flying over the edge, every success, every negative, politics, meetings, just kind of tunnel vision. Having Melissa just, [I'm] completely much more mellow about those things. I'm still very achievement driven, but when you go to China, you see this is how people are living. This is what's going to happen to other babies. And then you see this child. She says and does the funniest things, and she's loving, and then it's like this whole other part of your brain is firing, like okay, Cara, open your mind. There is joy. There is fun . . . you can be playful. You don't have to be so serious. I'd say more balanced, which I had wanted, and just like a kinder, more patient than I was. I care more about my own behavior. I can't come home on some rampage from work 'cause that affects her, so I have reined in a lot of those negative traits . . . worked on disciplining my mind more than I have before. I focus more on the positive because I would like her to have a more optimistic view. I think about the way I was raised, what I would like from that and what I don't want, and that's kind of pushed me to behave differently.

This change of perspective went beyond being more balanced and optimistic. It permeated how Cara saw herself and her interactions with others. She commented that she had come to "speak what I think is true, regardless of [others'] reactions." I asked to what extent she could do this, and she replied:

> Ooh, that's more, definitely, than I used to be able to, and actually to a point where I feel good about it, not that there's not room for growth. Before, when I said things, part of what I was doing was wanting something back, wanting to be validated, wanting to be heard, and then I would think there would be no point in saying anything unless people changed based on what I said. I don't need that as much anymore, or I can catch myself

sometimes getting into that cycle. Say what you think, where you are, regardless of whether they agree or not because I would rather others do that for me. I would rather know them even if they don't agree. I can't imagine running around thinking the only way I would speak would be to change somebody. Part of it, too . . . sometimes I don't need to speak. Before, I think, I needed to engage more than I do now. I needed to battle it out. [Now,] I'm more able to hear other people. I can just listen. I don't need to say anything, or I don't need to say as much as I used to. So, that's kind of paradoxical. Like on one hand, I feel more free to speak, but then on the other hand, I don't feel like I have to speak, or I don't regret as much not saying things sometimes because I think there's a time not to say anything. So, that has been big, and it feels a lot better to not care as much or to not obsess and ruminate, not that I don't do those things, but not like I used to.

As I listened to Cara's comments, it struck me that she had found her way through the external noise in her life. I asked how she came to this point:

There was something about the process of Melissa. I'm not exactly sure what it was except that at some point I just realized . . . it kind of just hit me on the head. Part of it was simply you are thirty-six years old, and now you have your own child, and this isn't just going to happen naturally unless you start making this kind of emancipation happen. You just have to do it. It is something that I really worked on, that I thought like I'm going to go one of two ways. I'm either going to be driving myself crazy and worrying and anxious all the time, or I'm going to try to get a grip on this, and so part of it was deliberate and doing some work on that.

After twenty years of interviews, Cara anticipated my next question about what this work involved:

I was doing a paper on moral disengagement and ethics. Why do we do bad things and the processes that we go through to disengage ourselves. That's what got me on this track. I started reading these books, seven perfections according to Buddhism. That's where I learned the calm-my-body-calm-my-mind thing. One thing that I've really picked up from this book that I just love was this notion of how do you stay engaged with people or just the world without being smothered by it, but then also not fully disengaging? That really fascinated me because that really spoke to me about how I saw myself as somebody that would get so engaged, be crushed under the weight of whatever it was, and then the only way I knew how to get out of that was to disengage completely. And so this perspective that you could actually have some equanimity, like you could sit and be engaged with somebody or something and let it go up and down, but you didn't have to come with it, and that was just huge, like the biggest, wow, that's obvious, but it wasn't. You don't need to be so extreme. You can stay engaged and still be separate.

Cara was so fascinated by these ideas that she began to listen to a series of tapes in the car called *Your Buddha Nature*. She explained how the messages related to how she was feeling about her family:

> Things were really intense emotionally with our families. I felt like I was drowning in my family, and I felt panicked. At that point, it was very intense, and that kind of worked its way in and I really heard it, and I'm not sure I would have heard it before. I started doing yoga. . . . It's about balance and breathing. So, there's something that goes on with yoga. I don't know what it is, but for me, at least, there is something about working through that same set of postures over and over, progressing through them and then doing really difficult postures. You do the same postures on each side, which is very balancing, and then some days you can do one thing, but then the next time you can't do it. It's maddening at first, like I could just do this, but it's like life. Go back and forth. You make progress; you come back. You make progress; you come back.

Cara's role as a parent and her realization that she needed to manage the intensity of all her emotions led her to a conscious decision to learn how to calm her mind and body. Using the lessons from Buddhism and yoga, she found a way to keep herself grounded in her internal foundation. She used this approach in parenting, teaching, and interacting with her colleagues. She also used it to stay grounded through the trauma of a violent murder of a member of her extended family. From first learning of this tragedy through the aftermath, Cara actively worked to stay balanced, reporting, "When I would feel myself getting angry at what they were doing, I was able to get re-centered." The strength of her internal voice and her mechanisms for staying in touch with it helped her calm her mind and body in the most difficult circumstances. She was grateful she had come to this place as she continued to struggle with life's challenges at age forty. She was now a good partner to herself.

Lauren's Story: Loss and Recovery

Like Cara, Lauren struggled with external influence in her twenties. She realized it when she found a man that she was sure was "the one" and took him home to meet her parents. After her parents said they liked him, but they were not sure, Lauren reported: "All of a sudden I didn't like him as much anymore. . . . It was because of what they said, all of a sudden I started changing my mind."[5] This realization prompted Lauren to go in search of what *she* really wanted. She moved to a different part of the country to pursue this relationship. She shared that the hardest part was leaving her parents, even though she had lived four hours away from them. I had the sense that what she found difficult was moving from her externally defined world to the uncertainty of finding her own voice.

Lauren worked diligently in the next few years to cultivate and trust her internal voice. Once she trusted herself, she committed to the relationship and married. Lauren worked out a balance between her career role in pharmaceutical sales and her role as a mother after the birth of her first child. At thirty-three, she and her husband were making progress on their plan to have four children; however, a complication with the second pregnancy resulted in an emergency hysterectomy. Although the baby was born healthy, Lauren's plan for two more children was derailed. She shared the effect of this experience:

> It was very, very traumatic. I'm glad I'm talking to you six months later. It's still hard now. I'm much better now, and I can talk about it more freely now. But it's something that is in your mind every day. The most important thing that it taught me was that life is not always what you plan it is. When you're younger, you have this plan of what's going to happen in your life, and things just go. But here we are in our thirties, and you start seeing life is not easy. Things do happen. And you need to learn how to respond to them. Maybe I need to feel fortunate that nothing bad has happened thus far. Who would have thought this would happen to us? It's just made me think about life, and then obviously everything that happened on September 11th puts things into perspective. You look at these families, and they didn't think they were going to lose a spouse or a father. It makes you really think twice. So, I had a tough situation, and I don't mind sharing this with you, I've never in my life experienced depression. My brother has had depression, and I've always just had the attitude: "Just snap out of it. It's no big deal. You can get through it."

But this situation also made me appreciate mental illness, and it is serious. It's not a situation of turning it on and off, and they need help. I was very depressed. I would say probably the first two to three months even until I started feeling like myself again. And I realized more of what my brother has been feeling. You hear all these stories about these people, and now I have more compassion for them. This year has been probably my toughest year. I feel like a baby saying that because I know people have a lot worse things going on in their lives.

Experiencing depression personally, Lauren gained insight into her brother's experience. I asked how she was coping with her own depression. She explained:

Time heals. I know I need more time, but the further you get away from it, the better. Having a clear mind of getting over the depression and just trying to see clearly and putting things into perspective helps. At my toughest point, when I was just so emotional, I did go on medicine. I did see a counselor twice, and then I went home to visit my parents, and when I came back, something snapped. I just became rejuvenated, and I just didn't feel the need to go anymore. The counselor has an open door. I know that she's there, and I just haven't had the need to talk to [her]. Maybe it's because I have been talking to my friends about it that that has really helped. And the other thing, sad but true, somebody always has a worse story. That makes you feel better, too.

Talking with her spouse, her parents, a counselor, and her friends was helping Lauren process her feelings and put her loss into perspective. They respected her feelings, and this helped her work through them. Recognizing that life is not always the way you plan it, Lauren was adjusting to not being in control and learning how to respond to the unexpected. She was also working on reconciling reality with her goals:

You have this plan in your head. I'm going to get married; I'm going to have four children. Our home has five bedrooms, and I always thought each room would be a child's room and then our room. When your plan is twisted, plan B has to come into play. That's been the other consuming thing of my life recently. There are other options in the future. That's something that my husband and I need to deal with when the time is right. The hardest thing I'm struggling with right now is being clear in my mind of my feelings. Are they because I really want something else in life or because I'm still emotional from being postpartum? I don't know the answer to that. I may never know that answer. But as far as my desire to have a larger family, I don't feel any different than I felt the day after it happened.

Lauren still wanted a larger family but knew she needed to sort out her internal feelings about not being able to have more children herself. She focused on putting her loss in perspective, clarifying her feelings, and taking the time she knew she needed to heal before considering how to construct plan B.

Lauren and her husband did decide to pursue a larger family. Over the next three years, they tried to have another child with a surrogate. This proved a challenging experience, as Lauren reported in our eighteenth interview:

It's almost like I have this second life that so many people don't know about. It has consumed so much of my thoughts, my energies, my emotions, but yet, my friends at work, maybe one or two people know what I went through. We have been trying to have another child, and it hasn't worked so far by using a surrogate. For the past two years, I've been working on that, and it is a huge commitment and a job in itself. First, we had to find someone that's willing to do this for you, and there's a whole medical community that gets involved. Having firsthand experience, it's nothing that I would wish upon anybody. But I can't imagine never trying. I have this separate inner turmoil going on. Other people may have other private turmoil that you don't know about, and as I'm getting older, I know everybody has it—everybody that you think is happy and has the world by the tail, everybody has some inner pain, and many times people don't discuss it.

Lauren's desire for additional children, a dream she still held on to once she got past postpartum and depression, led her to explore a process she initially described as bizarre. Securing her internal commitments enabled her to get past the issue of trusting someone else to do this for her. Although she was committed to this challenging process, she was also fully aware that it might not result in a larger family:

If nothing happens out of this, I've completed three tasks in my life. Number one, I've gained a new education that I never knew about before. I feel like I can help people, or at least talk to people on an educated level. Number two, I feel like I'm more compassionate with people suffering from infertility because it now affects me. You can't judge a person until you've walked in their shoes. I'm more in their shoes than I was before. Number three, when we decide to close the chapter, and this is one point I haven't reached yet in my life, I will have complete closure. My biggest thing of starting this whole process was I don't want to live life with regrets. I wish I would have, I should have done this, why didn't I do this? So whenever I get frustrated and think, "What the heck am I doing?" and all the money we're spending, and nothing's happening, at least I'll be able to say, "Okay, I gave it literally 110%. This was my fate. This was the plan from above, and I can walk away now." So, to me, there's no dollar value to have peace of mind and closure, and so that's a process I've been learning. I know this will come up again in my life, like I'm sure when I lose my parents, and it's a similar theme where you have to accept closure and continue life in a positive way because you can continue life in a negative way. I'm not there yet, but I'm much closer to there than when I spoke to you the last time.

Lauren knew what she wanted and she was willing to give 110% to trying to get it. Simultaneously, she knew that the outcome was beyond her control, and she might have to be satisfied with having tried. She was trying her best to prepare for accepting the outcome and continuing life with a positive perspective.

GAINING PERSPECTIVE

Creating a workable philosophy for adult life seems to be the key to becoming good company for yourself. For these participants, creating such a philosophy required developing their internal voices. Lynn, Heather, Lauren, and Cara all recognized the need to develop their internal voices to resolve pain they encountered in their lives. For these four women, resolution of their particular struggles lay in deciding to listen to their internal voices to make sense of the external messages they received and the unpredictable events in their lives. Kelly and Alice recognized the same need in the context of their work environments. They both succeeded in giving primacy to their internal voices to enable them to function in their work settings.

Each woman's cultivation of her internal voice led to acting on it to change her life. Lynn's internal voice led to her acceptance of the good in herself and a new positive foundation for her life. Similarly,

Cara's internal voice helped her see herself in a new way that created an internal foundation for both her professional and personal life. Heather's facing her fears and acting on her voice, despite the cost of doing so, established a new foundation that finally merged competing parts of her identity. Building an internal foundation was crucial for facing circumstances beyond their control. Kelly and Alice, both of whom viewed their faith as an act of free will, used the internal foundations they had constructed through faith to face frightening circumstances. Lauren relied on her internal foundation as she engaged a surrogate to have a child, while knowing all along that the outcome was beyond her control.

Thus, energy devoted to trusting your internal voice and developing an internal foundation contributes to the ability to shape your future despite limited control and to face life positively. This kind of perspective is what helped participants self-author their lives in an uncertain world—to achieve what Mark called grace in the dance with reality.

As these women worked through their struggles, they needed partners who respected their opinions, helped them think through their experiences, and collaborated with them to reframe their perspectives. The partners who helped most were those who stayed on the back seat of the bicycle. These partners—therapists, medical personnel, members of faith communities, family, spouses, or friends—focused on encouraging these women to develop their own voices, to stay in the captain's seat for the journey. Because they had good partners to help them cultivate their internal voices, they were able to strengthen those voices to serve as their own partners when necessary. The challenges they faced deepened their empathy and compassion for others, as well as strengthening themselves. Thus, they became increasingly able to both receive and give help. This enhanced ability to relate to others authentically, as a result of their own self-authorship, enabled them to find partners who would be good company on their journeys. Chapter 9 turns to the role of partners in supporting the development of self-authorship to gain perspective.

LEARNING PARTNERSHIPS: A TANDEM BICYCLE EXPERIENCE

PARTNERSHIPS: HOW TO PROVIDE GOOD COMPANY FOR OTHERS' JOURNEYS TOWARD SELF-AUTHORSHIP

As you have seen from the preceding stories, having good company for facing the challenges of adult life can make all the difference in your ability to adopt a positive perspective and move forward with your life. The participants whose stories you have read found good company from a wide array of partners: friends, significant others, parents, educators, employers, and professionals. Professional partners included doctors, personal trainers, therapists, management coaches, mentors, and clergy. If you are reading this book as a partner, this chapter will help you explore how to partner with those you care about to provide them with good company for their journeys.

THE NATURE OF GOOD COMPANY

As you have seen throughout this book, the shift from authority-dependence to self-authorship involved participants learning to share responsibility for their lives with those who guided them to the threshold of adulthood. Rearranging these relationships with important adults in one's life is like trading seats on a tandem bicycle. Whereas the adult (e.g., parent, educator) has been in the front captain's seat through early life, at some point, those who are moving into adulthood want to move up to the captain's seat to take increased responsibility for directing their own journeys. Self-authorship requires their willingness to take increased responsibility for the journey, and a willingness on the part of their partners to move into a supporting role. New partners acquired in adulthood (e.g., significant others, friends, employers) can offer good company by joining the support network on the back seat of the bicycle.

Being good company requires balancing challenge and support. Challenges often arise unexpectedly when people are faced with complexity at work (e.g., Kelly's teacher's strike) or with life decisions (e.g., Cara's decision to have children). These situations often demand developing personal authority to resolve them (e.g., Heather's marriage decision) and collaborating with others to solve mutual issues (e.g., Lauren and her husband's efforts to have additional children). If the challenge to listen to and cultivate an internal voice is already present, the partner provides good company by providing the necessary support to help the person facing the challenge. Moving toward self-authorship requires support for cultivating one's internal voice, particularly until the fragile internal voice becomes strong enough to hold its own against external pressure. You can help others learn to trust their internal voices (the first part of self-authoring one's life) by creating circumstances that help them build confidence in their internal voices and supporting them in learning to control their reactions to reality. To support those who are building an internal foundation (the second part of authoring one's life), you can offer guidance for creating a philosophy for managing their reaction to reality, support integration of aspects of their identity, and offer feedback that helps them refine their internal foundation. Thus, being good company means gradually shifting from forms of support designed to build confidence to forms of support designed to encourage integration.

Although support is the primary role of being good company, sometimes being good company means introducing challenge. For example, those who experience what Alice called "fairy tale" lives sometimes do not encounter the challenge to listen to their internal voices. Thus, good company can also involve helping others become aware of the complexity of issues in their lives, the need to develop their personal authority, and the importance of learning to collaborate with others to solve mutual issues.

Listening to my participants' stories over the years about what kind of support and challenge helped them develop self-authorship led me to define the characteristics of learning partnerships that effectively balance challenge and support.[1] The six components of learning partnerships (see Figure I.2) offer a framework through which to provide this good company.

Partners supported participants in developing self-authorship by:

- Respecting their thoughts and feelings, thus affirming the value of their voices,
- Helping them view their experiences as opportunities for learning and growth, and
- Collaborating with them to analyze their own problems, engaging in mutual learning with them.

By providing these three supportive functions from the back seat of the bicycle, partners helped strengthen participants' internal voices. Good partners also challenged participants to develop self-authorship by:

- Drawing participants' attention to the complexity of their work and life decisions, and discouraging simplistic solutions,
- Encouraging participants to develop their personal authority by listening to their own voices in determining how to live their lives, and
- Encouraging participants to share authority and expertise, and work interdependently with others to solve mutual problems.

Pointing out these challenges from the back of the bicycle, together with support for moving toward them, provides good company. For example, the autonomy that Dawn, Evan, and Sandra had at work helped affirmed that their voices were important in daily decision making. Their supervisors encouraged them to structure their own work, thereby situating opportunities for growth in their personal experience. Their supervisors acknowledged the complexity of the work at hand—whether it involved playing a character in theater, managing a real estate deal, or handling a social work case—and trusted them to bring their own expertise to these roles. Their supervisors collaboratively shared their authority and expertise with participants. This combination of challenge and support helped Dawn, Evan, and Sandra develop their internal voices. Similarly, Kurt's parents affirmed his internal voice by encouraging him to be true to himself. They acknowledged the complexity of finding a suitable career, encouraged him to trust his feelings, and stood ready to support his decisions. Mark and Lydia benefited from spouses who affirmed their voices and respected their perspectives in the mutual negotiation of marital relationships and life challenges. Although partnerships took various forms for different participants, good partnerships contained some mix of these six components. Combined, these components helped participants navigate the journeys to self-authorship and choose their own paths through it. The next set of stories illustrates these partnerships and their effect on developing self-authorship in more detail, so you can consider how you might create similar partnerships.

LEARNING PARTNERSHIPS

Some participants enjoyed good partnerships in their early twenties that helped them cultivate and sufficiently trust their internal voices to build their internal foundations. These partnerships also helped participants face challenging situations that arose in their thirties and supported them as they cycled through the process of trusting their voices, building internal foundations, and securing internal commitments.

Rosa's Story: Building Faith through Change and Crisis

Challenges came at Rosa fast. Upon graduation, she returned to her hometown, began teaching first grade, and married the man she had dated for seven years. Life's challenges began immediately, as Rosa became pregnant on her honeymoon. She shared her reaction: "Everything I do, I plan. I'm not spontaneous. So, that was really hard to spontaneously be pregnant. And there was nothing I could do about it. I think the biggest learning experience was just roll with the punches."[2] She also was surprised that her baby became her top priority and called her long-standing plan to be a teacher into question. Her husband provided good company, as she reported:

> He's more laid back about things. If a change comes, that's fine, and he deals with it. It's good because that helps me. It makes me realize: "Okay, things are going to be okay. Just calm down. It's a change, but you're going to work through it." That's why

he's good for me. Sometimes, I can really panic about changes. He gets me a little more down to earth with it, but I'm good for him because sometimes he can be too laid back. Sometimes, it kind of gets him to thinking, "Yeah, I do need to plan for this." We complement each other that way.

As Rosa worked to learn to roll with the punches, she was trying to control her reactions to reality. Her husband challenged her to recognize the uncertainty in planning life and also affirmed that she would be able to work through it.

Over the next four years, Rosa adjusted to her role as a mother. She learned to listen to her own voice in parenting by sorting through her experiences with her first child. She also tutored and returned to teaching part time, acting on a personal need for a career. At twenty-six, she was pregnant with her second child. As her own life appeared to be becoming settled, challenges in her extended family prompted further reflection. A stranger murdered Rosa's twenty-seven-year-old cousin. Rosa's aunt and uncle were able to forgive the man who killed their daughter, something that Rosa worked hard to understand. In the midst of reflecting on her faith and the meaning of life in light of this event, Rosa's twenty-eight-year-old sister was diagnosed with breast cancer. While Rosa was becoming adept at controlling her reaction to the reality of these circumstances, she was still working on her internal foundation. She shared with me the role her sister played in her examination of her faith:

> She is doing okay; it's been five years now. She thought she might beat it, but then she had tumors growing on her spine. I helped her because she couldn't do anything. It was a struggle to walk to the bathroom. She talked over funeral arrangements with me when she was thirty-two; she had things written down. She has become very religious. It has drawn us all closer to God. . . . I pray more; when I pray, I am more involved. I used to just recite prayers; now I really pray. I've become much more spiritual. I got away from that in college. I go to church sometimes during the week for my sister. She has made me a much more spiritual person. She is still here because of her prayers. . . . I still don't believe everything the Catholic Church does, but I do still have a strong faith.[3]

Faith became more meaningful to Rosa through her sister's experience. Rosa no longer accepted teachings of the Church at face value, but she was convinced that God had a hand in her sister's survival. Conversations with her sister over the next year helped Rosa clarify her beliefs. Her sister's attitude also helped her gain perspective:

> My sister really taught all of us just to have humor. I learned that humor can help you keep a little sane about things. Her whole attitude was: "Stop praying for me to live. You see how bad I'm getting? You see I don't want to live this way? Your prayers are canceling out mine." She always had that humor about her. That really helped us, even helped us accept that it was her time to go. One time, this cute little blonde her husband worked with came to the front door with a plate of brownies, and my sister made a comment like, "Okay, he's already moving on. Wife's not even dead yet," and she would joke about that, and I think that's how they kept their sanity. It helped us keep ours 'cause it was very hard going in there and seeing her like that.

While Rosa struggled with her sister's declining quality of life, her sister's attitude helped her use her faith to resolve it:

> She was so helpless that she could not do anything. So, you kind of just felt like, "Oh my God, just let her end," and she had such a strong faith. She's like, "You guys, and I'm going to a much better place." I mean it was so nice talking to her 'cause we were prepared. We knew it was coming, and we were . . . it's awful to say, but kind of looking forward to it. When she did die I felt more relief than grief, you know? It's like, "Oh, thank God, her suffering has ended." But she died with this smile on her face.

Rosa's sister lost her battle with cancer at age thirty-five but not before providing good company for Rosa to solidify her faith. Her sister's encouragement to work out her beliefs and face life's challenges with a positive attitude helped Rosa trust her internal voice and solidify her internal foundation.

In the midst of Rosa's sister's terminal illness, Rosa and her husband decided to have a third child and were surprised with twins. Rosa used her new perspective to manage life with four children. Her internal foundation enabled the spontaneity she had never had and led her to be much more flexible in how she handled her children and her overall life. She and her husband achieved a mutual partnership in which they openly worked out issues:

> He's a great husband. We keep each other going. We're a great team. He's willing to admit when he's wrong, but then sometimes he will stand his ground. That's good, 'cause I'm the same

way. I will give in sometimes, and sometimes, I will stand my ground. We respect each other. Because we do let each other stand our ground on certain issues, and other issues we do know, "Okay, we have to give in to this if we're going to make this work."

Rosa's life circumstances changed her career ambitions immediately after college. Adjusting to motherhood earlier than she had imagined and facing the reality of her cousin's and sister's deaths brought more than enough pain to trigger internal reflection on how to handle circumstances beyond her control. Her ability to engage in that reflection, cultivate her internal voice, gain a positive perspective on her life, and build her internal foundation was substantially strengthened by her partnership with her husband and her sister. Both encouraged her internal voice, explored life experiences with her, and worked mutually with Rosa to manage those experiences.

Will and Leslie's Story: Jointly Negotiating Life and Death

Will's post-college life began in a more predictable fashion than did Rosa's. He initially worked in collections and learned through experience how to judge alternatives in approaching people in differing circumstances. His supervisors afforded him maximum autonomy in this role, which allowed him to find his own voice in his work. Four years after graduation, he moved to automobile financing, where he continued to enjoy autonomy and a supervisor who was a good partner:

> I have a lot of autonomy. No two deals are the same. I use my judgment for who will and won't pay. Ninety percent of the time I can make my own decision, and the manager backs me. Most of the time, she'll back me no matter what she thinks. It is a guessing game—the only way we make money is to do loans. I use my past experience, trying to remember people who paid me well, showed stability, residents in the area for a period of time.[4]

Will had opportunities to gain direct experience, learn from it, and use his insights in making new decisions. Knowing he would have the support of his supervisor helped give him confidence necessary to make difficult decisions, as he reported:

> I've become a lot more confident in the last twelve months, and I guess most of that's from the workplace, but also a large part of that's because of my wife. In the business setting, I'm much

more outgoing, and it's just kind of to get by. I'm always willing to, although sometimes I don't like to, make decisions. As a result, people tend to look to you to solve their problems. If you're willing to take the risk and make the decision and sometimes suffer the consequences, then people kind of look to you for that, and as a result, you somehow start to think that you always make the right decisions, which obviously isn't true. I always look at the pros and cons of each one and decide to throw the dice and see how it comes out, so that's probably boosted my confidence quite a bit. Also being willing to take on the really tough problems. Because I was willing to do those and then got more and more comfortable with it, that'll always help to boost your confidence.

It was clear that the autonomy Will had been afforded in his work enabled him to act and build confidence in his internal voice. Intrigued about his attributing some of his confidence to his wife, Leslie, I asked what role she played in this. He explained:

We've grown a lot as far as our decisions and long-range goals. We're talking more about a family. Depending on how things go, I would imagine the next year or two that there may be a child, so that gives me a lot of confidence, too. One of the reasons we got married was because we've always felt like we did a good job of communicating and making decisions and haven't had many things that we can't negotiate out, whether it's buying a car or buying a house or planning long-range goals. We've always been able to somehow negotiate into something.

Will noted that he was still happily married after three years and that he and Leslie had transitioned into joint decision making fairly easily.

Having good partners at work and at home helped Will accept reality and work on controlling his response to it. One way he did so was to evaluate the likelihood and consequences of the worst-case scenario. He reported:

It's getting to the point where it's tough for people to get a rise out of me because . . . you have to take things in stride, and there's very little that's worth really worrying about for the long run. I like to work hard, and sometimes I will be momentarily stressed for five minutes at work, but I really feel that going home stressed is not a good idea, and I try not to do that. Occasionally it happens, but not very often anymore. Life will go on no matter what, and all that could ever happen at work is you could get fired. I guess I'm just not that concerned about that happening. Maybe that makes me more relaxed—and more willing to take chances.

As Will anticipated, he and Leslie did have their first child the following year. This led to a renegotiation of their work and personal roles:

> Not long after our daughter was born, my wife desired to work less. It wasn't possible; she made $10,000 more than I did. We liked the house we had [recently purchased.] Her desire not to work meant that I had to make more money. Simultaneously, an offer for another type of position came in; it was twice as much as I was making. The potential in a year or two would increase beyond what both of us could make. It included an opportunity to get another degree and met her desire to stay home with the baby. It met the need to make more money. We like to travel, and we need to pay for the little one's college. It was interesting talking through how to do me going back to school and trying to do day care. Our daughter was at day care for two months while we decided. Once we got comfortable with both doing part-time work for a while, while I went back to school, then we figured out how to do it. If you want to do something badly, you can do it. Taking a big risk doing this, I could fail in this new position, but I don't think so. We have taken out loans to make this work. If it didn't work, we would figure out another plan.[5]

Will and Leslie each expressed their desires and worked together to develop plans that would meet their joint needs. Will trusted his internal voice to take these risks. Their partnership and ability to authentically consider each party's needs made Will comfortable calculating risks in both his professional and personal life. Will then was able to take risks and envisage the positive outcomes because he trusted his internal voice. He shared that he felt lucky to be able to be with his daughter more and thought having done so would help him empathize with Leslie when she took over full-time responsibility for the children they anticipated having in the future.

Over the next few years, Will finished his graduate degree, and they moved to another city for his new position and had their second child. Will found more good partners there, one of whom was his father, who worked in the same company. Will bought small manufacturing companies that were in trouble to turn them around on behalf of his company. Success depended on his ability to calculate risks because mistakes would cost millions of dollars. His partners in the company, including his father, supported him in his work. Will had confidence in his experience in calculating risks and appreciated the autonomy his new colleagues provided for him to do so. Given the magnitude of the decisions, he also sought their advice. When he did so, they helped him sort through his perceptions to come to a good choice. As result of these experiences and his colleagues' advice, his ability to calculate risks became instinctive. He described how he operated in negotiations: "I'm used to being what I would call a straight shooter. You say what's on your mind and your position on the thing, and they say theirs, and that's it. Then you try to find some middle ground." Will did not see negotiations as particularly stressful because he had developed his internal foundation, and it served as a basis for authentic interactions in negotiations. He carried this perspective into his personal life, as well: "My wife and I don't sweat the small stuff. Don't worry about things not in your control or that have already happened. It's over with."

Will and Leslie now had two children and were discussing having more children. Will reported that both were pretty unsure whether to do so. Two years later, they did have a third child. Will explained that they had continued to sort it out together:

> It was funny when we . . . maybe even before we got married, I had wanted to have two and she had wanted to have three or four, and so I, of course, moved to one because I thought it was better negotiating. Start at one and try to settle it. So, when we had the second one, we kind of said, "Well, we'll see how it goes," and maybe a year and a half after we had the second one, we talked about it some more, and we said we would try to have three and then see if we could call it quits, so . . . which tells you that if we're having this conversation next year and there's a fourth one . . .

Will and Leslie had established a strong partnership in which they listened to each other and made joint decisions that balanced both their needs. Because Will had enjoyed strong partnerships in both work and personal life, he was securing his internal commitments in his mid-thirties.

Will continued to benefit from partnerships with Leslie and his father as he faced the biggest challenge of his life at age thirty-six—leukemia. Excruciating pain in his arm prompted Leslie to take Will to the hospital late one evening. Within hours, doctors diagnosed his condition as leukemia. Despite the shock of this unexpected crisis, Will and Leslie immediately set about tackling the challenge.

The next two years were filled with chemotherapy, stem cell transplants, 220 days of inpatient treatment, progress, and relapses. I never had another opportunity to interview Will after his diagnosis, so his wife Leslie generously agreed to share their story. They decided together to be open with their children throughout the process and would make treatment decisions jointly. Leslie reported that Will immediately turned to his strengths: calculating the risks of treatment outcomes and the probability of his survival, and organizing their finances to ensure she and the children would be financially stable. His father partnered with him in working out their financial affairs, and Leslie partnered with him to cope with treatment and help him stay connected to the children. Will was preparing for his third stem cell transplant when he suffered another relapse, which reduced the chances of a successful outcome to 1%. At that point, he and Leslie mutually negotiated their most difficult life decision—they decided to discontinue treatment. Will left the hospital, told each of his children what to expect in the coming weeks, and then organized a trip the following weekend to Disneyworld that they had postponed twice due to his health. He personally called thirty-eight family members and friends to join them, and every person attended what Leslie described as a very upbeat weekend. Will died six weeks later.

Leslie and I talked about their partnership and how it played out in the major decisions in their lives. She described it like this:

> He approached the disease the only way that we knew how to approach anything, like when we decided to get married, when we decided to buy our first house, when we decided to have kids. It was very systematic. Let's look at the pros and cons. Let's make this list, and that's how he handled all the major decisions in his life. When we had our first child, and he was offered the position with his dad to come up here, it was a major decision in our life. Let's talk about the pros and cons. Is this going to benefit us in the end? That's how he approached everything and always the underlying thing that drove all of our decisions in our life. . . . Before the kids were born, it was he and I. Is this going to be a good decision for he and I? Is this going to be good for our marriage? How is this going to affect our life? Will it make us happier? Once the kids came, every decision we made, big decisions, we talked about together, and

it was how is this going to affect our family? When this disease, this diagnosis hit us . . . it hit him . . . he approached it the same way. Okay, this is what we're facing. This is the decision, and how is this affecting my life. How can I make it the best for the family? How can I make it the best for me? That's just the systematic way that he always approached everything, we always approached everything together, that we were hit with this biggest event of our entire life, and the only way to approach it was to go back to what we knew and go back to the way he always addressed everything.

This approach to negotiating life included careful reflection on everyone's needs, weighing options, and making choices accordingly. This approach was second nature to Will, in large part because he had secured his internal commitments. Will's solid self-authorship, and the fact that he and Leslie had used this approach successfully in negotiating their lives, led them to use it to negotiate Will's death:

Will and I said oftentimes the last six weeks that his death is going to be a life-changing event for me, for the kids, for him obviously, but it's going to be a life-changing event. How do we want to approach it? It wasn't quite this clear-cut in our conversations, but we got to it over time, but we decided together that we did not want it to be a traumatic event. We didn't want them to look back on this time, as this was such a horrific time. It's always forever going to be "before Daddy died" and "after Daddy died." But we didn't want it to traumatize them, if that makes sense. So, everything we did and every decision we made and how we approached it and how I've approached it since then is from that perspective of trying to make it life changing but not traumatizing.

Leslie did her best to carry out their plan to minimize the trauma of Will's death for their three children. It was a struggle, and her reflection about it revealed the nature of their partnership:

I feel like Will and I kind of grew up together. We didn't have to make a life on our own after college 'cause we had each other. I've been with him since I was nineteen . . . half my life. So, I'm trying to create a person that I've never been before. It's trying to unravel yourself and figure out what parts were him, what parts were me. It very much blended while we were married, and that's what a good marriage is about, being your own person but being better as a whole, and that's who we were. We were each very much our own people and very independent people, but when I think about our marriage, we were better as a whole. We complemented each other. We brought out the best in each other, and because of that we were better as a whole. So, trying to take the best of that and separate it out is where I'm at, and it's coming to grips with the fact that maybe what I used to do and what I used to be is not all going forward and that's okay. I'm confident I'll come out on the other side, that's very much how I approach things. It's a decision to keep moving forward and trying to make a life for yourself. That's my new job. That's the cards I've been dealt, and I can sit around and pout and wonder why and feel bad for myself, or I can get myself up off the couch and figure out how to make it work. So, right now, that's the path I'm trying to take.

Leslie's resilience in the face of recreating herself and creating a "new normal" for her three children stemmed in part from her partnership with Will. They each brought themselves to the relationship, communicated honestly, and worked mutually to balance their interests. The authenticity of their relationship and their mutual negotiations over the years had helped both of them build strong internal foundations. Their story also underscores the value of good company, even after the internal foundation is securely in place to face life's ongoing challenges.

Gavin's Story: Educational Partnerships

Gavin sold insurance upon graduating from college. He was immediately given a level of autonomy for which he was not quite ready:

> My company is saying: "Here's your desk. Here's your office. Here's your phone. Here's the mailbox. Here's a little bit of clientele to get started. Start your own business. Here's some suggested ways to do it. Here are people who have done it and been successful. But this isn't necessarily the way you have to do it. See if you can build yourself a business."[6]

Gavin reported that the office where he started did not even have a manager. Another insurance agent served as Gavin's first work partner by helping him put the rejection agents routinely experience into perspective and not take it personally. The following year, Gavin had the benefit of a manager:

> At times, he's there to be a cheerleader: "Hey, you can do it. Do this. Do that. It'll come." Certain days, he'll be the accountant

and say: "Look, here's your numbers. Here's what you have. Here's what you have to have." Sometimes, when you have questions about things you don't know the answer to, he's your teacher. But it helps a lot. He's kind of a little bit of both. As long as you're an agent, though, it all comes down to what you do yourself because as much as he wants to help you, as far as your schedule, you make it yourself.

Gavin realized that a lot of his success rested on his own shoulders. Yet, he found it helpful to interact with other agents to put things in perspective and to have a manager who served as a teacher who also valued Gavin's abilities. After two years, Gavin moved to a different company where he found a learning partnership with his boss, a senior person in the field. Gavin's boss went beyond dispensing advice and answering questions. He supported Gavin in working through his questions and offered him autonomy in his work. Gavin described how his boss helped him learn to think for himself:

It's really nice to know that I can just say, "Mr. Smith, I'm having trouble with—I don't understand this." He doesn't always give me the answer. A lot of times, he'll throw back questions like, "Well, what do you think about it?" He always tries to get you to answer it yourself. And if he feels differently, he'll tell you. I'm still kind of nervous just because I feel like what I'm asking him is going to be stupid or silly. But he never makes you feel bad. His method of getting people to learn is he always thinks that if you're a bright enough person, you really do know the answer, or it's easy enough for you to find out. If we disagree, then he says, "Well, if that's the way you see it, do it your way and if it works out let me know." . . . It gives me the impression that if my mind-set is that I'm going to do it my way, I can do it that way. If it doesn't work, I'll tell him. And a lot of times he'll say, "Well, you'll feel a lot better with yourself because you tried it." So, it's a very, very relaxed atmosphere with very, very professional people. They just know how to—it's like they're being a mentor. It's neat.[7]

Gavin's boss invited Gavin to listen to his internal voice by encouraging him to reflect on his own ideas and use his own expertise to think through his work. He provided help when Gavin needed it without making Gavin feel incompetent. He supported Gavin trying his own way, even if he disagreed with it. Even when Gavin did make mistakes, his boss still encouraged him to try out his own thinking in order "to feel better about himself." His boss offered a strong partnership that helped Gavin cultivate and trust his internal voice. Learning to trust his internal voice led Gavin to realize that selling insurance was not a career fit for him.

After four years selling insurance Gavin decided to return to school to become a teacher. He explained the shift in perception that prompted this:

> It goes along with a shift in perception from I'll be rated by how much money I make to what makes me happy, a shift from what do my friends and relatives think versus what do I think. I've always been surrounded by peers, thought of everything in that mentality: How will I be perceived by others? I am the only one who has to worry about what I think. Your circle of contacts shifts from personal to professional relationships—smaller and tighter groups—you realize that you are true friends. They will support you no matter what, do what you feel will make you happy. Impressing others doesn't go away, but it is much smaller—that enables you to do what you want. You realize that friends and phases of life are temporary—crazy to please them. Pleasure with what you are doing won't be as transient.

Gavin had harbored the idea of being a teacher in college, but at the time, external influences had overpowered his internal voice and led him to believe that teaching was not a suitable male career. The dissatisfaction he encountered in selling insurance, along with good partnerships with supervisors who helped nurture his internal voice and a tight-knit group of true friends who supported him "no matter what," led him to listen to the internal voice over the noise of his peer groups' expectations. The shift to focusing on what made him happy enabled him to make a career change in keeping with his internally defined notion of success. He returned to school for a master's degree in teaching and took part-time jobs to support himself financially.

Gavin continued to find good partners when he began his student teaching two years later. They helped him with his teaching and offered perspectives that opened up his thinking about where he might teach:

> It is a different experience because it is all girls. Basically, there are three full-time male teachers out of fifty. It is an interesting perspective being the minority. It is neat to be in a school where most teachers love what they are doing. You can

get into material, there is a lot of flexibility, and you're allowed
to offer new courses. Two or three teachers can teach the same
thing. You can go at your own speed. The principal doesn't
review lesson plans. This caused me to turn my head. I didn't
think I'd be interested in a parochial school but my opinion has
changed.

Gavin enjoyed the autonomy to which he had become accustomed in
business. He particularly appreciated being able to teach in a way
that matched his personality:

My personality is exactly how I teach. I'm usually quiet when I
first meet people, then open up after I get to know them. This
happened in teaching, too. I'm starting to integrate other
things into this basic style. At no point has my supervisor told
me to do something another way. The only criticism was in the
first week about a lesson on Hinduism; my supervising teacher
showed me how to explain it, another way of doing it. I was not
told not to do it or what to talk about. There have been suggestions or creative ways of doing something I'm already doing.
They are supportive of ways I did things. I came up with some
projects, anything I want to do, and they've let me try it. Sometimes, what I wanted to do was the biggest flop. Now I know it
didn't work.

Because Gavin recognized the value of autonomy, flexibility, and collaboration with partners in the insurance business, he valued them
in his educational experience. Just as these types of partnerships
had helped him find his voice in business, they were helping him
craft his identity as a teacher. His trust in his internal voice led him
to be open to his supervising teacher's perspectives.

Over the next two years, Gavin finished his degree, substitute
taught while trying to get a permanent teaching position, ran a
business installing swimming pools on the side, and held a night job
to make ends meet financially. He landed a summer teaching job
that turned into a full-time position teaching social studies in middle school. He was pleased to land a position in a school with a
diverse student population. He explained his affinity for helping
students from backgrounds different than his own:

I have a student from our district, who was expelled from our
school, then kicked out of another school—I work with him five
hours a week. One-on-one, he is a wonderful kid. I know he has
made mistakes, but it is fun. His teacher provides me with all

the materials; I essentially help him do his work. He has a violent tendency. I do score book for the girls' basketball game, so I
take him, and he helps me keep the scores. I really enjoy trying
to help the kids who aren't the best students. Some teachers talk
about students they can't stand—and I kind of like them. A lot
of these kids come from households where parents work two jobs
and don't see them often. I have a student in seventh bell class
who got in a fight. She was angry because her mom just got sen-
tenced to four more years in prison. That kind of stuff, I can't
relate to, but I can at least try to help them a little bit.

Gavin also took up coaching the girls' volleyball team and immersed
himself in the school and the students. He felt he had found his calling and was satisfied with his career change. He trusted his internal voice and began incorporating his talents into his everyday life.
In the midst of building his internal foundation at age thirty, Gavin
was shaken a bit by his girlfriend's unexpected pregnancy. He
trusted his internal voice as they made the decision to wait to
marry, but he struggled with sharing the news:

I have never felt that nervous in my life, telling my parents.
She just told her mother! It didn't cause her any mental
anguish. I was thinking, I am nine years older than her, I
should be ready for this, and it shouldn't be that hard for me to
tell my parents. I worried for weeks, for weeks! We went to my
parents' house—I told them, they reacted. Of course, I knew
they couldn't possibly get mad, and they didn't, but nonethe-
less, my mom said, "Oh, so when are you getting married?" Dad
did the same thing. I was a little surprised. As much as my parents wanted us to get married as soon as possible, they understood. I said I have to wait. We feel we made a good decision,
and we are glad we waited.

Gavin knew his parents would accept the situation, yet he still worried about telling them. He found them to be good partners, however, in understanding his position. He found the same among work
colleagues, when he showed up at the summer party at the principal's house with the baby. Reflecting on his hesitancy in revealing
this information, he said:

It's funny because I always consider myself pretty much, at
school and work, [unconcerned] about what people think. I
can't control it, and it never bothered me. And this, it didn't
bother me, but obviously, by my actions, it must have because
otherwise I would have been more forward with information.

Gavin's internal foundation was strong enough for him to reflect on his concern about others' reactions. Through such reflection, he was continuing to work on securing his internal commitments in order to be comfortable sharing news with which others might disapprove or disagree.

Gavin continued to refine his role as a teacher and also became the summer school principal. He attributed his satisfaction with his work to good partners:

> I have a number of people that I've developed into friends on the faculty . . . even though you're not 100% thrilled with every-thing, you have people that you can have good relationships with. You don't realize how important it is to have administra-tion that just lets you teach without a lot of unnecessary struc-ture, or to have teachers that you actually get along with and like. One of the nice things about our old principal was he was a very hands-off manager, so if he knew that you did a good job, in whatever ways he assessed that, he just left you alone. If he thought that there were some things you need help with, he would help you. I know a lot of schools where the administration is a lot more confining than ours. The first principal I had was very much "I trust you as a professional. You need to do what you need to do in your classroom." The lady that replaced him was very much the same. "I trust you as the professional. You are going to do what you need to do in your classroom, and I'm going to come by a couple times a year and observe it to make sure that there are no significant mistakes. I don't need to see your lesson plans every week. I don't need to talk . . . you're the professional. You do it." From that respect I've been very lucky.

Gavin's success with work partners throughout his career, along with his affinity for those students who needed assistance, prompted him to join a five-person teaching team for a special proj-ect involving forty-eight students who did not qualify for Individual Educational Plans but needed more than the typical classroom experience. Explaining his decision to apply, he said:

> It was a combination of I knew the teachers that were doing it were good. I knew the principal of our high school who started this similar program. I liked him, and I knew what he was doing over there was working well. And it was just one of those things where sometimes you just got to take a risk, and this seems like a great idea. And when else would you ever have an opportunity to basically start from scratch, just have a few guidelines and parameters, and then run it all the way through?

The autonomy all of Gavin's good partners had afforded him became a mainstay of his professional life and helped him build his internal foundation and secure his internal commitments. As a result, he jumped at the opportunity to start a new program in which he could have a significant impact.

CREATING LEARNING PARTNERSHIPS

These stories demonstrate the important role of partners in developing self-authorship. How can you create these partnerships with those you care about? You can provide good company by using the six components of learning partnerships.

Life Partners

If you are reading this book as the life partner, you can use the six components of learning partnerships to promote your partner's internal voice and simultaneously strengthen your relationship. Framing your relationship as a complex combination of both your perspectives conveys to your partner that her/his perspective is an integral component in the relationship. Managing life decisions— career choices, family relationships, finances, major purchases, whether to have children, parenting, and health conditions—is one context in which you can offer good company. When you approach these decisions as complex and informed by both your perspectives (and sometimes those of others who are involved as well), you create a shared setting in which you and your partner can express your internal voices. Bringing your voice to this decision-making process provides a model for your partner. Affirming your partner's perspective in the decision-making process supports your partner in listening to and cultivating her/his voice. Working to share authority as a means to arrive at a mutually agreeable decision frames your relationship as one of mutual negotiation to meet both parties' needs and interests. Throughout this negotiation, expressing your beliefs, values, and feelings clearly and supporting your partner to do the same helps strengthen both your internal voices and enhance the authenticity of your relationship. Disagreements will inevitably occur and can be framed as opportunities for each of you to clarify your beliefs, values, and feelings. These conflicts are also an opportunity to learn how to work through differences so that they strengthen rather than weaken your relationship.

For example, Rosa and her husband had very different reactions to their surprise pregnancy. It interrupted Rosa's external formula for her early adult life and caused her considerable anxiety. Her husband, however, took it in stride. He emphasized that it was beyond their control and that they could work through it. He helped Rosa manage her reaction to reality, and they worked together to make decisions that met both their needs. They did disagree and admitted when they were wrong. Yet, they stood their ground when they thought they were right. Because her husband offered a context in which she could express herself freely, she learned to trust her internal voice to bring it into their relationship. Similarly, Will and Leslie engaged in complex negotiations about how to blend their careers and family needs in which both expressed their beliefs, values, and feelings, and they debated them until they came to solutions. The process helped strengthen their internal voices and their connection to each other.

Sometimes partners assist each other with decisions that rest primarily with one partner. In this case, engaging in conversations to help the partner clarify his or her beliefs, values, and feelings can help cultivate the partner's internal voice. These types of conversations encourage your partner to make his/her own decision while evaluating multiple options or opinions. Supporting a partner's voice when it is in conflict with external pressures can help sustain it. Kurt's construction of his management and leadership philosophy (chapter 4) is a good example. He spent considerable energy figuring out how to be effective as a manager and a leader in his work. Although he had work colleagues who provided good company for this task, he also credited his relationship with his wife as a crucial aspect of his success. Kurt experienced unconditional love from his wife. He was free to be himself, and she freely expressed herself in the relationship, and this helped Kurt in finding his authentic self. He saw the benefits of open and honest communication. As he and his wife made joint decisions, Kurt realized the value of integrating multiple perspectives. This relationship modeled the authenticity he wanted in his work relationships and also built his confidence in his internal foundation. This confidence enabled him to let go of his long-standing concern about how others viewed him to become a straightforward, authentic leader.

As Will and Leslie's story conveys, partners are equally important once internal foundations are in place. Lydia's story (chapter 6) shows how her husband's trust of her parenting in his absence strengthened her internal foundation. They also mutually created a framework for managing the on-going ambiguity of Navy life. In their thirties, Mark and his wife continued to negotiate how their career paths and parenting meshed. Dawn's partner supported her in integrating her talent for cooking and her multiple sclerosis (MS) into her identity. Honest feedback from her partner also assisted Dawn in reevaluating parts of her internal foundation. Alice and her husband and many other parents negotiated careers, child care, and parenting philosophies in ways that encouraged both partners' voices to be heard, affirmed the needs of all involved, and focused on collaboration to find solutions that were consistent with their internal voices and foundations. The six components of learning partnerships are interwoven in all of these life partnerships.

Parents

If you are reading this book as the parent, you can use the six components of learning partnerships to promote your daughter or son's internal voice and construct an adult-adult relationship. As a parent, one of your challenges is to step back from your position of authority (or move to the back seat of the bicycle) to enable your son or daughter to take up his or her personal authority. Because children become accustomed to the parent-child hierarchy, you are in a better position than your child is to reframe the relationship as adult-adult. Engaging your sons or daughters in reflective conversations that enable them to clarify their beliefs, values, and feelings helps convey the importance of their internal voices and affirms that you value them. Inviting them to bring their internal voices to your relationships creates a setting in which to practice expressing themselves authentically with loved ones. Also, offering increasing responsibility and autonomy for decisions over time can help them listen to their internal voices. The more opportunities they have to directly put their voices into action (even, or especially, when doing so holds important implications), the more they learn to trust their internal voices. Gradually transferring authority from parent to child does not mean that anything goes, however. Sharing authority and expertise in mutual decision making means parents afford their children a meaningful role in decision making yet still bring to bear their parental expertise when it is appropriate in arriving at a mutual decision. Autonomy also comes with responsibility. Freedom to make choices and experience the consequences helps people refine their internal voices. As late adolescents take up adult roles (e.g., employee, college student, parent, partner), parents can still be important partners by maintaining mutual relationships. At this point, parents offer an authentic adult-adult relationship in which their children can refine their internal voices and find support in facing the challenges of adult life.

Many participants enjoyed these learning partnerships with their parents. Mark cherished his mother's advice of "to thine own self be true" and talked routinely with his father about career and life issues. Kurt tried to be true to the man in the glass as his parents encouraged. They also engaged Kurt in reflective conversations about his career choices and offered unconditional support for his decisions. Dawn's parents engaged her in conversations about her nomadic existence in her twenties yet supported her explorations and her coming out. Dawn also enjoyed a good partnership with her grandmother, as did Sandra, whose grandmother engaged her in reflective conversations about her faith and her career options. Evan called his grandfather to talk about life issues. Cara's parents formed an adult-adult relationship with her in her twenties that helped her cope with her in-laws' expectations. This foundation enabled Cara to maintain her relationship with her parents when they were hesitant about the decision she and her husband made to adopt an international child. Other participants found adult-adult relationships with their in-laws that supported their internal voices. Parents, grandparents, or in-laws were often key partners in sorting out parenting roles and work roles. The key in all of these relationships were parents and grandparents who were willing to challenge participants' thinking, encourage them to cultivate and refine their internal voices, and support them in taking responsibility for their lives.

Participants tried to enact these partnerships with their young children. They found it challenging, however, given the increasing prevalence of violence, kidnapping, and sexual predators that required closer parental supervision than was the norm when they were growing up. They shared their concerns about how to balance their children's safety with teaching their children responsibility and autonomy. Barb and her husband hesitated to allow their daughter Cathy to run ahead of them walking in the neighborhood. Barb said: "I'd rather just sit at home in my living room with all the doors locked. At least then I can relax." Barb and Jimmy were not taking any chances with Cathy's safety, although they wished they could offer her more freedom. Al, noting the same issue with his children, speculated that his concern for safety contributed to his children's lack of creativity in "making their own fun":

> When I was a kid, I could ride my bike a mile to somebody's house or a basketball court or the baseball field and play, and now you can't do that because you're scared to death somebody's going to nab your kid. My perception is you just can't leave them out of your sight. I think almost in some ways we've reverted from making your own fun, which when we were kids was a good thing because it forced you to be resourceful, creative. Now, everything's organized, in part because of this whole safety issue, so we lose probably some of the spontaneity and creativity that kids used to have.

Al was not sure that he and his wife were doing the right thing by having their three-year-old daughter in dance and cheerleading, but he didn't want her sitting home playing video games either.

My participants were often unsure about how to balance their children's educational success with teaching them responsibility and independence. Al reported:

> You always wonder if you're doing the right thing, and who knows? There are lots of books about parenting, but I don't think anybody really knows exactly how to do it. When Joseph has homework, we try to let him do it himself, and then we check it, and if there's some that we need to go over, we do. I'll look at his answers, and if there's any that I think he needs to look at again, I'll say, "Well look at this one again." That's one way of dealing with it to try to give them some responsibility.

Many parents were torn between helping their children succeed in competitive school environments and teaching them to figure things out on their own.

Alice enlisted God to help her create a learning partnership with her daughter. You will recall that Alice suggested that her daughter talk with God about how to treat her brother and how to conduct herself when she felt peer pressure (chapter 8). Alice did not step back from her responsibility as a parent in these instances, but afforded her daughter some autonomy to figure some of this out for herself. Alice and her husband also offered their daughter the freedom to choose being baptized in their faith. Alice's story shows that despite the challenges, learning partnerships with children are possible.

Peers: Friends, Siblings, Co-workers

If you are reading this book as a friend, co-worker, or sibling, you can use the six components of learning partnerships to help others develop their internal voices and simultaneously strengthen your relationships. Friends and co-workers often share similar concerns. They rely on each other for support in facing life's challenges. Siblings often have strong connections and know each other's histories. The nature of the support you offer to friends, co-workers, and siblings may make all the difference in helping them find their internal voices. As a peer, it is important to resist giving advice or turning the conversation to your concerns. Focus instead on drawing out your friend's concerns and asking questions to help her or him clarify what is really at issue in a particular situation. Questions that help them sort out how they are making sense of a situation, what evidence they have for that interpretation, what about it bothers them, and what other possible ways there are to view it all help people listen to their internal voices and identify beliefs, values, and feelings they are bringing to the situation. Engaging them in working through the benefits and drawbacks of various alternative responses helps cultivate their internal voices. Reflecting back what you hear them saying sometimes helps them hear it more clearly. Helping people sort out their priorities in a situation can help them listen to their internal voice and recognize it as a sound basis for decision making. Offering expertise that you have is appropriate as long as it does not eclipse your peer's own voice. Conveying that they are in the front seat of the bicycle for their journey is important to help them concentrate on their internal voice rather than on other external voices.

Sandra (chapter 5) relied heavily on her friends and co-workers as she struggled with her career dilemmas. Co-workers helped her process situations with patients and talk about best courses of action. They consistently asked questions and provided moral support but did not give advice. When they had mutual expertise, they shared their interpretations, but they always encouraged Sandra to make her own decision. Her friends helped her process her career frustrations. They encouraged her to talk about her values, explore other ways they might be implemented, and reframe how she saw changing careers. As an only child, Sandra relied on her cousins for some of this support, as well. Rosa's sister, who was battling cancer, was a good partner for her; she helped Rosa clarify her faith and develop her internal foundation as they coped with the implications of cancer together. She engaged Rosa in explicitly exploring her beliefs and sharing their feelings about the disease. Her sister modeled authenticity and engaged Rosa in an authentic relationship.

Participants sought out support networks when they were unavailable in their work or personal settings. Lydia connected with Navy wives to figure out Navy life. Other Navy wives served as models of what is possible and of how to manage ambiguity. She also sought out mothers as she adjusted to being a parent whose partner was often away. Cara sought out academic women who did not have children when determining whether to have children. Participants described true friends as those who supported them doing what made them happy.

Employers

If you are reading this book as an employer, you can use the six components of learning partnerships to promote your employees' internal voices and enable them to be more productive and capable of negotiating the complexity of work. Participants thrived in work settings in which they were afforded autonomy yet given enough structure to succeed. Employers who portrayed the complexity of work roles and work decisions helped employees see that most aspects of their work were complex and required negotiating multiple perspectives. These employees also saw that they would have to bring their own voices to the process of shaping their work and meeting their employers' expectations. Many managers, through their style of leadership, affirmed employees' internal voices and expressed the need for them to be evident in the workplace. For example, Gavin's insurance supervisor asked him how he viewed situations, helped him figure things out for himself, and encouraged

Gavin to try his own methods. Will's boss supported his decisions on risky loans and thereby helped Will build his confidence through taking risks. Her supervisor's insistence on asking for the rationale for her decisions led Sandra to adopt a rationale for decisions. Dawn's directors invited her to bring her voice to the characters she played. Kurt's supervisor modeled not allowing others' perceptions to control his decisions. These work environments that participants encountered early in their careers served to draw out and affirm their internal voices. Knowing their supervisors would help them and share expertise as needed enabled them to take the risks to try out their new internal voices in their work roles.

As employees' internal voices became surer, employers still played a key role as learning partners. Will's father and other company officials trusted Will to purchase companies on their behalf. Their trust strengthened Will's trust in his own perspective and skills. Gavin continued to refine his identity as a teacher, as his principals afforded him autonomy in his teaching and trusted that he knew what was best in the context of his particular students. Sandra entered into a mutual partnership with her social work supervisor in which they supported each other through difficult situations. Participating in this partnership helped Sandra refine her internal foundation and form a framework for managing her reaction to reality. Mark consulted with the owner of his company on major decisions but, for the most part, made lightning-fast decisions on his own. Cara's department chair disagreed with her handling of a student grade complaint, but he respected and supported her position. This enabled her to act on her internal foundation and maintain her integrity. Essentially, these employers treated their employees as trusted adults who were capable of analyzing workplace problems, gaining expertise in handling these problems, and negotiating workable solutions. The guidance employers offered in refining their employees' abilities also supported the latter's internal voices and foundations. Growth toward and within self-authorship increased participants' productivity as employees, as well as their job satisfaction. The key to good company as an employer is balancing autonomy and guidance to enable employees to develop internal foundations upon which to ground their work.

As employers, participants tried to help their employees develop their internal voices. It was a struggle given their employees' prior experiences. Lindsey worked in a government agency in which he tried to offer his employees autonomy. He noted:

> We present numbers to a team of directors. My job as a supervisor is to answer questions only if the people who are actually putting these numbers together are truly stumped. I tell them, "I don't want to intrude here, and please speak up and answer those questions and I'll keep my big mouth shut, and if you give me a wink, then I'll chime in and explain something." I do think that I need to try to take a step back more and let these people sort of fend for themselves. I'm really trying to foster an atmosphere where these analysts have a sense of ownership with their statistics, and it's really a challenge right now to try to get these people to take ownership. If you need to explain something you have to dig in there and figure it out. They know that I'll get it.

Despite Lindsey's clear communication with his employees and his willingness to support them as needed, their preference was to rely on him rather than take responsibility themselves. They hesitated to dig in and figure things out. They were also hesitant to tell him when they made mistakes, despite the fact that he reacted positively. His experience demonstrates the challenge of creating learning partnerships with people who have been socialized to rely on authority rather than to develop their internal voices. Kurt's story in chapter 4 further illustrates that it is a struggle as a supervisor to create these partnerships unless you have developed your own internal voice.

Educators

If you are reading this book as an educator, you can use the six components of learning partnerships to promote your learners' internal voices and enhance their ability to handle ambiguity. Many participants reported that in their secondary schools, and sometimes in college, knowledge was portrayed as something students acquired from teachers. Learners were viewed as receptacles of this knowledge rather than active partners in learning. As a result, learners had no idea that they should use their internal voices to form their beliefs. In college, participants encountered instructors who involved them in learning and asked them what they thought about topics they were studying. These instructors respected students' opinions and thus affirmed their ability to learn and decide what to believe. Problem-based learning, inquiry learning, service learning, and other forms of teaching that actively engaged learners in exploring ideas encouraged them to listen to and cultivate their internal voices. These approaches engaged students in actively researching ideas, conducting experiments, considering multiple perspectives on a problem or question, reflecting on their own ideas and what they had studied, and applying these in understanding concepts. These students' involvement challenged them to bring their internal voices to learning. The teachers who engaged students' thinking helped refine it by asking for a rationale for students' conclusions and thus affirmed that students were capable of thinking and learning. These teachers also shared their expertise in these interactions but did so differently than the traditional "telling students" what they had to know. They offered their expertise as part of the exploration and engaged students in developing reasonable beliefs by evaluating evidence. Participants who encountered these learning partnerships recognized the need to develop their internal voices and, as a result, were better prepared for the complexity of college study, and of life beyond college.

Participants who attended graduate and professional schools reported finding good company for developing self-authorship. Their instructors valued their experience and ideas and expected them to share these in class discussion. Learners were routinely asked to offer evidence for their perspectives and explore the benefits and limitations of various viewpoints. Instructors emphasized the complexity of learning and invited students to develop their personal authority in the learning process. The instructors offered their expertise but encouraged learners to weigh it with other perspectives to make their own decisions about what to believe. These educators provided guidance but remained on the back of the bicycle, insisting that the learner take the captain's seat. Thus, the key to being good company as an educator is to encourage students to think for themselves and teach them how to learn. Good examples of such partnerships are available if you are interested in reading about them in more detail.[8]

Educators who participated in my study reported that creating learning partnerships was not always easy, given the nature of schools and colleges. Lynn, who as a result of substitute teaching and permanent teaching jobs in multiple districts had wide experience with multiple grade levels, shared that school administrators' focus on "teaching to the test" meant not teaching children what they really needed to know or to learn. Lynn was not opposed to assessment of learning, but she was opposed to programs that did not promote learning. Her experience echoed that of other teachers in the study. They generally had minimal autonomy in their work to do what they felt would really advance students' learning. Justin, who after years of teaching in special education became a school principal, struggled with these same issues in his administrative role, noting that the focus on achievement scores was "short-sighted." Justin reported that his building was "hovering right underneath the standards" and that he spent the majority of his time trying to figure out how to raise scores. Justin worked to focus on his school's curriculum to align it with state standards. He hoped that teaching the curriculum would yield higher test scores. Thus, while he worked to focus on student learning, he reported that the pressure of test scores was distracting.

Cara's story in chapter 8 about her university's grading culture reveals another challenge to creating learning partnerships. The routine practice of raising students' grades subverts the educational principle that giving them honest feedback about their performance improves learning. In the case of the student who harassed Cara and his peers, colleagues encouraged her to just raise the grade rather than attempt to teach the student that his behavior was inappropriate. Such educational environments work against students developing their internal voices. Educators such as Lynn, Justin, and Cara who want to create learning partnerships with their students have to work around these challenges. In contrast, Gavin's school environment offered him more autonomy to create learning partnerships with students.

Professional Partners

Anyone can be a learning partner. Evan described an elderly man who was his mentor in refereeing hockey. He talked routinely with his mentor about hockey issues and was always comforted by seeing him in the stands when he was on the ice refereeing a game. Kurt appreciated his management coach, who helped him develop his management philosophy and clarify his own values as they related to his career. Seasoned professionals, who have more experience in a particular arena, can provide the challenge and support those who are new to it need to increase their confidence and expertise. When professional partners use the components of learning partnerships, they essentially take the back seat of the bicycle. Doing so enables front riders to take account of professional counsel while working toward developing their own voices, philosophies, and approaches. These relationships are often highly important over the course of both parties' lives.

Medical and mental health professionals can also be learning partners. Sandra's doctors and personal trainer were important partners for her in managing her health. She specifically sought doctors who respected her experience and who engaged with her about how to stave off hip replacement until later in life. She valued her personal trainer's approach because he shared authority and expertise with her as they jointly determined how to maintain her physical health. Dawn appreciated her neurologist's interest in her philosophy of life as they discussed how to manage her MS. Dawn also enjoyed good company from her therapist, who helped her acknowledge her talents and integrate them into her identity. Many of the study participants took advantage of counseling opportunities to face life's challenges. Although some approaches to medicine and therapy are, by their nature, learning partnerships, some can foster authority dependence. Using the components of learning partnerships can help you actively engage patients and clients in taking responsibility for their health. Will's story conveys the importance of being able to make wise decisions about medical treatment.

Some participants turned to members of the clergy to help them address life's challenges and how their spiritual beliefs were evolving. Sandra enjoyed a good learning partnership with one of her priests because he listened to her perspective and worked together with her to sort out her call to serve. Likewise, Reginald enjoyed a good learning partnership with his senior pastor as he was growing into his own role as a minister. He and the senior pastor worked as colleagues and shared authority as they conducted their every day work in the church. This helped Reginald cultivate and trust his own voice as a pastor. He, in turn, created learning partnerships with his parishioners by encouraging them to take the front seat as they sorted out their beliefs and life issues. Similarly, Sandra and Alice respected the thoughts and feelings of their clients and helped them sort through their problems while staying on the back seat. Al emphasized that respecting his patients' opinions and concerns was central in advising them to choose the best medical treatment.

Understanding Your Partner's Journey

As the diverse narratives in this book show, the journey toward and through self-authorship varies widely because of individual characteristics and environmental influences. Being a good partner requires understanding the nuances of your partner's journey. What might this journey look like for people different from those included in this study? To explore that question, the next chapter introduces additional stories from other studies involving people of different backgrounds. If you did not yet find stories that were consonant with your experience, I hope you will find them in the next chapter. These additional stories add to our ability to understand the multiple variations of the journey toward self-authorship.

CHAPTER 10

DIVERSE SELF-AUTHORSHIP STORIES

THE LIFE NARRATIVES IN THIS BOOK OFFER A RARE OPPORTUNITY—a window into possible ways internal voices develop in all their messy glory! To hear these participants reflect on prior years, and to be able to compare those reflections with their narratives at the time, draws out complex interactions of personal and environmental factors. The variation in the journeys for the group of adults who you have met so far in this book underscores that authoring our lives is a unique process for each of us, as we constantly balance who we are becoming with our relationships with those around us. The stories of self-authorship in this book are intended to raise possibilities for authoring your life, to highlight possible pathways into and through adulthood, and to open you up to reflecting on your life in a new way. I do not assume that these stories capture the experiences of any adults other than those who lived them. They represent one group of people who attended one college in a particular time period. They do not represent the larger group of students who attended college with them, students at other colleges, or others their age who did not attend college.

Only you, the reader, can determine the extent to which these stories resonate with your life and the lives of those about whom you care. The best way to use this book is to consider how the stories relate to your life—what resonates and what is different? You can also engage others in your life in conversation to see how the themes from these stories relate to their lives. Some aspects of these stories might offer good company to you; other aspects might offer good company to others with whom you interact.

Another way to explore the utility of these stories for your life and for the lives of those around you is to compare them with stories of others who differ from those you have read about so far. The participants in this book are now forty years old. What different possibilities and challenges do students face who are currently in college and twenty years younger? The participants in prior chapters are all white. What different possibilities and challenges do the stories of people of color reveal? Dawn is the only participant we have met who openly identifies as gay. What can the stories of those who identify as gay, lesbian, bisexual, transgender, or queer add to our understanding of the path to self-authorship? Participants in the stories you have read all attended college. What additional lessons can stories of those who enter the workforce after high school provide?

This chapter presents the stories of adults from these additional groups to broaden the context for authoring your life and to further explore how personal and contextual factors affect that process. I have included current resources that specifically address the process of authoring your life; there are many other sources of information about adult development that are not included here.

STORIES OF CONTEMPORARY COLLEGE STUDENTS

Interviews with current or recent college students of multiple races, ethnicities, sexual orientations, and social classes provide insights into additional dynamics that mediate the journey toward and through self-authorship. These stories show that unique combinations of personal and contextual dynamics can prompt self-authorship any time from late high school through one's thirties.

Self-Authorship: Latino/a College Students' Stories

To understand the college experience and ethnic identity development of Latino/a college students, Vasti Torres, an adult development researcher, interviewed twenty-nine Latino/a college students over the course of their college experiences.[1] Nine of these students began college in 2000, thirteen in 2002, and seven in 2003. These students attended four different urban universities located around the country. Two universities were predominantly white, with 4% Latino/a students, and two were Hispanic-Serving Institutions that had 25% and 95% Latino/a students, respectively. Collectively, these interviews revealed many similarities with the journey toward self-authorship my study participants experienced. The Latino/a students' stories, however, also revealed additional aspects of the evolution of the internal voice. These included recognizing their cultural reality, incorporating an informed Latino/a identity into their daily lives, and renegotiating their relationships with others based on their Latino/a identity.

Recognizing how their cultural history affected them was a central dynamic for Latino/a students as they made choices based on their internal voices, designed plans of action, and advocated for themselves. For example, Antonio's lack of legal residency thwarted his aspirations to attend medical school. Once he recognized this limitation, he changed his major to pursue a more realistic path; however, he simultaneously worked actively to gain support for a legislative bill that would offer temporary residency to students who did not have legal status. He explained his situation:

> When one graduates from a four-year university, a lot of the medical schools require that the student have a Social Security number . . . And besides, medical school is very, very expensive, so if I was to have papers, the government might be able to help me, and I might be able to apply for scholarships, which require me to have a Social Security number. So, more doors will be open for me to study medicine.[2]

Antonio's career choice was a blend of his internal voice and his cultural realities. He simultaneously accepted these realities and advocated for himself and other undocumented students by working to change these realities.

Another dynamic evident in these students' stories was incorporating an informed Latino/a identity and the cultural choices that stemmed from it into their daily lives. Araceli demonstrated this dynamic as she described what it meant to be Chicana:

> I knew the main facts and the main ideology. I knew it, and I thought I related [to it], but I didn't feel I was that strong of one. And now, going out to the capital [city] and rallying helped a lot. And not just the political aspect, but learning about the past and being able to go out to a high school and being able to

tell them this [is] what your past is about, letting them know that we [Mexican Americans] are here, and we want you to succeed. Even though we're a minority doesn't mean it's a bad thing. And I now feel like that applies to me, and I say it with pride.[3]

Once Araceli understood and solidified her own cultural identity, she shifted to mentoring others to advocate for Latinos/as. Advocating for their culture reflected another dynamic of self-authorship for Latino/a students.

The Latino/a students Torres interviewed also renegotiated their relationships with others based on their Latino/a identity.[4] For example, Susie achieved an informed Latina identity, and as a result, discontinued her friendships with former gang friends in order to embrace her college student identity. Elizabeth maintained her circle of friends but interacted with them differently after refining her Latina identity. Achieving interdependence for Latino/a students requires maintaining their own cultural values while adapting to living in a diverse society. Thus, cultural identity and values were a central thread as these students moved toward, into, and through self-authorship.

Torres emphasized that dealing with racism and the dissonance it caused mediated the journey toward self-authorship. For example, Sagi, a community college student who had been in the United States for only five years, explained her sense of being in college:

I feel ashamed . . . because I have an accent. If I am confused, people judge me more because you have an accent. But if you are an American, and you say something and it doesn't come out right, then they say, well, can you explain that a little more, and they can explain it. They have more words to explain it. And when you are a second-language learner, you don't. Besides, when [the professor] gives you this look, then she makes you feel embarrassed, it makes it hard to come up with a word.[5]

Sagi internalized negative stereotypes about herself and noted, "When I have an accent, I see myself as not being well [educated]."[6] Sagi gained confidence during college through a job in which she spoke English, earning a scholarship, and having interactions with a Latina role model (Torres). All of these experiences helped her reject negative stereotypes that interfered with her development. In some cases, racism was overwhelming enough to stifle growth; in other cases, the dissonance and students' resilience in coping with it helped them shift to self-authorship.[7] This contributes to growing evidence that those who face marginalization, and thus must work to accommodate dissonance related to their identities, relationships, and beliefs, may be challenged to develop self-authorship earlier in life. This is another example of how the appropriate balance of challenge and support can help adults develop their internal voices.

Self-Authorship: Lesbian College Students' Stories

As was the case with the Latino/a students in Torres's research, lesbian college students have to forge their identities in resistance to social norms that emphasize heterosexuality. Interviews with lesbian college students reveal the dynamics stemming from this resistance in the journey toward and into self-authorship. Elisa Abes, an adult development researcher, interviewed ten lesbian students ages eighteen to twenty-three to understand their identity development and its relationship to self-authorship.[8] She interviewed them again two years later.[9] The group included five Caucasians and five students of color. Their stories revealed that contextual influences and the degree to which students developed their internal voices affected lesbian identity construction. Those with internal voices were better able than those who relied on external influences to decide how contextual influences shaped their identity.[10]

One participant whose internal voice was still somewhat fragile talked about the challenge of listening to her internal voice in the midst of external noise. Gia, a fourth-year student, was dating a woman whose family disapproved of their relationship. She explained:

> I'm having to deal with my girlfriend's family, and they're not very happy about me. . . . So, I've been thinking a lot more about people and how against gay people they really are. . . . It makes me angry, and it makes me also I think, somewhere inside, I want to hide it. Even though I know hiding isn't right. It's starting to have that kind of effect on me, and it's bothersome. And that's what makes me angry. It's like why are these two people, who are ignorant, going to get me to think badly about myself or my relationship? . . . And it's so funny because

> I know what I know about the gay community, my life, how I feel about me. I'm very secure about myself. And then to have these two people who are challenging that, and I'm allowing that. So it really frustrates me . . . That's where the anger comes in. Because inside I'm like, why should I want to melt into the mainstream, just because these two people don't like it? . . . Their homophobia is like starting to seep into me. . . . Why should I let their ideas like start seeping into me? . . . It's like this really complex problem right now.[11]

Although Gia was secure about herself, she felt the contrary external messages were undermining her sense of self. She was keenly aware of the tension between her internal voice and external influence, a sign of being in the crossroads, yet she was not able to resolve this tension in a manner consistent with the sense of self to which she aspired. The homophobia of her girlfriend's family simultaneously challenged her to strengthen her internal voice and thwarted her progress in hearing it.

Jacky, a 21-year-old college junior in Abes's study, used discriminatory experiences to develop her internal voice. She used discrimination as a stimulus for "researching various political and identity-based issues, reading in-depth about all sides of an issue and then reaching her own conclusions after a logical analysis of multiple perspectives."[12] Describing a financial struggle caused by the lack of domestic partnership benefits, she said:

> It doesn't make me feel sorry that I'm gay or anything like that, but it makes me wish I could be more able to change the system . . . I'm Black, gay, and female, and leftist . . . and I'm not a Christian. . . . It makes me follow politics that much more. . . . It helped me shape my opinions and my politics and my point of view.[13]

Jacky explored and self-authored her beliefs and identity as a result of the discrimination she experienced on multiple fronts.

Beth, another of Abes's participants, had come to trust her internal voice. As a junior in college, she described how she was making sense of the contextual influences on her identity:

> I'm seeing so many things as not so defined . . . my religious identity, for example, which has always been very primary to me, is still very important to me, but it also is a lot less defined, exists along a continuum and less in a specific label. There are issues with that I'm still working out with myself. . . . If I don't

believe in God and don't want to have a traditional Jewish marriage, can I still identify as culturally Jewish, what does that
mean? . . . How does that intersect with queer identity? . . . But
I don't see my Jewish identity as my prime role in my life. I
don't see being queer as the prime role in my life. I don't see
being white or middle class or a student or maybe somebody
who wants to be an academic someday as the one thing that
must define me. I am this collection of things . . . some of which
are label-able, some of which are stories or experiences or the
exact combination that only exists within me, or how I interpret them. I know, I've been kind of going through an anti . . .
not anti-labels phase because obviously labels are important to
communicate, but . . . I don't feel comfortable as defining
myself as a list of identities. I just see myself as a combination
of those and a lot of other things that I don't label. . . . I recognize that there are aspects of my identity that if taken out of
the whole picture are defined as or are definable, mostly as
sexuality, or religion, or career goal, or family, or whatever. So,
in that way, I do recognize that they are definable by separate
terms, but I also don't think that the way I think about any
one of them would be the same if I didn't have all those other
things. The way I think about my relationship with my family,
for example, might be this is how I relate to my mother, this is
how I relate to my sister, this is how I relate to my stepfather,
and my outside family, and everything else. That said, that
relationship with them would be entirely different if it weren't
influenced by that—all those other things, you know, sexuality, religion, etc.[14]

Beth resisted seeing herself as any one of many social identities and
instead integrated them into a complex portrait based on the values
she was choosing with her internal voice. In authoring her identity
and life, she and her peers faced the additional dynamic of working
against contextual influences, particularly those that suggest being a
lesbian is not the norm. Whereas students from dominant cultures
are often able to readily find at least some contextual influences
that support their identities, relationships, and beliefs, lesbian
college students have to grapple with contextual influences that
oppose and serve as sources of discrimination against their identities, relationships, and beliefs; as a result, they encounter more
challenge and less support than majority students. Leah, another
participant who also integrated her lesbian and Jewish identities,
used her self-authored system to reject external perspectives that

she felt were discriminatory. Recounting an exchange with a peer who insisted that Leah could not be both gay and Jewish, she said:

> It was beyond her conception that I was a gay Jew. . . . She was afraid of me. I was foreign to her. I was impossible. And it opened my eyes. . . . It made *me* feel a little conflicted, though not about, I mean of course I'm happy with both my sexuality and my religion and all these things, but it made me feel this really sucks that there's people in my community, in both my communities, that don't like me because I'm religious or don't like me because I'm gay, and that's just stupid. This is so dumb.[15]

Leah found having to deal with these kinds of reactions frustrating, but the strength of her internal voice helped her frame discrimination as a problem outside of herself rather than a question about her identity.

Based on her collective interviews, Abes suggested that this dynamic of resisting social norms yielded a form of self-authorship that involved social change because students had to change social norms in order to redefine the meaning of their identities.[16]

Self-Authorship: First-Year High-Risk College Students' Stories

As was the case with Torres's Latino/a students and Abes's lesbian students, for high school students for whom college attendance required going against community or family values, resisting social norms also promoted self-authorship. Jane Pizzolato, an adult development researcher, interviewed thirty-five college students who were at high risk of dropping out of college because of poor prior academic preparation, low grades, or simply belonging to a population with a low historic incidence of college success. This group of mostly first-year students included students who identified "as Black or African American (sixteen), Asian (one), Hispanic or Latino/a (eight), or multiracial (three)."[17] Attending college was often in conflict with what their peers and communities expected of them, and their peers' negative behavior often served as the dissonance that prompted high-risk students to internally define their goal of attending college. Pizzolato learned in her interviews that it took a provocative experience that created enough disequilibrium for high school students to make an internal commitment to college. For example, Hollis was considering college, in part, because athletic recruiters had shown some interest in him. It was not until he was arrested for manufacturing drugs, however, that he was sufficiently provoked to reevaluate his goals. He explained:

> A lot of my friends didn't look at [getting arrested] like I did because I had something to give up, to lose. They didn't. They might be out the game for awhile, but soon as they out [of jail], they right back at it . . . but as soon as you get put with all this stuff, that'll prevent you from getting a scholarship altogether. That was the turning point in saying, "You know, I'm going to get serious about this s———."[18]

Going to jail was the impetus for Hollis to change his goals and seriously pursue college. These types of provocative experiences prompted students to aspire to possible selves that resisted the social messages they received; thus, they developed self-authorship prior to attending college.

The degree to which these high-risk students were able to maintain their visions of their possible selves and their self-authorship at college varied with the circumstances of their college admission. For example, some student athletes enjoyed the privilege of having others complete their application materials and handle their financial matters. Thus, they sometimes arrived at college without having learned how to manage college expectations. Tye, a student athlete who had done well in high school, quickly questioned his competence when he heard his peers in English class talking about ideas he had never heard of:

> I never even heard of these people or these things, and people are just talking about them so fluently. I feel so left out. And I'm not stupid, but I've felt that way a lot in class. I wasn't sure I should ever have been let in [to college].[19]

Because Tye had already developed internally defined goals, he worked to overcome this setback:

> I'm pretty sure that there's something that I know that other kids don't know, but not academic stuff. They kinda got the upper hand there, but you know it just means that I gotta get in there and learn too. I got skills, too; they just not as good as the other kids' [skills] yet.[20]

Taz, another student athlete, found it difficult to transition from the street mentality he used in high school to the mentality the college expected. He reported being his old self, which he described as being

disrespectful and fighting with others. He then had to work to construct a way to merge his past social identity with his new possible
self. He reported:

> In the street, you gotta read between the lines and draw con-
> clusions. You gotta figure out what people really mean. And the
> schoolboy mentality . . . you gotta read between the lines with
> your books and with your teachers to figure out what's really
> going on. You gotta read between the lines and draw conclu-
> sions in school. I think the schoolboy mentality, it goes along
> with the street mentality—but it's a little bit different. I'm still
> not sure how you mix them, but I'm on the verge of doing it.[21]

These students realized that they needed to make changes to
achieve their new goals. Because they had already begun to self-
author, they looked for ways to bring what they already knew to this
new environment instead of looking for external formulas.

Some high-risk students were disadvantaged in the admission
process because their families were unable to provide procedural
support in the college application process. These students had to
figure these processes out on their own. They also had to establish
priorities and ways to achieve them on their own. Jordan described
figuring out how to meet her individual goals while maintaining her
commitment of providing for her family:

> Thinking about how I could get a degree and really help my
> family, I decided I had to go to college. If I was to stay at home,
> and knowing what it's like, I knew what I would become—most
> of my friends are pregnant or have kids. . . . So, I chose to come
> to college and try to help my family from here.[22]

Pizzolato reported that Jordan moved beyond the external formulas
she had seen her peers follow to construct her own formulas for
achieving her goals.

For some high-risk students, self-authorship wavered early in
college as others' doubts about their capability and marginalization
of their identities pushed them to behave in ways to gain acceptance
rather than in ways consistent with their internal goals.[23] Cosette,
who identified as Hispanic, encountered resistance from people who
saw her as white due to her skin. She described this struggle:

> I feel like I don't know who I am or what I'm talking about—
> anywhere—because the whole attitude of these people saying,
> "Oh, that's not right." And, "Oh, you aren't that," and just

always opposing me. It seems like now the majority of the time I'm just doing things to make people happy, and I'm saying, "I don't know," "I don't know," just to have an opinion—in class or not—just so people stay friends with me, and so I can actually get through a day.[24]

This initially sounds like Cosette reverted to external formulas to gain approval; however, the fact that she is aware of her behavior and dismayed about acting in ways to make others happy reveals that she is still working on listening to her internal voice amid the external noise.

Personal characteristics and coping strategies influenced the ways these students made sense of these challenges and their ability to maintain self-authorship. Those who were clear about their goals and used effective coping skills were able to solidify their self-authored vision of themselves.[25] Of the twenty-seven first-year students Pizzolato interviewed, seven blamed external sources for their frustrations and sought external formulas to resolve them. Six exhibited self-regulatory behavior to move past their initial frustrations and reflectively solve problems based on their internal goals. Fourteen used what Pizzolato called supported coping, which involved seeking relationships to help develop clarity about their challenges and plans for overcoming them. In many cases, friends challenged students to reconsider their behavior. Conversations with peers, advisers, and counselors helped students clarify their feelings and devise plans to adapt to college. Thus, these students' experiences suggest that learning partnerships are crucial even to students who enter college having developed self-authorship.

Self-Authorship Stories of Students in a College Service-Learning Course

Lisa Boes, an adult development researcher, interviewed eight Harvard University students (one sophomore and seven juniors; of whom four were men and four women; with the group consisting of one Asian American, two Latino/as, five Caucasians) who recently took a course in community organizing.[26] The course incorporated many of the components of learning partnerships. The instructor supported students by respecting their opinions and feelings, helping them sort through their experiences, and collaborating with them to solve problems. Their projects in various communities challenged them to address complex issues, develop their personal authority, and work collaboratively with others to solve issues about which they all cared. These characteristics helped these students cultivate, and in some cases trust, their internal voices. Through these interviews, Boes explored students' self-authorship and the effect the course had on these students' journeys toward self-authorship. Of the eight students in the course, two demonstrated that they were listening to their internal voices and three were working on self-authorship. Because the course focused on students taking responsibility for their own community organizing projects, it likely attracted students who were ready to or already listening to their internal voices.

Celia was struggling to listen to her internal voice. This was apparent in the tension she felt between those she served and her own needs:

> [Sometimes, I am] overwhelmed by feeling like I couldn't do enough to make things right with these people that I cared about. . . . When you get so involved and so committed to people or to what you're doing, it's really hard to take sanctuary, and it feels . . . I feel guilty about taking that sanctuary.[27]

Celia recognized that she did need to take sanctuary and did so despite feeling guilty about it. She was listening to her internal voice to figure out boundaries for her service.

Jane was engaged in a slightly different struggle with listening to her voice. She developed principles about community organizing and used them to guide her decisions. Yet she struggled to express her voice with her immigrant parents:

> The very people who give me a reason to do the work that I do—my parents—are also the ones who disagree most with what I do. I see them work so hard, and I want to help people like them. . . . The longer I have worked in organizing Asian American students, the more I have come to realize that most of us either don't tell our parents anything about our activist work or do so at the expense of having our parents ask us to stop wasting their time getting into trouble. Many times, the louder we are in the public arena, the more silent we are in our private one.[28]

Jane was also struggling with integrating her school and personal life, evident in her analysis of whether to introduce a boyfriend she was confident her parents would disapprove of because he attended a community college:

> It's hard enough without putting my life into cubbyholes with this [being my school] life, and this is home life. Ideally, like I would want to integrate the two. [But I feel] I'm being a bad person by not introducing [my boyfriend] to my parents. But I saw my brother go through [a similar situation] that they didn't approve of, so I'm doing sort of a cost-benefit analysis.[29]

Jane's internal voice was under construction but not yet strong enough to emerge from the external noise of her parents' perceptions. She was doing the cost-benefit analysis to weigh the cost of risking their disapproval versus disappointing herself for not honoring her internal voice. She had cultivated her internal voice in her college life but remained uncertain how to express it in her Asian American family culture.

Neil, Maura, and Stephen were in the process of building self-authored systems during the course. Neil's initial community organizing project was with a local church and focused on leadership issues. He ran into difficulty because of a conflict within himself:

> I had difficulty returning to the mindset of a weekly church-goer, and I always felt something of a disconnect at affiliate meetings (though no one I met with ever mentioned this, I worry that they may have noticed some awkwardness in that). Thus, one of the reasons the project first appealed to me turned into one of its difficulties: I was not always plausible in the role of a concerned churchgoer trying to work for change, and may have been, as a result, less able to connect with people and persuade them that certain courses of action were the correct ones. Plausibility, however, is not just an external phenomenon. For the project to be successful, I had to be plausible to myself as well as others; whether or not I was plausible to others, I was never able to convince myself that this was something I should be directly invested in, and as a result, I had difficulty marshaling a sense of passion for the work.[30]

Although Neil worried that others may have questioned his plausibility, his own questioning of it led to his leaving the project. He trusted his internal voice sufficiently to use it to guide his actions.

Maura began her community-organizing project to create an epilepsy network, and she had a clear sense of what she wanted. She recognized that she wanted to control the project on one hand yet knew from her course readings that the point was to empower others. She struggled with this contradiction throughout the project. Near the end of her project, she recounted this experience:

> I was participating differently, and in a different kind of conversation: listening rather than promoting my own agenda, doing my part of the facilitation work, rather than running the show, and trying to move the group forward. Afterwards, I realized I hadn't listened to or legitimately sought to understand the interests, needs and resources of my constituents until the end of the project.[31]

Throughout the project, Maura grew increasingly able to trust her internal voice enough to share authority with others. She began to recognize that interdependent relations with others helped her grow:

> [I realized that] what's important to me is that no one has any control. . . . I can [try to] control everything . . . but that's not true. . . . I guess what's become important to me in the last couple years is developing . . . and identifying things that are more important to me in the sense that they move me or teach me things . . . or they expand my world or they connect me to others in new ways. What's important to me is developing a capacity to have those things and develop those things. So it's sort of like, out to the world, back into me, out into the world, back into me.[32]

Maura appears to be saying that identifying the things that move her, teach her, expand her world, and connect her to others in new ways are the mechanisms for building her internal foundation. Maura's notion of "out to the world, back into me" sounds similar to Dawn's (chapter 2) knowing when to let things happen versus when to make them happen. Evan's (chapter 7) notion of floating on the waves seems similar to Maura's willingness to let go of control.

Stephen trusted his internal voice as he built relationships with Columbian immigrants in his project with a Community Development Corporation. Faced with explaining why a Harvard student would be involved in an immigrant neighborhood, he shared with people he met the story of his grandfather immigrating to the United States. He explained how this helped him build connections:

> Once the woman I was visiting saw my intentions as genuine, it was easy for her to buy into some of my motivational energy. Once she viewed my story as credible, it seemed to inspire motivation in her, as if she thought, "If someone who doesn't

even live here is motivated to improve my community, I want to help, too." With motivation present on both sides, the last part of the process is to build hope. It is great to go out and motivate residents of [this community] to come together to affect community change, but it is equally important that they believe they can affect a change. . . . This, I think, is where the plausibility-motivation-hope process comes full circle. Hope, once realized, redefines what is plausible. The woman I visited may not have any idea right now what she and a handful of her neighbors are capable of, but through our shared stories, she gets motivated to bring a few people together for a house meeting. At that meeting, we will sit down and pick one thing, one problem to try and solve, one problem we have hope in. The leadership developed in solving that problem and the empowerment that comes from solving it generate new and greater hope and open up an entire new range of what this community believes it can plausibly accomplish. This is how [the organization] and I are building leadership in [this community].[33]

Unlike some of his peers who were uncomfortable unless they were in control of their projects, Stephen was comfortable with working collaboratively with neighborhood residents on a project they jointly considered feasible. Although he did not know where these relationships with people different from him would lead, he trusted that they would solve a problem, develop leadership, and become empowered to see new possibilities. Despite this comfort, Stephen struggled with organizing according to ideas being taught in the class versus working with the community through an already existing organization. It was not until a long-time member of the organization voiced these same tensions that he began to think differently. He reported:

It was like a wall inside my head fell down. I was immediately struck by the enormity of all of the disconnects that I now saw for what they truly were. . . . I struggled most of the class to try and *resolve* the tension between in-class theory and my out-of-class project. . . . By the end of the class, I started to see the *tension itself* as important and helpful. I *accepted* the dissonance instead of trying to minimize it.[34]

Stephen's ability to endorse these tensions and work with them instead of explaining them away reflected that he sufficiently trusted his internal voice to explore these contradictions. Near the end of the course, he began to see them as a source of growth.

These students' stories reinforce that it is possible to develop self-authorship during college if sufficient support is available. The responsibility involved in their community projects, combined with the learning partnership the course offered, helped many in the class move toward self-authorship at ages earlier than those whose stories you read earlier in this book. The opportunity to use what they learned in class in a real-world setting seemed central to their personal growth.

Self-Authorship: Stories from The Wabash National Study of Liberal Arts Education

Interest on the part of college educators in what kinds of experiences promote growth during college prompted a group of researchers to start the Wabash National Study of Liberal Arts Education (WNSLAE).[35] This is a large-scale study involving nearly 7,000 college students attending twenty-five institutions. The study focuses on the educational conditions and experiences that foster growth on seven outcomes: effective reasoning and problem solving, moral character, intercultural effectiveness, leadership, well-being, integration of learning, and inclination to inquire and lifelong learning.[36] The study also explores how these experiences affect students' journeys toward self-authorship. This study offers stories of a diverse group of students who are in college now, so we can compare them to the stories of my study participants who were in college twenty years ago.

The first phase of this project occurred in 2005 and involved, in part, interviewing 172 students at four institutions (two community colleges, one major research university, and one large comprehensive university) to explore the practices and conditions that promote liberal arts learning outcomes and self-authorship. The study team interviewed ninety-five first-year students, seventeen sophomores who were completing their second year of college at community colleges, and sixty seniors. Of these students 80% identified as white, 8.6% African American, 7.5% Asian, 5.2% Hispanic/Latino, 2.3% Pacific Islander, and 1.7% Native American. Although 63% of these students expressed opinions that reflected using external formulas, 31% expressed views that reflected arrival at the crossroads, and 6% demonstrated that they were moving toward self-authorship.[37]

One of the college seniors whom the team interviewed grew up in a large city in the Midwest, was a part of a blended family, and was dramatically affected by her opportunity to study abroad in England. When asked how the insights she gained in her classes affected her personal life, she responded:

> I mean, a lot of those things play out in my personal life, in the conversations I have . . . in the people I choose to spend time with, in the career I choose, and the path of the career I choose. The . . . the different topics of film that I would actually like to pursue. . . . I think every aspect of my life have been influenced by those ideals, I guess. It was building of ideals for me, and it's regulated every action I've taken . . . I think they're conscious, and . . . I try to challenge myself, and challenge other people, and that's why I get into so many arguments. . . . I try to make sure that I'm thinking of my ideals in every sense, and from every angle. . . . I challenge myself in that way. (Laughs) . . . [I] sometimes provoke people in the process, but . . . I've seen it through a lot of people in my life, especially my family, and their choices in their lives, and just how (pause) either unmotivated, or almost sociologically predetermined they were—having knowledge of them, you get to create your own pathway—I mean, at least as much as you can, as much as opportunity allows you. But, to have that freedom to look at things more objectively, to have a lot more choice in it than a lot of people I've grown up with, or have known through my family—people who haven't gone to college.[38]

This student's college experience offered her the opportunity to pursue her ideals. Inherent in this process was coming to trust her internal voice. This yielded a freedom to make her own choices and realize that she could influence her future. She appeared ready to take up the responsibility to chart her life course. The eleven students who were listening to and cultivating their internal voices chose what to believe and used their beliefs to guide their actions. They chose actions that were consistent with their identities, that benefited them, and that also benefited others.[39]

In the longitudinal phase of the WNSLAE, the interview team interviewed students at six diverse campuses over the course of their college careers to learn more about the practices that foster liberal arts outcomes and promote the development of self-authorship. The six campuses include three small colleges and three large universities. Two are Hispanic-serving institutions and one enrolls

approximately 50% African American students. The study team
interviewed 315 students on the six campuses in the fall of 2006 and
interviewed 226 of those same students in the fall of 2007. The
majority of these students are of traditional college age, and sixty-
nine identified as students of color (thirty-four African American,
thirty-five Hispanic). Additionally, thirty-two were born in countries
other than the United States.

Initial interviews reveal that the majority of these students
were following external formulas to guide their lives as they entered
college; however, a few were traversing the crossroads.[40] One sophomore African American woman offered these thoughts in identifying the themes of her first year of college:

> Growing is a theme. Being open to new ideas, finding out more
> about yourself, learning more about yourself, a voicing of your
> opinion and knowing your opinion before voicing your opinion,
> and the standing up for your opinion. . . . I think the overall
> thing would be more empowerment, and empowerment of just
> yourself in general, empowerment of others, empowerment of
> whatever you're doing, whatever decisions you're making. Um,
> a kind of, a source of pride, I guess, pride in what you're doing,
> knowing that you're right, a source of responsibility. A sense of
> overall, like I don't know if contentment would be the word, but
> an overall satisfaction with yourself and with what you're
> doing or with what I'm doing and where I'm going, and how I'm
> getting there; and I got my roadmap, I got my directions. I'm
> going where I want to go, and I'm going there how I want to get
> there, and I don't feel that I'm letting anyone or anything out-
> side, or even letting myself, stop me from reaching my goals or
> following my dreams. But being realistic. The sky is the limit,
> but you have to be realistic.

She discovered her own voice and is working hard to listen to it to
guide her journey. She shared that her classes and serving as a res-
ident advisor helped her see multiple perspectives and understand
her own emotions more deeply:

> So, I've been more open to realizing that there's more than one
> side to a story and also with just supporting my beliefs actually
> more. I voice my opinion, and I support it with facts. I don't just
> throw out an idea there and don't support it. So, I think that
> definitely makes a difference. And also with my interpersonal
> communication skills, they have greatly improved because I
> used to just get mad and not say anything, or just leave the

room or something like that. But now it would be like, "It angers me when you do this and this and this," and I just say, "I'm mad, and this is why I'm mad." So, it helps you control, um, this experience has helped me control my emotions, especially my interpersonal communication class. It helped me deal with conflict better and not just be mad, and learn that there's a whole lot of different, um, emotions besides anger and being furious. There's kind of, behind that a lot of times is sadness, or it's embarrassment or it's hurt, and it's not, it's coming off as anger but it's not. So, and just me understanding that in myself, I can understand that in other people.

Finding resources to understand her own voice helped her listen to it more intently and articulate it more carefully to others. This story reinforces that one can develop one's internal voice at age eighteen or nineteen if support is available.

A Hispanic male participant explained that he chose a small liberal arts college to learn to deal with conservatives. He came from a high school located in a large urban area where students spoke twenty-five different languages. Reflecting on his first year at the beginning of his sophomore year, he offered:

One thing here that I was afraid of was the whole religious aspect and the whole attitude toward minorities and homosexuals. I'm a very open person. I'm a very liberal person, and I know here [is] a straight man such as myself supporting a homosexual or even, you know, last year my roommate was gay. Then, since I didn't squat or reserve a room this year, I got a random roommate, and he ended up being gay, also. (Laughs) So, you know for most, for a lot of people here, it's an eye opener like, "Oh, why the hell didn't you move out?" I'm just like, "It's not really that big of a deal for me." They're like, "what do you mean?" I'm sorry, the way I grew up even though my parents, there was conflict. They're as open as they can be growing up in a third world country in Latin America, so they're very conservative on a lot of issues but very liberal on other issues. Homosexuality, now that they're born-again Christian, is a taboo. Even with my sister, who's educated and a little more liberal, it still seems taboo for her; I'm the black sheep from the family. I'm the deist. I'm the liberal. I'm the one that's been arrested for protesting. Like when I'm going about it, and I just tell them that's the way I see things. I don't see them as any different. Then it'd be ridiculous for me not to hang out with them or to treat him differently because he was gay. It's like him treating me differently because I'm straight. I have my belief system. I know that is natural and I know that he didn't choose to be gay. I know that he's going to suffer because of the way that, of the injustice that mankind is, the way that man is. We're just, we're a prejudiced bunch. I know we have our quirks. I know that, if anything, I would help him out because I know it's going to be harder for him being on campus here because of, you know, who he is. So, they just stare at me. They just shake their heads.

This student trusted his internal voice to choose his beliefs and his actions toward others. He was active in a gay ally group, despite disapproval from many of his peers. He actively disagreed with his parents on religious matters. Yet, he maintained positive relationships with conservative peers and his family. Asked how he determined whether he agreed with a point of view, he responded:

I think a lot of it has to do with, before I actually take anything in, I really have to think about it. I'll look at it both ways. For example, let's take welfare in econ class. We'll talk about the downfalls of welfare, and I'll understand that. It has a huge impact on the economy. It is true [that] people sometimes are lazy, and welfare can facilitate that, and then knowing people on welfare it sort of adds fuel to the fire, in a sense, because I know that there are a lot of people like that and, sad to say, a lot of them are minorities. You know, it's not politically incorrect to say minorities don't receive, you know, aren't as educated as Caucasians because it's true. Minorities don't graduate, don't have the same graduate rate as Caucasians do. There are reasons for it, of course. That's the thing, you have to be very specific about it, and I think in a case like when I'm trying to make a decision about something, I have to look deep into it. I have to consider both situations, and I have to even stray off a little bit and think about the two options, how I can [think about] those two options and this thing in general. So I have to think a lot.

It appears that this student's exposure to diverse perspectives in his high school and family helped him cultivate his internal voice prior to college. As a sophomore, he trusted it enough to use it to analyze information to determine what to believe. Because students in the Wabash National Study entered college at varying places on the journey toward self-authorship, the interview team hopes to learn more about the evolution of self-authorship among this diverse group of current college students as they progress through college.

Insights from Contemporary College Student Stories

The emergence of self-authorship prior to or early in college, evident in the stories of students currently in college, suggests that multiple personal characteristics and environmental factors contribute to authoring your own life. Students who experienced marginalization and discrimination were challenged to develop self-authorship early in order to overcome these barriers. Students who were exposed to diverse ideas in their family environments were better able to let go of external formulas than those who had not. College environments that challenged students to develop their internal voices and supported them in doing so in effect offered their students learning partnerships that helped some of them to trust their internal voices. I hope the diversity of these stories expands on those of my study participants to broaden your sense of the possibilities for authoring your life.

OLDER ADULT LEARNERS' STORIES

Very few projects involve interviewing older adult learners about their journeys toward self-authorship. One such project followed forty-one Adult Basic Education/English for Speakers of Other Languages adult learners from all over the world.[41] Their stories reveal the nuances of self-authorship for learners attending a pre-college English for Speakers of other Languages program in a community college, for adults participating in a family literacy program, and for adult employees participating in a high-school diploma program. These stories offer the opportunity to hear about self-authorship among adults, many of whom are from countries other than the United States.

Self-Authorship Stories of English for Speakers of Other Language Students

Seventeen learners ranging in age from eighteen to thirty participated in repeated interviews over the course of a year while they attended a precollege program for English for Speakers of Other Languages (ESOL) at Bunker Hill Community College.[42] They were all enrolled in courses together and came from ten different countries and four continents. Of these, three participants were at the phase of working to listen to their internal voices, and three were cultivating their internal voices.

Benetta, a woman from Central America who hoped to be a nurse, was working to listen to her internal voice. She lived with her husband and worked part time. Her struggle to listen to her internal voice is apparent in her relationship with her mother, whom she described as her best friend:

> I have a big problem with my mother because she says that I have to go, I *have* to go back to my country, and get my career there, my degree. She says it's too difficult for me to get it here because it will take long time, and she says: "Baby, there's school for you if you come back to our country. It will be easy for you, and it's your language." But, that is not what are my plans to do because I want to get my career here with English. And that's why I want to stay here, and she say, "No, baby, come back to your country, to my country and do it." But it's my decision. I am going to stay here. It is hard when we disagree about important things. But I think she understands. She understands. Maybe not right now, but she will.[43]

Benetta had her own perspective on her education and career, yet she found it difficult when her mother disagreed. She wanted to believe that her mother understood her wishes. Benetta reported progress in her psychology class that suggested she was following her internal voice:

> I feel more comfortable talking to people. Before, I couldn't speak with you, like look in your eyes directly. I only, like, with my head down. And now I can do it. I can see you directly, and I feel comfortable talking to you. I don't know at what point I changed, but it was in psychology class. Something happened this semester. I can't explain to you exactly how it just happened because it just changed. I didn't know how. I didn't know how. Every time I read a chapter, I say, okay, maybe that is one of my problems. I'm going to change this. I went to the next chapter, and I would say, "Okay, I have to change this myself." This was a big change for me. My personality, everything. Now, my work, I'm talking with everybody. I'm saying, "Oh hi, how are you doing?" And I'm making a conversation with everybody, all my co-workers. And here, I have more friends in college. Before, I was only alone, and just, I came to class, different classes. I went to the learning center, do my homework, and go home. I went to work. I did my work. Never talked to nobody. Now, I spend more time with people. I'm talking. Now, I have

more friends. I think it's a big improvement for myself. I say, how I change like that? That personality that I had before, and now I'm more open. I think that is the word. I'm open now. More friendly. I have more communication with others. That's good because they say, "Okay, she's a nice person."[44]

Identifying her "problems" through reading her text, Benetta set about changing aspects of her personality. She was pleased with the results and evaluated them as improvements, in part, because she liked herself better and, in part, because others approved.

Serge, a man in his mid-twenties from the Caribbean, was also concerned about his mother's approval. He was trying to choose between physical therapy and pharmacy as a career. He worked full time and lived with an uncle and cousins. Serge described making some decisions by himself, yet he was concerned about "if everyone around me is going to be supportive."[45] He was particularly concerned about his mother's approval:

I think it is a part of the way we grew up, and it is a part of my culture that you have to listen to your parents and respect your parents and honor your parents. And it is a part of my religion, too. Sometimes, you don't want to take advice. Sometimes, they can give you it, but you don't want to take it. You think it is bad. Sometimes, if you sit down and go over what they told you, you will see that sometimes there is positive things that you can take for yourself. . . . I don't think it is a problem for me. Sometimes, taking advice from your parents is really good. Some decision I want to take, I don't go to them. Like if I wanted to take a decision about I wanted to have a house in [my native country], and I know they don't want me to. That's a decision for myself. And I say that I want to have a house because when I am retired and I can go back. They say "no." They know they not going to have a house [in my native country] because it is too dangerous now. Well, that is their opinion about it. I have my own opinion about it. I have my own country. We have a little, not a fight, but a little discussion about it. But I really know if I want to do it in the future, to build a house, I am going to build it. Because it is my idea, and I am going to do it, and nobody's going to take it from me.[46]

Serge honors his parents as he has been socialized to do in his culture. He clearly considers their ideas, even when he does not want to, yet, in some cases, he listens to his own voice. He is trying to hear his own voice amid the cultural and religious messages to honor his parents. He also reported making progress in his psychology course:

> When people say something to me I usually get, even I don't show you that I'm angry, but I'm angry inside. Now, it's like there's not anything that make me angry. . . . I think the learning is, like they say the language, is really good thing for human to experience. And when you're learning those things, you behave in a new way. You understand yourself in another way. And then you see the world, and then you understand the world another way, in your own way. And now I know how to tolerate people. I know how to understand and know everybody. Because everybody behave in that way, in their own way, in their own world. And I have to be in my own world and have my own world. And I have to tolerate and understand the value of everybody. We learned the social learning. We learned a lot of things about people, about, you know, a lot of things that we have inside and we don't know. And then maybe by studying psychology, we understand the things that we have that needs to be changed but that needs to be shaped again.[47]

Serge is learning about himself, why he behaves the way he does, and how he might understand himself and others differently. These insights lead him to change aspects of his behavior and to accept others. These insights are assisting him in cultivating his internal voice.

Sonja, a woman in her early twenties, started to study law in Europe prior to moving to the United States with her family. She worked part time and wanted to work in radio. Sonja also reported a close relationship with her mother but noted that her mother allows her to decide for herself. Sonja was already cultivating her own voice and expressing it:

> What does it mean to me to have a best friend? My best friend has to feel with me. I am very complicated person. I know that. I am very complicated because I am very honest. Sometimes, I am like cruelly honest. And my best friend and person who is with me has to know how to deal with it. I don't like to pretend. . . . I always say what I think. And I have very strange way of making jokes, but I always say them. And that's why. I just feel that I don't have anything to hide from people. I don't have anything to be ashamed of in my life. That's why I feel comfortable to say everything. Even something that most people would not say, I say. It's very important for the relationship for people to understand that, and I don't want to lie to them even about that.[48]

Although her honesty sometimes puts people off, Sonja was committed to being herself in relationships. She was also committed to following her internal voice in career decisions:

> I don't do anything in my life that I don't like. Sometimes, you have to do something. I know that, but if I have to study something that I don't find interesting, I don't have success in that because that gives it like for three or four hours. Let's say the computers. I know computers are very important here, and that's a very good career, easy money and everything. You have a big salary, but I just don't like it, and so then I have to choose between these, too. My friends and my family are like, "You should take computers." But I did not want to take it because I know if I took that, then I would not have success as much as I have in psychology because I really like it. And I think that if you really want something, and if you really like something, you have determination, I think. You have to know what you want, how much that is really important to you because if you know that that's really important to you, you are ready to give up a lot of other things. If you are there just because you should be, you think, "I should be." So, it all depends on what you think about it.[49]

Sonja listened to her internal voice in determining what she would do with her life. She was well aware of others' perceptions but put more stock in her internal sense of what was important to her.

These stories demonstrate that relationships with parents play a substantial role in the ability to listen to one's internal voice. Sonja's mother's encouragement for Sonja to decide for herself supported Sonja in establishing her own voice. Benetta and Serge worried about their parents' approval and how to honor them while still listening to their own voices. Their cultural heritage was an important factor in how they developed their internal voices to honor both their parents and their own internal desires. The increased understanding of themselves they gained through the ESOL program helped them understand how to relate to others more effectively. Thus, as they cultivated their internal voices, they also paid attention to how to maintain good relationships with their parents. This delicate balance of maintaining relationships while coming to self-author one's life is important for everyone—from college students to adults—who struggles to balance deep connections with parents and their internal voices.

Self-Authorship Stories of Adult Learners in a
Family Literacy Program

Interviews with fifteen adults participating in a family literacy program called Even Start yielded self-authorship stories from adults, most of whom immigrated to the United States. The program involved an ESOL course, basic computer instruction, and assistance to help the adult learners advocate for their children's education. The adult learners ranged in age from twenty-two to forty-four and came from eleven countries with only one from the United States. Three (ages twenty-two to thirty-seven) were working on listening to their own voices, and two (age thirty-one and forty-four) were building self-authored systems.[50]

Linn, a thirty-four-year-old woman from Asia with two children, was unable to practice her profession once she moved to the United States. She chose to stay home with her children but joined the family literacy program to learn English and help her children. She reported her inner conflict between staying at home to raise her children and expanding her knowledge:

> My desire is I want to study more, but my family situation is not, I have to stay home. So, I have very many conflicts with myself . . . So, I think it's not time to study or going to outside. I want to stay with the home. . . . In my experience, when I stayed with my children, sometimes it's good, but sometimes it makes me depressed because I don't have any chance to meet other people. Most of the time, inside of me, I want to do something to improve my life. This time, I'm very happy with this program. . . . I want to [do] something to study and to be other things . . . but in my mind I can't do that cuz I can't [speak] English, I have to take care of the children, I'm too old to study other things. After this program, I'm getting good to learn English, and then I saw other students. They have a hard life, they study here, and they work, and they have to take care of the children, many children. When I look them, I feel I'm not lonely. Many other immigrants, they live very hard, too, very hard time. So, I can do my life positively. . . . When I stay home, I don't have any motivation to learn something. Only for housework. But when I study here, I meet the other student and meet good teachers, and meeting good people is another learning to me. Not only English.[51]

Although Linn claims the desire to stay home with her children as her own, there is some indication that she feels compelled to take this role. Her internal voice is most clearly expressed in her desire to study more to reclaim her professional identity. The literacy program gives her an opportunity to develop herself through learning English and meeting other immigrants. She is listening to her internal voice and trying to find ways to reconcile her need to raise her children with her desire to expand her own horizons. Her internal voice is also clear on the subject of parenting, in which she reported that the U.S. education system meshed better with her values:

> When I live in my country, my parent is the same thing, pushing me to study more and more. At that time, I followed my parents' value. But in my mind, I don't like that. When I move here to U.S.A., the education system is more comfortable the student. They are respect students, student's way, student's mind, they respect students individually. . . . We [she and her husband] think the same way for the children. I thought in my country it's not good. That the parenting in my country, I don't like it there. So, after move here, I'm content to meet this American education system. . . . Also, I know some people in the U.S.A., their parents want to maybe, for example, high-level people want to [be] sure their children to go high-level living, but most of American people, they emphasize their content with their life, enjoy their whole life. . . . The parent want to, their children is going to be a doctor, but their children doesn't like that, the parent need to, um, respect their opinion. Then, their children make enjoy their life.[52]

Linn has a clear vision of how she will approach her children's education. In this case, she is able to choose a path different from the one her country advocates in order to remain true to her beliefs and values.

Hamid, a forty-four-year-old man from the sub-Sahara with nine children, articulated the struggle many immigrants faced in the United States where their professional credentials were not valued. In his home country, he held a position of responsibility in a health-related profession. When he came to the United States, he reported, "If you don't have paper, they think you know nothing."[53] By paper, he meant a college degree. Hamid trusted his own voice to evaluate his worth based on his own standards yet understood that in the context of the United States, he would have to gain the credentials to reclaim his professional work. The other self-authored adult learner articulated a similar position. Dalia, a 31-year-old woman from the Caribbean who has five children, trusted her internal voice and sought opportunities to develop herself:

> I wanted to always keep my mind fresh and organized and learning new things. I never felt like I knew as much as I wanted to. . . . Getting a college education to me would be like a way to have a door open for me. . . . With a college degree . . . nobody is going to tell me . . . you are not qualified. School, I think, basically what it says to me . . . I'm doing something for myself. . . . I think I'm more proud of myself. I feel like I'm accomplishing something for myself. . . . Being active doing things, communicat[ing] with other people, talking about whatever we read, who agrees, who disagrees . . . our feelings about it . . . so to develop ourselves more.[54]

Dalia and Hamid both realized they would need U.S. credentials to reach their goals; however, the lack of affirmation they encountered did not alter their views of themselves. Because they created their own internal standards, they were less susceptible to accept external valuations of their worth. Other researchers also noted this resiliency on the part of self-authored adult learners:

> Self-authoring students seem better able to evaluate and critique the messages they receive about race, class, linguistic, and cultural differences. As they move away from Socializing ways of understanding, they develop the ability to reflect on the standards and values of their cultural surround, reviewing them according to their own internal standards and values. Thus, even if the culture messages imply their inferiority, they are able to reject these messages and disregard negative feedback that contradicts their own values and standards.[55]

Linn, Hamid, and Dalia were able to reflect on the standards they encountered and judge them against their internal standards. Their self-authored systems were crucial as they faced the challenges of professional credentialing in the United States.

Despite already building self-authored systems, these older adult learners appreciated the support and diverse perspectives of their peers in the Even Start program. Dalia articulated this:

> I feel very supported here, that I am to learn because that's something I didn't have before. I was the only one supporting myself to learn, the only one pushing myself in the back. I'm not saying people are on my back pushing me, but they are there for me. So, the fact that they are there for me to learn,

> that makes it even easier for me to push yourself and say, there are people here to support me, and that's going to give me a hand to help me.[56]

Dalia pushed herself, but she found it easier with support from her peers. She and her peers often exchanged ideas about parenting. She offered, "Like I was getting other people's ideas, and then I was trying to put my ideas, I was getting more ideas."[57] Another learner, Ho, noted, "I . . . listen to other people's opinions and ideas, but compare their ideas and my ideas . . . think about it, see what would happen."[58] These self-authored learners carefully considered new ideas but also weighed them against their internal standards.

These self-authorship stories reveal that a wide range of personal attributes and outside influences can enable adults of multiple ages to cultivate their internal voices and self-author their lives. Although these stories sound different on the surface, given that English is a second language for these immigrants, they affirm that self-authorship helps adults face difficult challenges. In that way, their stories are congruent with those of the Latino/a, lesbian, and high-risk students, whose ability to self-author their lives helped them overcome the barriers of their marginalization.

PERSONAL AND CONTEXTUAL FACTORS IN DEVELOPING SELF-AUTHORSHIP

The diverse stories in this chapter augment the stories of my study participants to convey the richness and variation in how we develop our internal voices. They also show that developing internal voices and foundations can take place at a variety of ages and in multiple contexts. The stories of those who experience marginalization and discrimination based on gender, race, ethnicity, sexual orientation, socioeconomic status, or faith affiliation demonstrate how developing one's internal voice can help overcome these barriers. Facing these challenges prompted some adults to abandon external formulas even before they went to college. For others who did not encounter these challenges, it took some form of tension in their experiences such as struggles at home, work, school, or in relationships to disrupt their external formulas. The stories of those whose cultural contexts emphasize family connections and loyalty reveal how complicated it is to deepen relationships with family while simultaneously cultivating your authentic internal voice to enhance those relationships. Stories of those who enjoyed good partnerships—whether with their families, friends, teachers, or employers—illustrate how supportive partners can help you gain confidence as you learn to trust your internal voice. The stories of older adults convey that attempting to meet new demands of family or work life can lead to opportunities to cultivate and trust your internal voice later in life.

So, the journey each of us takes depends on our personal set of realities—our personal characteristics, the environments we find ourselves in, the others with whom we are in relationship, and how we react to it all. These stories show that multiple pathways can lead to self-authorship. Collectively, the stories support the notion that developing one's internal voice is advantageous in learning, work, parenting, and personal relationships. The next chapter revisits the insights and strategies from the collective stories and offers you an opportunity to apply them to authoring your life.

CHAPTER 11

MAPPING YOUR JOURNEY

I PROMISED THAT THIS BOOK WOULD PROVIDE YOU with a compass for your journey through your twenties and thirties. I hope the detailed stories throughout this book offer you a vision of how to develop your internal voice and how to be good company to those around you in their journeys toward self-authorship. You have read about multiple pathways out of external formulas, through the crossroads, and into and through self-authorship. You have seen how strengthening their internal voices helped people succeed in their education, enjoy more meaningful relationships with friends and family, be more effective in their work, and be good parents. You have no doubt noticed throughout the stories that those who were able to strengthen their internal voices reported being better able to handle the ongoing challenges of adult life—health problems, losing loved ones, discrimination, relationship conflicts, work problems—than those who were still struggling to discover and heed their internal voices. One more important lesson the stories teach us is that it takes hard work, reflection, risk, and persistence to develop one's internal voice.

Now, it is time to consider the pathways you have taken or will take to self-author your life and the ways you can provide good company to others. This chapter offers you the opportunity to apply the key insights and strategies from the stories in this book to authoring your life. Let's revisit some of those key insights and strategies so that you can ask yourself how they might work for you. I offer guiding questions throughout this chapter to help you do the kind of reflection that leads to developing your internal voice. Often, we are too busy in our daily lives to stop, get off our bikes, and think about how we react to situations and interact with others. Keeping a journal of your thoughts and feelings is one way to record them, look at how they develop over time, and learn more about your own behavior. You may see areas in which you want to grow and then can identify opportunities that will help you. Keeping a journal is one way to listen to and trust your internal voice, sort out what you believe, and build your internal foundation.

KEY INSIGHTS & STRATEGIES

In chapter 8, I noted three common experiences that moved participants toward self-authorship: experiencing pain, gaining perspective, and having good partners. Here, I have organized the key insights and strategies around those three dynamics.

Pain

As Mark stated in chapter 8, we learn from trying to resolve the pain in our lives. Much of this pain stemmed from participants being socialized to follow external formulas for success in learning, work, and relationships. For example, Anne (chapter 1) recounted succeeding in college without developing her internal voice:

> I wish teachers wouldn't do so many multiple-choice questions and have some more thinking-type things because life is not multiple choice. I've been realizing out here, I mean, there's so many things I have to think about and look up and research and think about more. It seems like in college and high school everything is just so multiple choice: "Memorize this and spit it out." And that's mostly all I ever did, memorize, memorize, memorize, and learn facts and just spit it out to someone and circle answers and that was it. I wish we'd done—I don't know—more thinking things or stuff like that.[1]

As an accountant, Anne needed an internal voice; as a college student, all she needed to do was memorize. Similarly, Mark reported that he never had to "feel" in a college classroom:

> Nothing in college or in the classroom ever prepared me to really deal with those feelings. . . . One thing I learned in my

childhood is not to trust relationships very much. . . . Maybe that's why I did so well in the classroom is because I was used to not going with feelings. I can listen to radicals on both fringes, right and left, shove my feelings aside, listen to it, and then develop rational critiques of both sides. I can get to a point where I don't feel anything.[2]

Thus, he was able to succeed academically without attending to his internal voice. This came back to haunt him (see chapter 3) when his academic achievements won him entrance to the law school of his dreams. Many participants disclosed the formulas they had automatically accepted about the appropriate time to marry, have children, purchase a home, or move up on the career ladder. They also learned formulas for who should care for children (remember Anne's concern that she should be staying at home?) and how they should use their education. Often, pain emerged in their lives as a result of the tension between these formulas and what actually happened in their lives. There is considerable evidence in today's world that competition for entrance to college and good jobs often has the unintended result of teaching young people how to follow formulas rather than to develop their internal voices. Stop here for a moment and think about how you have been socialized (and write in your journal if you are keeping one).

- Can you identify any external formulas that you were taught to follow?
- How prevalent are they in your life right now?

My study participants and those in other studies discovered limitations in following external formulas. For example, Sagi (a participant in Torres' study; see chapter 10) came to understand how her acceptance of stereotypes about herself (a form of external formulas) limited her success in college. Similarly, the lesbian students in Abes' study realized how formulas about relationships hindered developing their internal voices. Al (chapter 1) and Mark (chapter 3) discovered that following the formulas for success in work and law school left them unfulfilled. Lynn (chapter 8) tried to follow the formulas for getting a teaching job but came up against their limitations because they did not work for her. Many of the stories in preceding chapters reveal the discovery of the limitations of formulas for making relationships work. Take a moment here to consider these questions:

> • Can you identify limitations to any external formulas you follow?
> • If so, how do these limitations play out in your attempts to develop your internal voice?
> • Make a note about any external expectations that make it difficult for you to do what you want to do with your life.

Discovering the limits of external formulas often led participants to the realization that they needed to develop their own voices to be happy. As Barb said (chapter 1), "I probably won't be happy until I can forget that." She was referring to worrying about what other people thought. Lauren shared her insight in chapter 8 that she needed to find out for herself how she felt about a significant relationship. By attending a workshop, Kurt (chapter 4) realized that he allowed others to make him happy or sad. Cara (chapter 8) realized that her worry about others' perceptions was ruining her graduate school experience. Gia (chapter 10) became aware that her concern about her girlfriend's parents' disapproval of their relationship inhibited her ability to be open about it. Gavin (chapter 9) learned that following his heart to go into teaching, a role he thought others viewed as inappropriate for men, would make him happier than struggling to sell insurance. Think for a moment about whether you have encountered any of these realizations:

> • Have you experienced times when you were unhappy with relationships? With your work? Even with yourself?
> • During these times, what messages were you receiving from external influences? [List these in one column]
> • During these times, what was your internal voice telling you? [List these in a second column]
> • Were there conflicts between the external influences and your internal voice?

Pain and tension prompted people to reevaluate their lives and acknowledge the need to strengthen their internal voices. Sometimes, it was in the form of what Mark called the quiet pain of lack of fulfillment. Mark, Al, and many others found this to be the case in their work. In other cases, it was explicit pain. Heather's struggle with her marriage is a good example of the latter (chapter 8), as is Reginald's experience with his church's discrimination regarding his bipolar diagnosis (chapter 1). Some participants described tensions in their lives that encouraged them to strengthen their own voices. Sandra's stress in her work life was in conflict with her call to serve (chapter 5). Kurt struggled to balance his loyalty to his supervisors with his philosophy of managing employees (chapter 4). Cara, Barb, Anne, and many others experienced tension between what others expected of them as women and their own desires. Many reported tension in relationships with coworkers, peers, partners, and family. Certainly those who were marginalized on account of some personal characteristic experienced these tensions. In fact, nearly all of the stories contain some version of this tension. Pause here and consider how this has played out in your life:

- When have you encountered tension or pain in your life?
- How does this tension or pain relate to the strength (or lack of strength) of your internal voice?
- If your internal voice were stronger, how would that affect your reaction to the tension or pain?

Gaining Perspective

Participants worked hard at listening to, cultivating, and trusting their internal voices. Kurt spoke at length (chapter 4) about the struggle he encountered to look inside, to be true to "the man in the glass." Dawn (chapter 2) worked to extract herself from the "clutter" and external noise people threw at her to embrace herself as a gay person. Similarly, Cara spoke eloquently in chapter 1 about pushing against the invisible external force to listen to her intuition. Mark (chapter 3) described learning to listen to internal cues through meditation. Dawn shared with us the cyclical nature of this process, reporting that she would take two steps forward and one back. Her descriptions of the shadow lands also conveyed that it took persistent work to trust one's internal voice. Participants used a wide variety of resources as they worked to strengthen their internal voices. Mark and Sandra reported using books to guide their thinking; Cara listened to *Your Buddha Nature* tapes in her car. Many used exercise—Dawn's bike riding, Cara's kick-boxing and yoga—to find time to reflect on their internal voices. Sandra, Alice, and Rosa used spiritual resources to help with their internal work. Consider for a moment how you can listen to your internal voice:

> - What are some ways you can listen to, cultivate, and trust your internal voice?
> - Reflect on the realities of your life. What things can you control, and what things are beyond your control?
> - What resources have you found that help you strengthen your internal voice?
> - What other resources might you look for to help you strengthen it further?

Often, the work participants undertook to strengthen their internal voices led them to take risks to bring life into alignment with their growing internal desires. Mark (chapter 3) took a risk in rearranging his career and relationship priorities by proposing to Michele. Although this meant scaling back his aspirations at law school, he felt confident that marrying Michele would improve his life in more important ways than career success. Evan (chapter 7) took risks in tackling tough work assignments because he was convinced that it would help him learn more and refine the way his mind worked. Heather (chapter 8) left her husband when she was four months pregnant because she knew in her heart that she could not make the relationship work. Despite the negative reaction from her friends, Heather persevered because her internal voice guided her toward what was best for her and her unborn child. Lauren (chapter 8) left her job and family to move to another part of the country to explore a relationship she knew she had to figure out for herself. Those who had already come to trust their internal voices continued to take risks to build internal foundations or secure internal commitments. Whether these were relationship risks (as in Dawn's case), career risks (such as Sandra's career change), or personal choices (including having children and balancing parenthood with career), they all involved action to bring life into line with one's internal voice. Stop here and think about how this has played out in your life:

- What risks have you taken? What did you learn about yourself as a result?
- Were these risks guided by your internal voice?
- What risks could you take to more closely align your life with your internal voice?

Through these risks and other varied experiences, participants opened themselves to new ways of seeing things and gained perspective on their lives. Mark's relationship with Michele offered him a new perspective on happiness. Surviving on her own during her pregnancy helped Heather gain perspective on her strengths and priorities. Lauren's move away from her parents helped her gain perspective on deepening family relationships. Lydia's Navy life opened her eyes to new ways of living her life; her son's illness put daily problems into perspective. Similarly, Kelly's husband's service in Iraq cast her everyday concerns in a new light. Dawn's multiple sclerosis (MS) helped her gain perspective on her priorities just as others' health problems changed their outlooks. These experiences helped participants build philosophies to ground their lives or revise their philosophies. For example, Lynn chose to adopt a more positive outlook, and Evan revised his notion that he had to control everything. Pause here to think about your experiences:

- What kinds of experiences have helped you gain exposure to new ways of seeing things, to new perspectives?
- What experiences could you seek out that would help you build or refine your philosophy of life?

Throughout the journey toward self-authorship, participants talked about reflecting on their experiences to sort out what they believed to be important to them. Dawn articulated this best and her words from chapter 2 are worth repeating here:

> The whole thought process of just taking stock of where you are in your life. It's like putting your life through a sieve, getting the big awkward chunks out of your life, getting the nice finely sifted residue—it is kind of sorting it all out. What is the essence of you and what isn't?[3]

Participants used this sorting and sifting to decide what to keep as part of their internal foundation and what to let go. This sorting included what to believe, what to value, who to become, and how to relate to others. Reflect for a moment on what this sorting process is like for you:

- In what ways have you sorted through ideas you've encountered about what to believe?
- How have you sorted out how you want to relate to others?
- What are you keeping as important to the "essence" of you? Make a list of things to keep, reconsider, and let go. Pay particular attention to your strengths and talents. How can you make the best use of your strengths and talents to shape your life in satisfying ways?
- How could you organize what you want to keep to build or strengthen your internal foundation?

The stories show that diverse personal characteristics made a difference in how people responded to their experiences and how they approached life. Evan's drive to excel simultaneously enhanced his success at work and hockey yet led him to burnout in his early twenties. Dawn's knack for self-exploration prompted her to turn inward routinely to reflect on her life; this worked to her advantage when she was diagnosed with MS. Lydia's resilience helped her cope with Navy life and her son's illness. Sandra's strong faith and call to serve guided her thinking about her career for most of her twenties and thirties. Many of the adult learners in chapter 10 approached learning and life in the context of the realities of their lives. Lynn's pessimism in her twenties made her miserable, and her conscious choice to embrace a more optimistic approach improved her outlook in her thirties. Pause here to consider your personal perspectives and characteristics:

- What personal characteristics or values do you possess that help you strengthen your internal voice?
- What characteristics or values might you consider changing to help you strengthen your internal voice?

Partners

The stories reveal the importance of having supportive partners to strengthen your internal voice. You have read about participants who enjoyed good company from their parents, grandparents, life partners, siblings, friends, or coworkers. Some, like Gavin and Sandra, benefited from strong partnerships with their employers. Kurt similarly grew as a result of his partnership with a management coach. Some of the stories include partnerships with teachers that helped learners strengthen their internal voices. Other participants found good professional partners. For example, many took advantage of opportunities for counseling to help build their internal voices and cope with challenges they encountered. Clergy, medical personnel, workshop leaders, and mentors provided good company in many of the stories. Although you can proceed on your own, it is easier to have the support of good partners. Take a moment here to think about your partners:

> - Who can you identify as supportive partners in your journey? List them here, along with why you identified each as a good partner.
> - What can you do to benefit from the support of these partners?
> - How can you find good company for your journey in your family, friends, coworkers, or community?
> - How will you explain to partners that they can best help you by taking the back seat of the bike?

If you found it difficult to respond to these questions, you may want to revisit chapter 9 to read about what makes a person a good partner.

Strengthening your internal voice helps you participate more effectively in relationships because you can be yourself. This authenticity helps you be a better partner because you are not worrying about what the other person thinks of you. Kurt captured this idea when he reported that he and his wife came to their relationship as whole people and not in need of the other to complete them. Their authentic relationship helped Kurt strengthen his internal voice, which in turn, helped him shift from managing to leading his employees. The authentic relationship Will and Leslie developed helped them provide good company for each other as they negotiated how to manage their life circumstances and, ultimately, Will's death. Dawn's internal foundation helped her see the work she still needed to do to be part of a loving, authentic relationship. Al's internal foundation helped him be a good partner in encouraging his patients to decide what was best for them. Alice's internal foundation helped her afford her daughter some autonomy in sorting out how she should behave. All of these stories suggest that the more settled you are in your internal voice and foundation, the better able you are to respect others' thoughts and feelings and collaborate with them to work through their problems—two of the key components of learning partnerships. Reflect here for a moment on your role as a partner:

> - For whom do you serve as a partner?
> - In what ways are you providing a good learning partnership to your partner(s)?
> - In what ways could you be better company than you currently are?

BEST WISHES FOR YOUR JOURNEY

No matter where you are on your journey, I hope the stories convinced you of the value of developing your internal voice to meet life's challenges. I hope you found insights and strategies in this book to help you guide your bicycle and envision how to help your partners guide theirs. I wish you the best as you turn your bike toward the path to authoring your life.

CHAPTER 12

A THEORY OF SELF-AUTHORSHIP DEVELOPMENT[1]

THIS CHAPTER IS AIMED PRIMARILY AT READERS WHO FOLLOW STUDIES OF COLLEGE STUDENT and adult development, or anyone else interested in the underlying theory, and how it illuminates the stories in this book. It shows the patterns in the participants' journeys to self-authorship and uncovers how they are shaped by individual personality, background, and experiences. Although the narratives show participants reaching similar destinations, the paths they took vary because of their differences as people and the unique circumstances of their lives. Each person's way of making sense of the world, themselves, and their relationships with others affected how they approached experiences and how they interpreted those experiences, as did the support systems they had available to face life's challenges. For some, their personal set of realities (to borrow a phrase from Evan in chapter 7) yielded a fairly straightforward path toward authoring their lives. For others, their personal set of realities resulted in their taking a more roundabout path to that same destination.

A deeper understanding of the phases of the journey toward and through self-authorship and the steps in each phase can help partners provide the challenge and support to enable adults to shift to the internal coordination of their beliefs, identities, and social relations. I use the word *elements* for the steps to convey that there are certain components, or building blocks, that comprise what developmental psychologist Robert Kegan calls the self-authored system; the term *system* stems from Kegan's notion that self-authorship is "the mental making of an ideology or explicit system of belief."[2] This system does not emerge full-blown but rather in a gradual, cyclical fashion.

This chapter offers a theory of self-authorship development that emerges from participants' stories. It offers an overarching storyline of development, and patterns of movement within it—particularly movements in beliefs about the world, oneself, and relationships— how they intertwine in multiple ways across that journey, and how the phases cycle and recur for different participants. It is important to note that this is my construction of this theory, influenced by my study of self-authorship over the years. It is one possible interpretation based on one group of participants (see the methodological appendices for a detailed discussion of this point).

A Cyclical Overarching Storyline

Participants began to discover the need to develop an internal voice when, in interacting with the external world, they found shortcomings in the values and points of view they had acquired from the authority figures in their lives (the crossroads). Most participants recognized the need to listen to this internal voice to guide decisions regarding their beliefs and values, identity, and social relations soon after graduating from college. Cultivating this voice fully, to stand at the center of how they viewed the world, themselves, and their relations, took substantive effort and time. The stories reveal that the path toward self-authorship is not a steady march forward. Instead, it could be described as two steps forward and one step back or, at times, one step forward and two steps back.

Movement away from the crossroads was halting, as participants extracted themselves from external control only to be sucked back into it. As their internal voices gained strength, it became easier to avoid being pulled back. Dawn's analogy of learning to walk then being able to run captures the distinction between moving *toward* a new phase and moving *into* it. Kurt articulated this recurrent cycling between his awareness of his proclivity to sacrifice his needs to meet those of others, his attempts to stop doing so, and his slipping back despite his intentions. This same back-and-forth motion took place among trusting the internal voice, building an internal foundation, and securing internal commitments.

The storyline starts with participants' movement out of the crossroads—the juncture where external expectations and the internal voice compete for dominance. Next, I describe three elements of self-authorship, followed by movement beyond self-authorship. The map of the journey toward self-authorship, with which you are, by now, familiar, portrays the cyclical nature of this overarching storyline.

The three phases of the journey—*Moving Toward Self-Authorship, Building a Self-Authored System,* and *Moving Beyond Self-Authorship*—represent three qualitatively different *meaning-making structures.* Meaning-making structures refer to the underlying organizing principles of how we make sense of our world.[3] We organize meaning using a particular structure, or rule, until we encounter discrepancies between our structure and reality. As Swiss developmental psychologist Jean Piaget described, we attempt to hold onto our structure for as long as it is feasible, assimilating new experiences into that rule as exceptions. When we can no longer resolve discrepancies this way, we alter the structure enough to get our rule and experience back into balance (see page 3 on how change happens). For example, study participants found using *external formulas* as a structure during college to be effective. When they encountered problems with these, they first assimilated those experiences into their external formula structure; however, after college, they encountered tensions they could not resolve with external formulas. They then recognized the need to develop their own internal voices and take responsibility for reevaluating the external influences in their lives. This move to the *crossroads* reflects moving to a new rule or structure. Similarly, *Moving Toward Self-Authorship* reflects their movement out of the *crossroads* toward the new structure of *Building a Self-Authored System*. The underlying principle of that structure is internally determining one's beliefs, identity, and social relations. *Moving Beyond Self-Authorship* is a new structure characterized by a move toward self-transformation, or the ability to reflect on one's self-authored system.

Moving Toward Self-Authorship

Emergence from the crossroads was a gradual process for my participants. Two distinct elements of this phase of moving toward self-authorship were evident in the stories: listening to the internal voice and cultivating the internal voice.

Listening to the Internal Voice. In this first element, participants' internal voices edged out external influence as their primary way of seeing the world. I use the phrase "edged out" to convey that the external authority on which participants had relied for most of their lives was still present and influential. They were *aware* that their internal voices needed to be developed and strengthened to determine their beliefs, establish their internally defined identities, and guide their relationships. Awareness, however, did not automatically translate to action. Participants had to actively work on *listening* to their new and fragile internal voices. As Dawn and Heather put it, they were trying to hear above the clutter the external world threw at them, to hear above the external noise of daily life. Consistently keeping the newly formed internal voice in the foreground was a challenge for most.

Cultivating the Internal Voice. As their internal voices grew stronger, participants were increasingly able to keep them in the foreground in this second element. Their primary focus in this element was *cultivating* their internal voices. They analyzed their interests, goals, and what made them happy. They began to use their internal voices to make decisions about the direction of their careers and personal lives, and who they wanted to become. They began to critically analyze external influence, as opposed to uncritically accepting external formulas as they had earlier. External influence still pressured their internal voices on some occasions, and sometimes stifled them on others. For example, work and family environments sometimes inhibited participants' internal voices. Genesse's story (chapter 1) is a good example of work relationships that inhibited her development. Because she worked for many years for supervisors who did not afford her autonomy, she had a hard time gaining confidence in her internal voice in the work context. The ups and downs of her relationship with her mother over time also mediated her ability to trust her internal voice. Her story reveals that this can be a long struggle and result in an unevenness of the development of the internal voice. Continued relegation of external influence into the background to the point that their internal voices became more dominant prompted participants to shift into a new meaning-making structure: building an internal self-authored system to guide their lives.

Building a Self-Authored System

Building an internal voice requires moving the source of one's beliefs, identity, and social relations "inside" oneself. Thus, the internal voice must be built in all three developmental dimensions (see pages 9 amd 10) to yield a self-authored system. This system becomes the lens through which individuals interpret their experience and form their reactions to the external world. Three elements of the phase of building a self-authored system emerged from participants' stories: learning to trust their internal voices, building an internal foundation, and securing internal commitments. These three components, or building blocks, are what participants used and reused in building a self-authored system.

Trusting the Internal Voice. Participants' key insight in this element was making a distinction between reality and their reaction to it. They recognized that reality, or what happened in the world and their lives, was beyond their control, but their reaction to what happened was within their control. Mark articulated this in chapter 3 when he said he was, "still at the mercy of fate, but I interpret fate, decide what it is going to mean to me and take action in my environment." Trusting their internal voices heightened their ability to take ownership of how they made meaning of external events. They recognized that they could influence their own emotions and happiness by choosing how to react to reality. This led to a better sense of when to initiate making something happen versus when to let something happen. This way of seeing things enabled them to be more flexible and move around—rather than trying to change—the obstacles they encountered. In chapter 2, Dawn called this the "art of controlling without controlling" and was using this approach to work with her multiple sclerosis (MS). Similarly, Evan noted in chapter 7 that he expected things to go wrong and was satisfied to do what he could to resolve issues. Whereas participants were aware of the need to develop their internal voices in moving toward self-authorship, they now had developed confidence in their internal voices. Thus, they came to have faith in and trust their internal voices and the internal commitments they were making based on these voices.

In many cases, participants moved from awareness of, to confidence in, their internal voices multiple times as they worked to trust their internal voices in each developmental dimension (i.e., knowing what to believe, who to be, and how to relate to others) and in multiple contexts (e.g., work, personal relationships, parenting). Awareness often prompted exploration, which sometimes led to what Dawn called the shadow lands. These were times of confusion, ambiguity, fear, and even despair as individuals struggled to analyze and reconstruct some aspect of their beliefs, identity, or relationships in various contexts. As Dawn noted, it was not possible to be "in the light" all the time. By reflecting on these challenging experiences, participants emerged from the shadow lands with a clearer vision of themselves and greater confidence in their ability to internally author their lives. Their personal reflection skills and the extent to which they had good support systems influenced the intensity and duration of excursions into the shadow lands. Once they had sufficient confidence to trust their internal voices in multiple dimensions and contexts, participants were able to begin building an enduring internal foundation.

Building an Internal Foundation. In the element of trusting their internal voices, participants consciously set about creating a philosophy or framework—an internal foundation—to guide their reactions to reality. They worked to refine their personal, internal authority in determining their beliefs, identity, and relationships. They reflected on how they had organized themselves and their lives, and they had made the necessary rearrangements to align arenas of their lives with their internal voices. This often meant accepting personal abilities or characteristics and incorporating these into their identities, as Dawn did with her gift in cooking. They made additional choices using their internal voices as guides. Their ability to explain how and why they made particular choices gave them the assurance that they could rely on their personally created identity, decision, or relationship, even amid uncertainty. Synthesizing their beliefs, identity, and relationships into one internal foundation yielded what Dawn called the "core of one's being," or what Mark called a "truer identity." These phrases reflect the enduring nature the internal foundation acquires when all of the threads of one's development become integrated into one entity.

Participants acted according to their internal foundations as they were building them. This often yielded feedback that they used in refining their internal foundations. As they built some parts of the internal foundation in a new dimension or context, they found that they needed to cycle back to the element of trusting their internal voices to gain additional confidence. They returned to strengthen their confidence, while they continued to build other parts of the foundation. Similar to a physical construction project, it is often necessary to return for additional materials or to revise a blueprint to address an unanticipated twist. Cara's story in chapter 8 offers a good example. Despite her success in extracting herself from external forces in her twenties, Cara faltered when her parents and grandparents expressed their desire for her to have a baby. Although she did not return to the crossroads, she did further reflect on her internal voice to settle for herself where children fit into her vision of her life. Similarly, Dawn revisited her internal voice upon learning of her MS diagnosis. Visits to the shadow lands occurred in this process as well, perhaps because the participants hadn't fully developed their skills of reflection or lacked good support. Their increased confidence helped them work through painful experiences and use the conclusions they reached to strengthen their internal foundations; however, participants pointed out that initially the beliefs and perspectives they were forming were, as Kurt said, in their heads rather than in their hearts. Mark described this as admiring a set of convictions one has constructed versus living them. While they were building the internal foundation, they perceived that they were beginning to live their convictions. In retrospect, many could identify the transition from admiring to living their convictions that led them to securing internal commitments.

Securing Internal Commitments. Participants identified this third element of building a self-authored system as "crossing over" from understanding their internal commitments to living them. Dawn called it crossing over into wisdom. Mark also used the crossing-over metaphor in noting that there came a time when he had no choice but to "cross the bridge" to live his convictions. When the internal foundation became the enduring core of their being, participants felt that living their convictions was as natural and as necessary as breathing. This element was a time of living the internal foundation and securing the internal commitments they had made.

Many participants described inner wisdom as the blurring of their knowledge and their sense of self. Dawn described it as living the facts and absorbing that information into her entire being, which led her to "know" as second nature. Kurt described it as his convictions becoming part of his heart rather than existing only in his head. This merger of knowledge and sense of self seems to reflect not only the bringing inside of personal authority but making personal authority one's very core. In this element, participants integrated their internal foundations and infrastructure with their external personal realities. Evan referred to this as floating on the waves, accepting that sometimes things were over his head and taking life as it came. Mark's aspiration for grace in the dance with reality, to be able to work with it instead of fighting it, is a similar notion. Dawn portrayed this as acting and watching what happens with the confidence that she could create something positive. Participants' increased certainty that things would work out stemmed from knowing becoming second nature. This allowed them to move forward with faith and trust in their internal foundations even when, on the surface, it would be legitimate to question a course of action. Dawn's riding in the MS 150 bike ride in the summer heat and Lydia's immediate acceptance of Navy life's challenges are good examples of participants moving forward with faith and trust.

The certainty that came with living their internal foundations also yielded a greater sense of freedom for participants. They were no longer constrained by fear of things they could not control and trusted that they could make the most of what they could control. They were open to learning about and developing new parts of their self-authored systems, often recognizing contexts in which they needed to refine or develop some aspect of themselves. In these instances, they returned to building that portion of the foundation or, in some cases, recycling back to gaining confidence in that area. Cara captured this in comparing yoga to life: "It's like life. Go back and forth. You make progress; you come back." In the securing internal commitments element, the internal foundation became increasingly open to the possibility of further reconstruction because participants had the internal security to see reconstruction as positive and exciting. They accepted new versions of what counted as normal and enjoyed the dynamic process of living their internally authored systems. They were adept, as Lydia and Evan put it, at rolling with whatever came their way.

Trusting the Internal Voice, Building an Internal Foundation, and *Securing Internal Commitments* appear to be three increasingly complex elements of the meaning-making structure, *Building a Self-Authored System.* Each element reflects a distinct focus, yet all three are based on the same underlying organizing principle: internally determining one's beliefs, identity, and social relations. The initial element involves developing the internal voice to use in these decisions. The intermediate element involves using the internal voice actively to build and solidify one's internal belief system by making internal commitments. The advanced element involves securing internal commitments, thus refining and strengthening the internal system to become the core of one's existence. The solidification of this structure yields the security to explore more freely and continue personal evolution, and it opens the possibility for moving beyond self-authorship.

Moving Beyond Self-Authorship

Dawn's story offers a preview into what moving beyond self-authorship might entail. In our twentieth interview (see chapter 2), Dawn shared with me that she had made, and acted on, some bold, risky decisions from the space that she called her essential self. She reported "existing in that space for several days" and was certain that these moves came from the ability to be in that space of her essential self; however, she also reported having trouble staying in that space. She found herself reverting to an old space where she had been previously and wondered how to navigate staying in the new one. My interpretation of Dawn's story is that although she was still embedded in her internal foundation, she was gaining a new ability to reflect on it or to stand back from it to get a glimpse of it. This reflects developmental movement because it is a shift of what was subject to us (or, in other words, something that is so much a part of us that we cannot see it) to object. When something becomes object, we can stand back from it, see it as a part of ourselves, and reflect on it (see page 3 for more on how change happens). Dawn's beginning ability to see the "old space" of being embedded in the foundation suggests that it was becoming object. Rather than being embedded totally in her internal foundation, she was on the verge of being able to have a relationship with it that would allow her to further reflect on it.

This is possibly an example of the shift from self-authorship to self-transformation.[4] The ability to transcend the internally self-authored system allows one to reflect on it and, thus, opens one to transformation that leads to recognition of opposites and contradictions and the ability to hold them together.[5] Self-transformation is possible when we recognize that various forms of our selves exist in relationship to each other.

DIVERSE PATTERNS OF MOVEMENT AND EVOLUTION

This overarching storyline of participants' twenties and thirties reflects both a consistent storyline and diverse patterns of movement within it. The consistent storyline can be characterized as moving toward the meaning-making structure of self-authorship, building and solidifying that meaning-making structure, and moving beyond it toward self-transformation. Although this storyline runs through all the participants' stories, their movement along that path varied widely in terms of which of the three dimensions of development were in the forefront of the journey, the degree to which the journey was cyclical, and the variations they experienced in various phases of the journey.

Clarification of Misconceptions of Self-Authorship

The participants' stories clarify two common misconceptions about self-authorship. First, the cyclical nature of the evolution of self-authorship just described suggests that self-authorship is more complex and nuanced than a simple linear trajectory. Although all the participants moved toward increasing self-authorship, they took numerous paths in this journey based on their personal characteristics, experiences, the challenges they encountered, and the support available to them. Personal characteristics, such as participants' socialization based on their gender, sexual orientation, faith orientation, race, or ethnicity, predisposed participants to seek particular experiences (e.g., jobs, relationships, travel). These characteristics influenced how they approached experiences they sought and experiences that happened to them, either at a personal level (e.g., relationship struggles, work challenges, health problems) or societal level (e.g., 9/11, the Iraq war). Their meaning making at any given point affected how they approached experiences and how they interpreted those experiences, as did their particular combination of the beliefs, identity, and relationships. Participants' work, family, and personal environments offered a range of challenges and support systems to face life's demands. Evan referred to all these dynamics as a "personal set of realities." Particular sets of personal realities yielded a complex set of factors that influenced developing self-authorship. For example, Dawn's sense of spirituality fueled the self-exploration she engaged in through theater and travel. Her coming out in her twenties was a salient experience that enabled her to cast off external expectations to listen to her own voice. MS, relationship struggles, and trying to support herself via theater work presented major challenges in Dawn's thirties. Her capacity to self-reflect—an intrapersonal strength—and her appreciation of multiple perspectives—an epistemological strength—predisposed her to seek out experiences to explore herself and helped her process challenges she encountered. The support of her family, friends, and medical community combined to help her listen to and trust her internal voice. Trusting her own voice, her spirituality, her willingness to continue digging deeper, and her ongoing support from others enabled her to build her internal foundation and return from the shadow lands with greater strength.

Second, self-authorship enhances, rather than constrains, relationships. The longitudinal stories demonstrate that self-authorship refers to shifting the source of one's beliefs, identity, and social relations from the external world to the internal voice and foundation. Doing so initiates a reframing of relationships that become more authentic because they honor one's internal commitments. Connections based on these internal commitments result in interdependence in which parties to the relationship act authentically and support each other in doing so. Thus, self-authorship strengthens relationships and enduring ties with the external world. Dawn's work on her internal foundation enabled her to enter an authentic relationship in her late thirties because she was finally able to bring her internal voice to the relationship. Cara's ability to listen more openly to others' ideas and speak what she viewed as truth, regardless of others' reactions, led to more authentic relationships for her. Kurt's internal foundation allowed him to engage in authentic relationships at home and work. Some of the stories in chapter 10 also demonstrate this intersection of self-authorship and connection. The remainder of this chapter explores the diverse pathways toward and through self-authorship.

Variations on How the Three Dimensions Intertwine

Perhaps due to individual characteristics or their contexts, many participants had a default dimension; in other words, one of the three developmental dimensions was in the forefront of their developmental journey. If they gained complexity in meaning making in this dimension, it often came into tension with their meaning making in another dimension. This tension, then, sparked growth on the other dimension; thus, their default dimension "led" development. If meaning making in the default dimension lagged substantially behind the others, it made integration of the dimensions and forward movement on the journey difficult. Those for whom the three dimensions evolved together enjoyed a smoother journey than did those who experienced greater gaps among dimensions.

Mark's story is a good example of the epistemological dimension leading development. He identified with literature in high school, often defining aspects of his identity through novel characters such as William Faulkner's Joe Christmas and Henry James's John Marcher. He was enthralled with history, feminism, Marxism, and a variety of other perspectives during college. His intellect was his default mode of operating, as he calculated what classes to take, how to interact with professors, and how to engage his peers. Although he modified his behavior in discussions from tearing apart others' arguments to building toward other arguments late in college, he still operated on an intellectual plane of logical and rational analysis when he entered law school. The dissatisfaction he encountered there led him to realize that he needed to listen to internal cues. Despite his ability to consider multiple perspectives and weigh relevant evidence in deciding what to believe late in college, he had used rationality at the expense of how he felt. The success he reported from avoiding feelings in the classroom reinforced his rational approach throughout college and into law school.

To address his unhappiness at law school, Mark turned first to his intellectual default. He used a "cost-benefit analysis"[6] to determine whether to propose to Michele and what role he might play as an attorney. Later, he used Tony Robbins' concept of installing beliefs to create positive emotions that would make him happy.

Recognizing that being intellectually right meant nothing in arguments with his wife, he began to look beyond the intellect. His exploration of what would make him happy and how to sustain his relationship with Michele led him to pursue Chinese philosophy and his spiritual self. This marked his shift to working on meaning making in the identity and relational dimensions. Mark's evolution in these dimensions did not replace his use of his intellect but rather put it in the context of his overall meaning making. He described it as a knife he could use as appropriate but also something he could let slip from his hand. At this point, he was able to include his own feelings and those of others in weighing evidence to decide what to believe, who to be, and how to interact with others.

Dawn's story offers an example of the identity dimension taking the lead. Her interest in introspection was evident in college, and her conscious quest to develop her identity was interwoven in her theater work. She was constantly searching for "all the little truths" within her so that she could bring them to characters she played in theater productions. Her identification of her sexual orientation as "out of the mainstream" no doubt influenced this search, as did her MS diagnosis a decade later. Reflecting on her identity, sorting out the essence of herself, and determining what was important to her were routine activities in Dawn's life, and her intentional work on them aided her increasing complexity in the identity dimension. Her intrapersonal meaning making also supported how she decided what to believe. She often compared new information to what she already knew, deciding if it fit or not and whether to add it to her repertoire. For example, the cooking she took up as a financial measure became an outlet for her creativity. As she learned to cook professionally, she learned what ingredients naturally went together, what substitutions worked, and what a teaspoon of salt looked like in the cup of her hand. Her willingness to look at multiple perspectives, experiment, and handle ambiguity in how she came to know something (the epistemological dimension) all hinged on her growing trust in her core sense of self (the intrapersonal dimension).

Dawn's story also illustrates that one can move forward on the identity and epistemological dimensions, and yet the relational dimension can lag behind. Dawn told of numerous relationships in which she lost sight of herself—ironic given her focus and attention to refining her sense of self. This extended to losing sight of taking care of her physical health, which also caused problems in relationships. After a particularly painful breakup, Dawn again descended into the shadow lands to work on parts of herself that she felt needed improvement, mainly allowing herself to be vulnerable emotionally. To address her relational needs, she turned to identity work. Although she trusted her core sense of self to make career and life decisions, she still protected it in relationships. It was not until her late thirties that Dawn was able to translate the complexities she had achieved in the identity and epistemological dimension to the relational dimension. Her motivation to participate in a meaningful significant relationship, her adeptness at self-exploration, and her trust in her core sense of self merged to make this possible.

Kurt's story illustrates the relational dimension in the foreground of development, although in this case, it complicated movement rather than supported it. Recall Kurt's insight in his early twenties from the workshops he attended—that he relied on others' perceptions for his self-worth. He knew instinctively that this was not a good idea, yet he could not immediately stop doing it. Although he articulated being true to the "man in the glass," he routinely looked beyond the man in the mirror to see what others thought of him. As he reported, he spent the entire decade of his twenties getting in touch with who he was. In the course of doing so, he often sacrificed his own needs to meet those of others. This complicated his finding and succeeding in a career path.

As Kurt moved into management at his workplace, he found himself between supervisors and employees, a difficult place to be for someone who is concerned about others' perceptions. He had developed a sense of himself and universal principles he wanted to apply in his work. Although he was no longer looking for approval in these relationships, he was still concerned that others recognize his contribution and sometimes defined his worth based on his success at work. Working to support the company and to keep employees from feeling disenfranchised, he built a new set of beliefs about how to manage people that involved helping them think that their ideas were driving company practice. As Kurt was promoted to increasingly responsible positions, he had to give responsibility to his employees to stay afloat. Simultaneously, his internal sense of self was getting stronger, and he came to believe in himself. The combination yielded a significant paradigm shift in his coming to genuinely believe in his employees as decision makers.

In Kurt's case, his relational development constrained his identity development because to strengthen his internal voice, he had to work against his desire for others' approval. It also constrained his epistemological development because he struggled to implement his beliefs in the face of others' disapproval. Once he freed himself of others' perceptions, in part by trusting his sense of self, he was able to move forward on all three dimensions to engage in more complex professional and work relationships. Having one of these interdependent relationships with his wife, one in which approval was not an issue, helped him along this path. He was able to experience expressing himself authentically and functioning interdependently in this relationship; this increased his confidence that work relationships could take this same form.

Collectively, the stories suggest that one can move along the storyline in one dimension without parallel movement in another until the tension between the two becomes unsustainable. Humans' interest in being in balance, articulated in detail by Jean Piaget[7], prompts noticing tension between dimensions and an urge to resolve it. For example, Mark's recognition that his intellectual calculus was not sufficient for his personal happiness led him to turn to developing his sense of self the way he had his intellect. Similarly, Dawn's awareness that the interpersonal relationships she wanted required additional intrapersonal complexity led her to work on resolving that tension. This unevenness in the movement on the dimensions accounts for some of the cyclical nature of the journey.

Personal Variations of the Journey

Individual characteristics predisposed participants to seek particular experiences (e.g., jobs, relationships, travel) and influenced how they approached those that happened to them either at a personal level or societal level (e.g., 9/11, the Iraq war). Individual characteristics included participants' socialization based on their gender, sexual orientation, faith orientation, race, or ethnicity. Aspects of their personalities (e.g., Evan's drive to excel, Dawn's self-exploration, Lydia's resilience) also influenced their experiences. Their personal meaning-making structures (e.g., moving toward self-authorship, building a self-authored system), and preferences or styles within meaning-making structures (i.e., separate or connected styles) reflect another level of individual characteristics. I describe each of these levels of individual characteristics next using examples from participants' stories.

Personal Characteristics. Gender socialization affected participants' choices during their twenties and thirties. Alice, a successful counselor with a master's degree, wanted to start a family in her twenties. She shared her struggle with tension between her career and having children:

> Honestly, my initial thoughts were "That isn't fair that I have to balance because I am the woman; nothing will change for him. Why should I have to give up what I have worked so hard for?" Probably six months I felt that.[8]

Alice and her spouse worked out a balancing act, which was later complicated by her health, that helped her maintain her professional and family priorities over the next decade (chapter 8). Cara's struggle with gender socialization was clear in her dilemma about having children and her role as a professional woman (chapter 9). These gender-related issues took energy away from her professional goals. Many of the women in the study struggled with this issue, as well as with the choice of staying home with their children. Gender expectations mediated Gavin's journey (chapter 9) in a slightly different way. He pursued insurance sales after college despite a longing to go into education. He was socialized to think that men were to succeed financially and that education would not yield that success. After a few years being miserable selling insurance, Gavin returned to school for a master's degree and went into teaching. There, he found his niche working with students with learning challenges.

Dawn's sexual orientation influenced her journey because it was, as she put it, "out of the mainstream." Although she was aware of it during college, it took a long time to become comfortable going against societal expectations. As she noted in chapter 2, the need for inner strength to stand apart from the mainstream helped her develop confidence. Thus, she attributed part of how she saw things and how she thought about life to her sexual orientation.

Participants' faiths or spirituality played a part in their developmental journeys. As Sandra described in chapter 5, her quest to serve God through her faith played a major role in her career path and her personal depression during her twenties and thirties. Dawn's spirituality (chapter 2) played a powerful role in her quest to understand her core sense of self. Mark's notion of spirituality was an important factor in his development of a philosophy that extended beyond how one knows what to believe (chapter 3). Some participants renewed their interest in religious involvement as they worked through their experiences. Al, a family doctor, returned to his Christian roots to focus on things that he found satisfying, such as volunteering or focusing his career on helping others (chapter 1). Rosa turned to her faith to make sense of tragedies in her family, including her sister's breast cancer and her cousin's murder (chapter 9). The diverse ways participants interpreted their spirituality influenced their journeys regardless of their particular religious or faith beliefs.

Personality characteristics also affected participants' journeys. Lydia's resilience helped her make the most of Navy life and use her various experiences to develop self-authorship (chapter 6). Dawn's penchant for self-exploration prompted her to see experiences to develop her internal voice and process them in ways that helped her deepen her internal foundation (chapter 2). Evan's drive to excel enabled him to always be in a learning mode and to push himself to develop further (chapter 7). Lynn's tendency to view life negatively constrained her development, and she intentionally chose to alter this part of her personality in order to move forward (chapter 8).

Meaning-Making Structures. The meaning-making structures participants used affected the pace and texture of their developmental journeys. For example, those who had enjoyed success using external formulas were surprised and disheartened when these failed to work in life after college. Mark was shocked at his disappointment at law school. Similarly, Gwen, who had lived by the mantra "Plan your work and work your plan, and you're going to get where you want to go,"[9] found it hard to let go when she realized that this was a lie. Those for whom external formulas had not worked as effectively were more amenable to letting them go. Dawn was willing to let go of external formulas about sexual orientation to embrace her own. Phillip (chapter 1) had entrusted his fate to the process of getting a college degree and getting a good job. When the job did not automatically follow the degree, he lost confidence that he could pursue his dreams. His unhappiness led to letting go of the formula and moving east to try to break into the business he desired. Those who had let go of the external formula in at least one developmental dimension were more prepared to work on their internal voices having seen some need to do so.

Within the meaning-making structure of building a self-authored system, those who had constructed strong internal foundations found more strength to handle crises than those whose structures were still being built. For example, many participants faced serious health problems—their own or those of their partners or children. Will and Leslie (chapter 9) faced the ultimate crisis with Will's leukemia and subsequent death. Because both had secured their internal commitments at the time of Will's diagnosis, they were able, to the extent that anyone could, manage treatment decisions, maintain an authentic relationship, and provide a healthy environment for them and their children to face the inevitable. The strength that stemmed from their internal commitments helped them cope with this tragic situation. In contrast, Genesse desired greater strength as she coped with her husband's heart condition. Because she was still struggling to trust her internal voice and build her foundation, the possibility of losing her spouse shook her to the core. Although both of these cases reflect intense crises, participants' coping capacities varied based on how they made meaning of themselves and the world around them.

Patterns or Styles. Participants' preferences about their meaning making also affect the developmental journey. In the college phase of the study, I identified these preferences as gender-related patterns within participants' approaches to learning and knowing.[10] "Gender-related" conveyed that they were not gender exclusive, but women in the study tended to use relational or connected patterns more than men in the study, who tended to use agentic or separate patterns. Relational-pattern participants listened carefully to information, valued rapport among peers, and appreciated peers sharing perspectives. Agentic-pattern participants expressed themselves through mastering material, debating with their peers, and learning to think independently. The contrast between these two patterns reflects the connected and separate knowing that researchers Mary Belenky, Blythe Clinchy, Nancy Goldberger, and Jill Tarule identified in their study of women.[11] They described connected knowers as believers who tend to look for what could be right about a perspective whereas separate knowers are doubters. Connected knowers tend to move "into" others' knowledge and the subjects they are trying to know, whereas separate knowers tend to stand back at arm's length from others' perspectives and the subjects they are trying to know. These distinctions are also reminiscent of earlier descriptions of the human tendency toward communion (or connection) versus agency (autonomy).[12]

One of the most valuable insights of the college phase of my longitudinal study was that relational and agentic gender-related patterns were equally complex.[13] For example, in absolute knowing, where participants believed knowledge to be certain, two gender-related patterns emerged: receiving and mastering. Receiving-pattern knowers preferred to take in the information, whereas mastery-pattern knowers preferred to practice in order to learn. What students using both patterns shared is an underlying belief that authorities had knowledge, and it was their role to acquire it. Thus, their patterns reflect different preferences within the same meaning-making structure of absolute knowing. Similar relational and agentic patterns emerged in transitional knowing (where knowledge is perceived as sometimes certain and sometimes uncertain) and independent knowing (where most knowledge is perceived as uncertain). For example, relational independent knowers found it easier to listen to others than to themselves, whereas agentic independent knowers found it easier to listen to themselves than to others.

The gender-related patterns evident in absolute, transitional, and independent knowing merged in contextual knowing when participants evaluated relevant evidence to arrive at justifiable beliefs. Those who used relational patterns now found value in standing outside of the context to gain perspective; those who used agentic patterns now found value in moving into the context to gain perspective. Despite this merger, it is still possible to lean toward one or the other style. Developmental psychologist Robert Kegan eloquently articulates the distinction between structure and style and notes that each structure can favor either preference (relational or agentic).[14] For example, he suggests that one can be relationally self-authorizing or separately self-authorizing. He described the connected employee as one who

> exercises personal authority on behalf of inclusivity, keeping communication lines open for maximum participation and input, preserving connections and surfacing threats to colleagues' collaborative capacities; personally evaluates employer

expectations and own performance relative to these kinds of priorities.[15]

In contrast, he described the separate employee as one who

exercises personal authority on behalf of advancing or enhancing one's own position, status, advantage, agenda, mission, or profile; relates to others on behalf of furthering unilateral ends rather than deriving ends out of relationship; personally evaluates employer expectations and own performance relative to these kinds of priorities.[16]

Both employees are self-authored and evaluate expectations and their performance based on their internally established priorities; however, their stylistic preferences prompt them to generate different priorities. Kurt (chapter 4) is a good example of a connected employee because of his focus on drawing his employees into decision making. He seeks maximum participation and removes obstacles to his employees' success. He evaluates his performance on how well the team is working to meet the company's goals. Lindsey, an economist for the federal government, is also relationally self-authorizing (chapter 9). His management style hinges on letting his employees solve problems themselves and supporting them as needed. Lindsey enjoyed digging around in the numbers, so he had to resist helping out at presentations and giving his employees too much support. He held back, or tried to, in the interest of getting them to take ownership for their work. He did this despite the risks involved, which he described:

I always try to let people know where I stand. I think that you lead by example; I put in a lot of hours, and they know that. If something does go wrong, I take the blame, and I handle it from there. If there's an error, they come to me. We had a relatively large . . . biggest mistake that I've ever been around for. It happened to be in an area that I'm responsible for and ironically . . . it happened when I was out sick for four days. On the one hand, there's a silver lining in every cloud because there was a big error, and it reflected on me because these are people that work for me, but at the same time, people were saying, "If you were here, that wouldn't have happened." That's all good and dandy, but it still did happen, and it reflected on the bureau, and we're still feeling ramifications from it now. Once you publish the statistics, they're on the World Wide Web instantaneously, and if there's an error, you have to issue a press release to tell the world that you made an error, and it's exactly how we are. One of the major ways in which we are judged is based on magnitude and number of errors or revisions. It makes it very stressful when you release numbers and you haven't really had a chance to fully review them. There's always going to be mistakes, and what you hope is that you catch the big ones, and this was a big one that did not get caught. Whether or not I would have caught it, who knows? It doesn't really matter at this point.

Lindsey took responsibility for this mistake because he oversees the employees who made it. Rather than blaming them, he focused on how to get them to take more ownership. He also described how he handled encouraging employees to share mistakes with him:

> If someone makes a mistake, especially a doozy, I'll make a very conscious effort to not show any displeasure. I'm not sure that's necessarily the right angle, but my philosophy is if I jump up and down and scream at this guy who just told me he made a mistake, he's never going to tell me he made a mistake again. He'll try to hide it from me. The first thing I tell people when they come to work for me is: "Look, the minute you think you made a mistake, just please tell me, even if you're not sure. Please tell me as soon as possible, and maybe we can correct it before we publish these numbers." People will make mistakes, and they may have caught them a day before they get published, but they're afraid to tell anybody. For that very reason, when they do come to me and say, "I made a mistake," on the inside, my stomach may have just fell through the floor, but I'll make a very conscious effort to not have this shocked look on my face and say, "Okay, let's take a look at it. Let's see what we have." And that's something that I learned from another supervisor of mine, and I think that was a good lesson. Unfortunately, the director doesn't share my philosophy, and when I have to go to the director, he gets angry, and I can't blame him 'cause that reflects on him, too, obviously. So, [it's] a very fine line in a lot of these management type issues that you have to try to find a happy medium, and it really varies from person to person. Some people need more coaching and guidance than others, and some people are just naturally more independent. These are all things that you try to learn as you go.

Even though Lindsey incurred the wrath of his boss when things went wrong, he maintained his stance that coaching employees to take ownership of their work and share mistakes with him without penalty was the best approach.

Evan (chapter 7) is a good example of a separate employee because of his focus on getting his part of the job accomplished. He gives full attention to making sure that anything that is his responsibility is taken care of effectively. Although he is friendly with his colleagues and works collaboratively to meet company goals, his primary focus is on completing his assignments effectively. Justin, an elementary school principal, uses this same form of self-authorization. He described his decision-making process in the context of multiple constituents who all wanted something different from him:

> I've got fifty people that I work with, and that's just teachers. I have 550 kids and their parents, so it just feels really overwhelming sometimes. It's difficult because you certainly can't please everybody. People have preconceived notions of what kind of person is a principal. It doesn't matter who I am or what I do, I'm the principal, so I'm the evil guy. People don't really give you a chance sometimes. You just have to let it roll off your back. It's just part of the job, so you just do what you feel like you need to do and move on. I value what I do. It's not an easy job. It's not always very fun, but at other times it is. I get a kick out of having a difficult situation turn out okay. I get a real sense of satisfaction out of that. There's a lot of frustration if a bad situation gets worse or doesn't get resolved. Then, I feel kind of self-defeated. It's something that's almost like an art form. One thing that one group of people wants is something that the other group of people do not want, and I get stuck in the middle because both groups of people are demanding different things of me. So, I have to make a decision—what's going to benefit the kids most?—and go with it, and let the chips fall.

Justin's approach is to exercise personal authority on behalf of advancing the mission of the school. He uses what is best for the kids as his criteria for decision making even if constituents disagree with it. He offered an example:

> You look at what your goals are and what's going to be best for the kids involved, academically or socially. You look at what the research says and what other people have done, what's worked in the past. You try to combine all those things to make a decision. People throw up roadblocks, they try to sabotage things,

and then other people will support you the whole way. Sometimes, you try to get support for things that you think are good, and you don't get that support because people have their own self-interests in mind. That's the toughest part because it seems like, a lot of the time, people are just really self-interested. If it's inconvenient for them or if a change of routine doesn't benefit them directly somehow in making their life easier, then they won't do it even if it is better for kids. Our PTA is a good example of a group [of] people who are very supportive and work hard at our school but are really mainly interested in number one, their own kids. They're not really interested in academic achievement of all the kids in our building, like handicapped kids or kids from really low incomes or kids who have a lot of family problems. That's frustrating for me because I feel like we should all be in it together to help everybody in our building. I haven't found out yet how I can change that mindset. Helping kids that are struggling is really going to help the whole school, and that will in turn help their own kids. It's going to change the culture of the school a little bit, and then maybe that year that their own kid starts to struggle a little bit, people will care about them a little bit more.

Although Justin tried to enlist support for his philosophy that helping all kids benefits the whole school, he wasn't optimistic about gaining much support. So, he proceeded to gather information, use it to judge the likelihood of reaching the school's goals, and make decisions despite various constituents' displeasure with him.

Complexities of Personal Variables. Socialization, personal characteristics, meaning-making structures, and styles within meaning-making structures all influenced how participants approached their adult lives. Understanding how these factors affect personal and work life helps partners understand the multiple ways people make sense of what to believe, who to become, and how to interact with others. Remaining open to multiple pathways people might take based on their personal set of realities helps partners support these paths.

Contextual Variations: Holding Environments

As the stories in chapters 8 and 9 illustrate, the environments in which participants lived and worked enabled them to move forward or held them in place to varying degrees. Robert Kegan called these *holding environments* and described the three functions of a developmental holding environment as confirmation, contradiction, and continuity. Confirmation provides support for the person's current meaning making and "holds on" to the person as he or she is. Contradiction challenges the person's current meaning making and "lets go," as she or he moves to a new structure. Continuity "stays with" the person as he or she reintegrates the previous self into a new self.[17] Holding environments that offer all three functions are more effective contexts for development than those that do not. Learning partnerships offer all three functions.

Participants who enjoyed good learning partnerships in multiple dimensions of their lives also had an easier journey than those whose holding environments did not function as learning partnerships and sent inconsistent messages. For example, Kurt's parents encouraged him to focus on the man in the glass (his internal voice), and they would support him. They respected his thoughts and feelings and invited him to bring his personal authority to his decisions. He also had mentors in the form of supervisors and his management coach, who confirmed him as he was yet invited him to be something more and stayed with him through the change. They respected his thoughts and feelings, helped him work through his experiences, and shared authority and expertise with him as he built his leadership philosophy. His wife provided an authentic partnership in which he could express himself freely, reflecting all of the learning partnership components. In contrast, Cara had less effective holding environments throughout her graduate education, with the exception of one female mentor. Gender socialization also offered a difficult holding environment for her. Her thoughts and feelings were rarely respected, she was not invited to bring her personal authority to her graduate work or personal decisions, and only her mentor engaged in collaborative learning with her. She did have an authentic partnership with her husband that helped her as she worked against the constraints of her other holding environments. His invitation for her to bring herself to their relationship and decisions supported her personal authority and her ability to interdependently work through issues.

Some participants faced holding environments that worked against their growth. Heather's holding environments actively constrained her ability to develop her internal voice. Her family dynamics and her role as the oldest complicated her listening to her internal voice. Her work supervisors varied in their support of her internal voice. Her personal relationships with her husband and her friends were active forces against her developing her internal voice. Although she managed to move forward despite these holding environments, it was a far more painful journey than it would have been had she had learning partnerships in which her internal voice would have been supported.

Personal and contextual variations intersect. For example, Mark's confidence in his internal voice, supported by the effective learning partnerships he enjoyed with his parents and spouse, enabled him to work through ineffective work holding environments without shaking his confidence (chapter 3). In contrast, Anne (chapter 1) reported that one of her work holding environments eroded her confidence to the extent that it affected her personal life. She wanted to become something more, but her colleagues perceived her as an overachiever. Reginald's (chapter 1) work holding environments made it more difficult for him to develop his internal foundation because they did not confirm him as he was, at a time he was struggling to adjust to his bipolar diagnosis. The myriad of possibilities of personal circumstance, individual characteristics, and multiple holding environments make for a complex set of dynamics that shape developing self-authorship.

The Potential of a Cyclical Theory of Self-Authorship

The theory of self-authorship I have articulated here reflects a varied and messy path from authority-dependence to and through self-authorship. At first glance, this map of multiple divergent pathways does not readily translate to how educators, employers, parents, partners, friends, and others who support those on this journey might do so more effectively. It certainly does *not* lead to standard practices that can be applied to all people across contexts. This map of possibilities does, however, illustrate the characteristics of partnerships through which we might authentically engage others in developing their internal voices and foundations.

I attempted to shape this book as a learning partnership. I have used language that conveys respect for your thoughts and feelings. I have shared stories that might help you sort through your experiences. I hope the stories helped you consider the complexities in your life and how developing personal authority might help meet those challenges. Stories of partnerships model how you can acquire support for your journey, as well as offer support for those of others around you. For those of you who are educators, I hope the tone and style of the book offer a new way to envision working in partnerships with learners to guide their journeys toward self-authorship.

The "Three Elements of Self-Authorship" discussed in this chapter are reprinted with permission from the American College Personnel Association (ACPA), One Dupont Circle, NW, at the Center for Higher Education, Washington, DC 20036.

APPENDIX

LONGITUDINAL STUDY METHODOLOGY AND METHODS

I have operated from a constructivist perspective from the start of the longitudinal project because I view the dimensions of development as constructed by individuals making meaning of their experience. Both Perry[1] and Belenky et al.[2] emphasized their theories as possible windows through which to understand epistemological development, rather than the objective truth. Thus, although I used their theories to inform the college interview (Phase 1), I employed an open-ended interview and an inductive analysis to allow new possibilities to emerge from the context. In sharing the findings of the college phase, I emphasized them as possibilities stemming from a particular context, useful in other contexts depending on the reader's judgment of transferability.[3] I continued this constructivist approach in the post-college phase (Phase 2) to continue to allow participants' constructions of their experience to emerge.[4] Consequently, the intrapersonal and interpersonal dimensions became major themes in the interviews. Because this book synthesizes data from the post-college phase, I will concentrate here on post-college methods, highlighting college-phase methods as necessary. Descriptions of this method have been previously published due to the longitudinal nature of the study.

347

Participants

The 30 people upon whom this book is based are participants in a
twenty-two-year longitudinal study that began in 1986 when they
entered college. I interviewed 101 traditional-age students (fifty-one
women and fifty men) when they began college at a midwestern
public university in the United States. Seventy percent of the entering class of which the participants were a part ranked in the top
twenty percent of their high school class. Their majors included all
six divisions within the institution (i.e., arts and sciences, education, fine arts, interdisciplinary studies, business, engineering and
applied sciences), and co-curricular involvement in college was high.
Of the seventy participants continuing in the post-college phase of
the study, twenty-one pursued additional academic preparation
after college graduation, including law school, seminary, medical
school, and various graduate degrees. Their occupations included
business, education, social service, ministry, and government work.

Attrition over the past fifteen years resulted in thirty participants, all of whom are Caucasian, by year twenty. Of these thirty,
two were single, one was in a committed relationship, twenty-six
were married, and two were divorced (one of whom remarried). Of
these eighteen women and eleven men, twenty-two had children.
Seventeen had been or were pursuing advanced education: twelve
had received master's degrees in education, psychology, social work,
business administration, and economics. One had completed seminary, two received law degrees, one completed medical school, and
one completed a doctorate. The most prevalent occupations of these
thirty participants were business (sixteen) and education (nine).
Areas within business included sales in varied industries, financial
work, public services, real estate, and marketing. Educators were
primarily secondary school teachers and administrators; one was a
college professor. The remaining participants were in social work,
law, homemaking, and Christian ministry.

One dynamic of this context is the small number of students
from underrepresented groups on the campus. Only three of the
original 101 participants were members of underrepresented
groups, two of whom continued into Phase 2. Although none of these
three withdrew from the study, all were unreachable by Year Ten
because of changing addresses. This book offers a portrayal of the
evolution of self-authorship based on these thirty participants. This

portrayal is offered as a possibility, and it is not assumed to fit any young adults outside of this context. Transferability to other students and contexts is left to the judgment of the reader, based on the thick description of participants' stories.[5]

Interviews and Rapport: Developing a Partnership

I continued the qualitative nature of the college interviews during Phase 2 to allow participants' stories to be the primary focus. Phase 2 interviews were unstructured.[6] Because few researchers have explored development after college via a longitudinal approach, it was particularly important for the interview to allow participants to set the agenda and to allow their perspectives to emerge freely. I began the annual interview with a summary of the focus of Phase 2 of the project, which was to continue to explore how participants learn and come to know. I then asked the participant to think about important learning experiences that took place since the previous interview. The participant volunteered those experiences, described them, and described their impact on her or his thinking. I asked questions to pursue why these experiences were important, factors that influenced the experiences, and how the learner was affected. Each year, I used participants' reactions to the conversation to revise and improve the interview process. The interview became more informal as the study progressed and addressed what life had been like for participants since we talked last. These conversations included discussion of the dimensions of life they felt were most relevant, the demands of adult life they were experiencing, how they made meaning of these dimensions and demands, their sense of themselves, and how they decided what to believe. Inherent in these dimensions was their sense of themselves in relation to others and their involvement in significant relationships. I conduct the majority of the interviews by telephone, but I visit approximately one-third of the participants for face-to-face interviews in their homes. Interviews range from one to two hours.

Rapport established from our long association contributed to the richness of the interviews. Throughout the project, I provided direct information to participants about my research interests and procedures. I shared annual summaries of my interpretations of the collective interviews and invited participants' reactions. Upon completion of the college phase of the study, I sent copies of *Knowing and Reasoning in College* to all remaining participants. During the next few years, I continued to send annual summaries, including excerpts from published works, and copies of *Making Their Own Way*. These efforts on my part to both keep them apprised of my interpretations and to solicit their interpretations altered our relationship from the traditional researcher-participant to partners in understanding young adult life.

This partnership contributes to the intimate nature of the interviews, apparent in narratives throughout this book. Participants routinely commented that they had few opportunities to talk about themselves with someone who listened. Their friends and families tended to give them advice, share their own similar experience, or try to alleviate participants' concerns. My focus on hearing their stories, constantly asking for the meaning behind their thinking or how they arrived at their current perspective, provided opportunities for self-reflection. As Ned shared, the interview was an opportunity for introspection:

> I don't often get the opportunity for someone to ask these tough questions to figure out my framework. It is very parallel to discussions with my close friend—at the beginning I had no idea what I'd say; then, I recognize things I need to think more about.[7]

Over the years, participants became accustomed to this opportunity to explore during our conversations. They also came to anticipate the questions in my mind as they shared their stories. The informational, conversational nature of the interview meant that I gave them autonomy to define and pursue significant topics. I had no predetermined questions; instead, I asked questions to gain an indepth understanding of the stories they told. My questions included: "What does that mean for you?" "What do you mean when you say that?" "How did that perspective come about?" or "What are the experiences that led you to that notion?" I also asked how various perspectives related to each other or to earlier perspectives from previous interviews.

I conveyed my respect for participants' privacy in numerous ways, another important dynamic of our partnership and participants' willingness to share intimate reflections on their lives. I invited them to choose the focus of the interview and to offer dimensions of their experience for discussion. Participants were aware of my interest in the epistemological, intrapersonal, and interpersonal dimensions of development from my writing and our previous interviews. In cases where our interview focused on one dimension over another, I often noted this observation and asked if there were other dimensions that warranted our exploration. Participants knew, however, that I would not push them to discuss areas they were uncomfortable sharing. Their willingness to share insights across dimensions, including personal and relationship issues, was likely heightened by my emphasis on confidentiality. I have never revealed their identities over the twenty-two-year study and have routinely consulted with participants when I wanted to publish their stories extensively. Although I have had participants' permission to share some very personal experiences because participants believe this would benefit others, I have sometimes chosen to withhold those stories from published work out of concern for their privacy. Our overall rapport has conveyed to participants that I have a genuine interest in their well-being and respect their privacy.[8]

Interpretation: Mutually Constructing Narratives

My constructivist approach to this project and the partnership developed over the course of the study both mediate data interpretation. My constructivist approach led to using grounded theory methodology[9] to analyze interview responses. Each year, I reviewed transcriptions of the taped interviews and identified units of the story. I then sorted the units into categories to allow themes and patterns to emerge from the data. I also reread data for each participant across years to develop successively evolving interpretations and further develop patterns. Credibility of the themes and patterns is enhanced through prolonged engagement to build trust and understanding, and member checking to ensure accuracy of interpretations. Two research partners joined me to reread and analyze parts of the post-college data. Each of us prepared summaries of themes individually, followed by meetings in which we discussed and synthesized our perceptions. This use of multiple analysts helped mediate our subjectivities and increase the adequacy of our interpretations.

Despite these methods, the question of whose story is told in this book is important. Numerous scholars have explored the issue of representation, or the degree to which a qualitative inquirer presents participants' stories versus his or her own. In light of my constructivist bent and the three core assumptions of the Learning Partnerships Model, I approach this question using those three core assumptions. Viewing knowledge as complex and socially constructed (the first core assumption) yields the notion that no one true journey toward and through self-authorship exists; rather multiple journeys abound. These journeys stem from the personal characteristics of individual participants, their meaning making of their experience, and their social construction of meaning with those in their social contexts. From this vantage point, the evolution of self-authorship—in fact, the concept of self-authorship itself—is offered as a possibility for understanding how young adults view knowing, themselves, and their relationships.

Social construction of knowledge is inherent in another core assumption: Authority and expertise are shared in the mutual construction of knowledge among peers. My participants and I mutually constructed the narrative of this book. They offered their narratives and their meaning making in the context of my questions and quest for understanding their lives. I interpreted their meaning making by merging their stories with my understanding of human development. I routinely consulted them, sharing my interpretations for their reaction and feedback. My part in this mutual construction was mediated by another core assumption: Self is central to knowledge construction. The meaning I made of their narratives was mediated by who I am—my personal experience of my own development, my experience as a student and scholar of human development theory, and my experience as a faculty member who interacts intensely with students of this age group.

Although not professing to write the "true" story of these participants' lives, I am committed to offering a reasonable interpretation of their narratives. This has involved balancing what Clandinin and Connelly call "falling in love" with participants and maintaining some distance from them.[10] Full involvement with participants—or in this case going into their stories, gaining access to intimate details of their lives, and caring about their well-being— yields rapport and understanding. Yet, Clandinin and Connelly emphasized that researchers "must also step back and see their own stories in the inquiry, the stories of the participants, as well as the larger landscape on which they all live."[11] This tension is congruent with the tension between self as central to knowing and knowledge as mutually constructed. One must bring the self to the knowing process, yet simultaneously make space for others' narratives, and from the two, construct a perspective.

The story told here—trusting one's internal voice, building one's internal foundation, and securing one's internal commitments—is my construction. It is mutually constructed with others, primarily my longitudinal participants. My construction has benefited from the perspectives of others, including colleagues who provided feedback on my interpretations. I offer it here for continued mutual construction with readers to contribute to our understanding of young adult life and the nature of good company for that journey.

NOTES

Introduction

1. Baxter Magolda, M. B. (1992). *Knowing and reasoning in college: Gender-related patterns in students' intellectual development.* San Francisco: Jossey-Bass.

2. For more detailed stories of these participants' twenties, see Baxter Magolda, M. B. (2001). *Making their own way: Narratives for transforming higher education to promote self-development.* Sterling, VA: Stylus.

3. Ibid., p. 119.

4. Baxter Magolda, M. B. (2004). Learning Partnerships Model: A framework for promoting self-authorship. In M. B. Baxter Magolda & P. M. King (Eds.), *Learning partnerships: Theory and models of practice to educate for self-authorship* (pp. 37–62). Sterling, VA: Stylus.

5. Baxter Magolda, *Making their own way,* p. 44.

6. Ibid., pp. 267–268.

7. Kegan, R. (1994). *In over our heads: The mental demands of modern life.* Cambridge, MA: Harvard University Press.

8. Baxter Magolda, M. B. (2004). Self-authorship as the common goal of 21st century education. In M. B. Baxter Magolda & P. M. King (Eds.), *Learning partnerships: Theory and models of practice to educate for self-authorship* (pp. 1–35). Sterling, VA: Stylus.

Chapter 1

1. Baxter Magolda, M. B. (2001). *Making their own way: Narratives for transforming higher education to promote self-development.* Sterling, VA: Stylus (p. 118).

2. Ibid., p. 262.

3. Ibid., p. 272.

4. Ibid., p. 145.

5. Baxter Magolda, M. B. (2004). Self-authorship as the common goal of 21st century education. In M. B. Baxter Magolda & P. M. King (Eds.), *Learning partnerships: Theory and models of practice to educate for self-authorship* (pp. 1–35). Sterling, VA: Stylus (p. 14).

6. Baxter Magolda. *Making their own way,* p. 128.

Chapter 2

1. Baxter Magolda, M. B. (2001). *Making their own way: Narratives for transforming higher education to promote self-development*. Sterling, Va.: Stylus. (p. 151)

2. Ibid., p. 154.

3. Ibid., p. 151.

4. Ibid., pp. 152–153.

5. Ibid., p. 182.

6. Ibid., p. 183.

7. Ibid., p. 178.

8. Ibid., p. 178.

9. Ibid., p. 179.

10. Baxter Magolda, M. B. (2004d). Self-authorship as the common goal of 21st century education. In M. B. Baxter & P. M. King (Eds.), *Learning partnerships: Theory and models of practice to educate for self-authorship* (pp. 1–35). Sterling, VA: Stylus. (pp. 18–19).

11. Ibid., p. 20.

12. Baxter Magolda, M. B. (2004c). Preface. In M. B. Baxter Magolda & P. M. King (Eds.), *Learning partnerships: Theory and models of practice to educate for self-authorship* (pp. xvii–xxvi). Sterling, VA: Stylus. (pp. xx–xxi).

13. Ibid., p. xxi.

14. Ibid., pp. xx–xxi.

15. Baxter Magolda, M. B. (2007). Self-Authorship: The foundation for twenty-first century education. In P. S. Meszaros (Ed.), *Self-Authorship: Advancing students' intellectual growth, New Directions for Teaching and Learning* (Vol. 109, pp. 69–83). San Francisco: Jossey-Bass (p. 71).

16. Ibid.

17. Baxter Magolda, *Making their own way*.

18. In *Making their own way*, I interpreted Dawn's twelfth-year interview as reflecting an internal foundation. Now, with the benefit of eight more annual interviews, her twelfth-year story seems to convey her first access to an early internal foundation. Her story suggests that these phases are not discrete but rather cumulative, gradual evolutions that overlap as they develop. See Chapter 12 for further discussion of this point.

Chapter 3

1. Baxter Magolda, M. B. (1992). *Knowing and reasoning in college: Gender-related patterns in students' intellectual development*. San Francisco: Jossey-Bass.

2. Baxter Magolda, M. B. (2001). *Making their own way: Narratives for transforming higher education to promote self-development*. Sterling, VA: Stylus (p. 46).

3. Ibid., pp. 46–47.

4. Ibid., p. 55.

5. Ibid., p. 55.

6. Ibid., p. 57.

7. Ibid., p. 63.

8. Ibid., pp. 64–65.
9. Ibid., pp. 67–68.
10. Ibid., p. 65.
11. Ibid., p. 66.
12. Ibid., p. 66.
13. Ibid., pp. 66–67.
14. Ibid., p. 68.
15. Baxter Magolda, M. B. (2007). Self-Authorship: The foundation for twenty-first century education. In P. S. Meszaros (Ed.), *Self-Authorship: Advancing students' intellectual growth, New Directions for Teaching and Learning* (Vol. 109, pp. 69–83). San Francisco: Jossey-Bass (p. 72).

Chapter 4

1. Baxter Magolda, M. B. (2001). *Making their own way: Narratives for transforming higher education to promote self-development*. Sterling, VA: Stylus (p. 78).
2. Ibid., p. 98–99.
3. Ibid., pp. 126–127.
4. Ibid., p. 127.
5. Ibid., pp. 172–173.
6. In *Making Their Own Way* (Baxter Magolda, 2001, p. 173), I interpreted Kurt's perspective in these two quotes as reflecting the internal foundation. In light of subsequent interviews reported here, it is more likely that he was still cultivating his internal voice.
7. Baxter Magolda, *Making their own way*, pp. 181–182.
8. Baxter Magolda, M. B. (2004d). Self-authorship as the common goal of 21st century education. In M. B. Baxter Magolda & P. M. King (Eds.), *Learning partnerships: Theory and models of practice to educate for self-authorship*. Sterling, VA: Stylus. (p. 24).
9. Baxter Magolda, M. B. (2003). Identity and learning: Student Affairs' role in transforming higher education. *Journal of College Student Development, 44*(2). (p. 234).

Chapter 5

1. Baxter Magolda, M. B. (2001). *Making their own way: Narratives for transforming higher education to promote self-development*. Sterling, VA: Stylus (p. 266).
2. Ibid., pp. 267–268.
3. Ibid., p. 166.
4. Ibid., p. 168.

Chapter 6

1. Baxter Magolda, M. B. (1992). *Knowing and reasoning in college: Gender-related patterns in students' intellectual development*. San Francisco: Jossey-Bass (pp. 309–310).

2. Baxter Magolda, M. B. (2001). *Making their own way: Narratives for transforming higher education to promote self-development.* Sterling, VA: Stylus (pp. 289–290).

3. Ibid., p. 290.

4. Ibid., pp. 165–166.

5. Ibid., p. 169.

Chapter 7

1. Baxter Magolda, M. B. (2001). *Making their own way: Narratives for transforming higher education to promote self-development.* Sterling, VA: Stylus (p. 76).

2. Ibid., p. 94.

3. Ibid., p. 121.

4. Ibid., p. 120.

5. Ibid., p. 121.

6. Ibid., pp. 121–122.

7. Ibid., p. 122.

8. Ibid., pp. 122–123.

9. Ibid., p. 123.

10. Ibid., p. 120.

11. Ibid., p. 156.

12. Ibid., p. 156.

13. Ibid., pp. 156–157.

14. Ibid., p. 157.

15. Ibid., pp. 157–158.

16. Ibid., p. 158.

17. Ibid., p. 158.

Chapter 8

1. Baxter Magolda, M. B. (2001). *Making their own way: Narratives for transforming higher education to promote self-development.* Sterling, VA: Stylus (p. 102).

2. Ibid., p. 129.

3. Ibid., p. 118.

4. Ibid., p. 163.

5. Ibid., p. 99.

Chapter 9

1. Baxter Magolda, M. B. (2001). *Making their own way: Narratives for transforming higher education to promote self-development.* Sterling, VA: Stylus; Baxter Magolda, M. B. (2004b). Learning Partnerships Model: A framework for promoting self-authorship. In M. B. Baxter Magolda & P. M. King (Eds.), *Learning partnerships: Theory and models of practice to educate for self-authorship* (pp. 37–62). Sterling, VA: Stylus.

2. Baxter Magolda, M. B. (2001). *Making their own way: Narratives for transforming higher education to promote self-development*. Sterling, VA: Stylus (p. 82).

3. Ibid., p. 176.

4. Ibid., pp. 254–255.

5. Ibid., pp. 148–149.

6. Ibid., p. 39.

7. Ibid., p. 265.

8. See Baxter Magolda, M. B. (1999). *Creating contexts for learning and self-authorship: constructive-developmental pedagogy* (1st ed.). Nashville, TN.: Vanderbilt University Press; Baxter Magolda, M. B., & King, P. M. (Eds.). (2004). *Learning partnerships: Theory & models of practice to educate for self-authorship*. Sterling, VA: Stylus; and Bekken, B. M., & Marie, J. (2007). Making self-authorship a goal of core curricula: The Earth Sustainability Pilot Project. In P. S. Meszaros (Ed.), *Self-Authorship: Advancing students' intellectual growth, New Directions for Teaching and Learning* (Vol. 109, pp. 53–67). San Francisco: Jossey-Bass.

Chapter 10

1. Torres, V., & Hernandez, E. (2007). The influence of ethnic identity development on self-authorship: A longitudinal study of Latino/a college students. *Journal of College Student Development, 48*(5), 558–573.

2. Ibid., p. 563.

3. Ibid., p. 566.

4. Ibid., pp. 558–573.

5. Torres, V., & Baxter Magolda, M. B. (2004). Reconstructing Latino identity: The influence of cognitive development on the ethnic identity process of Latino students. *Journal of College Student Development, 45*(3), 333–347 (p. 338).

6. Ibid., p. 338.

7. Torres, V., & Hernandez, E. (2007). The influence of ethnic identity development on self-authorship: A longitudinal study of Latino/a college students. *Journal of College Student Development, 48*(5), 558–573.

8. Abes, E. S. (2003). *The dynamics of lesbian college students' multiple dimensions of identity*. Unpublished Dissertation, The Ohio State University, Columbus, OH.

9. Abes, E. S. (2007). Applying queer theory in practice with college students: Transformation of a researcher's and a participant's perspectives on identity. *Journal of LGBT Youth, 5*(1), 55–75.

10. Abes, E. S., & Jones, S. R. (2004). Meaning-making capacity and the dynamics of lesbian college students' multiple dimensions of identity. *Journal of College Student Development, 45*(6), 612–632.

11. Baxter Magolda, M. B., Abes, E., & Torres, V. (2009). Epistemological, intrapersonal, and interpersonal development in the college years and young adulthood. In M. C. Smith (Ed.), *Handbook of research on adult learning and development* (pp. 183–219). Mahway, NJ: Lawrence Erlbaum (p. 198).

12. Abes, E. S., Jones, S. R., & McEwen, M. K. (2007). Reconceptualizing the Model of Multiple Dimensions of Identity: The role of meaning-making capacity in the construction of multiple identities. *Journal of College Student Development,* 48(1), 1–22 (p. 11).

13. Ibid., pp. 11–12.

14. Epistemological, intrapersonal, and interpersonal development, pp. 204–205.

15. Abes, E. S., & Jones, S. R. (2004). Meaning-making capacity and the dynamics of lesbian college students' multiple dimensions of identity. *Journal of College Student Development,* 45(6), p. 624.

16. Abes, E. S., & Kasch, D. (2007). Using Queer Theory to explore lesbian college students' multiple dimensions of identity. *Journal of College Student Development,* 48, 1–18.

17. Pizzolato, J. E. (2003). Developing self-authorship: Exploring the experiences of high-risk college students. *Journal of College Student Development,* 44(6), 797–812 (p. 801).

18. Ibid., p. 804.

19. Ibid., p. 806.

20. Ibid., p. 806.

21. Ibid., p. 806.

22. Ibid., p. 808.

23. Pizzolato, J. E. (2004). Coping with conflict: Self-authorship, coping, and adaptation to college in first-year, high-risk students. *Journal of College Student Development,* 45(4), 425–442.

24. Ibid., p. 432.

25. Ibid., 425–442.

26. Boes, L. M. (2006). Learning from practice: A constructive-developmental study of undergraduate service-learning pedagogy. Unpublished Doctoral Dissertation. Harvard University.

27. Ibid., p. 174.

28. Ibid., p. 201.

29. Ibid., pp. 201–202.

30. Ibid., p. 150.

31. Ibid., p. 181.

32. Ibid., p. 184.

33. Ibid., p.131.

34. Ibid., p. 222.

35. Blaich, C., & King, P. M. (2005). *Student Achievement of Liberal Arts Outcomes: A Study of Claims and Causes.* Paper presented at the Association of American Colleges and Universities; see http://liberalarts.wabash.edu/cila/nationalstudy.

36. King, P. M., Kendall Brown, M., Lindsay, N. K., & VanHecke, J. R. (2007). Liberal arts student learning outcomes: An integrated approach. *About Campus: Enriching the Student Learning Experience,* 12(4), 2–9.

37. Baxter Magolda, M. B., King, P. M., Stephenson, E., Kendall Brown, M., Lindsay, N., Barber, J., et al. (2007). *Developmentally Effective Experi-*

ences for Promoting Self-Authorship. Paper presented at the American Educational Research Association.

38. Ibid., 2007, pp. 30–31.

39. Baxter Magolda, M. B., King, P. M., Stephenson, E., Kendall Brown, M., Lindsay, N., Barber, J., et al. (2007). *Developmentally Effective Experiences for Promoting Self-Authorship*. Paper presented at the American Educational Research Association.

40. Barber, J. P., & King, P. M. (2007). *Experiences that Promote Self-Authorship: An Analysis of the "Demands" of Developmentally Effective Experiences*. Paper presented at the Association for the Study of Higher Education; King, P. M., & Baxter Magolda, M. B. (2007). *Experiences that Promote Self-Authorship among Students of Color: Understanding and Negotiating Multiple Perspectives*. Paper presented at the Association for the Study of Higher Education.

41. Adult Development Research Group. (2001). *Toward a new pluralism in ABE/ESOL Classrooms: Teaching to multiple "cultures of mind." National Center for the Study of Adult Learning and Literacy Report #19.* Cambridge, MA: Harvard University Graduate School of Education.

42. Helsing, D., Broderick, M., & Hammerman, J. (2001). A developmental view of ESOL students' identity transitions in an urban community college. In Adult Development Research Group (Ed.), *Toward a new pluralism in ABE/ESOL classrooms: Teaching to multiple "cultures of mind"* (pp. 77–228). Cambridge, MA: National Center for the Study of Adult Learning and Literacy, Harvard Graduate School of Education.

43. Ibid., p. 139.

44. Ibid., p. 168.

45. Ibid., p. 140.

46. Ibid., p. 140.

47. Ibid., p. 169.

48. Ibid, pp. 149–150.

49. Ibid., pp 166–167.

50. Portnow, K., Diamond, A., & Pakos Rimer, K. (2001). "Becoming what I really am": Stories of self-definition and self-expansion in an Even Start ABE/ESOL family literacy program: A developmental perspective. In Adult Development Research Group (Ed.), *Toward a new pluralism in ABE/ESOL classrooms: Teaching to multiple "cultures of mind"* (pp. 229–377). Cambridge, MA: National Center for the Study of Adult Learning and Literacy, Harvard Graduate School of Education.

51. Ibid., p. 271.

52. Ibid., pp. 303–304.

53. Ibid., p. 274.

54. Ibid., pp. 273–274.

55. A developmental view of ESOL students' identity transitions, p. 179.

56. "Becoming what I really am," p. 355.

57. Ibid., p. 356.

58. Ibid., p. 356.

Chapter 11

1. Baxter Magolda, M. B. (2001). *Making their own way: Narratives for transforming higher education to promote self-development*. Sterling, VA: Stylus (p. 193).

2. Ibid., p. 42.

3. Baxter Magolda, M. B. (2004d). Self-authorship as the common goal of 21st century education. In M. B. Baxter Magolda & P. M. King (Eds.), *Learning partnerships: Theory and models of practice to educate for self-authorship*. Sterling, VA: Stylus. (pp. 18–19).

Chapter 12

1. Portions of this chapter are adapted with permission from Baxter Magolda, M. B. (2008). Three elements of self-authorship. *Journal of College Student Development, 49*(4), 269–284. Reprinted with permission from the American College Personnel Association (ACPA), One Dupont Circle, NW at the Center for Higher Education, Washington, DC 20036.

2. Kegan, R. (1994). *In over our heads: The mental demands of modern life*. Cambridge, MA: Harvard University Press (p. 91).

3. Kegan, R. (1982). *The evolving self: Problem and process in human development*. Cambridge, MA: Harvard University Press; Kegan, R. (1994). *In over our heads: The mental demands of modern life*. Cambridge, MA: Harvard University Press; Perry, W. G. (1970). *Forms of intellectual and ethical development in the college years: A scheme*. Troy, MO: Holt, Rinehart, & Winston; and Piaget, J. (1950). *The psychology of intelligence* (M. P. a. D. Berlyne, Trans.). London: Routledge & Kegan Paul.

4. Kegan, R. (1994). *In over our heads: The mental demands of modern life*. Cambridge, Massachusetts: Harvard University Press.

5. Boes, L. M. (2006). *Learning from practice: A constructive-developmental study of undergraduate service-learning pedagogy*. Unpublished Doctoral Dissertation. Harvard University; Debold, E. (2002). Epistemology, fourth order consciousness, and the subject-object relationship or how the self evolves with Robert Kegan [Electronic Version]. *Enlightenment Magazine, Fall-Winter*. Retrieved July 27, 2007, from http://www.wie.org/j22/kegan.asp.

6. Baxter Magolda, M. B. (2001). *Making their own way: Narratives for transforming higher education to promote self-development*. Sterling, VA: Stylus (p. 42).

7. Piaget, J. (1950). *The psychology of intelligence* (M. P. a. D. Berlyne, Trans.). London: Routledge & Kegan Paul.

8. *Making their own way*, p. 7.

9. *Making their own way:* p. 43.

10. Baxter Magolda, M. B. (1992). *Knowing and reasoning in college: Gender-related patterns in students' intellectual development*. San Francisco: Jossey-Bass.

11. Belenky, M., Clinchy, B. M., Goldberger, N., & Tarule, J. (1986). *Women's ways of knowing: The development of self, voice, and mind*. New York: Basic Books.

12. Bakan, D. (1966). *The duality of human existence: An essay on psychology and religion.* Chicago, IL: Rand McNally & Company.

13. *Knowing and reasoning in college.*

14. *In over our heads.*

15. Ibid., p. 225.

16. Ibid.

17. Kegan, R. (1982). *The evolving self: Problem and process in human development.* Cambridge, MA: Harvard University Press.

Appendix

1. Perry, W. G. (1970). *Forms of intellectual and ethical development in the college years: A scheme.* Troy, MO: Holt, Rinehart, & Winston.

2. Belenky, M., Clinchy, B. M., Goldberger, N., & Tarule, J. (1986). *Women's ways of knowing: The development of self, voice, and mind.* New York: Basic Books.

3. Baxter Magolda, M. B. (1992). *Knowing and reasoning in college: Gender-related patterns in students' intellectual development.* San Francisco: Jossey-Bass.

4. Baxter Magolda, M. B. (2001). *Making their own way: Narratives for transforming higher education to promote self-development.* Sterling, VA: Stylus.

5. Denzin, N. K. (1994). The art and politics of interpretation. In N. K. Denzin & Y. S. Lincoln (Denzin, 1994). (Eds.), *Handbook of qualitative research* (pp. 500–515). Thousand Oaks, CA: Sage.

6. Fontana, A., & Frey, J. H. (2000). The interview: From structured questions to negotiated text. In N. K. Denzin & Y. S. Lincoln (Eds.), *Handbook of qualitative research, second edition* (pp. 645–672). Thousand Oaks, CA: Sage.

7. *Making their own way*, p. 132.

8. This kind of rapport is essential to an in-depth study of human development. Peers who suggest that this rapport has altered the participants' development, a matter seen as a potential problem from a positivistic perspective, have sometimes challenged me. I concur that participation in this project probably has altered participants' development due to the self-reflection involved, the opportunity to read about others' development, and exposure to the overall developmental process. I remind readers, given this issue, that I make no claims that these participants' stories or my interpretations of them are generalizable to others but rather particular constructions that may be transferable.

9. Charmaz, K. (2003). Qualitative interviewing and grounded theory analysis. In J. A. Holstein & J. F. Gubrium (Eds.), *Inside interviewing: New lenses, new concerns* (pp. 311–330). Thousand Oaks, CA: Sage; Charmaz, K. C. (2006). *Constructing grounded theory: A practical guide through qualitative analysis.* Thousand Oaks, CA: Sage.

10. Clandinin, D. J., & Connelly, F. M. (2000). *Narrative inquiry: Experience and story in qualitative research.* San Francisco: Jossey-Bass (p. 81).

11. Ibid., p. 81.

INDEX

Abes, Elisa, 285, 288
Absolute knowing, 339
Adult Basic Education, 301. *See
    also* English for Speakers of
    Other Languages (ESOL)
Adult learners
    in family literacy program,
        306–309
    of other language students,
        301–305
Adult learners, self-authored,
    308–309
Adult life, challenges of
    Al's experiences. *See* Al, story of
    Anne's experiences, 33–36
    Barb's experiences, 28–31
    career choices, 22
    Dawn's experiences. *See* Dawn,
        story of
    external influence, problem
        with, 21–22
    Genesse's experiences, 24–28
    getting ready for, 215
    health problems, 23
    Kurt's experiences. *See* Kurt,
        story of
    learning new skills, way of han-
        dling, 207–208
    Lydia's experiences. *See* Lydia,
        story of
    Mark's experiences. *See* Mark,
        story of
    personal life choices, 22–23
    Phillip's experiences. *See* Phillip,
        story of

Reginald's experiences, 31–33
Sandra's experiences, 12–13. *See
    also* Sandra, story of
stress problems, 24
supporting yourself in, 217–218
Agentic gender-related patterns,
    338–339
Al, story of
    internal commitments, securing,
        37, 38
    internal foundation, building, 36
    role of good citizen, performing,
        38–39
    stress in work, facing, 37–38
Alice, story of
    clear communication, 232–233
    faith, role of, 230–231
    Guillain-Barré syndrome, expe-
        riencing, 230
    internal foundation, building,
        231–232
    life before challenges, 229–230
    parenting practices, 233–234
Anne, story of
    internal foundation, building,
        33–35
    personal crisis, facing, 35–36
Authenticity, in self-authoring,
    68–70

Barb, story of
    career mindedness, 28–29
    dilemma between work and
        motherhood, 30–31
    motherhood, prioritizing, 29–30

Being true. *See* Kurt, story of
Benetta, story of
  disagreements with mother, 302
  listening to internal voice,
    302–303
Boes, Lisa, 291
Building a self-authored system,
  329
  building an internal foundation,
    326–327
  securing internal commitments,
    327–328
  trusting the internal voice,
    325–326

Cara, story of
  depression, experiencing,
    237–238
  external noise in life, wiping
    out, 240–241
  force of external influence, expe-
    riencing, 21–22, 234,
    235–237
  internal foundation, building,
    238–240
  successful academic/professional
    life, 234–235
Career decisions
  free will, exercising, 100
  internal voice, importance of,
    142, 145, 305
  making choices, 22
  philosophy of life, influencing,
    87
  priorities in life, 98
  sense of values, helping, 99
Challenges in life, role of, 250–252
Christmas, Joe, 332
Cognitive development, 9–10
College education
  growth during, 296–300, 301
  high-risk students in, 288–291

Latino/a college students,
    282–285
  lesbian students, 285–288
  life after, 22–23, 322, 323
  peer pressure during, 288
  self-authorship during, 16
College-service learning course,
    students in
  internal voice, cultivating,
    291–293
  self-authored systems, 293–296
Connected employee, 339–340
Contextual knowing, 339
Co-workers. *See* Peers
Crossroads, 6–7, 134–141, 162–163
  story about, 47–48, 76–79,
    105–106

Dalia, story of
  Even Start program, views on,
    308–309
  internal voice, listening to,
    307–308
David (Lydia's husband)
  parenting philosophy, 173, 179
  strong marital relationship,
    sharing, 177–178
Dawn, story of
  alternate sexual orientation,
    accepting, 48
  art of controlling without
    controlling, following, 52–53
  bringing humanity to herself,
    67–68
  cooking, creative venue, 46–47
  crisis in personal
    relationship, 50
  defining moment in her life, 45
  essence of her relationship with
    the world, finding, 51–52
  internal foundation, building,
    56–58

internal foundation, developing, 63–65

internal voice, listening to, 48–50

intuition, describing, 49

lessons learned from, 70–72

MS diagnosis, handling, 52

multiple sclerosis, facing, 50–51

personal/professional crisis, 54–55

quest for her spiritual core, 58–59

self-authorship, moving beyond, 68–70

self-discovery, effects of, 47–48

spiritual core of herself, cultivating, 52

spirituality, opinion about, 49, 53–54, 55–56

spiritual perspective, change in her, 62–63

struggles in self-discovery, 66–67

theater, influence of, 45–46

transformation from knowledge to wisdom, 59–62

understanding own self, focusing on, 65–66

Depression, 146

confidence lapse and, 136

faith, impact on, 158

leading to realignment of priorities, 191

versus positive attitude, 136, 154, 194

stress and, 26, 146, 154, 158

supportive environment, dealing with, 158–159, 213–214, 242–243

uncertainties leading to, 86

Developmental holding environment, 343–345

Developmental journey

changes in, 3, 9–11

epistemological dimension to, 332–333

and gender-related patterns. *See* Gender-related patterns of participants

holing environment and, 343–345

identity dimension to, 333–334

meaning-making structures affecting, 337–338

personal characteristics of participants affecting, 335–337

personal variables, complexities of, 343

relational dimension to, 334–335

three dimensions of, 9–10, 332

Dissonance and self-authorship, 284–285

Educational partnerships, 261–267

Educators, 275–277

Employees, 273–275

connected employee, 339–340

maintaining relationship with, 122–123

as partner, 273–275

separate employee, 340, 342

English for Speakers of Other Languages (ESOL), 301–305

Epistemological dimension, 332–333

ESOL. *See* English for Speakers of Other Languages (ESOL)

Evan, experiences with internal voice

cultivating internal voice, 191–192

listening to internal voice, 190–191

Evan, story of
  awareness of mind's work, 192–193
  internal voice, cultivating, 191–192
  marriage, views on, 190
  problems in being perfectionist, 190–191
  problem-solving approach, development of, 193
  reflection on college life, 189
Evan, story of building of internal foundation
  additional responsibility in family, taking, 196
  knowledge and skills, acquiring, 195–196
  parenting responsibility, taking, 197–198
  personal and professional commitments, balancing, 195
  personal life, crisis in, facing, 197
  personal realities, new approach toward, 196–197
  relationship with wife, improving, 198, 205
Evan, story of securing internal commitments
  emergency situations, being ready for, 202
  floating-on-the-waves philosophy, embracing, 198–199, 211–213
  key interest area, identifying, 206–207, 209
  learning new skills, 207–208, 209–210
  maturity as key to success, 204
  opportunities, taking up, 205–206, 211
  parenthood, views on, 199
  parenting philosophy, 210–211

personal crisis, handling of, 201, 203–204
priorities in life, importance of sorting, 201–202, 203
professional life, experiencing success in, 199–200
refereeing hockey, growth in, 204, 208–209
self-criticisms, 200–201
self-improvement, working on, 200
Evan, story of trusting internal voice
  challenges in marital life, dealing with, 194
  drive for perfection, compromising, 194–195
  priorities, identification of, 193
  relationships, reframing of, 193
  sense of self, refinement of, 193
Even Start
  Dalia's experiences, 308–309
  Hamid's experiences, 307, 308
  Linn's experiences, 306–307
  scope of, 306
External formulas, 6
  disruptions of, 309
  followed by college students, 298
  limitations of, 15–17, 313–314
  in meaning-making, 337
External influence
  internal voice, conflict between, 286, 324
  invisible force of, 21–22
  purpose in life, 1
  in twenties, 242. *See also* Adult life, challenges of

Faith
  convalescence, role in, 230–231
  crisis in personal life, role in overcoming, 227–229

developmental journey, affecting, 336–337
parenting practices, 233–234
Faulkner, William, 332
Finding peace and calm, story of, 36–39
Floating-on-the-waves, 198–199, 328
advantages of, 203–204
self-criticism of, 200–201
Frankel, Victor, 87
Free will, 95
faith as an act of, 246
internal commitments and, 232–233
in personal relationships, 97, 98
relationships with God and, 228
in shaping life, 96–97
Friends, 272–273

Gaining perspective
internal foundation, importance of developing, 245–246
self-authorship, road to, 217
strategies for, 315–318
Gavin, story of
boss, learning partnership with, 262–263
internal commitments, securing, 265–266
internal voice, listening to, 263
manager, learning partnership with, 261–262
students, partnerships with, 263–265
success in teaching, experiencing, 265, 266–267
Gender-related patterns
absolute and contextual knowing of, 339
developmental journey, affecting, 338

relational and agentic, contrast between, 338–339
stylistic preferences of participants and, 340–343
Gender socialization, 336
Genesse, story of
parenting problems, 26
professional crisis, 25–27
stress, dealing with, 27–28
Good company
characteristics of, 12–13
model of learning partnerships, 11
nature of, 249–252
and self-authorship, 218. *See also* Supporting yourself
Guillain-Barré syndrome, 230
Gwen's experiences
of good company, 12
of meaning-making, 337

Hamid, story of, 307, 308
Heather, story of
crisis in personal life, identifying, 221–222
internal foundation, 224
internal voice, trusting, 222–224
High-risk students
circumstances of college admission, impact of, 289–290
coping strategies, influences of, 291
marginalization of identities, impact of, 290–291
provocative experiences, impact of, 288–289
Holding environments, defined, 343–345

Identity
components of, 129
contextual influences on, 285. *See also* Lesbian college students

development of, 82
ethnic, 282. *See also* Latino/a
   college students
forging of, 285
internal, 57, 169
of lesbians, 285
personal, 138
professional, 138, 152
Identity development
ethnic, 282–283
personal, 152
professional, 152
self-authorship, relationship
   with, 285
Identity dimension, 333–334
Internal commitments, securing,
   9, 38
by cultivating relationship with
   God, 231–232
to deal with risks involved in
   work, 37
to deal with tragic situation, 338
and effect on relationships, 331
to face adult challenges, 41–42
to face external challenges of
   life, 202
for meaning-making, 327
by self-authored system, 327
by self-exploration, 71
sorting and sifting for, 318
Internal foundation. *See also* Self-
   authorship
to attract opportunities in work,
   130
development of self-authorship,
   in building, 70–71
difficulty of maintaining, 71,
   336–337
enduring nature of, 326
to face circumstances beyond
   control, 246
to frame external influence on
   behavior, 110

to guide career and life
   decisions, 41
intrapersonal, 66
to maintain relationship with
   employees, 122–123
and making decisions, 35
and personal talents, 56
positive attitude and, 220–221
process of building, 8–9
professional training, for building, 231
strengthening, 33, 269
well-developed, 63
Internal stability. *See* Lydia, story of
Internal voice
adult challenges, role in facing,
   41–42
cultivating, 7
difficulties faced in trusting,
   222–223
listening to, 7, 31–33
new perspective, supporting,
   219–220
strategies for developing, 315–316
struggle for listening to, 24–28,
   28–31
trusting, 8, 164–167
Interpersonal development, 10
achieving wisdom in, 71–72
awareness of, 350–351
in professional life, 185–186
relationship with partner, 71
Interviewees
career choices, 22
depression, 24
health problems, 23
internal voices, 41
in thirties, challenges faced,
   41–42
in twenties, 41–42
Intrapersonal development, 10
awareness of, 350–351
difficulties in, 158

intellectual approach in, 100
in professional life, 185–186
in relationship with partner, 71

James, Henry, 332

Kegan, Robert, 15–16, 321–322
Kelly, story of
  believing in her faith, 228
  faith, exploring, 225
  good partnership with spouse,
    sharing, 227–228
  internal voice, trusting, 225–226
  relationship with God,
    understanding, 226–227
  stress, handling, 228–229
  "there is hope" philosophy,
    embracing, 226
Kurt, story of
  continued development, ultimate
    goal of, 128–129
  control over own reactions,
    109–110
  crisis in professional life,
    108–109, 110–111
  crossroads, traversing, 105–106
  dilemma in career path, 104,
    111–112
  external formula, relying upon,
    104–105, 116–117
  implementation of principles,
    challenges in, 118–119
  inner voice, listening to, 105
  interaction with penchant for
    people, 103
  internal commitments, securing,
    122–123
  internal foundation, effects of,
    116
  internal sense of self, effort in
    cultivating, 107–108
  new philosophy of management,
    efforts in attaining, 113–114

parenting philosophy, 123, 124
positive approach toward
  challenges, attaining,
  125–127
power of choice, achieving, 110
self-belief, learning, 120–122
self-exploration, importance of,
  114–115
spirituality, opinion on, 109

Latino/a college students
  cultural history of, effects of, 283
  identity, effects of, 283–284
  racism, impact of, 284–285
Lauren, story of
  depression, dealing with, 243
  external influence, dependence
    on, 242
  internal commitments, securing,
    244–245
  reality with her goals, reconcil-
    ing, 243–244
  trauma from pregnancy issues,
    experiencing, 242–243
Learning
  definition of, 105
  internal voice, 263. *See also*
    Learning Partnership Model
  new skills, 208
  vulnerability, 58–59
Learning Partnership Model
  components of, 251
  educators, 275–277
  employees, 273–275
  good company, part of, 12–15.
    See also Good company
  in life and death. *See* Will,
    story of
  life partners, role in, 267–269
  objectives, 11
  parents, role in, 269–272
  peers, role in, 272–273
  professional partners, 277–279

Lesbian college students
  contextual influences on
      identity, understanding,
      286–287
  discriminatory experiences,
      overcoming, 286, 286–287
  identity, forging, 285
  internal voice, challenges in lis-
      tening, 285–286
Leslie, story of
  partnership with husband, 256,
      257, 258–259
  personal loss, overcoming,
      259–261
Life partners, 267–269
Linn, story of
  parenting philosophy, 307
  professional and personal roles,
      conflicts between, 306
  professional identity, reclaiming,
      307
Loss and recovery, story about,
      242–245
Lydia, story of
  Alex's food-intake, efforts in
      managing, 181–182
  Alex's health problems,
      handling, 180–181, 182–183
  crossroads, traversing, 163–164
  family and military lifestyle,
      problems in balancing, 171
  "figuring it out" philosophy,
      184–185
  internal sense of identity, main-
      taining, 169
  internal voice, listening to, 163,
      165–166
  military life, influences of,
      167–168
  military life, perspective on,
      162–163
  momentary frustrations,
      overcoming, 168–169

motherhood, experiences of,
      170–171
  "new normal" constructing, 167
  overseas tours, influences of,
      164–165
  parenting, views on, 172–173
  parenting philosophy,
      developing, 174–175,
      178–179
  personal life, facing problems in,
      179–180
  planning skills, optimizing, 183
  positive attitude, adopting,
      171–172, 176–177
  priorities in life, sorting out,
      166–167
  reactions to husband's redeploy-
      ment to sea, 175
  resilience, developing, 175–176
  shy college student to resilient
      adult, transformation,
      185–186
  skepticisms about moving to a
      new place, 169–170
  strong marital relationship,
      maintaining, 177–178
  successful college life, 161–162
  taking decisions about child
      rearing, 173–174
  uncertainties of husband's mili-
      tary life, handling, 183–184
Lynn, story of
  internal voice, trusting,
      219–220
  pain, experiencing, 218–219
  positive thinking, maintaining,
      220–221

Making own music, story of, 39–41
Making Their Own Way (Baxter
      Magolda), 138, 224
The Man in the Glass, 106
Marcher, John, 94, 332

Mark, story of
  challenges of life, facing, 84–86,
    88–89
  crisis in professional life, 98–99
  crossroads, traversing, 77–79
  disappointments in professional
    expectations, 76
  external formula,
    disappointments with, 76–77
  faith, importance of, 91–92,
    93–94
  focused attitude, 76
  foundational philosophy, impor-
    tance of, 86–88
  "go with the flow" philosophy,
    89–91
  identifying pain, 76
  inner voice, trusting, 79–81
  internal cues, listening to, 77
  major decisions in life, handling,
    92–93
  marriage, approach toward,
    97–98
  new perspective towards life,
    83–84
  organized religion, approach
    toward, 94–95
  parenting philosophy, 95–97
  Taoism, influences of, 81–83
Mastery pattern knowers, 339
Maturity, as key to success, 204
Maura, story of, 293–294
Meaning-making, 323, 337–338
  elements of, 32
  external formulas and, 337
  participants involvement in,
    324–325
Misconceptions of self-authorship,
  330–331
Motherhood, 30. *See also*
  Parenting/parents
  balancing work, 186, 255
  challenges of, 170

Moving beyond self-suthorship,
  329–330
Moving toward self-authorship,
  323–325
MS. *See* Multiple sclerosis (MS)
Multiple sclerosis (MS), 50
Multi-tasking, 213

Neil, story of, 293
No Exit (Sartre), 50

Pain
  internal foundation, motivating,
    312–314
  revaluation of life, motivating,
    216–217, 314–315
Parenting/parents, 172–173
  career decisions and, 17
  challenges in, 13, 23, 181–182,
    229
  experiences in life, influences of,
    209
  faith and, 231, 233
  floating-on-the-waves philosophy
    of, 199
  internal foundation, impact on,
    224, 232, 241
  internal voice, listening to, 253,
    307
  key partners, 270
  life partners, role of, 267–269
  life's philosophy and, 130–131
  philosophies, 95–96, 124,
    173–174, 210
  practices, 27–28
  role in partnership, 269–272,
    305
  self-authorship and, 309
  stress in, 26
  trials and tribulation of, manag-
    ing, 233–234
  work and, balancing, 30–31,
    229–230

Parenting philosophy
  child's views, listening to,
    173–174
  free will, belief in, 95–96
  insights into, 179
  involvement of children,
    210–211
  situation and response model,
    124
Partners
  educators, 275–277
  employees, 273–275
  life, role of, 267–269
  parents, role of, 269–272
  peers, role of, 272–273
  professional partners, role of,
    277–279
  self-authorship, role in,
    251–252, 319–320
  understanding journey of your,
    279
Partnerships. *See also* Learning
    Partnership Model
  building faith through, 252–255
  educational. *See* Educational
    partnerships
  negotiating life and death
    through, 255–261
  partners' role, 251
Peers, 272–273
Personal characteristics, 336–337
Personal life
  calculating risks in, 257
  complexity of work and, 220
  good partners in, 230
Phillip, story of
  challenges in life, facing, 40
  internal commitments, securing,
    39–40
  refection on himself, 40–41
Piaget, Jean, 335
Pizzolato, Jane, 288, 290, 291
Positive attitude, 175, 218,
    220–221

Priorities in life
  importance of, 201–203
  as key to success, 205
Professional partners, role of,
    277–279

Racism, and self-authorship,
    284–285
Receiving pattern knowers, 339
Reginald, story of, 31–32
Relational dimension to
    development, 334–335
Relational gender-related patterns,
    338–339
Risk in life, 316–317
Robbins, Tony, 78, 332–333
Rosa, story of
  gaining perspective, 254
  husband's support, 252–253,
    254–255
  sister's support, 253–254

Sandra, story of
  challenges of life, 142–143
  depression, dealing with,
    146–147
  dilemmas in profession,
    147–149
  external formula, relying on,
    144–145, 148
  in local library, 153–154
  in paralegal professionreasons of
    joining, 141–142
  praying, importance of, 143–144
  profession, challenges in, 12–13,
    135–137, 138
  professional internal voice,
    listening to, 134–136,
    138–139, 153
  relationships, opinion about,
    145–146
  relationship with God, 149–151
  responsible for herself, quest for,
    139–141

self-confidence, understanding, 151–152

sense of identity, nurturing, 137–138

taking control of her life, 154–156

values and beliefs, vision of, 133–134

Sartre, Jean Paul, 50

Self-authorship. *See also* Supporting yourself

building a self-authored system, phase of, 325–329

challenges, role of, 250–252

in college-service learning course students. *See* College-service learning course students

contextual factors in developing, 309–310

crossroads and, 6–7

cyclical theory of, potential of, 345–346

demands of contemporary society and, 15–16

developmental changes and, 3, 9–11

developmental dimensions and, 332–325. *See also* Developmental journey

ESOL program and, 302–305

in Even Start adult learners, 306–309

external formulas and, 6

in first-year high-risk college students. *See* High-risk students

gaining new perspective, way toward, 217

good partnerships, way toward, 217. *See also* Good company

internal commitments, securing, 9. *See also* Internal commitments

internal foundation, building, 8–9. *See also* Internal foundation

internal voice, trusting, 8. *See also* Internal voice

Kegan's notion about, 321–322

in Latino/a college students, 282–285

in lesbian college students. *See* Lesbian college students

Mark's description of, 7–8

misconceptions of, clarification of, 330–332

and pain, experiences of, 216–217

partner's role in helping, 251

racism in, 284–285

WNSLAE studies on, 296

Self-confidence, 147, 185

internal foundation, building, 155

internal voice, trusting, 158–159

painful experiences, dealing with, 147

self-discovery and, 47

self-reliance, distinction between, 151

Self-criticism

advantages of, 201

floating-on-the-waves philosophy, 200–201

Self-discovery

effects of, 47

internal voice, 56, 70

Self-exploration

developing strength, 59

discovering own self. *See* Self-discovery

internal foundation, 71, 72

internal voice, developing, 46–47, 142, 337

parents' role in, 270

self-confidence, developing, 80. *See also* Self-discovery

sense of spirituality, fueling, 331, 333

Self-reliance
  internal foundation, building, 155
  internal voice, 158–159
  self-discovery, distinction
    between, 151
Self-transformation, 68–70
Separate employee, 340, 342
Serge, story of
  cultivating internal voice,
    303–304
  mother's approval, depending
    on, 303
Sexual orientation, 336
Siblings, 272–273
Sonja, story of
  controlling her own decisions,
    304
  listening to internal voice, 305
Spirituality
  in motivating life, 49, 109
  in personal development,
    336–337
  in self-exploration, 331
Stephen, story of, 294–296
Stress
  and carving out time for
    yourself, 229
  caused by depression, 24. *See
    also* Depression
  cause of, 10
  coping with. *See* Stress, dealing
    with
  emotional, 154
  expectations leading to, 31
  intellect and, 84
  parenting, 26, 228–229
  personal growth in
    relationships, leading to,
    22–23
  physical illness, leading to, 25,
    228
  sense of independence, 146
  at work place, 31, 54, 108, 153

Stress, dealing with
  internal commitments, 223
  internal foundation, 198
  internal voice, trusting, 51–52,
    158–159, 214
  in male-dominated
    environments, 234
  self-confidence, 28, 180–181
  sense of independence, 146
Supporting yourself
  in adulthood, 217–218
  Alice's experiences. *See* Alice,
    story of
  by being grounded in faith. *See*
    Kelly, story of
  by changing perspective, 218–221
  by facing fears, 221–224
  Lauren's experiences. *See*
    Lauren, story of
  for other's journey, 250
  proceeding step-by-step. *See*
    Cara, story of
  self-authorship, helping, 251.
    See also Self-authorship
  for yourself. *See* Supporting
    yourself

Taoist principles, 81, 82–83
Three dimensions of development
  cognitive development, 9–10
  interpersonal development, 10
  intrapersonal development, 10
Torres, Vasti, 282–285

U.S.S. Cole, 178

Wabash National Study of Liberal
    Arts Education (WNSLAE)
  findings of, 297–300
  first phase of, 296
What Color is Your Parachute?, 144
Will, story of
  father, partnership with, 259

impact of good partnerships,
256–257
personal crisis, experiencing,
258–259
success, experiencing, 257–258
supervisor, partnership with,
255–256
wife, partnership with, 256, 257,
259–261

Wisdom
absolute knowing, 339
contextual knowing, 339
WNSLAE. *See* Wabash National
Study of Liberal Arts Education (WNSLAE)

Your Buddha Nature, usage of
tapes, 241

MARCIA B. BAXTER MAGOLDA
Making Their Own Way

Narratives for Transforming Higher Education to Promote Self-Development

"...provides long-awaited answers to critical questions regarding how college impacts students' lives. Through an accomplished interview technique, the author provides us with an inside tour of the lives and minds of hundreds of college graduates. The longitudinal design allows us to comprehend more fully the lifelong impact of higher education. The author weaves these stories into a highly usable framework for educational improvement. Her concrete suggestions help the reader transform insights gained from the interviews into current college curricular and co-curricular practices. This book will be immediately useful for anyone connected to the college experience." —AAHE Bulletin

EDITED BY MARCIA B. BAXTER MAGOLDA & PATRICIA M. KING
Learning Partnerships

Theory and Models of Practice to Educate for Self-Authorship

"Those interested in strengthening the ties between theory and practice and between faculty and student affairs can find inspiration here. Those committed to developing the co-curriculum to promote self-authorship will have a better sense of how to do that from this book. *Learning Partnerships* could serve as a text for courses on epistemological development or teaching and learning. It could provide a foundation for professional development for faculty or student affairs practitioners (and examples for doing so are included)....With its focus on practice and experiential education and its personal tone, readers are invited into the worlds of the authors to see the assumptions and principles of the [Learning Partnerships Model] in practice." **—Journal of College Student Development**

DANNELLE D. STEVENS & JOANNE E. COOPER

Journal Keeping

How to Use Reflective Writing for Learning, Teaching, Professional Insight and Positive Change

"A superb tool for educators who want to be reflective practitioners, and help their students become reflective learners. I hope this fine book will be widely read and used." —**Parker J. Palmer** (author of *The Courage to Teach, Let Your Life Speak, and A Hidden Wholeness*)

"This book describes a practical strategy for promoting learning and thinking artfully grounded in adult development and learning theory. Stevens and Cooper remind readers that reflection is a key element of learning and offer multiple ways to reflect meaningfully through journaling. They use their own and others' journal entries to reveal how journaling helps reflect on one's experience, develop one's internal voice through making meaning of experience, transform one's assumptions and knowledge, and organize and communicate one's perspective. They offer multiple possibilities for readers to use journaling for personal growth, fostering their own and others' learning, and managing professional life." —**Marcia B. Baxter Magolda**

Sty/us

22883 Quicksilver Drive
Sterling, VA 20166-2102

Subscribe to our e-mail alerts: www.Styluspub.com